THE
MILDER
GARDEN

Also by Jane Taylor

Collecting Garden Plants
Fragrant Gardens
Gardening for Fragrance
Kew Gardening Guides: Climbing Plants
Kew Gardening Guides: Tender Perennials

THE
MILDER
GARDEN

Jane Taylor

J. M. Dent & Sons Ltd
LONDON

First published 1990
© Jane Taylor 1990

Printed in Great Britain by
Butler & Tanner Ltd, Frome and London
for J. M. Dent & Sons Ltd
91 Clapham High Street
London SW4 7TA
This book is set in
11 on 12 point Monophoto Bembo

British Library Cataloguing in Publication Data
Taylor, Jane, 1944–
The milder garden.
1. Gardens. Vegetables. Cultivation
I. Title
635

ISBN 0–460–86022–4

Contents

List of colour photographs. vii

Preface 1

I   The Potential and the Pitfalls 5

II   The Early Years. 23

III   Mixed Borders 49

IV   Shrubs and Trees 88

V   Using Walls 129

VI   Hot and Dry 149

VII   The Mature Milder Garden 178

VIII The Tropical Look 223

Appendix 1   *Some more plants for the milder garden* . . 232

Appendix 2   *Note on plant availability.* 240

Bibliography 241

General Index 243

Index of Plant Names 244

Colour photographs

Crocosmia 'Lady Hamilton' with *Helichrysum petiolare*
Beschorneria yuccoides
Fuchsia splendens 'Karl Hartweg'
Isoplexis sceptrum
Watsonia fulgens
Alstroemeria pulchella growing through *Helichrysum petiolare*
Osteospermum 'Whirligig'
Convolvulus sabatius
Salvia involucrata
Senecio scandens
Tropaeolum tuberosum
Dianella sp.
Penstemon 'Taosensis'
Clematis paniculata
Rhododendron eximium
Rhododendron 'Lady Chamberlain'
Senecio candicans
Pseudopanax crassifolius
Plumeria alba
Tea Rose 'Mme Berkeley'

Preface

WHEN I began to garden in a mild, coastal climate, in a garden already mature and well provided with shelter, I found that the standard works of reference I had hitherto relied upon – Bean, *Hillier's Manual*, Graham Stuart Thomas's *Perennial Garden Plants* prominent among them – all too often failed me. Their (dare I say it) Home Counties perspective, most noticeable in Bean, meant that many of the plants I wanted to look up were simply not mentioned, for they were considered too tender. W. Arnold-Forster's *Shrubs for the Milder Counties* covers a lot of the ground missed by Bean, but only in an impressionistic manner; and it is by now much out of date, for many plant names have altered as taxonomic research reveals new data, and new plants have been introduced since it was published in 1948. The North American *Hortus Third* covers a much wider range of plants, but the descriptions are so brief as to be almost useless to the gardener searching for the helpfully subjective comments of an Arnold-Forster, and – again, because of new taxonomic research – it is not very accurate.

Again and again, I was obliged to make trips to London to search through the volumes in the Lindley Library of the Royal Horticultural Society, in order to track down details such as country of origin and botanical authority. I longed for a book which would guide me in the right direction with a mixture of ingredients: a touch of the subjective descriptions of Arnold-Forster; up-to-date nomenclature, so far as possible; references to a much wider selection of the plants that were coming my way through purchase, exchange or gift; and the basic botanical details of family, country of origin and authority. Failing to find it, I decided to write it myself. All those hours in the Lindley Library had left me with a sizeable card index; a far greater number of hours in the garden had given me the experience of growing several thousand different plants suited to the milder corners of Britain.

1

Believing that the object of growing plants is first of all to enjoy them, I decided to write a subjective narrative, not an encyclopaedic text. Taxonomic details, after all, can perfectly well be incorporated into the index; and clearly, a book of the size envisaged must have an index. The bulk of the text, then, consists of a discussion of many plants that I have grown, and some that I have merely coveted, more or less arbitrarily divided into chapters on the basis of the growing conditions they need. Because my gardening experience began, effectively, on a bare and windy site, I am very aware that gardens do not just happen, they have to be created, often in defiance of such obstacles as poor soil, bad drainage, lack of water, too much wind, vandalism, and an ever-widening gap between one's aspirations and one's bank balance. The chapters that follow recognize this, starting – after an initial chapter in which I attempt to suggest the potential of the milder garden – with the plants that will help you to create shelter, and concluding with the kind of 'tropical' jungle that you can expect in a mature garden. For those whose magpie instincts are as well developed as mine, an appendix lists some more plants that might be worth trying, relating them to the preceding chapters. Clearly, no book can fulfil all your needs; the bibliography will suggest where you can obtain more detailed information about the plants than I have been able to give in this book.

Other gardeners, too, are often a source of invaluable information about the plants you want to grow, or have acquired without really knowing much about. Many generous gardeners have helped me with both information and plants, ready-made or in the shape of cuttings or seeds. It is always hard to know whom to thank; cravenly, I shall begin by acknowledging my debt to three people now no longer with us. My late husband Dick put up with my passion for gardening with remarkable patience, and helped with much of the heavy work until his health failed. Both Dr Mark Smith, of the University Botanic Garden, Bristol, and Basil Fox, of the Aberystwyth Botanic Garden, were extremely generous with plants and advice. Tony Collett showed me what could be done on an apparently unpropitious site, for he gardened on a windswept Welsh hillside; Wanda Pugh, when she was obliged to move from her Welsh woodland garden, gave me many choice rhododendrons which did surprisingly well in the colder, harsher Forest of Dean. From Christopher Lloyd I had not only a warm welcome each time I visited Great Dixter, but also encouragement to experiment with tender plants. Many other people have helped me: Colin Rogers, Tony Lord, Christine Skelmersdale, Roy Cheek, Mike and Jane Henry, Charles and Brigid Quest-Ritson, Keith and Ros Wiley, Penelope Hobhouse, Michael Hickson, Richard Fulcher, Walter Magor, Jim Russell, David and Barbara Barker, Philip and Helen Ballard, Joan Wilder, James and Louisa Arbuthnott, John

Treasure, Peter Healing, Neil Lucas, David McClintock, the late Percy Picton, and many others.

Finally, I thank my mother, who has never failed in her love and practical support; and Risal, who knows how much I owe to him.

London
January 1990

I

The Potential and the Pitfalls

ENGLISH gardens are admired throughout the world, in a partly idealized image of broad, velvety lawns, herbaceous borders, banks of hybrid rhododendrons, and rose gardens. Like most stereotypes, this tells only part of the story. In the milder areas of Britain and Ireland are many gardens where large-leaved rhododendrons grow in place of the iron-clad hardy hybrids; where rocky hot slopes are carpeted with the Hottentot fig and streamsides lush with arum lilies; where *Amaryllis belladonna* proliferates to fill autumn days with its apricot-scented pink trumpets; and where the Chilean *Luma apiculata* (*Myrtus luma*) self-sows to form groves of cinnamon-barked trees.

In Britain, where I have learned more than half my gardening, the Gulf Stream is responsible for the mild coastal climates that make such gardens possible. Its waters wash the Isles of Scilly and the coasts of Devon and Cornwall, Wales and Ireland, and the Isle of Man, and extend their benign influence as far as the north-western coast and isles of Scotland. The southern, Channel coasts, too, feel the tempering effects of the Gulf Stream; the Channel Islands, the shores of Brittany and the Atlantic coast of France also enjoy a maritime climate milder than their latitudes suggest. There are, as well, some surprisingly warm areas inland, especially in large cities where massed buildings and their occupying humanity create a more benign microclimate than in the surrounding countryside. In central London I can overwinter, unprotected outside, pelargoniums and tobacco plants that could not be fully relied upon to survive mild Devon winters.

Similar mild but often windy cool-temperate climates, where frosts are seldom severe, are common to most parts of New Zealand (except the northern, tropical tip of North Island and the mountain climates of the uplands), Tasmania and parts of southern Australia, along the more northerly parts of the Pacific coast of North America from Oregon to Vancouver, and in southerly parts of South America: all areas where a

5

great ocean exercises its tempering influence. Then there are always to be found unexpected microclimates, as for example in the heart of Switzerland, which (excepting the transalpine, Italian canton of Ticino) has a typically Continental climate of hot summers and cold, crisp winters. Yet on the shore of Lac Léman near Vevey, in the village of Saint Saphorin, the climate is more Mediterranean than Continental, with hot summers still but mild, damp winters: so that olive trees grew and thrived for decades until the great freeze of 1956. Along the Rhône valley, away from the tempering influence of the lake, is the privately owned botanic garden of Saint Triphon, where loquats (*Eriobotrya japonica*) and *Musa basjoo* grow outside without even the shelter of a wall.

Thus, although a study of a map giving climatic zones may be a useful starting point to suggest what plants you may or may not succeed with, these maps perforce work in broad sweeps and ignore local effects. Then again, not every work of reference gives a hardiness rating to the plants described; and even when it does, the findings of the authors may conflict with the practical experience of other gardeners and growers. In Britain, for example, though the winters are comparatively mild as a rule, summers are generally dull and overcast, the brief interlude of cloudless skies insufficient to ensure a thorough ripening of woody plants or of certain bulbs. This in turn means that many woody plants especially are less able to survive cold than in other areas which, though rated identically in the zoning categories, enjoy hotter summers. It is wise to consider Britain, for practical purposes, as one zone lower than the mean winter temperatures suggest: zone 6, instead of 7, for the bulk of the country, and zone 7, instead of 8, for the milder counties. This does not alter the undoubted fact that many shrubs and trees rated as Z8, Z9 or even, in some cases, Z10, seem to thrive in mild British gardens, while others rated Z6 have succumbed to frost because they are accustomed to Continental climates where the summer ripening enables them to survive the cold of winter.

The zones here referred to are those most commonly encountered in North American, British or European works of reference, such as *Hortus Third* (US), or Krüssmann's *Manual of Cultivated Broadleaved Trees*. They are those prepared by the US Department of Agriculture, extended and adapted for Europe but not, so far as I have been able to discover, for other areas. To some extent, no doubt, equivalent climatic zones for, say, New Zealand, could be deduced from the zone hardiness attributed to New Zealand plants in cultivation, given a knowledge of their habitats.

It doesn't do to put too much stress on the hardiness rating for any given plant. My files are full of notes about Z5 or Z6 plants which lost no time dying in a putative Z8 garden, and – more encouragingly – of Z9 or Z10 plants that have done well for several years in that same alleged Z8.

Nor is the feel of the climate to us humans a reliable guide to its effect on plants. The milder coastal areas of Britain can seem bitterly inhospitable. I have felt colder, in that almost frost-free, coastal Devon garden where, away from the shelter of great belts of Monterey pine, there is no escape from the relentless westerly winds laden with Atlantic moisture, than ever in our Swiss garden at midwinter, with the thermometer registering a crisp − 10°C and the sun shining from a clear and windless sky.

Those blustery winds off the sea do damage at all seasons by carrying salt particles inland. After the turn of the year the prevailing westerlies give way to searing east winds, blowing off the Urals and uninterrupted in their passage over the lowlands of northern Europe and the chilly North Sea by any calming or warming influence. The temperature may register above zero − it is, rather, the still nights that are most to be feared, when frost descends untimely from a clear sky − but the desiccating effects of a dry, cold easterly wind can be devastating to tender young growths. Even in summer, sea breezes can bring a chill to a sunny day. This is the kind of weather described by seaside tourist boards as 'bracing'. Yet it is in a sense illusory: the thermometer reveals that in such areas winter frosts are not severe, and the growing season is long. The problem, for plants and gardeners alike, is the chill factor of those strong prevailing winds.

The first need, then, in many mild but windy areas, is for shelter. An adequate shelter belt can cut the force of the wind so that the chill factor, and the parching effect of drying winds or scorching by airborne salt particles, is much reduced. Comparatively few plants are equipped to withstand gale force winds. Those that are can be used as the first line of defence to create a sheltered atmosphere in which a wide range of decorative plants can be successfully acclimatized. In Chapter II I will consider some of the trees and shrubs that I and others have found best able to create this vital shelter so that, within their protective range, we can get on with the business of exploiting the full potential of a mild climate. Just how essential this shelter is to the creation and continued existence of a garden in exposed areas can be seen if you visit any of the great coastal gardens of Devon and Cornwall, south-western Ireland, or the west coast of Scotland, then walk to a nearby, exposed stretch of coast. Without shelter, all is barren cliffs and moorland. A few distorted thorn trees may show clearly, in their wind-blown outline, the direction of the prevailing wind.

In most areas, a fairly constant pattern of wind can be discerned at various times of the year. Any planting you undertake for shelter must give protection from both the prevailing and any intermittently recurrent winds. Then, of course, there are freak storms, differentiated usually by their force rather than their direction; these do most damage when trees are in leaf. The resistance offered by a broadleaved tree in full sail is very great, as many of us were dismayed to discover when the gales of 19 October 1987 destroyed 15 million trees in southern Britain. The hurricane showed how fragile can be the root system of even a large and seemingly established tree; for though many trees were broken by the gale, others were simply tipped out of the ground to reveal pitiably small root systems. Another area of weakness may be the union of stock and scion of grafted trees; in some, the whole superstructure was shown to have survived on the frailest of unions, perhaps with no more than ten to fifteen percent of the tissue united. Such trees snapped off at the graft leaving the rootstock still sturdily held in the ground.

By definition, in the milder gardens of which I write, frosts are less severe than in cold inland areas. Yet it does not do to rely too entirely on plants that are not fully hardy: there will always be some seasons when it will be colder than normal. If your garden is planted entirely with trees and shrubs that are apt to be damaged or even killed by more than a few degrees of frost, you are going to be faced from time to time with the need to start again more or less from scratch, which is a depressing and expensive business as well as inefficient. But if you play safe with all your plants, you will be wasting much of the potential of your climate and site. The wise gardener grows a range of plants of varying hardiness, and for key components and elements of design such as windbreaks, hedges and important specimen trees, will choose plants that should survive the worst frosts likely to occur. The more important a given plant or planting may be, whether as a design feature or for shelter from the elements, the more certain you should be that it will withstand the worst that your local climate may do.

As well as frosts of freak severity, there is another kind of frost damage you may need to guard against. Because the winters are mild, the plants scarcely cease growing; warm spring days spur them on; and an untimely frost may singe their young growths or early flowers. The plants most at risk, paradoxically, are those from areas with colder winters and warmer, sunnier summers. In these areas woody plants experience a season of dormancy when their metabolic processes are slowed, and in summer a period of ripening which produces wood able to withstand the frosts to come. In a mild climate, both the extended dormancy and the full summer ripening are lacking. The growths of summer remain soft, so comparatively light frosts may cause damage; mild spells in late winter encourage new growth which is then vulnerable to a subsequent cold snap. Typical of such plants is the pomegranate, *Punica granatum*, which thrives – and even self-sows – as a free-standing bush in our Swiss garden, where it forms wood able to stand − 10°C or worse. Yet in coastal Devon, it needed a warm wall.

As well as the individual frost-resistance of the plants you grow – about which more later − and the general climatic conditions with which you have to contend, you may well find parts of your garden far more suitable for tender plants than others. Especially, you should guard against impeding the free movement of air down a sloping site. If you live at the bottom of a valley there may be little you can do to improve air drainage, and your sheltered corners may turn into treacherous frost traps in winters that are colder than normal. Elsewhere, since cold air is heavier than warm, it tends to sink and to roll down any slope, which is often why one garden in a given area may be a congenial environment for plants that are too tender for another, nearby, with less efficient katabatics (air drainage). In practical terms, this translates into ensuring that there are no solid barriers that can prevent cold air from sliding downhill, away from your garden and its less hardy components; and, to the extent that this is not possible, into planting only the toughest species where there is a risk of frost settling. You may find yourself involved in a trade-off between creating shelter from wind and allowing the free movement of air; here the deciduous wind-sifters (see Chapter II), which present less of a barrier in winter, may be useful. The business of ensuring that the air drainage in your garden is as free as it can be is just as important as seeing to soil drainage, and may be as critical to the survival of less hardy plants.

The potential

It is a characteristic of all but the most timid gardener to be tempted by plants that are on the challenging borderline of hardiness. Thanks to the plant hunters, past and present, who have introduced to cultivation so many good things from other countries, the choice available to gardeners is now very wide. It is further increased by an ever greater range of cultivars in certain genera, as for example *Leptospermum*, *Osteospermum* or *Phormium*. I intend to describe many of these half-hardy plants in the following pages, and − as you may have surmised if you began by studying the table of contents − I shall also share with you my experiences both of making a garden from a bare site with such plants and of the entirely different opportunities and problems of a mature garden with ample shelter. In these two gardens, and in the course of running a small nursery garden seeking to provide a wide choice of unusual plants, I have been on familiar terms with many thousands of plants. I cannot say how many of them will find their way into these pages, but I can promise you that, almost without exception, the plants I shall write about are those I have known and grown. And because plants in a garden cannot be seen in isolation from their neighbours, I intend to share with you throughout these pages my interest in plant groupings and associations. In attempting always to create plant groups that are visually satisfying, I have borne in mind also the needs of the individual plants. Here a knowledge of their native habitats is a great help. If one did not know that *Olearia insignis* (*Pachystegia insignis*) was a plant of dry, hot, rocky slopes and *Senecio candicans* of moist and sheltered valleys, one might think that they would complement each other very happily. But with such differing requirements, inevitably one would suffer where the other throve. And even if by devoted care both could be made to do well, their juxtaposition would still look incongruous to anyone who knew how each grows in the wild. Then again, the plants from certain regions may have a compatibility with one another, visually speaking; deriving, no doubt, from the evolutionary impact of similar climatic conditions.

Before I begin with the practical considerations of what to grow on an exposed headland or in a warm, wet valley, I would like to give you a geographical foretaste of the range of plants from which a choice can be made.

The southern hemisphere

Plants from the southern hemisphere are, in the main, later arrivals in our gardens than those from the Old World or North America. It is with these that I shall begin, however, for many have still, to our eyes, the fascination of the unfamiliar. We have collectors such as Harold Comber to thank for many of the plants introduced to our gardens from these regions.

Chile is rich in handsome evergreen shrubs and trees, some with spectacular flowers, requiring conditions emulating their native forest margins, including high atmospheric humidity. They include members of the Proteaceae such as *Embothrium*, the much less familiar *Gevuina avellana* which is a foliage tree of the first rank, and *Lomatia ferruginea* with leaves like some magnificent fern. From Chile too are the woody gesneriads *Mitraria coccinea* – which will cover the ground like some tiny-leaved ivy, but that no ivy ever bore lopsided trumpets of piercing vermilion – and the more demanding *Asteranthera ovata*; and shrubby genera which some botanists assign to Philesiaceae, others to the portmanteau Liliaceae: *Philesia* itself, *Luzuriaga*, *Sarmienta*, and the magnificent *Lapageria rosea*. *Desfontainea spinosa*, so like an opposite-leaved holly until it opens its scarlet and yellow, tubular flowers; the climbing *Berberidopsis corallina* with toothed leaves and hanging sprays of crimson flowers; and the two *Crinodendron* species: all these are Chileans enjoying sheltered, shaded sites.

Not all Chilean shrubs are red-flowered, of course. *Laurelia serrata* is grown for its headily aromatic, bright green leathery leaves; *Abutilon vitifolium* more for its cupped mallow flowers in ice-white or clear pale lavender than for the downy, vine-shaped leaves which earned it its specific epithet. Nor should we overlook the southern beeches or *Nothofagus*, nor the myrtles of which the cinnamon-barked *Luma apiculata* is the most familiar Chilean representative.

These two genera are not exclusively Chilean. For just as there are frequent parallels between the North American and Japanese floras, so we find that in the southern hemisphere many genera are represented in both South America and Australasia. Among them are such familiar genera as *Fuchsia*, which is so widespread in our gardens and greenhouses that we scarcely remember it has a native land; *Eucryphia* and *Drimys* and *Weinmannia*, *Sophora* (also found in Asia) and genera such as *Nothofagus*, *Lomatia* and *Myrtus* already mentioned. I shall return to these when I come to antipodean plants.

For we cannot yet leave the South American continent, which has many more good things to offer, from Brazil, Argentina and other countries as well as Chile. Nor do all South American, even all Chilean plants require sheltered woodland conditions. *Fuchsia magellanica* is one of our best defences against Atlantic gales, though, being deciduous, it should perhaps yield its claims for supremacy to *Escallonia macrantha* and its kin, or the less familiar, and less colourful, *Baccharis patagonica*. Others, though less suited to full exposure to gales, thrive in warm and sunny positions: among them *Senecio vira-vira*, better known as *S. leucostachys*, a Patagonian shrub whose garden value lies in its silver, comb-like leaves on insinuating stems. Lemon verbena (*Aloysia triphylla*) needs sun and shelter: so, also, *Jovellana violacea*, closely allied to the calceolarias but with helmeted, not pouched flowers, and *Calceolaria integrifolia* itself; *Feijoa* and *Fascicularia*; the blue-berried *Rhaphithamnus spinosus* and elegant *Schinus molle* or pepper tree, so called for its bunches of rosy-red fruits; *Diostea juncea,* which looks entirely like a broom until its verbena-like flowers open to reveal its true identity, and the tree-heath mimic *Verbena tridens*; *Fabiana imbricata* looking even more heath-like until its white or lilac trumpets open; the Brazilian *Caesalpinia gilliesii* or bird of paradise flower; climbers such as *Tropaeolum tuberosum* and *Eccremocarpus scaber*; and the subshrubby *Grindelia chiloensis*, a yellow daisy redeemed from banality by its white, sticky-capped buds. Alstroemerias and their climbing cousins the bomareas, verbenas, *Canna iridiflora*, tobaccos: these are all South American and all but the last prefer sun.

Before I am tempted by the mention of cannas to move northwards, to the bright flowers of Mexico and the Caribbean, I want to scan the Australasian flora, beginning with New Zealand. The New Zealand genera which interest us fall broadly into three groups: the wind-hardy, tolerant of full exposure to sea winds but resentful of freezing conditions; those which need warm, sheltered sites in full sun; and those, such as *Pseudo-wintera colorata*, which prefer sheltered, humid woodland conditions, like many of the Chileans already noted. Let us consider this group first, remembering that some plants may be sufficiently adaptable to grow in sheltered or in exposed positions, and that others which thrive in exposure where frosts are rare will need more protection in colder areas. Among them are perennial, non-woody plants such as *Arthropodium cirrhatum*, as well as woody plants which include *Lophomyrtus bullata*, *Carpodetus serratus*, and, most notably, the tree ferns, which need shelter from wind at all times.

There are many New Zealand plants suited to full exposure to maritime winds. Foremost among them are the senecios (now mostly in *Brachyglottis*) and olearias, which reveal in the felted or waxy coating or the thick leathery texture of the leaves of many species, the adaptation won by evolution to the gales of their native coasts. Sword-leaved phormiums, with leaves so tough they can be used in an emergency as tree ties; *Metrosideros umbellata* and others, brilliant in scarlet or crimson flower; *Muehlenbeckia complexa* with tiny leaves borne on a tangle of wiry black stems; soapy-leaved griselinias, which in mild gardens can grow to immense size, and the smaller, heath-like cassinias: these are just a few of the shrubs and trees suitable for exposure that I shall describe in the next chapter.

For full sun, but not necessarily appreciating a wind-buffeting, are the New Zealand members of the pea family: *Notospartium*, *Carmichaelia* and *Chordospartium*; the parrot's bill or lobster claw, *Clianthus puniceus*, which comes in white and coral-pink as well as the scarlet which gave it both its vernacular names; and the sophoras, which bear their mustard-yellow, claw-shaped flowers among foliage composed of many tiny leaflets.

A particular problem with many New Zealand plants is their ability to withstand wind only when the thermometer is registering temperatures above freezing, even if they may be hardy enough to take a few degrees of frost in still conditions: for in their native lands, the combination of frost and wind is rare. Clearly, where freezing winds may be a feature of the climate even though it is generally mild, such plants need to be planted where tougher evergreens provide shelter. Among them are some conifers, including several of the more desirable *Podocarpus* species and the related genus *Dacrydium*; and broadleaved shrubs such as *Fuchsia excorticata*, which makes a tree in favoured sites to reveal its peeling bark; *Aristotelia serrata*; the evergreen hoherias; and *Pseudopanax*, a genus of striking foliage plants to which New Zealand nurserymen and breeders have lately turned their attention. The colder the area in which you are attempting to establish New Zealand plants, the larger this group will become, taking in many of the shrubs and trees that in favoured gardens make dependable wind shelter.

A particularity of the New Zealand flora is that many of its representatives have white flowers, even those of which the old-world relatives are coloured. The genus *Hebe* is one of the most notable and well-known exceptions, with flowers of, as well as white, every shade possible on the blue side of the spectrum except pure, gentian blue itself, through to crimson but not pure red. It is also a polymorphic genus, comprising tiny alpine shrublets on the one hand and large shrubs on the other, with leaves equally variable, from the conifer-like whipcords to the oval, fleshy leaves of the brightly-coloured *H. speciosa* hybrids.

Except for the odd outlier in South America, hebes are essentially confined to New Zealand. Not so other genera such as *Olearia*, which crosses into Tasmania and southern Australia. With such a range of habitats, olearias vary from extremely wind-resistant shrubs, some more, some much less tolerant of frost, to soft-leaved, soft-wooded shrubs grown largely for their abundant flowers. But without doubt the best known representative of the Australian flora is the genus *Eucalyptus*, with *Acacia* not far behind. These and other genera, indeed even some individual species, occur in both Tasmania and mainland Australia, but the Tasmanian flora also includes some extremely desirable shrubs and trees for our gardens occurring only on that island. Among them are spiky *Richea* species; the slender climber *Billardiera*, prized its royal blue fruits; evergreens such as *Anopterus glandulosus* and *Acradenia frankliniae*, both white-flowered; and conifers such as *Diselma* and *Athrotaxis*. Blue-berried, evergreen perennial *Dianella* and the exquisite blandfordias or Christmas bells occur in both Tasmania and Australia, along with shrubs and trees that include *Leptospermum* (also found in New Zealand), *Melaleuca* with bottle-brush flowers, and some of the showiest olearias, those of the *O. stellulata* Splendens group with flowers of lilac, mauve or rose as well as white.

Much of the Australian mainland is desert, and parts have a steamy tropical climate; but in the south of the continent are areas with more equable climates where grow plants adaptable to the Atlantic littoral and equivalent zones. Some plants from western Australia may also grow for us, though the flora of this region is generally less ready to adapt. It is thus in the states of Victoria and New South Wales that we are likely to find most of the shrubs and trees suitable for our purposes. Indeed, some may well be hardier than many Tasmanian plants, for the temperate island climate is without extremes except those dictated by altitude. Almost as familiar as the eucalypts and acacias from these parts are the callistemons or bottlebrushes, easy and quick from seed and mostly hardier than *Melaleuca*. The protea family is well represented in Australia also, with genera such as *Banksia* (few of which will take any frost), *Telopea* and *Grevillea*.

There remains in the southern hemisphere for our consideration the southern part of the African continent. South Africa is rich in plants of

the great flowering monocotyledonous families, Liliaceae (in the broad
sense), Amaryllidaceae, Agavaceae and Iridaceae, as well as in a variety of
brilliant daisies. Among monocots, *Agapanthus*, *Nerine* and belladonna
lilies, *Crocosmia* and *Gladiolus* need no introduction, and freesias are well
known as cut flowers. Of irids other than these last three genera, scarcely
less familiar are *Ixia* and *Sparaxis*. Genera that deserve to be more widely
grown are pure blue-flowered *Aristea*, the peacock moraeas and *Watsonia*,
which unlike *Gladiolus* has scarcely suffered the attentions of the hybrid-
izers. In Liliaceae we have the great range of kniphofias, a genus which
extends northwards across the equator to Uganda and Abyssinia, with
outlying species in Madagascar and southern Arabia. And there are lesser
genera in all these families, from which we can pick such as the bizarre or
freakish *Ferraria*, or the dainty *Homeria*. The climate in the extreme south
of South Africa is dry in summer and wet in winter, so bulbs from this
region tend to spend the summer months in a state of dormancy. Further
north the rain falls chiefly in summer, so species from these areas are
dormant in winter and can consequently, when transferred to other
climates, withstand much colder temperatures than the winter-growing
species from further south.

Showy composites include not only the familiar annuals or cut flowers,
Arctotis, *Venidium*, *Ursinia*, *Gerbera*, but also the blue felicias and genera
such as *Gazania* and *Osteospermum* where new cultivars are yearly brought
to our notice. Then there are the arum lilies; succulents – notably *Carpobrotus*, *Lampranthus* and *Aloe* – and the delightful genus *Diascia*, lately
reintroduced to cultivation in Europe and already justifiably popular.
Indeed, such is the contribution to our gardens of these and other plants
that South Africa's shrubs have been somewhat overshadowed. In the
same family, Scrophulariaceae, as *Diascia*, we have *Phygelius*, a genus of
softwooded shrubs which for years was represented in cultivation only by
P. capensis and, more rarely, the refined *P. aequalis*, and which now offers
several cultivars, following the almost instant success of *P. aequalis* 'Yellow
Trumpet'. From South Africa also we have *Melianthus major*, a foliage
plant of the very first rank, a shrub in fact but behaving in a herbaceous
manner when cut back by winter frosts. Nor should I wish to forgo
Freylinia lanceolata; for its little buff-yellow trumpets, borne in panicles in
winter, are deliciously fragrant and its slender foliage is comely all year.
And could anyone, having once grown it, dispense with *Helichrysum
petiolare*, in all its variants a rapid filler and interweaver linking neighbouring groups with its heart-shaped grey, variegated or buttery yellow
felted leaves? Some buddlejas, including fragrant, winter-flowering *B.
auriculata*, are South African also. And there are the Cape heaths, of which
Erica canaliculata and yellow-flowered *E. pageana* are among the few likely
to withstand light frosts.

The northern hemisphere

Because of the long historical connections between northern Europe and the Mediterranean, plants from this region and the wider theatre of southern Europe and the Iberian peninsula have long been cultivated in cooler climes. Among early introductions were evergreen shrubs: laurustinus (*Viburnum tinus*), *Phlomis* or Jerusalem sage, *Quercus ilex* and myrtle, and aromatic or medicinal shrubs such as rosemary and sage. Of more purely ornamental trees and shrubs, the Judas tree or *Cercis siliquastrum* was introduced early, around the sixteenth century, followed by several *Cistus* species and some of the brooms: plants that have become so familiar that we scarcely think of them as foreign. Similarly, such well known perennials as acanthus, *Paeonia officinalis* and *Anemone pavonina* are all from southern Europe, yet all are frost-hardy and completely integrated immigrants. There are less frost-resistant plants from these regions, some worthy occupants of the garden: *Artemisia arborescens* and the silvery centaureas, and *Scilla peruviana* (the specific name is a solecism, but we are stuck with it) among them. Also somewhat tender are many of the shrubs that compose the vegetation known as *maquis* or *garrigue*: the *Cistus* and *Myrtus* and *Phlomis* already noted, *Pistacia lentiscus* the mastic tree, from the bark of which resin is obtained and used as a flavouring for raki and for medicinal purposes, and – where the soil is reasonably fertile – *Arbutus unedo*, the strawberry tree.

As we move further south, or further east, we find many plants worthy of warm corners. To the south and west of mainland Europe lie the Atlantic islands which form the region known as Macaronesia: Madeira, the Canary Islands, the Azores and the Cape Verde islands. From these islands come the shrubby daisies once called *Chrysanthemum frutescens* (the Paris daisy) and *C. foeniculaceum*, but now given their own genus, *Argyranthemum*; the giant blue echiums; huge geraniums of the *Geranium palmatum* type; fleshy aeoniums; and shrubby foxgloves. Here, too, we find *Clethra arborea*, most beautiful of its genus, with glossy foliage and sprays of white flowers like lily of the valley; brooms of both the major genera, *Cytisus* and *Genista*; and, for warm shade, species of *Vaccinium* (*V. cylindraceum* and *V. padifolium*). The Canary Islands have their own pine, *Pinus canariensis*, and their own holly, *Ilex perado*. In nearby mainland Morocco we find the silvery, silky-leaved *Cytisus battandieri*.

We can also turn our attention eastwards from the Mediterranean, to south-west Asia and, particularly, to the region eastwards of the Himalayas, that great range which separates the climates of Siberia, the hot south of India and Indonesia, the warm dry areas of Iran and Turkey and the humid, warm-temperate or subtropical areas of Assam and Burma, southern China and Japan. In south-west Asia the summers are hotter, the winters drier than in mild maritime climates, with the consequent likelihood of winter damage to insufficiently ripened wood, as in the case of the pomegranate which thrives in our Swiss garden but not in a milder, coastal British one.

From the foothills of the Himalayas, Bhutan, Assam and Upper Burma, and Yunnan have come to our western gardens many fine trees and shrubs; so many, indeed, that tender perennials from these regions – *Hedychium*, *Rehmannia*, and the Evansia irises among them – have been almost over-shadowed. One of the great plant collectors working in this area was Frank Kingdon Ward. Some of his introductions are not truly frost-hardy: *Leycesteria crocothyrsos*, *Prunus cerasoides rubea*, *Sorbus insignis*, and the large-leaved *Cornus chinensis*. He was not the only collector to introduce plants of special interest to gardeners in mild areas, but – unlike, say, George Forrest who first introduced *Sorbus harrowiana*, now believed to be part of *S. insignis*, and whom we may remember also when we grow *Jasminum polyanthum*, *Buddleja fallowiana* and much else besides, or Ernest Wilson (*Magnolia delavayi*, *Jasminum mesnyi*) – very many of Kingdon Ward's introductions are more or less susceptible to frost.

The area of the Himalayan ranges bordering China, Tibet and Upper Burma is the heartland of the huge genus *Rhododendron*. The three col-lectors already mentioned, with Joseph Rock and, earlier, Sir Joseph Hooker, as also other, less-known collectors, introduced many species which need sheltered conditions to reach their true potential. There are those most desirable, blood-red forms of *Rhododendron arboreum*; species in the subsections Maddenia, Edgeworthia and Fortunea; and the large-leaved species of subsections Grandia and Falconera. It is hard, after living at close quarters with fine specimens of these species and the best of their primary hybrids, to feel much affection for the hardy hybrids. Some of the finest *Camellia* species, too, can be grown to perfection in mild, sheltered gardens, whether in woodland, as befits many, or in the sunnier positions which better suit *C. sasanqua*.

Many other familiar genera from the east, which we know chiefly through their winter-hardy representatives, have less-known species worthy of growing in milder gardens. I have already referred to *Prunus cerasoides rubea*, Kingdon Ward's carmine cherry; and to *Magnolia delavayi*. The hardy dogwoods are well-known for their colourful winter stems or their massed white or pink floral bracts in late spring; from the Himalayas comes the evergreen *Cornus capitata*, with primrose bracts followed by fruits looking somewhat like a strawberry and tasting like an overripe banana, and full of pips. The very varied ornamental brambles include *Rubus lineatus*, with dark green palmate leaves silvery-silky beneath, and virtually no prickles. Also for those who admire foliage above, or as much as, flowers, there are several hollies; some fine mahonias; and a handful of acers so unlike the popular concept of a maple that few would recognize them at first meeting. Viburnums, a large and varied genus, include some tender species valued for foliage or for flower: among the former, *Viburnum odoratissimum* comes from as far south as Malaya yet will thrive in sheltered, mild gardens. Buddlejas have much more to offer than *Buddleja davidii*, colonizer of bomb sites and London Underground embankments: not least the winter-flowering *B. asiatica*, or the large-flowered, raspberry-pink *B. colvilei*. There are some beautiful tender clematis from these parts, among them silvery-silky *Clematis phlebantha* and evergreen *C. uncinata*, which bears large sprays of starry-white flowers, faintly scented, in summer.

Other Asiatic climbers for mild gardens include the very tender giant honeysuckle, *Lonicera hildebrandiana*; and *Rosa bracteata*, the Macartney rose. A host of lesser, or less-known, genera and species also come from these areas. *Wattakaka sinensis* and *Trachelospermum jasminoides* are climbers; *Cupressus cashmiriana* is one of the most graceful conifers we can grow; *Neolitsea sericea, Euonymus lucidus, Stranvaesia nussia, Cinnamomum camphora* are first-rate foliage plants; and for flower we can choose from such as *Colquhounia coccinea* with orange-scarlet flowers and leaves a little like a buddleja's, but apple-scented; the *Hamamelis*-like *Loropetalum chinense*; *Stachyurus himalaicus* with pink instead of the expected primrose flowers; *Clethra delavayi*; and blue-flowered *Ceratostigma griffithii*. The *Camellia* relatives, *Cleyera, Ternstroemia* and *Eurya*, with good glossy foliage, occur in Japan also.

Indeed, the same is true of several other genera; while yet others, introduced originally to the west from Japan, have later proved to originate in China. The specific epithet 'japonicus' should be treated with circumspection, as in *Cleyera japonica* (found also in China, Formosa and Korea), or *Mahonia japonica*, which is a Chinese native though long cultivated in Japan. The late Michael Haworth-Booth claimed that with experience of growing plants from Japan, China and America, the perceptive gardener can begin to form a mental picture of what he called 'the Chinese look'. However beautiful the flower, he maintained (citing as examples *Magnolia denudata, Campsis grandiflora* and *Rhododendron simsii*), Chinese plants have a coarseness, 'a faint, earthy, toad-like quality', which is not present in their Japanese or American counterparts. Be that as it may, from Japan have come many fine plants to enrich our gardens: *Prunus campanulata, Stachyurus lancifolius, Viburnum japonicum*, and scores of plants hardier than these. Many Japanese perennial plants introduced to the west are hardy, but *Farfugium japonicum*, cultivated for its variegated forms (and better known, more descriptively, as *Ligularia tussilaginea*) needs shelter. The near-hardy banana, *Musa basjoo*, with bold paddle leaves, is Japanese also. Nor can one overlook the holly fern, *Cyrtomium falcatum*, with a distribution extending to Hawaii.

And so, finally, we cross the Pacific to the continent of North America, where many Japanese plants have their close counterparts. Much of the continent has such bitter winters that native plants are hardy in all temperate areas. But in the southern USA, where the summers are warm and humid, parts of the Pacific coastal areas of California, and in some parts of Mexico, the climate varies from warm-temperate, through sub-tropical to deserts both cool (a relative term in these areas) and hot. Both in the Mexican flora and the Californian are plants adapted to dry conditions, from which a selection can be made to evoke, if you wish, the desert atmosphere – agaves and yuccas, the prickly poppies (species of *Argemone*), *Beschorneria yuccoides*, echeverias, and *Tradescantia pallida* 'Purpurea' to add a sombre note to the grey and glaucous tones.

Not all the plants from these areas are xerophytes or succulents. Dahlias, many *Salvia* and *Penstemon* species, lobelias, *Abelia floribunda* with narrow magenta trumpets like some *Fuchsia triphylla* mimic, the familiar *Choisya ternata* and plants less well known – *Rhodochiton atrosanguineum*, the cestrums, *Eupatorium ligustrinum* – all occur in Mexico and neighbouring countries.

Mexico and Central America, too, have their own fine conifers, *Pinus ayacahuite* with long, glaucous needles, *P. patula*, and the brooding *P. montezumae*; *Abies religiosa*, the sacred fir; and *Cupressus lusitanica*, among them. Further north, California is the home of two conifers which, more than any other trees, have made possible the great coastal and island gardens of Britain: Tresco, the Cornish and Irish and west of Scotland gardens that have been made largely in the last one hundred years. For both *Pinus radiata*, the Monterey pine, and *Cupressus macrocarpa*, the Monterey cypress, are resistant to the salt-laden Atlantic gales which stunt and distort all the native plants of those areas, even the tough hawthorn and sycamore.

California is also the home of the genus *Ceanothus*, chiefly blue-flowered shrubs forming a major constituent of the chaparral, the brush of the Californian foothills. In stony, starved, free-draining soil they grow with *Yucca whipplei*, *Arctostaphylos* and native oaks. Also Californian, also sun-loving, are the tree poppies, *Dendromecon* and *Romneya*; the lowly *Epilobium canum* subsp. *angustifolium*; and the shrubby musks. Californian mahonias, unlike their Asian counterparts, are also happiest in sun, as suggested by their glaucous-blue colouring. Growing in moister soils in the wild is the madrona, *Arbutus menziesii*, which has bloomy, cinnamon bark almost as beautiful as that of its Grecian counterpart *A. andrachne*.

Hardiness

It must be evident that the choice of plants for mild climates is very wide, whether your garden is fully exposed to salty ocean gales or sheltered by tall trees, sun-baked or wet with running streams. Each of these extremes will form the subject of a chapter to come. Though no amount of contrivances will persuade a plant of hot and rocky slopes to thrive in a boggy dell, or save a woodland plant from scorching, perhaps to death, in a hot or windlashed site, there remain some general principles that can be applied to any situation, to help young plants reach their full potential. So successful have some garden-makers been in creating ideal conditions for their plants that we may see, in sheltered Cornish gardens for example, far finer specimens of exotic plants than ever in their natural habitats. In the famous garden of Ludgvan Rectory, Canon Boscawen grew many New Zealand plants sent to him by his brother. Comparing notes after the plants had been established in the garden for some years, the brothers found that the Ludgvan plants were superior to any seen in the New Zealand bush. In more than one English garden on the Atlantic littoral or even along the Channel coast, trees and shrubs have been planted and successfully established – at least until a freak winter damaged or killed them – which might have seemed impossible to grow except in a frost-free climate. As long ago as 1856 the *Illustrated London News* published an article about Salcombe on the south Devon coast, where 'orange, citrons, lemons and limes come to perfection in the open air'. More recently, much success has been achieved by planters in the south of England growing in a cool greenhouse young trees and shrubs likely to be very tender, until they had formed some well-ripened wood and had reached a height of, say, 1–1·5 m/3–5 ft. At this stage they are planted out, late in spring, and carefully nurtured through their first season outdoors, staked if need be and regularly watched to see that they do not lack moisture. While still in the glasshouse, the plants are regularly potted on, the greatest care taken to prevent them becoming potbound or checked. In a garden at Salcombe itself, where frosts of −5·5°C/10°F are common, by a further refinement a greenhouse was constructed of which the roof could be removed in summer. Plants successfully grown outside for several years after this treatment included *Grevillea robusta*, *Nicotiana glauca*, and *Myoporum laetum*, all rated Z10, where the temperature range is −1 to −5°C/30–40°F.

Many supposedly tender plants – albeit hardier than these – have gained their reputation because they are susceptible to damage from frost when young, before they have formed well-ripened wood, yet are reasonably hardy once safely through their first few years. In oceanic climates, where the summers are not hot enough to ensure quick formation of mature wood but the winters are comparatively mild, plants of this kind are especially vulnerable in their early years. Others – *Cistus* and *Ceanothus* are familiar examples – are actually hardier when young than when senescent, a stage they reach comparatively rapidly, just as they rapidly grow to mature size. Another group of plants, which must be set out when still small even if vulnerable to frost, are those such as eucalypts or acacias which have deep, far-ranging roots adapted to seeking out all available moisture from very dry soils, and quickly outgrowing the cramped conditions of a pot. A pot-bound eucalypt will very likely never become rootfast, and before long may be blown over, or killed by the accumulation of water around the collar as windrock chafes a crater around the base of the stem.

For every species there is a critical minimum temperature below which it will be killed; but this is not to be expressed in terms of absolute degrees of temperature. It is affected by several factors, one of which is the amount, and just as important the pattern of distribution, of rainfall. A plant which is adapted in its native land to a fairly constant level of precipitation through the seasons, even if frost is rare, is more likely to survive in a mild oceanic climate than one from a region with colder but drier winters. Such winters are often accompanied by hotter summers than we experience in our temperate regions, so that – as we have seen – the plants may suffer through inability to form sufficiently mature wood to survive the less cold but wetter winter which follows. Plants which are adapted to survive extremes of drought will also be very vulnerable to damage in a milder, but wetter winter.

A pattern of rainfall which is entirely different in its native land may leave a plant unable to survive when required to acclimatize elsewhere, even though the temperature range may not differ greatly. If the precipitation is markedly seasonal, plants will begin to grow at the beginning of the wet season. If this coincides with winter, and is followed by a dormant season during the dry summer, a species from such a climate, transplanted to a region where rainfall is more constant, may fail to adapt and continue to grow in winter, with damaging or fatal results when even a light frost follows a mild damp spell. Such are many South African plants, for example nerines from the Cape region, which are more tender than species from further north where the average temperature is higher but the growing pattern corresponds more closely to that imposed by a temperate, uniformly moist climate. Plants from monsoon regions frequently make their new growth late in the season, and are damaged because the new wood has not had time to ripen before the onset of winter.

The level of atmospheric humidity also affects plant growth. Xerophytes will be more susceptible to cold damage where the air is moist, while those accustomed to very high atmospheric humidity may suffer in regions where the air is drier even though the total precipitation may be much the same.

Plants that are able easily to regenerate from below ground, though their topgrowth may not ripen sufficiently to form frost-resistant wood, can often adapt to growing in a colder climate by adopting a herbaceous habit of growth, or can be treated as if they were herbaceous, the topgrowth cut back each spring.

What goes on below ground level may also have a profound effect on a plant's ability to survive in an alien climate. Few plants relish soggy, cold soils in winter; xerophytes, and those from regions where the winters are invariably dry, especially resent such conditions. On heavy clay soils, it may be difficult to succeed even with comparatively hardy plants if the soil lies wet in winter. This may be so even if the species or genus in question grows, in the wild, with its feet in the wet. Kniphofias, for example, often found by streamsides in South Africa, are resentful of the hostile combination of cold and wet which may beset them in other climates. All too often we have to contrive, for the benefit of our plants, the very opposite of what the climate provides: we must arrange for ample moisture in the growing season, and impeccable drainage in winter. Even a grey-leaved plant such as *Helichrysum petiolare*, its felty coating seemingly an adaptation to a dry climate, can suffer badly if short of water in summer; yet it may survive even severe winter frosts if quite dry at the root. At the foot of a wall, where tender plants are often planted to benefit from both warmth and shelter in winter and improved summer ripening, the soil is frequently very dry and if extra water can be laid on in summer they may thrive. In the open ground you may need to lay drains, make raised beds, or dig-in quantities of coarse grit to improve the soil texture. Sandy soils, on the other hand, will need improving with abundant dressings of humus; though there are plants, apart from evident xerophytes, which are so well adapted to growing in coastal regions that they will thrive in almost pure, blown sand.

Given all these considerations about the likely hardiness of a plant, and assuming that you have chosen the plants best adapted to the conditions you can offer, what more can be done to give half-hardy subjects a good start in life and a fair chance of survival? For protection against wind and cold, plants should be set closely together – much closer than the usually recommended distances. They will much more quickly afford each other shade at the roots and shelter, and support each other against wind-rock and twisting. All growing plants give off minute amounts of heat; if they are close-packed, more of this heat will be retained instead of being dispersed by the wind. As they grow, some of the plants must be removed to allow the others to develop without distortion. Some can be moved to new quarters, others may be dispensed with altogether; in this second category will come fast-growing, comparatively cheap plants such as brooms, cistuses, tree lupins, or those that are naturally short-lived. Other plants, which resent disturbance, should be sited in their permanent quarters and protected by portable or dispensable nurse plants, or by artificial shelter of the kind I shall consider in the next chapter. There, also, I will discuss other aspects of planting in exposed gardens.

II

The Early Years

THE great enemy of gardens on the eastern Atlantic littoral – and to a lesser extent of other coastal gardens – is wind. The storm-force westerlies, laden with salt and with sand particles, damage most plants so severely that without some shelter, living or artificial, little gardening is possible. There are, fortunately, trees and shrubs that will tolerate even these damaging gales. To these we can turn for the provision of shelter within which, once it is established, we can fully exploit the advantages of a mild climate.

The sheer force of these coastal gales is not the only way they do damage, by breaking limbs from trees or whipping and twisting shrubs until they snap or even are torn from their anchorage in the soil. Salt particles carried on sea winds scorch the leaves of plants which have evolved no natural protection against this assault. And particles of blown sand may prove as abrasive as emery paper to the stems of your plants. As soon as there is enough shelter to filter the wind, reducing its speed, the sand particles are dropped: but the salt still remains until a dense barrier of salt-resistant plants has grown up within which pockets of stillness can be created.

Artificial windbreaks

In the early years it is helpful, and in some gardens essential, to put up artificial barriers to filter the wind. A wall is expensive, and not necessarily the best form of defence; for a solid barrier creates strong down-draughts and turbulence which can be almost as damaging as the gales you are trying to deflect. Better is a more or less temporary construction of a permeable fence designed to reduce windspeed by a minimum of 40%. There are many proprietary windbreaks available, made of woven plastic netting, or of strips of plastic. All are rather unsightly, but serviceable and comparatively cheap. Dearer, but smarter, are lath fences composed of vertical 2·5 cm/1 in laths nailed parallel to cross members, leaving 2·5 cm/1 in gaps between the laths. All the timber used should be tanalized to protect it against rot. Whether you use a proprietary windbreak, lath screening, or even chestnut paling or hurdles, the supporting posts should be stout and strong. Tanalized stakes 5 × 7·5 cm/2 × 3 in, set deeply in the ground no further apart than 2 m/6½ ft for netting or 3·3 m/11 ft for laths should be used. With any of these, the effective shelter extends for about seven times their height in very windy sites, up to ten or even twelve times where the wind is less violent. Within this zone it will be easier to establish living windbreaks than if you plant even the most wind-tolerant shrubs and trees without any shelter to give them a start.

Living windbreaks

In extremely windy gardens the shelter belt will need to be much wider than where the winds are moderate. On the most exposed headland you will need to plant an outer line of defence of low-growing shrubs to sift and deflect the wind and permit your more substantial sheltering trees to develop within their protection. A sloping outer line of shelter, gradually increasing in height towards the leeward, better deflects the wind than a vertical wall of vegetation, even supposing you were able to achieve this without the outer line of lower shelter. Some of the taller trees suitable for windbreaks tend, too, to become bare at the base with increasing height; the shrubby plants give vital protection at ground level also.

Shelter belt trees and shrubs should be planted when still small, so that they can form sturdy roots able to withstand the worst gales while the topgrowth still offers little resistance to the wind. Among the few exceptions are *Griselinia littoralis* and *Rhododendron ponticum*, which move well when large; but there remains the difficulty of staking to steady the top-hamper, which is not necessarily adequately balanced even by their heavy rootballs, until the plants have gained a new roothold.

I shall discuss specific ways and means of planting shelter belts and wind-hardy trees and shrubs later in this chapter; for it is time now to consider the plants themselves.

Most protective shrubs should be evergreen, to give year-round shelter; though as we shall see, some very twiggy deciduous shrubs are also efficient wind sifters, even when leafless in winter. The plants that withstand salty gales most successfully are those with grey or silver foliage, or with a high gloss or waxy finish to the surface of the leaf: though this is a less reliable indicator as many woodlanders have polished leaves also. Most grey-leaved plants have their characteristic colouring from the coating of fine hairs felting one or both surfaces of the leaf; salt particles are trapped on the tips of these hairs, to be washed off by the next rains without harming the sensitive surface of the leaf itself. Such plants, which include many extremely wind-hardy shrubs from New Zealand, also blend into a seaside landscape, their gentle colouring according well with the prevailing greys and blues, purples and sea-greens of the ocean and sky. The varnished film on the leaves of such plants as *Euonymus japonicus* also prevents salt from being absorbed into the soft and vulnerable tissues of the leaf. Hebes, a largely New Zealand genus, have adapted by developing not only a tough epidermis, but also a system of protecting the growing point of the leaf, which is held in the shielding clasp of the next pair of leaves. Just how important this protection is we can see by looking closely at, for example, the distorted thorns on Cornish headlands, their tortured shapes caused not by the wind physically bending the young branches to a form they gradually come to adopt permanently, but by the combined effects of windburn and salt spray damaging irreparably the emergent buds on the windward side, so that only those to leeward can develop.

Other salt-resistant plants have evolved a sticky, gummy exudation as extra protection. *Escallonia macrantha* and other species in this South American genus are among the finest of seaside shrubs for this reason. Some gummy and felted *Cistus* species are also very wind hardy. And once you have contrived enough shelter to reduce the wind speed to a point where blown sand is no longer a threat, leafless plants such as *Spartium junceum* are also able to withstand much wind provided they can be made root firm.

In districts where the winds are cold as well as salty some deciduous trees may be useful as the very first line of shelter. *Alnus glutinosa*, the common alder; willows such as *Salix caprea*, the goat willow, or bloomy-stemmed *S. daphnoides* and *S. acutifolia*; sea buckthorn, *Hippophae rhamnoides*; *Lycium chinense*; or even poplars such as *Populus trichocarpa* or *P. alba*: all these can be used. At the University campus at Aberystwyth on the west Wales coast, *S. acutifolia* was the most successful shelter tree in the early stages, being quick to grow and very cheap – cuttings stuck direct where the shrub is needed usually root.

But in milder districts, and especially in smaller gardens, you will hardly want to give too much space to these, when there are many first-rate evergreens to choose from. Some of the finest for mild windy gardens are the escallonias, such as *Escallonia macrantha* already noted, which has crimson flowers among its glossy, aromatic dark green leaves. In small spaces it can be a nuisance, for it is a greedy shrub with an extensive root system that resents disturbance, and wide-spreading branches needing regular trimming. More suitable derivatives of this species have been developed in Cornwall: 'Crimson Spire' and 'Red Hedger'. Both will reach 2 m/6½ ft in four or five years, and with their narrow outline are less demanding of space. 'Crimson Spire' is probably the more satisfactory of the two, with a stiffer, more upright habit and better flowers. Of similar vigour and height are 'Exoniensis', a graceful shrub with large polished leaves and white or blush flowers; 'Ingramii' with aromatic foliage and deep pink flowers on upright growths; and 'Newryensis', which has white flowers blushing pink. 'C. F. Ball' is another hybrid of *E. macrantha*, rather less tall at 3 m/10 ft (against up to 4 m/13 ft for the parent), with similar large aromatic leaves and crimson flowers. *E. rubra* (*E. punctata*) varies from pink to crimson, another good wind-sifter which can even be established from cuttings stuck where they are to grow. *E. revoluta* departs from the usually glossy style, for it is grey-felted all over; it bears white flowers in late summer.

Quite different from the escallonias is another surprisingly wind-hardy shrub from South America, *Buddleja globosa*, which can reach great size in mild gardens. It is showy when set with golfball-sized globular clusters of orange, honey-scented flowers in late spring, but is rather coarse in leaf and far from wholeheartedly evergreen. Not so the fresh, yellow-green *Griselinia littoralis* and the darker green *Euonymus japonicus*, both good evergreens. They are often seen, free-growing or clipped into hedges, in maritime areas. Both are first rate windbreaks, able to take the full strength of ocean gales, and the euonymus will even grow right on the seashore. *Griselinia littoralis* will grow to 4·5 m/15 ft as a shrub, or if allowed to develop tree form may reach as much as 10–15 m/33–50 ft.

Also suitable for seashore hedges are *Baccharis patagonica*, a small-leaved evergreen, and the grey, scurfy *Atriplex halimus*, which does not grow much over 1·5 m/5 ft. Of similar stature but greater solidity is *Bupleurum fruticosum*, one of the few shrubby members of the Umbelliferae to be at all frost-hardy. Wind-hardy and suitable for seashore planting it certainly is, though it needs staking at first unless planted very small. With its dark glaucous-green, oblong leaves and typical umbellifer heads of small, acid-green flowers, it is a satisfying if not showy plant. Entirely different is *Muehlenbeckia complexa*, a scrambling New Zealander with wiry black stems and tiny, sparsely borne, rounded or fiddle-shaped leaves. It needs support to reach any height, but could be used to conceal a reasonably robust artificial windbreak, for it is an ideal wind sifter tolerant of maritime exposure.

Many other New Zealand shrubs are well suited to our purpose. *Pittosporum ralphii* is less familiar than *P. tenuifolium*, but is a hardier shrub reaching 3 m/10 ft or so, with thick-textured, leathery oblong leaves, dark green above and white-felted below. It should be planted when small and will grow even near the shore, in sand. The similar *P. crassifolium* is suitable for the mildest districts only; a friend of mine who was the curator of a botanic garden used to say, only half joking, that the only way he could tell them apart was to plant them side by side and see which survived the winter. Much larger in leaf is *Brachyglottis rotundifolia* (*Senecio rotundifolius*, *S. reinoldii*). At Aberystwyth in the campus, this and the very similar *B. elaeagnifolia* (*Senecio elaeagnifolius*) have made large, rounded shrubs, well clothed with thick, leathery, rounded leaves, buff-felted beneath and dark grey-green above. Grown in too much shelter they lose their character to become gangling shrubs, displaying peeling bark which is not sufficient compensation for the loss of their satisfyingly pudding-shaped outline.

Probably as tender is *Hebe dieffenbachii*, a fast-growing, wide-spreading shrub from the Chatham Islands, with almond-green, pointed leaves set in formally tiered ranks along the stems. In autumn it bears clear lilac or white, showy flower spikes. Unlike many hebes it is extremely tolerant of drought. A hebe which is much seen in coastal gardens is *H.* × *franciscana* 'Blue Gem', not very blue, but a bright lilac-mauve in flower, and only a gem in the sense that a dependable but boring acquaintance could be described as one. It has rounded leaves and a hummocky habit well adapted to deflecting wind, but unlike the Chatham Islander it is not tall enough to provide much shelter. *H. salicifolia,* on the other hand, may reach 2 m/6½ ft, and is more appealing, with pointed fresh green leaves lacking the hint of smugness of 'Blue Gem'; the flowers are white, sometimes with a hint of lilac, and very sweetly scented.

Several olearias can be counted among the finest seaside shrubs for shelter and ornament alike. The hardiest, and dullest, is *Olearia* × *haastii*, with small sombre green leaves and off-white flowers quickly dirtying, in late summer. But it is a fine coastal hedge for wind- and wave-battered shores, seldom needing clipping. Also with oval, but compensatingly larger and bolder leaves, are two members of a confusing species often referred to in earlier literature as *O. albida*, which is quite another species. They are now given cultivar status as 'White Confusion', a singularly apt name, and 'Talbot de Malahide', in recognition of the peer of that name who did so much to bring New Zealand and Tasmanian plants to European gardens. The first is considered to be a form of *O. avicenniaefolia*, a big shrub with somewhat pointed oval leaves off-white below and olive green above, flowering in late summer, after 'White Confusion' itself. 'Talbot de Malahide' is the *O. albida* of earlier writers; a very tough shrub, it may be a hybrid of *O. avicenniaefolia*.

No less tolerant of seaspray, and considerably more alluring, is *O. macrodonta*, sometimes called New Zealand holly though unrelated to the genus *Ilex*. It resembles holly in leaf shape only, for it lacks the vicious spines, and is of the grey-green colouring, silvered by the white under-surface of the leaf, that is so appropriate in seaside gardens. If cut hard back at intervals, O. *macrodonta* will remain clothed to the ground with foliage, but allowed to grow unhindered it develops the form of a small tree with peeling papery stems deserving to be seen. The flowers are the usual white daisies, small but borne in great profusion in wide heads in summer. The form 'Major' lives up to its name in all respects, for it has reached a size of 6·5 m/21½ ft high and twice as wide in at least one coastal garden.

Olearia solanderi, and its near lookalike *Cassinia fulvida* (*C. leptophylla fulvida*), also tolerate full exposure on the shore. Both are twiggy shrubs, with short needle leaves, the whole plant given a yellowish cast by the colour of the stems and leaf reverse. The flowers are fluffy creamy heads of tiny daisies, which in the cassinia smell delectably of honey; the olearia wafts from both leaves and blossom a fragrance of heliotrope. The drawback to growing them in a very exposed spot is that much of their perfume will be blown away on the wind. *Olearia virgata* var *lineata* has longer, narrower, greyer needles, and is equally wind hardy. Though it has no beauty of flower, it is an appealing shrub, with long, elegantly whippy stems. The temptingly named O. *odorata* is similar, but less graceful, with stubby leaves and stouter stems. The perfume imputed by the specific name has always eluded me, but that could be because I grew it in the teeth of the wind.

Equally wind-hardy, but more sensitive to frost, are *Olearia furfuracea* and the very similar O. *arborescens*, both with wavy-margined olive green leaves, satin-silvery below, and white daisies in abundant wide heads. O. *arborescens* flowers first, in late spring and early summer; the other follows in late summer. The plant known as 'Rowallane Hybrid', and believed to be O. *arborescens* × O. *macrodonta*, has the toothed leaves of the second parent and the abundant, hanging flower heads of the first; with such parents, it is imperturbably wind-hardy. I would expect O. *capillaris* to be wind resistant also, for it is closely related to, and was once described as a variety of, O. *arborescens*; but it is superficially quite different, a densely branched shrub to 2·4 m/8 ft, with small, rounded leaves grey-white beneath, and corymbs of white flowers. Once it grows tall enough, it displays papery, pale bark.

More tender than these is O. *traversii*, a plant for mild gardens only: it must be grown in the open or it will lose its character. It grows extremely rapidly to a height of 6 m/20 ft, so fast indeed that you should top it once at least, when it reaches 1·5 m/5 ft, cutting back to half its height to help it gain a strong roothold. Its blunt silvery-grey leaves resist the full force of sea spray and wind, and the plant will grow even in sand, but like many Chatham Island shrubs is sensitive to more than a few degrees of frost. The true O. *albida*, a large shrub with big, soft green, wavy-edged leaves, is also remarkably wind-hardy and scarcely resistant to frost. It is something like *O. paniculata*, a shrub of great beauty which, though a little more frost-resistant and just as unperturbed by wind, is so deserving of a sheltered position if one is available that I will say no more about it until a much later chapter.

The genus *Corokia* also includes some fine shrubs of the greyish cast that looks so appropriate by the sea. The hardiest of those of sufficient stature to serve as wind filters is *C. × virgata*. The small, obovate olive-green leaves are white beneath and set on slender, erect stems. In late spring the bush is spangled with yellow starry flowers, which give way to small but showy fruits, orange-red in the type; forms selected for fruit colour have been named 'Red Wonder' and 'Yellow Wonder', and a coppery-leaved form with handsome burnished foliage is known as 'Bronze King'. *C. macrocarpa* is a Chatham Islander more suitable for milder climates than *C. × virgata*, with larger leaves of similar colouring and red fruits; *C. buddleioides* is a little smaller in growth, with slender stems and narrow leaves, white-felted beneath.

Before I leave the New Zealand flora, I must not forget to mention the species of *Metrosideros* from that country. All are more or less frost-tender; some are extremely wind-hardy; and many are spectacular in flower, the brushes of crimson or scarlet stamens set among glossy green or grey-felted foliage. The hardiest species is *M. umbellata*, a native of South Island, New Zealand, and also of the much windier islands to the south. The burnished leaves, from which it had the name we used to use, *M. lucida*, are myrtle-like, coppery mahogany in new growth, some compensation during the twenty years or so that one must wait before it becomes mature enough to flower freely, or at all. Plants in a few Cornish gardens had reached this stage by 1948 when Mr W. Arnold-Forster wrote *Shrubs for the Milder Counties*; by then, too, the severe frosts of 1947 had tested the plants of *M. umbellata* in his own garden, killing or badly damaging them. But even gorse was killed in that winter, and the southern rata had by then survived in his garden, as elsewhere in mild Cornwall, for well over twenty years to make substantial bushes.

In milder climates *M. excelsa* may also be used as a large wind-breaking shrub; for its home is the shore of North Island, New Zealand, where it reaches 15 m/50 ft in the wind and salt spray. Thick, dark green leaves, felted below, are borne on adult plants, but at the juvenile stage the thin-textured leaves are vulnerable to frost. *M. excelsa* succeeds well in the cool coastal strip from San Francisco to San Diego; where in British terms 'cool' is a relative term, for the winters are extremely mild, though the summers can be distinctly chilly in San Francisco – colder than many a British summer's day. *M. excelsa* also grows in the Isles of Scilly in Tresco Abbey gardens. Reportedly hardier forms are offered commercially, and should be tried where there is a chance of success however slim, but if

frosts of more than a degree or two occur regularly, it cannot be considered
as a shelter tree. *M. kermadecensis* differs from *M. excelsa* in its smaller size;
it derives its name from the Kermadec Islands to the north-east of North
Island of New Zealand, and as this suggests it is very tender. The leaves
are greyish, the scarlet flowers borne intermittently almost all year. It
has two variegated forms, very jazzy and and scarcely suitable, visually
speaking, for wind shelter: 'Variegata' is margined with yellow, 'Radiant'
has the leaves splashed at the centre with yellow. A new hybrid selection
of unspecified parentage, said to be suitable for coastal planting in mild
areas, is 'Minstrel', a compact shrub with vivid red flowers. Other species
of *Metrosideros* must wait until a later chapter.

This is not the only genus to offer shrubs and trees that are fully resistant
to salt spray and a wind buffeting where the climate is mild, yet in
colder gardens need the shelter of mature woodland. The same is true of
Myoporum laetum, a New Zealander which quickly grows into a small,
round-headed tree where the climate is very mild. The bright green,
pointed leaves are slightly fleshy in texture, and characteristically speckled
all over with tiny translucent oil glands.

Among *Elaeagnus* species there are many excellent wind resisters, hardier
than the *Metrosideros*. Some are deciduous, some evergreen, the latter more
suitable as year-round wind shelter. None is showy in flower, though
deliciously fragrant, but many are handsome in leaf. The familiar *E.
pungens* is best known in its variegated form 'Maculata', which has too
artificial an air to look quite appropriate as informal wind shelter. But the
plain-leaved form is entirely in character with many of the shrubs already
considered; the foliage is dark green, and somewhat scurfy-silvery below,
and the young shoots are frosted with silvery scales also. The hybrid of
this, *E. × ebbingei*, is even better, with larger leaves; but finest of all is its
other parent, *E. macrophylla*, with broad leaves silver-plated on the reverse.
All make large shrubs bearing small silvery-scaly, intensely fragrant
flowers in autumn. *E. glabra* has narrower leaves, and the useful habit of
scrambling into the lower limbs of neighbouring plants, so that it can be
used to make dense cover at lower levels among shelter-belt pines which
with age develop a clean trunk. A similar scrambling habit belongs to
E. × reflexa, which differs in the bright coppery scales on the leaf undersides
and stems. Deciduous *Elaeagnus* species such as *E. angustifolia*, with narrow
white-felted leaves, and *E. umbellata* with leaves soft green above and
silvery below, are very hardy, and useful as first-line shelter against colder
winds. They are beautiful also, and fragrant in creamy spring flower.

Before I consider some of the conifers and other tall trees suitable for
filtering salty gales, I must mention a few low-growing deciduous shrubs
for milder maritime gardens, which though leafless in winter are twiggy
enough to act as wind-sifters. Foremost among these are *Fuchsia magel-*

lanica, its form *gracilis*, and 'Riccartonii', all so well established as hedging plants in exposed Cornish coastal areas that many people think of them as native to the area, not as South Americans. They are, it is true, hardy almost everywhere, but in cold areas they lose their top growth in winter; in milder parts they maintain a permanent superstructure and form shrubs up to 1·5 m/5 ft or more. Also entirely at home in full exposure to the sea breeze, provided the area is mild, are the forms of *Hydrangea macrophylla*, highly ornamental flowering shrubs which I will consider later in this chapter and elsewhere.

Some of the tamarisks are decorative also; those that are best pruned hard each spring, that is *Tamarix pentandra* and its selection 'Rubra', and *T. ramosissima*, belong in a later chapter, but the species flowering on last year's growths can be allowed to make large shrubs, pruning restricted to some shortening of the shoots immediately after flowering. Such are *T. juniperina*, *T. tetrandra* and *T. parviflora*, all with feathery foliage, pale, bright or sea-green in colour, on dark branches, and large plumes of many tiny pink flowers in late spring. Many will root even from cuttings pushed into the ground where they are to grow. *T. gallica*, a native of south-western Europe, has become naturalized along parts of the English coast.

I must here, before they slip my mind, mention some worthy and valuable wind-hardy shrubs about which I have never been able to enthuse: perhaps precisely because they are so easy, adaptable and undemanding. *Cotoneaster lacteus* is perhaps the least dull, its oval, leathery leaves, large for the genus, grey-felted below, and its red fruits in large clusters lasting well into winter. Like this species, *C. glaucophyllus* is evergreen; it flowers in summer after the other species and ripens its fruits correspondingly later. *C. pannosus* is especially wind-hardy, and graceful in habit, its slender arching branches set with small, sage-green leaves, and deep red fruits in late autumn. There are many other species, but only the evergreens are worthy of consideration in this context.

Many people are as prejudiced against *Rhododendron ponticum* as I am against the cotoneasters, on account of its invasive, self-seeding ways and washy, purple-pink colouring. But despite its faults, which demand that it be kept to the outer reaches of the garden and well away from all the beautiful scarlets and clear yellows which the genus *Rhododendron* can offer us, it is a valuable wind-resister and can be planted as big as you can handle it. It needs like all of the rhododendron tribe, an acid soil. Seen in evening light, its colouring softened to dusky mauve, it is an ideal filler at exposed woodland edges.

If you have space for large trees as your shelter belt, then you could well plant *Quercus ilex*, a handsome, broad-crowned evergreen that should be planted small, at say 30 cm/1 ft. It makes a noble tree in time, or can be clipped to form a hedge: but a big specimen is a bad neighbour, and a nuisance in the more ordered parts of the garden, shedding its hard, unrottable dead brown leaves, mixed with the scurf of its fallen catkins, inconveniently in early summer when one doesn't want to have anything to do with leaf sweeping.

Also needing plenty of space are the salt-hardy pines of which *Pinus muricata*, the bishop pine, and *P. radiata*, the Monterey pine, are the most valuable, tolerant also of sandy soils. The handsomer is *P. radiata*, a three-needled species with bright green foliage and long lasting cones, squashed flat on the side next the branches. But it is less frost-hardy than the two-needled, dull blue-green bishop pine; and it is intolerant of crowding. The Scots pine, *P. sylvestris*, is also resistant to salt winds; and the maritime pine, *P. pinaster*, is much grown both along the southern English coast and in western France, where it forms the aromatic resin forests of the Landes south of Bordeaux. The Corsican pine, *P. nigra maritima*, also thrives in sandy soil and grows rapidly. All the pines tend to grow barelegged with age, so you will need an outer belt of shrubby shelter, of *Griselinia* or *Olearia avicenniaefolia* perhaps, to stop salty draughts reaching the garden proper; but they are beautiful in outline against the sea. The Monterey pine is the fastest in growth.

Faster-growing still, and often recommended for shelter, is the Leyland cypress. It is wind hardy, and can be used to make a tall hedge or allowed to form massive columnar trees. One of the parents of this, *Cupressus macrocarpa*, has often been recommended for coastal areas; but it has drawbacks, not least its lack of stability especially in shallow soils. Having experienced the damage caused by a large *macrocarpa* that keeled over in a gale, and the difficulty of removing such a bulky carcase, I view this as a very serious failing. The Monterey cypress has the reputation also of turning brown after about twelve to fourteen years when grown as a hedge, perhaps because the dense growth promoted by regular clipping prevents air from reaching the trunk. For all that, a large specimen, which has been allowed to develop its spreading, almost cedar-like habit, is a noble tree. Some of the yellow-foliaged variants are surprisingly tolerant of salt spray, more so perhaps than the type: the old 'Lutea', brighter 'Donard Gold', and feathery 'Goldcrest'. To my eyes, however, this colouring, set firmly in the yellow half of the spectrum, jars in the grey and blue, purple and green context of a seaside garden, and needs very careful handling.

The various forms of *Chamaecyparis lawsoniana* are less suitable for gardens exposed to salt spray, though in some places the blue-green or the yellow cultivars have succeeded reasonably well. Thuyas, superficially similar in aspect, though quite different in aroma, are quite useless in maritime exposure.

Within the outer defences

Within the shelter provided by the plants just described a wide range of ornamental trees and shrubs that are almost as wind tolerant will grow. The strawberry tree (*Arbutus unedo*), for example, is surprisingly resilient in the face of gales that are only slightly filtered by front-line shelter. Indeed, I know of specimens growing on cliffs in south Devon, taking the full force of the salty sou-westerlies and of the cold, desiccating spring easterlies alike, yet well clothed with foliage barely scorched. Admittedly, there it does not flower much.

Many hollies, too, and several hebes other than those already mentioned, are remarkably tolerant of wind. *Cordyline australis* stands erect in the face of storm-force winds, though with its characteristic tall trunk and narrow sword leaves it is scarcely adapted to provide any shelter for its neighbours. With a little more shelter, *Luma apiculata* (*Myrtus luma*) and *Crinodendron hookerianum* will succeed: but they look better if spared the worst of the wind, so I prefer to save them for a later chapter. So too with *Brachyglottis repanda*: for although this New Zealander is tolerant of exposure where the garden climate is mild, its large, grey-felted leaves become torn and tattered by wind. It is much more handsome if settled in a spot out of the gales but fully open to light and air.

Taller evergreen trees and shrubs that can be used as the second line of protection where the climate demands and space permits a wide windbreak are several of the spruces (though *Picea abies*, the common spruce, is not suited to coastal exposure) and the Douglas fir, *Pseudotsuga menziesii*; *Garrya elliptica* and its hybrid offspring G. × *thuretii*, with good glossy dark foliage; and *Phillyrea latifolia*, an excellent evergreen tree or large shrub with something of the appearance of a small ilex (*Quercus ilex*, that is, the holm oak) but none of its antisocial garden habits. *Quercus phillyraeoides* sounds, from its name, as though it returns the compliment of imitation, but in fact usually remains as a large shrub reaching perhaps 5 m/18 ft: which may, indeed, be quite tall enough to be useful. *Pittosporum tenuifolium*, though less tolerant of full coastal exposure than *P. ralphii*, thrives and makes tall trees when grown within the outer line of shelter. *P. colensoi* is similar, with larger less undulate leaves; the two seem to intergrade, or perhaps intermarry. Both have little maroon flowers which smell strongly of cheap chocolate.

Grown fully exposed to sea spray and strong winds, *Laurus nobilis* and the larger-leaved, more tender *L. azorica* become scorched; but behind a screen of taller trees they are very fine as second-line shelter. Cherry laurel too, *Prunus laurocerasus*, and the Portugal laurel *P. lusitanica*, make fine shelter within woodland or behind salt-resistant pines or holm oak. In such a position too, *Photinia* (*Stranvaesia*) *davidiana* and its forms should make good wind screens.

Barriers within the garden may also take the form of hedges. Several of the plants suggested as suitable for full exposure will make good internal hedges also: escallonias (to which we can add the numerous named cultivars, most of them of more modest growth than *Escallonia macrantha* and its near derivatives); *Euonymus japonicus*; *Hebe* 'Blue Gem'; *Baccharis patagonica*, which flowers inconspicuously in spring, and the hardier *B. halimifolia* or tree groundsel, a tall shrub with sage green leaves and white flowers in autumn; and *Griselinia littoralis*. Even the despised privet, *Ligustrum ovalifolium*, may have its uses: it is fast and cheap, rooting from cuttings stuck where it is to grow. But it is greedy, easily gets bare-legged, and seems to succumb easily to honey fungus infections, which kill it off in stretches. In mild districts privet remains evergreen. I would hesitate to use the golden-leaved form, 'Aureum', as a clipped hedge, for it is too garish; but both this and, especially, the cream-variegated 'Argenteum' are pleasant things when allowed to grow freely into specimen shrubs. *Lavatera arborea* is a rather coarse-leaved shrub, but very well adapted to growing in coastal exposures; the purple-red flowers are quite showy but not a good colour. The Californian *L. assurgentiflora* is used in the same way for hedging. And the Japanese *Rosa rugosa* grows in the wild on sandy seashores, so is well suited to use as an informal flowering hedge in seaside gardens. It sheds its leaves in autumn, but is twiggy enough to act as a wind filter even when bare. Surprisingly, the bamboos *Arundinaria* (*Pseudosasa*) *japonica* and *Arundinaria* (*Pleioblastus*) *simonii* are remarkably wind-tolerant and can be used to screen sections of the garden; both can be invasive. A formal, but rather slow, hedge could be made from holly, *Ilex aquifolium*, for both this and the hybrid *I.* × *altaclarensis* are tolerant of wind. Their fallen leaves and clippings, however, are extremely hostile to ungloved fingers. In very mild gardens the plant which W. Arnold-Forster knew as *Coprosma baueri* can be used to make a fine evergreen seaside hedge, its highly polished leaves reflecting the play of light from sun and water. The true *C. baueri* may not be in cultivation; Arnold-Forster's plant was perhaps *C. repens*. Another of this style is *C. lucida*, with quite large elliptic leaves, very glossy on the upper surface.

A garden without shelter

Of the shrubs suitable for hedges and screens, several are very fast-growing: escallonias, *Olearia traversii*, Leyland's cypress among them. You should get a good hedge of 3–4 m/10–13 ft within five years from any of these. But what of the early years? And what if you are prepared to put up with a wind battering yourself, not just in the first few years but for the foreseeable future, for the sake of a fine view, but still want a garden of some kind? If this is your case, then you must grow plants that are resistant to wind, low-growing so as not to obscure your view, and ornamental as well.

The basis of your planting should be a firm framework of evergreen shrubs which will give the garden a furnished appearance at all seasons. There are many shrubs with persistent leaves that will thrive in windy gardens so long as the climate is kind. And because they have evolved various ways of withstanding the onslaught of wind, they come in a variety of textures both visual and tactile. To recapitulate, some have thick and leathery leaves with a tough epidermis or a highly polished protective film, or a waxy finish; others are shielded by a scaly or scurfy coating, by a felting of silvery or bronze fine hairs, or by a gummy resin: some even combine two characteristics, giving the typical glossy upper surface and thickly felted reverse of the leaves of many of the best wind-resisting shrubs; yet others bring an entirely different character to the garden by disposing almost wholly of their leaves, the necessary functions performed by evergreen stems.

If your garden runs right to the shore, you may need to choose plants that grow willingly in sand or shingle, as well as resisting salt spray. Some cistuses, unlikely candidates though they may seem, do well: *Cistus crispus*, with felted leaves and vivid magenta flowers, is just one. And with the mention of colour, I want to hark back to a suggestion made earlier: that – as Dame Sylvia Crowe has observed – the dominant colours in a seascape are greys and blues, purples and greens; and that the happiest results will be achieved if in the choice of plants this range of the spectrum is allowed to dominate. Contrasting colours of orange or red or bright yellow need to be used with discretion where they cannot intrude into the wider land- and seascape. The magenta of *Cistus crispus*, though vivid, is in the right sector of the spectrum and will not jar as would a strong scarlet. This species makes low mounded bushes, effectively covering the ground: another valued attribute, for the dense foliage helps to trap blown sand, keeping it from the vulnerable stems of your plants. Others that seem impervious to salt spray are pale pink *C.* × *skanbergii* and *C. parviflorus*, both with greyish foliage, and the greener, white-flowered *C. salvifolius*.

Lower, denser cover still for seashore gardens is the Japanese shore juniper, *J. conferta*. Its fresh apple green needles are painfully prickly to handle, but the visual texture of this spreading shrub is pleasantly uneven without harshness, the main branches growing horizontally but side shoots tending upwards, like waves on a choppy sea. The flatter-growing *J. horizontalis* will also thrive in sandy soils; some forms have grey, glaucous

or purple-tinted foliage, especially in winter, contrasting effectively with
J. conferta.

From New Zealand come many low-growing shrubs suitable for blowy
gardens, as well as the taller species giving wind shelter. Some of the
smaller *Brachyglottis* species (senecios) are unsurpassed. The familiar 'Sunshine', often labelled *Senecio laxifolius* or *S. greyi*, is in fact one of a group
collectively known as the Dunedin hybrids, in which the blood of both
these species and also that of *B. compacta* is said to run. *B. compacta* itself,
as the name implies, is dwarfer and closer-textured; its wavy leaf margins
are whitened by the dense felting on the undersides, and the flowers are
the usual handsome yellow daisies. The leaf margins of *B. monroi* are even
more crimped, and the whole plant has a pewter-grey cast, with leaves
white-felted beneath; it is impervious to the fiercest wind off the ocean
and forms a dense mound. If *B. rotundifolia*, already proposed as a large
shrub for the first line of defence, is too bulky, then there are smaller
alternatives for coastal gardens. A compact, 1·2 m/4 ft form of *B. elaeagnifolia* named 'Joseph Andrews' is often labelled *Senecio elaeagnifolius* var
buchananii, but the *Brachyglottis buchananii* of botanists has thinner leaves,
silvered below. Smaller in leaf, *B. bidwillii* slowly reaches perhaps 1·5 m/5 ft
in mild areas; it has rounded, extremely thick leaves of dark bluish green
with buff felting beneath.

Of similar colouring to these brachyglottis are many olearias, but their
ray florets are never yellow. Not all the species in this antipodean genus
are wind-hardy, and I shall reserve some for later chapters. But in the
open coastal garden, as well as the big wind-filtering species already
described, there are several smaller olearias that will add their own character to the predominantly grey or sombre green colouring. Least exciting,
perhaps, though pleasant in its smooth pewter grey foliage, is *Olearia*
'Waikariensis'. More markedly olive green above and white beneath in
leaf is *O. cheesemannii*, very like a small version of *O. avicenniaefolia*; it
covers itself in early summer with fragrant white daisies. *O. rani* and *O.
cunninghamii* are names sometimes attached to this species, suggesting that
it has provoked as much confusion in the minds of taxonomists as the
larger 'White Confusion' itself. But the complexities of these are as naught
compared with the doubt surrounding the true identity of '*O. mollis*', a
name of no standing whatever, botanically, in relation to the shrub that
usually bears it in gardens. Someone should boldly publish a suitable
cultivar name for this most silvered of olearias. A low mound of 1–
1·5 m/3–5 ft in most gardens (but – be warned – as much as
2·8 × 4·5 m/9 × 15 ft where well suited), '*O. mollis*' has waxy leaves, quite
small and neat, with wavy margins and a musky odour derived from one
parent, *O. moschata*; the flowers are typical heads of small white daisies in
late spring. The other parent of '*O. mollis*' is *O. ilicifolia*, which has leaves

much narrower than *O. macrodonta* and correspondingly less holly-like: though, apart from their grey colouring, one can imagine a resemblance to one of the more tender holly species if not to the common *Ilex aquifolium* itself. *O. ilicifolia* is coloured much like *O. macrodonta*, grey-green above and white beneath, with sharp toothed and seductively undulate margins; the white daisies appear at midsummer. I have not found it as accommodating in captivity as *O. macrodonta*, which has a miniature form, 'Minor', to use where the type would be too large.

Another of *O. ilicifolia*'s offspring is one of the most desirable of all shrubs, *O.* 'Zennorensis'. Its name tells us that it grew in W. Arnold-Forster's garden, battered by gales from both the north and south Atlantic coasts of Cornwall, so its wind-hardiness is not in question. Long, very narrow, olive-green leaves, buff felted below, are set all along their margins with small sharp teeth. The other parent, *O. lacunosa*, is a tricky beast to raise and must wait its turn in a later chapter.

Perhaps it is time for a little relief from so many thickly felted, silvered or grey leaves. We need not leave the genus *Olearia* to encounter some very different shrubs, suitable for exposed coastal gardens. The yellow-toned *O. solanderi* has already received mention. Only slightly less yellow-complexioned, but with minute, circular, stubby leaves close-set on the branches, is *O. nummularifolia*. The flowers are nothing much, though they do smell sweet. With *O.* × *scilloniensis*, however, we come to a shrub where the leaves are no more than an agreeable grey-green setting for the mass of white daisy heads that all but obscure the foliage in late spring. It is a rapid grower which should be pruned by removing the flowered shoots after blooming. Unlike other members of this soft-leaved, conspicuously-flowered group of olearias it is pretty wind-hardy, so that it has just earned itself a place in this chapter instead of the next. I hesitate, too, over *O. semidentata* (*O.* 'Henry Travers'), which of all the members of this desirable genus is perhaps the one leaving me weakest with admiration. It is not that easy to please, and the usually recommended recipe is for a moist yet not soggy soil and a constantly moist atmosphere. If the second is not in doubt – for all seaside gardens enjoy a comparatively moist atmosphere due to the presence of salt crystals in the air, which is why they feel so unhospitable when the temperature drops even a little – the first is less certain. W. Arnold-Forster tells us that the finest plants he ever saw were in full sun on a south-facing slope, among boulders. Perhaps the boulders were the answer, giving the olearia a cool refuge for its roots. Certainly salt gales are no threat to this Chatham Island species, which thrives at Inverewe, in western Scotland, right down to the shoreline. Here it is a wonderful sight at flowering time, each large, solitary, long-stalked daisy opening deep lilac around a violet-purple disk; as the ray florets fade with age, the bush presents a varied play of colour to which the narrow, pointed, toothed leaves, grey-green above and silver-white beneath, add just the right note. O. *chathamica* is similar, broader in leaf with pale violet rays fading to white around the sombre purple disk.

Though they have not the hold on my heart of olearias, hebes are also essential ingredients in the windy coastal garden. There are several of pewter, glaucous or silvery-green colouring, forming hummocks of pointed or blunt, waxy leaves: ideal small shrubs to clothe the ground at the front of your shrub borders, and perhaps to pull together, with their quiet tones, a disparate planting. Narrow-leaved *H. recurva* reaches 90 cm/3 ft; *H. colensoi* 'Glauca', *H. albicans*, 'Pewter Dome', and the similar but slightly bolder *H. clarkii* are of denser habit; all are white flowered, and the last two especially have spikes as triangular as kittens' tails, opening from pinkish buds and enhanced by chocolate anthers. The tiny shell-like leaves of *H. carnosula* are glaucous also; they are closely set on prostrate stems, somewhat like the better-known and greyer *H. pinguifolia* 'Pagei'. In amongst all these grey tones, the fresh apple-green of *H. rakaiensis* (better known, incorrectly, as *H. subalpina*), paler and dwarfer *H. topiaria*, or the widespreading 'White Gem' make a pleasant change; they are especially welcome in winter for their spring-fresh colouring.

As its name implies, *H. cupressoides* is quite different in aspect, resembling a small mounded conifer of glaucous tone, even carrying the mimicry as far as the juniperous aroma of its foliage; it bears tiny blue veronica flowers in late spring. The true whipcord hebes have green or, often, bronzed or old-gold conifer-like foliage closely appressed to the stems. Those that are suitable for our purpose include the low arching 'James Stirling' and the more upright *H. ochracea* (which is often miscalled *H. armstrongii*, a greener whipcord), both of ochre colouring. All these are remarkably frost-hardy as well as wind-tolerant. Another group, which have purple or bronzed, quite narrow leaves, are almost as resistant to cold. Names to look for are 'Mrs Winder' with purple foliage, and the lighter, bronzed 'Waikiki'; both have lance-shaped leaves and form domes of 90 cm/3 ft or so. Their flowers are lilac-blue and of no great consequence.

The group of hybrids deriving largely from *Hebe speciosa* is another matter. Here we have a race of frost-tender but brightly flowered shrubs of which the foliage, with a few worthy exceptions, is unexciting to boring, pointed oval with the characteristic tough epidermis that makes hebes so resistant to salt winds. With the exception of hydrangeas, no other group of shrubs brings so much vivid colour to coastal gardens in late summer; and as the colouring of both hebes and hydrangeas lies in the blue half of the spectrum, they bring no alien note to the landscape. Those who garden in cold inland areas are forced to treat the *speciosa* hebes, most years, as bedding plants, renewed annually from cuttings; in milder parts they become permanencies, covered in late summer with sweetly scented spikes. The hardiest, in my experience, is 'Midsummer Beauty', which may or may not actually have *H. speciosa* blood in it; its comparative frost-resistance derives from the tough *H. salicifolia*, which is also no doubt the source of its delicious fragrance. It makes a big mound of shrub 1·2 m/4 ft or more high and wide, and bears its long, slender lilac spikes from summer till early winter; to hold your attention in its short flowerless season, the foliage is plum-red on the reverse, especially when young.

An old cultivar variously known as 'Alicia Amherst', 'Veitchii', or 'Royal Purple' (they may, originally, have been separate but closely similar clones) has deep royal-violet flowers, a striking colour but to my eyes not one that assorts quite happily with the assertively green foliage. 'Amy' and 'Purple Queen' both have violet-purple flowers among bronzed foliage, and similar colouring belongs to the much hardier 'Autumn Glory', which has smaller, rounder leaves margined in red-purple, and shorter flower spikes. Getting nearer to crimson-purple is 'La Séduisante'; while the nicest of those with deep-toned flowers is 'Simon Delaux', of rich crimson set off by plum-suffused foliage. Lighter than this, in strong purple-pink, is 'Gauntlettii'. 'Gloriosa' (also known as 'Pink Pearl') flowers before this and is twice as tall, with flowers of a cleaner, bright pink. Paler pinks include 'Carnea', reaching like most of these hebes about 1·2 m/4 ft if not frosted; the foliage is light green, the flowers rosy pink fading to white to give a pretty two-toned effect. Similar, but much hardier, is 'Great Orme'. The Wand series, 'White Wand', 'Violet Wand', 'Pink Wand' and 'Blush Wand', are all good coastal shrubs reaching 1·8 m/6 ft and flowering in summer; they were raised in Cornwall.

I may have been cool about the foliage of these showy hebes; but no one could overlook, though they might dislike, the variegated kinds. The old 'Andersonii Variegata' has quite large, elliptic, pointed leaves, broadly margined in ivory-white and softened with grey-green at the centre. The spikes of scented flowers, deep lavender fading to white, are worth having. 'Ann Pimm' is very similar but that the flower spikes are bright pink. There is also a variegated form of the pink 'Carnea', in which the leaves are smaller and narrower. And last of the variegated hebes that I think worth growing is the plant I knew for years as *H. speciosa* 'Tricolor'; but we must now, it seems, call it 'Purple Tips', a name no more inspired and less expressive of its grey-green and cream, plum-suffused foliage. The flowers are of the same reddish purple that we find in 'La Séduisante'. Don't bother with *H. × franciscana* 'Variegata'; let it remain in London window boxes, where its stubby, cream-bordered foliage in ordered ranks is as smug as some of the City institutions whose edifices it adorns.

It is time to consider some plants other than those from New Zealand, and at the same time perhaps to suggest some specific associations. The only resemblance between *Lupinus arboreus* and the *Hebe speciosa* hybrids, apart from their tolerance of wind and sea spray, is that they have fragrant flowers in spikes. But the tapering lupin spires are quite different, composed of pea flowers less densely packed than in border lupins of the Russell type. The typical colouring is a soft yellow; seedlings vary slightly to deeper or more lemony or creamy tones, and there are also white and violet or lavender forms. Least desirable are the yellows into which a touch of lavender has crept. Tree lupins, which are natives of California, are so quick and easy from seed that unless you must have a particular colour it is hardly worth bothering with cuttings. They flower from midsummer onwards, filling the air around with their warm beanfield perfume, and out of flower are comely in fresh green, fingered foliage. There is no better plant for a quick filler or as a nurse to some less resilient shrub; but do not discard your tree lupins once they have fulfilled this role, for they are much too pretty. You could point up the contrasting form of their spikes by setting one against *Hebe* 'Midsummer Beauty', lavender and pale yellow together.

The south European *Lavatera thuringiaca* (*L. olbia* of gardens) is rather formless, even more soft-wooded than the tree lupin but surprisingly wind-resistant. What you get from seed, as often as not, has wretched little flowers of dirty mauve-pink; but named cultivars can be excellent. The old 'Rosea' has large, paler and clearer pink flowers, while those of 'Kew Rose' are deep rose-pink. 'Bressingham Pink' is pale pink, and the delicious 'Barnsley' has petals almost white, fading towards pink, heightened by the bright pink centre of the flower. 'Peppermint' is white with a green heart. If you find them too tall, at 1·5 m/5 ft or more, then you could try 'Shorty', which is like 'Rosea' but half the height.

Some *Ceanothus*, like the tree lupins a Californian genus, grow in nature on coastal sand flats and exposed slopes. They are valued for the great range of rich or tender blue they offer, as well as pale smoke, amethyst and lilac, and white. Many are extremely drought-resistant and will find a place in a later chapter, with a wider range of *Cistus* than those suggested a few pages back, and many other plants of hot, dry regions. *Ceanothus rigidus* (described in Chapter VI, p. 173) is a species that could be tried in very exposed gardens, for its home is the windy sand flats of Monterey. In the open it makes a mound of 1·2 m/4 ft or so. Much more vigorous, and more frost resistant, is *C. thyrsiflorus repens*; its dark glossy leaves are larger than those of *C. rigidus*, and its flowers a clearer but paler sky-blue, in spring. It assorts well with *Cytisus × praecox*, an almost leafless mound of arching green stems reaching 1·5 m/5 ft which erupt into massed, heavy-scented cream flowers in spring; the deeper 'Allgold' I find too strong a colour for the ceanothus. *Ceanothus griseus* is another coastal species, its prostrate form var. *horizontalis* often met, in gardens, as 'Yankee Point'.

In gardens it forms a 1·2 m/4 ft mound, wider than high, with flowers of bright blue.

So far I have been dealing almost solely with shrubs of mounded outline; and indeed, this profile, allied to leaves with a protective film or felt coating, is one of the best adaptations to strong wind, allowing it to pass as smoothly as possible over the surface of the shrub which offers no vertical resistance to the airstream. However, a garden that consists only of molehill-shaped shrubs would be unsatisfactory to the eye; an element of contrast is needed. This the phormiums are ideally adapted to provide. I shall reserve for the next chapter many of the recent, brightly coloured cultivars, for they seem to me to fit better into the more consciously gardened context of a mixed border than into the kind of planting I am considering here where the wind and the seascape impose practical and aesthetic limitations. But the muted green of *Phormium tenax* itself, or the quieter manifestations of purple or variegated-leaved forms, are entirely acceptable, as also is the shorter *P. cookianum* (*P. colensoi*). The two species have in common sword-shaped leaves of extraordinary, fibrous toughness. Those of *P. tenax* may measure up to 3 m/10 ft long and up to 12·5 cm/5 ins wide; they are normally held stiffly upright, displaying their somewhat glaucous reverse. Sometimes the leaf margins are thinly outlined in red-brown. The claw-shaped flowers are rust-red also, and borne on stiff, plum-dark stems as much as 4 m/13 ft tall. The leaves of *P. cookianum* are more flexible, often recurving gracefully; they measure up to 1·5 m/5 ft long and 6 cm/2½ ins wide. The flowers are less colourful. The smaller species does not appear to have produced any purple-leaved forms, but *P. tenax* has given us 'Purpureum', in which the leaves are overlaid with glaucous purple with a grape-like bloom on the reverse, deeper 'Atropurpureum', and massive, 3 m/10 ft tall 'Purple Giant', with broad, bronzed leaves. In a seaside garden I know, 'Purpureum' is used to great effect in bold alternating clumps with large bushes of the hydrangea 'Joseph Banks', which has mopheads opening cream and aging, on the acid soil of this garden, to pale blue. Seven or eight each of the phormium and hydrangea are set against a high, whitewashed wall. The ability to plant with such restraint is enviable: most of us surely would be tempted to experiment with a wide variety of plants that would enjoy the shelter of that wall, with results conceivably more interesting horticulturally, but scarcely so powerful visually. It may have helped the owners of that particular garden, in reaching their decision to opt for an uncomplicated design, that the planting is on the outside of their boundary wall, facing a lane where coast walkers pass in large numbers. We have all suffered from 'finger blight', the loss of plant material caused by those who seem to believe that stealing cuttings, or even whole plants, is not theft.

Purple-leaved phormiums often produce seedlings of similar cast, but variegated forms, whether *P. tenax* or *P. cookianum*, are much less likely to have variegated offspring. In informal settings I would be reluctant to use anything more jazzy than *P. tenax* 'Variegatum', with muted creamy-white margins, or perhaps the two 'Tricolor' variants, one from each species: for in both, the tricolouring is limited to a restrained cream margin with red edges. Unlike many other plants with sword leaves, phormiums bear their leaves in one plane, forming fans, instead of rosettes. They are best set among low-growing plants so that their bold outline is unobscured. The leaves rattle dismally in high winds, but seldom become tattered unless at the tips.

Because of their permanent foliage, phormiums are often classed as shrubs though they form no wood and are therefore more accurately regarded as perennials. They are not the only perennials that can be grown in exposed gardens where there is little shelter. Also with sword leaves, but of quite different character, is the genus *Kniphofia*. Again, I prefer to save mention of most of the red hot pokers until the next chapter; but two that grow well right down on the shore, one a species, the other a hybrid of unknown parentage, are fine plants of greater character than the old *K. uvaria*, which itself will grow in rough places exposed to sea spray. The species I would choose in its place is *K. caulescens*. Its broad, intensely glaucous blue leaves arising in rosettes from the procumbent stems that lie along the soil surface like elephants' trunks give it an almost tropical appearance, though it is remarkably frost hardy. It needs, to preserve the foliage in good condition all season, a well-drained but fertile soil; the generally moister climates of maritime areas suit it well, and it will grow right on the shore. The stout flower spikes appear from midsummer onwards; at first muted coral pink, they age to ice-green. 'Atlanta', also with glaucous leaves, has much brighter orange-red to bicolor pokers in late spring. It is equally tolerant of shore sand and seaspray.

One of the easiest low-growing perennials for wind-battered coastal gardens is *Erigeron glaucus*; but you will need to keep it well away from the kniphofias, for its stubby-rayed, mauve-pink daisies with wide yellow disks clash with warm colours. Broad greyish foliage on spreading stems makes this a good weed excluder. Forming much wider carpets are the Hottentot fig, *Carpobrotus edulis*, and its near ally *C. aciniciformis*, both from Cape Province, South Africa. They bear thick succulent leaves, triangular in cross section, and many-rayed daisy-like flowers in summer. The first is bright magenta-lilac in colour; the other runs also to orange-buff, lemon, and soft yellow. They can be seen growing on the cliffs at Dawlish and elsewhere in south Devon, where they receive full measure of the salt-laden winds and sea spray with equanimity. Somewhat more restrained cover is provided by *Osteospermum barberiae*, one of the most suitable of the genus for very windy gardens; it has mauve-pink daisies with bronzed reverse, a brighter colour with less blue in it than the soft lilac-pink *O. jucundum*, which could also be tried. *O. barberiae* of gardens is, I should tell you, actually *O. jucundum* according to *Index Hortensis*; one of them, I should not like to say which, has probably entered into the parentage of 'Hopley', 'Lady Leitrim' and 'Langtrees', all of them of spreading habit, the flower heads with yellow disk and pink-mauve or white, pink-splashed ray florets. Any of them would form ideal low cover about the feet of your phormiums. Osteospermums of upright habit, or those with long trailing stems that risk being twisted and torn by gales, are less suitable and will be described in a later chapter.

Some *Libertia* species are ideally suited to seaside gardens, thriving in the moist air, resistant to salt, and flowering abundantly even in the dark spaces under pines. *L. formosa* grows to 90 cm/3 ft or so and bears its vividly white triangular flowers, enhanced by yellow stamens, in early summer; *L. grandiflora* is similar. Both have decorative orange-brown seed pods in autumn, and self-sow freely to make wide carpets of dense, weed-excluding clumps. *L. ixioides* is smaller, and flowers a little later; its leaves may turn orange-brown in winter. But the most colourful in leaf is *L. peregrinans*, a smallish species with each narrow, stiff leaf bright orange and green; 'Gold Leaf' is a selected form.

This is not the total of plants woody and non-woody that can be grown in seaside gardens without shelter; and even where no wind- and salt-filtering screens are planted, as low shrubs grow and knit together they will create small pockets of shelter within which the less resistant plants can be tried. In later chapters we shall meet many other plants from which you can choose, as well as those − treated chiefly in the chapter on the mature milder garden − which must be protected from gales and salt spray.

Planting and aftercare

It pays, almost invariably, to plant small in windy districts. (The greater vulnerability to vandalism of small trees in public places need not, I hope, concern us in our private gardens.) And small means very small. An ilex or a *Pinus radiata* that is much over 30–45 cm/12–18 in is already too big if it is to have the best chance of establishing itself firmly in its new quarters. *Pittosporum crassifolium* and *P. ralphii*, *Brachyglottis rotundifolia*, *Olearia traversii*, shrubby wind-resisters all, should go out as little seedlings or rooted cuttings no more than 30 cm/12 in tall. Some escallonias can even be stuck as cuttings where they are to grow. This does admittedly imply more aftercare than if they were a little larger, in that they are more readily swamped by weeds, trodden on by invading livestock including the human variety, or simply overlooked if the garden needs watering in times of drought; but the benefits, as they mature into firm, windfast specimens, outweigh this extra trouble. And if you did plant them larger, gave them less attention as they grew, and then found yourself after an especially fierce gale with a sizeable hole in your defences where a four- or five-year-old *Olearia traversii*, say, had blown over: in this case you would surely regret your misplaced impatience. There are exceptions, as we have seen: *Rhododendron ponticum* and *Griselinia littoralis* both move well without serious loss of stability even when large; but you cannot rely on them to plug gaps at short notice where your own failure in the early years of a plant's life has led to its demise at an inconvenient moment in the life of your garden.

If ever the old adage 'sixpence on the plant, and a pound on the hole' applied, it does so in windy gardens. Just pause to adjust these figures for inflation and decimalization, and ask yourself if you have ever, having spent £3.50 or so on a shrub, then spent the equivalent – in time, effort and money – of £140 on the hole you put it in. These were pre-decimal sixpences, remember, forty of them to the pound sterling. And £3.50 is not much these days for anything but the most commonplace shrub.

There follow from this two points. First, your soil and site preparation should never be skimped: and the stronger the winds your plants will have to withstand the truer this is. Second, never attempt to plant at one session more than you can cope with in the time you have available. This is not so vitally important when your plants are growing in containers and can be left, suitably protected and kept moist, for another day if need be; but even then you run the risk of trying to prepare a bigger area than you can quickly plant, which may be wasted effort. Digging your planting holes beforehand, in the off-season of winter, and filling in when the shrubs and trees are ready, is no answer. Nature being what she is, almost certainly a downpour will follow, and unless you garden on almost pure sand your holes may turn into sumps, to the detriment of your plants' root systems when finally you get them in. And even digging over the whole area, incorporating humus and nutrients, and then leaving it for weeks or months, may not be such a good idea: for newly dug soils also become waterlogged more easily than undisturbed terrain. Much depends on the nature of your soil.

When is the best season to plant? Remembering that much of what you are planting is less than fully frost-hardy, and that even in mild districts the soil is cold and the winds feel even colder in winter, late spring planting is safest, at least for all your evergreens. But there is then another hazard to face: for, especially in maritime districts of Britain and northern France, fierce, desiccating and chilly easterlies blow relentlessly in spring, damaging many plants, especially those vulnerable, newly-set shrubs and trees making tender new growths. Even so, I still think this is a lesser hazard than winter gales, and when I come to the question of aftercare I will suggest some of the ways you can help your plants to cope. The ideal planting weather is mild and still with a light, fine drizzle; but we all know that such ideal conditions seldom occur when they should.

I hope that wherever you are thinking of planting, right out in full exposure or in a sheltered part of the garden, you will prepare the soil thoroughly, digging in plenty of humus, especially on sandy or heavy clay soils. Clay can be improved, too, by liberal helpings of coarse grit. You may, if your soil is heavy and lies wet in winter, need to lay drains. Water that is moving, as it might be from springs, is less of a threat than stagnant water, but few plants that are perhaps already required to cope with colder winters than they are well-equipped for will relish the extra stress of wet feet during the cold season.

At all costs you must ensure that the roots of your plants have room to travel, uncramped. This means not only preparing an adequate planting hole, but also ensuring that stony or shaly ground or chalk subsoil is well broken up. In the chalk garden at Highdown, Sir Frederick Stern found that provided the solid chalk was thoroughly broken up with a pick, almost any plant that was not calcifuge would thrive, for its roots were able to penetrate deep to sources of moisture; but if a hole only big enough to take the roots was dug and the surrounding subsoil left undisturbed, very soon the plant starved, as truly as if potgrown and never fed or potted on. Some thin, sandy soils, where you might expect drainage to be perfect, are deceptive; for an iron-hard, impenetrable layer known as a hard pan may be lurking some way down. And excessively rocky ground may need to be subdued with pick and crowbar. Once there is a way through for the roots, such soils can be more congenial to the plants than you would imagine, for there is coolness and moisture among the stones. Even more important, though, than the plants' need for moisture – for, water company restrictions permitting, this can at least be artificially supplied – is the matter of roothold. It was borne in upon many of us, after the near-hurricane gales of October 1987 in southern England, that many large trees had pitifully small roots; and trees depend upon their roots for anchorage as well as for sustenance. Freedom for the roots to travel underground, unimpeded by any obstacle, will ensure a firm hold as well as a greater ability to withstand drought as the roots explore ever wider in search of moisture.

And that brings me to the question of the size of planting hole. Never, on any account, make it too small for the roots. This may seem like elementary advice, but it is, I suspect, all too often ignored. These days you will be planting almost everything out of containers – which you will, of course, have previously soaked in a bucket of water so that the rootball is uniformly moist. Except in the case of plants with extremely sensitive roots, it pays to break that rootball a little: the way I do it is to tuck the fingers of both hands, back to back, into the bottom of the rootball and twist gently, feathering the rootlets outwards so that the roots – which will probably have begin to curl inwards in their containers – can be encouraged to start on their journey through the soil. Anything which has become potbound to the extent of showing a main root or two coiling around the base of the pot will never become windfast. This is another argument for planting small, before the roots have become cramped. Even if a plant which has reached this rootbound stage, once planted, survives being tipped sideways whenever there is a gale, nothing is more maddening than to have to go round setting things upright all the time. I once inherited a *Leptospermum* – one of the double crimson variants of *L. scoparium* – which had obviously been planted when too large. It fell over whenever the wind blew hard, though all around it were specimens far taller, either properly planted when tiny or in some cases self-sown seedlings, standing erect without any assistance.

If the soil, or the weather, or both, are at all dry, you should consider puddling-in your new plants. Set them in their holes, making sure that the roots are well spread out and the top of the root ball is level with the soil surface, then quickly pour in a full bucket of water. Fill in with friable, moist compost, some of which you will also have incorporated with the surrounding soil. Firm very positively, with your full weight on the backs of both hands or on your heel. Then, taking care that you do not pile it too thickly around the collar of the plant, apply a mulch to keep the moisture in. Coarse-ground bark does not blow about too much and looks quite appropriate in a woodland or shrubby setting; in more open areas, where perhaps you are trying to evoke a Mediterranean or desert atmosphere, a pebble or gravel mulch may be more suitable.

Aftercare consists of ensuring at all times that your new plants do not dry out. That means not just roots, but also the tophamper. The wind, blowing across the leaves of your plants, increases the rate at which they lose moisture through transpiration, and until they have taken hold and made new feeding roots they may be unable to make good that loss. Regular spraying with fresh water, perhaps with added foliar feed at intervals, and if need be temporary wind screens of netting or laths, will help. If, despite all your efforts by way of spraying and shelter, your plants begin to flag, indicating an unsustainable loss of moisture, you may have to resort to defoliating. This does not mean stripping off all the leaves; merely about half of them. Pick them off, or if the leafstalks are resistant snip them off cleanly with secateurs. You will immediately reduce by half the amount of moisture the roots are called upon to supply. Sometimes a newly-planted shrub or tree, stressed by lack of moisture, may respond by spontaneously shedding all its leaves. This is an encouraging sign, and provided you still spray the plant over from time to time so the tissues of stem and bark do not dry out, it will probably leaf up again once the roots have made headway. The plants to worry about are those that turn brown without shedding foliage.

In windy areas it pays also to plant closely: much more closely than in more tranquil gardens. The price of this is constant vigilance to ensure that your plants are not crowding each other: though more plants perhaps than we think will grow as interlacing colonies, to form what looks like one cohesive whole. The benefits of close planting are increased resistance to wind as the plants more quickly knit together and support each other; mutual shelter from both sun and cold for the roots; and even a tiny, but perhaps critical, increase in ambient temperature, as more of the minute amounts of heat emitted by each are retained rather than blown away on the wind.

Some plants can be moved – notwithstanding the comments about planting small – as they grow too large and crowd their neighbours. Perhaps by the time you need to shift them, enough shelter will be available in your garden to give congenial homes for larger plants. But more likely you will simply dispose of the now unwanted plants. *Cistus*, hebes (though these will move quite happily even when of a fair size, thanks to their fibrous root system), tree lupin, escallonias and many others are all so easy to increase by seeds or cuttings, and so quick to grow, that it is no real hardship to start them again elsewhere, provided they are furnishings, not wind-filters that cannot be dispensed with. Clearly, you must make sure that you get the placing of your permanencies right first time: ilex, pines, and all the major components of tall wind-screens among them.

If you plant small, you should not need to worry too much about staking even in full exposure, especially if you can check your plants regularly, and firm back into place any that have worked loose. Grown thus, which is how they would grow in nature (though without the benefit of the gardener's timely heel), the roots may be wrenched and torn from time to time, but they will at least make their own roothold without becoming lazy. If staking is essential, a single stake and one or more ties, as is usually sufficient inland, will hardly do as support against ocean gales. A cage of three or four posts united by cross-bars at the top is what you need for trees that have already formed a trunk when you plant them, not least because the wind may blow almost as violently from another direction as from the prevailing quarter, forcing single-staked trees onto their supports with dire results as the bark chafes and maybe even the heads are snapped clean off. In the cage the ties should be fixed to the cross-bars, with the tree held securely in the centre by the ties.

Shrubs of suitable habit, with branches close to the ground, can be pegged down as the branches develop. This is beneficial in several ways. The shrub is encouraged to form a rounded outline furnished to the ground, making its own root shading. It may even form roots where the branches are pegged to the soil, making it still more root firm. And with several points of attachment it is much more secure against the twisting and rocking effects of wind, that can be so damaging. I have seen plants twisted right out of the ground, or badly damaged with many broken stems, or more insidiously hurt as a conical hollow with sides of smooth, beaten soil forms around the main stem, trapping water. The result is rot at ground level, or bark split if frost is severe enough to freeze the water. The pegged stems can be held to the ground with stones – make sure they are heavy enough to do the job without risk of the stems being wrenched from under them by the wind – or with pegs. Sections of bamboo stem, with the side shoot forming the V of the peg, work well and are quick and easy to prepare if you have growing bamboo to hand. The sort of plants that gain from pegging down are *Cistus*, *Brachyglottis*, hydrangeas, rhododendrons and azaleas.

Quite different treatment is needed for shrubs such as *Olearia traversii*, which grow upwards at a great rate. Eucalypts also behave in this way, and though most never become windfast enough to form first-line shelter, *Eucalyptus coccifera* has proved quite successful. These should be topped when they reach about 1·5 m/5 ft; head them back to half their height, and when they again reach 1·5 m/5 ft, do it once more. There is then a good chance that they will develop a firm roothold; without this attention, they are also certain to blow over sooner or later.

III

Mixed Borders

IN open, windswept gardens lashed by sea spray, the plants that will grow willingly are sufficiently few to impose their own coherence upon the schemes you devise. But wherever there is established shelter against the gales, or in gardens – in a city centre, perhaps – where wind is not an enemy, the potential for incongruity and mismatches becomes the greater because of the immense choice of material available.

The same design principles will apply whether you are making a garden in a frost hollow or on a warm and sheltered site. Plants of firm structure can be used to frame the massed colour of perennials and annuals, or as key elements in composition where form is dominant, according to your taste. One difference is that in a mild climate a far wider choice of evergreens will be available to you, so that your borders need never have the undressed appearance so familiar in cold gardens in winters. A mild climate, too, allows you to use more of those long-flowering, rather tender perennials or subshrubs which in colder areas have to be overwintered under glass and cannot be planted out until the risk of frost is past.

This may be so far into the season that they can scarcely get going before the first frosts of autumn put an end to their floraison. In milder areas, however, the season of frosts is so short that you should be able to keep your borders looking colourful for nearly nine months, against the five or six or less favoured gardens.

In planting your borders, you can choose many of your plants with greater daring, for you will of course have made sure that your garden has a firm structure of hardy material. If the softer components of your mixed border should be laid waste by a winter of freak severity, they can be reconstructed without too much pain from precisely the kind of fast-growing plants which are so well suited to mild gardens.

Just what goes into your borders is of course a matter of personal taste. You must also consider the constraints, other than climatic, that may be imposed on your selection of plants: questions of soil, aspect and atmospheric humidity among them. I shall assume for the purposes of this chapter that the soil is neither very wet nor very dry – both these extremes will be discussed in later chapters – and that the aspect is open and chiefly sunny. A few plants that prefer light shade may well find their way into this chapter, for any border as it matures will, unless it faces straight into the midday sun, develop a few areas that are partly shaded by the tallest shrubs. But plants that demand shaded, woodland conditions will get a chapter to themselves, later. I shall also leave until the chapter after this one many shrubs, especially those that seem to me to have an undomesticated character making them less suited to the frankly artificial mixed border than, say, shrubs such as *Olearia* × *scilloniensis* or *Choisya ternata* 'Sundance'. This will be a very subjective selection with which you may not agree; but then I should be disappointed if you did not from time to time disagree with me.

Sword-leaved and spiky plants

Even when I am planning a border in terms of colour – and when I do, I am happiest working with a restricted palette, say of grey and glaucous foliage with lavender, mauve, pink and white flowers, or coppery foliage with sharper tones of scarlet and tangerine and yellow softened by apricot and cream – even then, I find it helpful to think first of form and structure. Only later come the more colourful, but also more flimsy ingredients, those that will fill in the framework and provide much of the concentrated impact of colour. Among the most striking outlines are those of sword-leaved plants, forming bold fans or rosettes of foliage in contrast to the rounded outlines of many flowering plants.

Beschorneria yuccoides is the very type of rosette-forming, sword-leaved plant I mean. It can become large, reaching 2·4–3 /8–10 ft in flower, with leaves up to 90 cm/3 ft long. These grey, glaucous-bloomed blades form substantial rosettes which remain in beauty all winter; they are not so like a yucca as the specific epithet suggests and lack the fierce spiny tips of *Yucca gloriosa*. In summer there arise leaning, rhubarb-red flowering stems, wrist-thick at the base, their upper halves clad in pink and coral bracts from which hang narrow jade bells.

Most yuccas will, in time, form trunks topped by rosettes of spine-tipped, sword-shaped greyish or dark green leaves. All are splendid evergreens, which add to their qualities of leaf and habit handsome branching spires of creamy white bells appearing in late summer. Different species reach varying sizes, giving a choice for borders of all dimensions. Small species, with rosettes of around 60 cm/2 ft wide, are *Yucca flaccida* and *Y.*

filamentosa. Both have greyish green leaves with thread-like hairs along the margins; as its name suggests, the first has leaves less stiff, arching at the tip. Both are free flowering, the 1·5 m/5 ft spikes of cream bells on more or less erect sideshoots in *Y. filamentosa* whereas in *Y. flaccida* the side branches are held nearly horizontally, making a more open and graceful plume of flowers. Both have variegated forms, which are very decorative but generally less vigorous, and correspondingly less suited to making a bold visual statement except at close quarters where their insistent leaf striping overrides their structure.

Much larger than these are the viciously armed *Yucca gloriosa* with sombre, leaden green leaves in rosettes up to 1·2 m/4 ft wide, and *Y. recurvifolia*, which is more elegant in its long, arching leaves. Again, both have variegated forms, which are extremely decorative; in flower *Y. recurvifolia* is superior, with open candelabra appearing earlier in the year than the autumn-flowering *Y. gloriosa*.

It is as foliage plants that I am considering these yuccas, as indeed I earlier considered *Beschorneria yuccoides*; but it is necessary to keep in mind the flowers also when you are planning a colour scheme. The sharp tones of the beschorneria's flowering stems and bracts disqualify it from any scheme in which grey foliage is to be linked with flowers of mauve and lilac and pink. But you could well use it as the keynote of a grey and glaucous scheme with shades of cream and primrose, tangerine and apricot, heightened by touches of scarlet, such as I shall propose later. The yuccas, whether distinctly grey-green as *Y. flaccida* or of more sombre dark green, albeit still with a greyish cast, as in *Y. gloriosa* or the splendid *Y. recurvifolia*, are fitted to a wider range of colour schemes. The plain grey-green forms are more suitable as strong design elements in a border than the variegated cultivars, which are too restless to be used as repetitive components. All, plain or variegated, look well with stonework, and with broad, bold leaves about them. Miss Jekyll used them with the wide paddles of bergenias, to form end-pieces to a section of her main 'mixed border of hardy flowers'. In mild climates it could be *Bergenia ciliata*, its round leaves densely furred on both sides; but it is not wholeheartedly evergreen. You might prefer to set your yuccas or beschorneria in a froth of something light and small-leaved, as it might be the invaluable *Helichrysum petiolare*, or with the wide, cobwebbed grey leaves of *Salvia argentea*. Whatever you choose, I believe it is important to set all these bold, sword-leaved plants among something lower growing, so that their characteristic outlines may not be blurred.

There are now a great many phormiums available, plain or coloured. Many of the newer, brighter cultivars are not fully hardy in cold gardens, but should be completely reliable where *Beschorneria yuccoides* thrives. If the scale is right, you could use some of those already described in Chapter

II, such as the colossal 'Purple Giant'. Of more modest dimensions is 'Burgundy', with stiff, dark oxblood purple, twisted leaves about $1 m/3\frac{1}{4}$ feet long. 'Dark Delight' is of similar colouring, with slightly longer leaves that droop at the tips; 'Bronze Baby' is paler, with flexible leaves. Other all-purple phormiums – 'Tom Thumb', 'Thumbelina', or the paler 'Surfer' and 'Jack Spratt' – are very much smaller. I cannot imagine them dominating anything larger than a trough. They might be better used with some feathery grey foliage, no attempt made to keep them standing boldly above their surroundings; or isolated in a rock pocket or in gravel.

The old *Phormium tenax* 'Variegatum' has the usual stiff leaves of the species, striped on the margins with yellow; 'Veitchii' has the reverse variegation, the centre creamy yellow, margins green. Both reach about $2 m/6\frac{1}{2} ft$; 'Williamsii' is brighter and taller. *P. cookianum* also has an old, striped form called 'Variegatum', with bands of yellow concentrated at the centre; like the type it is smaller than *P. tenax* and has flexible, arching leaves, giving it a height of around $90 cm/3 ft$. The 'Tricolor' forms of each species also follow the type in the stiff or arching carriage of their leaves; their creamy margins are finely edged with bright red. Most gardeners buying phormiums, however, are likely to be seduced by one or more of the newer and very much brighter cultivars which are of hybrid derivation. 'Yellow Wave' has arching leaves of citron and lime, green-edged; 'Cream Delight' is perhaps pure *P. cookianum*, and very fetching, with broad cream margins and green centre overlaid with narrower cream stripes. Inheriting the stiffer habit of *P. tenax* are 'Yellow Queen' and the creamier 'Radiance'. Any of them would look well in a scheme where yellow dominates, and could be set in a ground planting of *Helichrysum petiolare* 'Limelight' or a background of one of the yellow-leaved *Pittosporum tenuifolium* cultivars, such as 'Warnham Gold'. The erect-leaved cultivars deriving from *Phormium tenax* would contrast most strongly; if your taste is for less abrupt transitions, then a cultivar with flexible leaves might be your choice, for in these the vertical, spiky outline is moderated into a mounded pile of arching sword-leaves.

Even more striking than the yellow or cream phormiums are the now many cultivars with foliage in shades of pink and red, tan and bronze, some of them also with wine-purple or cream striping. 'Dazzler', despite its name, is one of the quieter cultivars in this group, with blood-red and chocolate foliage centrally striped with rose; the leaves are comparatively narrow, lax and twisted, about $75 cm/2\frac{1}{2} ft$ long. It looks well with a background of *Pseudopanax lessonii* 'Purpureum' in sombre metallic purple, with the more glittering black-maroon of *Pittosporum tenuifolium* 'Tom Thumb' nearby, and a ground planting of *Verbena* 'Silver Ann'. 'Pink Panther' is of similar size, its arching leaves carmine-red at the centre overlaid with tawny stripes, the margins chocolate-brown and the reverse glaucous bronze. The pink in its colouring could be picked up by *Pittosporum tenuifolium* 'Deborah', a cultivar with small, very wavy-edged leaves margined cream and heavily flushed with pink. These coloured-leaved forms of the pittosporum are as frankly unnatural as the phormiums themselves, and thus assort well in character, with the added piquancy that in both genera the wild species and many of the coloured cultivars originate in New Zealand. Their origin is made very clear in the group of phormiums bearing names prefaced 'Maori', all with leaves arching at the tips, all coloured in shades of pink, apricot, tan and bronze, and scarlet. 'Sundowner' is similarly coloured but has stiff upright leaves reaching 1·8 m/6 ft, 60 cm/2 ft more than the tallest of the Maori group, 'Maori Chief'. 'Sunset' is also stiff-leaved, but a little shorter, and paler in pink fading to creamy yellow. Named for the other end of the day are 'Aurora' and the taller, 1·5 m/5 ft 'Smiling Morn', both with arching bronze leaves striped with rose, burnt orange and apricot. 'Apricot Queen' is quieter, with lax leaves of creamy yellow and apricot margined with bronze-green, and 'Guardsman' is appropriately tall and upright at 2 m/6½ ft, the bronzed leaves striped pink with glaucous reverse.

Domes and hummocks

You will probably want some rounded outlines, to contrast with or instead of all these spiky profiles. You could choose some of the shrubs already mentioned, such as *Olearia macrodonta* or *Brachyglottis rotundifolia*. Just because they are resistant to salt gales they need not be relegated only to the outer reaches of the garden, for they have beautifully patterned foliage. But for less windswept borders there is a wider choice of evergreen shrubs with fine foliage or of characteristic outline. In the more domesticated setting of a mixed border, too, you can use shrubs with variegated leaves, or choose coppery-maroon or lime-yellow (nurserymen's 'purple' and 'gold') foliage that would look out of place among the grey and glaucous tones of the majority of wind-resistant shrubs.

Arbitrarily, I shall keep for a later chapter the many shrubs with handsome green foliage, though I do not mean to imply that green leaves have no place in the mixed border. Far from it, indeed; an all coloured planting may look hectic unless very carefully handled, and the relief of plain and solid green or grey is essential. No, it is simply that there is so much border material to consider that this chapter will become hopelessly unwieldy if it is allowed to appropriate to itself all the shrubs.

I have already mentioned some of the variegated and coloured-leaved pittosporums, which make rounded shrubs and, if they show signs of running up to tree form, can be clipped to form solid buttresses or domes.

The tougher texture of their evergreen leaves means that they are less liable to the sunscorch which can disfigure shrubs with deciduous, yellow-flushed or white variegated foliage. The all-yellow kinds strike an unexpectedly alien note in a naturalistic landscape, but, if carefully sited, bring a cheerful tone to a border of foliage and flowers. There are four or five of them available in commerce: for *Pittosporum tenuifolium* is one of those species that seems especially prone to sporting to odd-coloured or variegated forms. As well as the all-yellow cultivars, there are others more or less heavily variegated with yellow. All the pure yellow cultivars are especially bright butter-gold in winter; in spring and summer they are nearer to lime-green: 'Warnham Gold', 'Winter Sunshine', 'Golden King'. The foliage of 'Limelight' is enlivened with yellow veining, and the green-gold leaf of 'Wendle Channon' is tinted with red.

There are fewer purple-leaved pittosporums to choose from. The diminutive 'Tom Thumb', with lacquered black-purple, wavy-edged leaves, can be matched in larger size by 'Purpureum'. More numerous are the variegated cultivars; their small leaves create a rather fussy impression, so that they need to be used with great discretion. Not for me whole borders of variegation, where the effect is so busy, to the point of freneticism, that the impact of any individual plant is blurred. Be that as it may, the number of variegated pittosporums introduced over the years testifies to their continuing popularity. Of yellow-variegated cultivars I know four: 'Eila Keightley', in which the centre of the leaf is yellow and lime-green, with paler, creamy midrib and veins; 'Margaret Turnbull', its dark green leaves with a bold central variegation of bright to lime-yellow, and the similar 'Abbotsbury Gold'; and 'Sterling Gold', with smaller yellow and green leaves. I cannot say I love any of them.

I will come back to the silvery and pink-variegated pittosporums later, for I feel the need of some relief from all this rather bitty foliage. If it is variegations you want in your rounded, evergreen shrubs, but on leaves of bolder outline, then you could turn to *Griselinia littoralis*, which now runs to four variegated forms that I know, or know of. The original of them all is 'Variegata', with leaves conspicuously white-margined. It sported, in a Jersey, Channel Islands, garden, to 'Dixon's Cream', in which the centre of the leaf is variegated with creamy-white. This cultivar has proved rather unstable, with a tendency to revert to the white-edged form especially when propagated from cuttings. The very slow growing 'Bantry Bay' also has central markings of cream to pale jade: the leaf margins are noticeably wavy. I have seen only a young plant of 'Brodick', which is described as of compact growth, with leaves 'maculated gold'; but coming from the garden of that name on the west coast of Scotland, it is likely to be worth growing.

Another good hedging and shelter plant already mentioned, *Euonymus japonicus*, also has some variegated cultivars more suited, visually at least, to the inner parts of the garden than to the outer defences. They are often seen as rather assertive suburban hedges in mild areas, but can as well, or better, be grown as individual shrubs in a border context. Again, you have the choice of yellow-margined leaves or those with yellow at their hearts, as in 'Aureus' ('Aureopictus'). 'Ovatus Aureus' has some leaves entirely yellow, others margined yellow on green: these may represent reversions to 'Aureomarginatus'. Then there is 'Duc d'Anjou', with pale or yellow-green leaves splashed with dark green at the centre. 'Macrophyllus Albus' ('Latifolius Albomarginatus' – how tiresome all these synonyms are) has grey-green markings on leaves conspicuously margined with cream. All are cheerful evergreens with a highly polished gloss, more or less redeeming the unremarkably oval leaf form.

A yellow-variegated shrub that you may regard as a good thing spoiled is *Luma apiculata* (*Myrtus luma*) 'Glanleam Gold', found in an Irish garden. The small, dark, pointy leaves of this Chilean myrtle are not at all, it seems to me, enhanced by yellow margins, and still less by the slightly hectic red flush in youth. 'Penwith' blushes with even deeper embarrassment, as well it may. I would rather stick to the plain-leaved kind, which I will undoubtedly extol, in a later chapter, for its many other attributes. If I want a small, yellow-variegated leaf, I will plant *Coprosma* 'Beatson's Gold'. The arched stems are set with narrowly oval golden-bronzed leaves margined with deep green. As coprosmas go, it is pretty hardy; and very easy to make more of. It is smaller, admittedly, than the myrtle, at around $1\,m/3\frac{1}{4}$ ft; so much the less fussy variegation to contend with, and the rather angular, open branching is agreeable.

The genus *Pseudopanax* is chiefly notable for bold green foliage, or for the bizarre juvenile forms that seem to call for an accompanying fauna of pterodactyls and dinosaurs. But *P. lessonii*, which in its green manifestations and hybrids must wait until a later chapter, has given us both 'Purpureum' already described, and 'Gold Splash'. This has the same three- to five-foliolate, wax-finished green leaves as the type, but they are marked with bright yellow. In suitable climates, nearly if not wholly frost-free, it will make a well filled, many-branched shrub of up to $3\,m/10$ ft.

Considerably hardier than the *Pseudopanax* are the Mexican *Choisya ternata* and Mediterranean *Viburnum tinus*. Both are apt to meet, unfairly, with opprobrium from people who associate them with seaside boarding houses, or perhaps with boarding school. The Mexican orange blossom is a rapid-growing aromatic evergreen with handsome polished dark green trifoliolate leaves; it grows into a large symmetrical dome spangled with starry white fragrant flowers in late spring and again in autumn. I grew up with *Choisya ternata* and have a great affection for it; it earns a place here for its newish, yellow-leaved form 'Sundance'. In its basic form

laurustinus has an uninspiring oval leaf of leaden green, looming like a
thundercloud as a background to bright summer flowers and redeemed
only by its winter flowering. White blossoms open from pink buds,
lacking only scent. If you grow it for its flowers, then you will no doubt
choose one of the improved selections; but there is a variegated form also,
with leaves lighter green than normal, boldly marked with creamy yellow.
Viburnum tinus 'Variegatum' is, not surprisingly, much slower-growing
than the green-leaved forms, but builds up in time to the same cumulus
outline.

The colouring of the variegated laurustinus is pale enough to lead us
into the shrubs, some hinted at already, with white or cream variegation,
often described as silver: whether in old-style cultivar names such as
'Argenteum', or in the modern, vernacular versions 'Silver' this and that.
Why, I wonder, do we have so many 'Golden Kings' and 'Silver Queens',
but not the other way about?

So, for a white-variegated evergreen shrub of rounded outline, what
shall it be if not one of those that have crept into these pages already?
Predictably, the choice is largely from among the pittosporums. This
time, though, *Pittosporum tenuifolium* does not have things all to itself. Both
P. crassifolium and *P. ralphii* have forms, known simply as 'Variegatum', in
which the leaf is irregularly margined with cream. As the ground colour,
especially on the young foliage, is pale pewter-grey, aging to grey-green
above and remaining smooth-felted beneath, the effect is less strident than
on the brighter green leaf. Both species are so beautiful in their plain-
leaved forms that I cannot think them improved by fancy colouring; yet
many people disagree with me, and they sell on sight. With its smooth,
pale green, wavy-margined leaves, *P. eugenoides* creates a wholly different
effect; its form 'Variegatum' with cream margins is a most elegant thing,
apparently hardier than the type. It forms a tidy, somewhat columnar
shrub to about 4·5 m/15 ft in suitable climates; the newer *P. eugenoides*
'Platinum' grows to about 3 m/10 ft, forming a neat pyramid of pale,
shining green leaves edged with white, set off by dark stems. All these are
New Zealanders. The Chinese *P. tobira*, which bears its blunt-ended,
polished green leaves in whorls, is quite different in aspect. 'Variegatum'
is conspicuously cream-edged and not an improvement on the plain bright
green form.

Pittosporum tenuifolium 'Variegatum' was presumably the first variegated
form of this species to be named; others have the now compulsory
vernacular-style names. It is a pleasant shrub, its greyish-green foliage
narrowly margined with cream. 'Silver Queen' has bright green leaves
with an irregular, but bolder, white margin, giving a generally silvery-
grey effect. Both 'James Stirling', with neat little leaves on blackish-
maroon stems, and 'Silver Sheen', also appear silvery green. 'Katty' has

larger leaves with white variegations, and forms an upright, compact bush. Quite distinct is 'Irene Patterson', in which the very wavy-edged leaves are green heavily speckled with white: one nursery that I know of gives 'Snow' as an aptly descriptive synonym.

Any of these you could, if you wished, use as a pale backdrop to flowers of vivid, hot colours. But *P. tenuifolium* also runs to a number of cultivars and hybrids in which the white or cream markings are flushed, either seasonally or permanently, with pink or crimson. These must be kept well away from flowers of yellow-based colouring. 'Garnettii' is probably the best known; it is spotted and flushed with rose-pink especially in winter. I never feel quite comfortable with 'Garnettii', for its markings too much remind me of the hectic spotting on certain white roses, after rain. The similar 'Saundersii' is more compact in growth. I have already proposed the small-leaved 'Deborah' as a companion for a pink-variegated phormium; the leaves of 'Silver Magic' are even smaller, silvery-white turning pink.

There is a cultivar of *Coprosma repens* named 'Silver Queen' also (what did I tell you?). It has a rounded, dense habit, with the habitual thick, varnished leaves of almost circular outline, deep green margined with white. The variegation seems, if anything, to emphasize the symmetrical arrangement of the opposite leaves, each pair borne at right angles to the next. 'Pink Splendour' is even more jazzy, with the same gloss finish on leaves margined yellow; as they mature the yellow fades to cream and develops a feverish pink flush. For completeness I must mention the two yellow-variegated cultivars of *C. repens*, which should perhaps have found their way into page 54 with other shrubs of this colouring. If your climate is just a little too severe for them, so that they have to be bedded out each season – a treatment which suits them admirably – they will make low sprawling shrubs more suited to be fillers at the front of the border than to providing firm structural outlines. 'Picturata' has a central patch of cream to lime-yellow; 'Variegata' is margined with creamy-yellow and sprawls naturally. 'Williamsii' grows more upright, and has narrower leaves, less highly glossed, almost wholly cream, with a central flash of green overlaid with the marginal cream so that it is muted to a pale greyish-green.

No one who is not unreasonably besotted with variegations would wish to grow all of the shrubs I have just described, at least not all at once. But with so many to select from, if you decide that in such and such a position you must have a variegated shrub, you ought to be able to make an appropriate choice. And in the most aesthetically satisfying gardens, selection rather than collection is the rule.

The softer colours in the mixed border

I propose from here on, at least until another change of direction seems
desirable, to take you along a border – a series of borders, rather. I shall
discuss the plants – shrubs, perennials, bulbs and ephemerals – that grow
in the borders, and others that could have, in slightly different circum-
stances. That is, I will allow myself excursions into a consideration of
plants I could have used, had the border been of much greater extent and
my resources of time, money and plants similarly unbounded. As you
will see, I also like to change the plantings year by year, not wholly, but
by bedding out afresh plants that could well be left alone, in a sufficiently
mild climate, to become permanencies, but which equally are easy to raise
from cuttings or seed and quick to grow to flowering or foliage specimens
big enough to make an impact.

In the main, in the pages that follow, I shall be describing to you plants
that, in reality, were planted together in a border. It is, in fact, two borders,
terraced one above the other into a hillside curving south and west facing.
The lower, and wider, of the borders arches around a crescent of sloping
lawn; the upper runs alongside a mown grass path. Both are backed by
the retaining stone walls, no more than 1·8 m/6 ft at their highest, that
were built when the slope was first terraced.

I have already said that I feel most comfortable, in dealing with colour,
with harmonies rather than contrasts. Colours in the garden are seen in a
context of, most usually, the green of foliage and grass, together with the
colours of other flowers and possibly of foliage other than green. In the
double borders I propose to take you along, the dominant colour was less
the green of grass – despite the turfed path and the sloping lawn – than
the silvery-grey of the walls and the long, low house above them, set on
its broad paved terrace. This abundance of stone, the full south aspect of
the borders, and the presence of two fine surviving plants, one at each
end, each with grey-toned foliage, made me decide to emphasize grey
and glaucous foliage rather than green.

The progression of flower colours was also determined by these two
survivors from the borders' original planting. At one end is a massive
clump of *Beschorneria yuccoides*; at the other a large old plant of *Buddleja
colvilei* 'Kewensis', greyed of leaf and deep plum-red in flower, a better
colour than the crushed strawberry of the type. So the scheme was
determined: from shades of coral and primrose, tangerine and amber, with
base notes of deep coppery crimson at one end, to lavender and lilac, rose
and crimson at the other, with the unifying theme of glaucous and grey
foliage running all through. Pure blues and white formed the link in
flower colour between the two bands of the spectrum. Strong colours

were eschewed; these went elsewhere, in a walled garden where scarlet and hot yellow could not intrude an alien note into an essentially muted landscape of grass, pine trees and stone, with the varying but never brilliant tones of the sea always in view.

Around the beschorneria, which had spread back to the wall, were set several plants of *Helichrysum petiolare* and a wide clump of *Alstroemeria pulchella*. This, despite its Brazilian origins, is not really tender; it has rather pale green foliage, and 90 cm/3 ft stems baring narrow, ragged trumpets of coppery crimson tipped with green over a long summer to autumn season. Nearby, *Canna glauca* added emollient tones of primrose yellow over narrow, glaucous-blue foliage. For a more concentrated volume of flower colour than that provided by the modest cannas, I added a yellow crocosmia: lemon 'Citronella' or 'Canary Bird' would do, but my choice was the larger-flowered, Indian yellow 'Lady Hamilton', which has similar green, sword-shaped leaves. I set it in a ground-swell of the variegated *Helichrysum petiolare*. Warmer still in colour is the clear tangerine *Crocosmia* 'Solfatare', which has pale chocolate-bronze foliage. It assorts well with the shrubby foxglove *Digitalis obscura*, a 90 cm/3 ft bush with very narrow glaucous foliage and small, bright tan-orange flowers. Other plants with flowers of the same amber, maize and saffron tones as the two crocosmias joined this group: *Mimulus aurantiacus*, the Californian musk, with narrow, sticky green leaves and apricot-buff monkey-faced flowers, *M. longiflorus* in paler buff-yellow, and *Cestrum aurantiacum*, a leafy, semi-scrambling shrub with narrow ochre trumpets fragrant at night. *Osteospermum* 'Buttermilk' belongs here also: unusually for the genus, it has flowers of palest straw-yellow warmed by the coppery reverse to the petals and deep brown disk. Of upright habit, it is likely to need staking. *Hedychium greenei* was planted here for its wide, maroon-purple backed leaves. These are so fine that its reluctance to produce orange-scarlet flowers matters not. The deeper *Mimulus puniceus*, with coppery crimson flowers, can be used to introduce stronger colour without stridency.

In the upper border these same colours were picked up by some of the more muted *Watsonia* species: buff-orange *W. bulbillifera*, pale ochre *W. pillansii*, and tawny yellow *W. stenosiphon*. Their upright habit and spikes of small, gladiolus-like flowers are suited to narrow spaces. *Sphaeralcea fendleri* is in the same colour range of pale clear orange, the little mallow flowers set on upright stems clothed with greyish foliage. Many salvias found their way into these borders: appropriate to the warm-toned section is *S. africana-lutea* (*S. aurea*), from South Africa, a 90 cm/3 ft shrub with small aromatic, wavy-edged almond-green leaves and ochre flowers maturing to rust and brick-red. The calyces retain their maroon and acid-green colour long after the corollas have dropped. A bigger plant by far, needing the space of the lower border, is the Brazilian *S. confertiflora* (*S.*

bolivensis), which will reach 1·8 m/6 ft in a season. Its bold green leaves, brownish beneath, are held on red stalks; they smell revoltingly of burnt rubber when crushed. Above the ample foliage are long, unbranched inflorescences, close-packed with small cinnamon-brown flowers in plush-textured, tawny red calyces.

A special treasure tucked in against a sheltering angle – the terrace walls are supported at intervals by low, slab-topped buttresses – is *Grevillea* × *semperflorens*, its thread-fine green foliage the setting for spidery flowers of muted buff, orange and apricot pink. Hardier than this and the salvias are the two species of *Phygelius* from South Africa, and their newer hybrid offspring. The better-known of the two is *P. capensis*, a subshrub growing to 1 m/3¼ ft or so, with hanging curved tubular flowers of orange-scarlet with yellow throat, making it rather bright for this border. But *P. aequalis*, which is shorter in growth, has nodding tubes of softer, buff-pink flushed with pale orange, enlivened by the yellow throat and crimson lobes. Their more vivid hybrid descendants will have their turn later; here we might grow dusky, reddish-pink 'Winchester Fanfare' or pale salmon-orange 'Salmon Leap'. The best form of *Lobelia tupa* belongs here too, for its broad soft foliage is grey-green, forming a plinth for the tapering 1·8 m/6 ft spires of claw-shaped, coppery crimson flowers.

To cool so many tan and buff tones, I set some warm ivory-white flowers and grey foliage. *Leonotis leonurus* 'Harrismith White' is a form of the usually rich orange-flowered lion's ear from South Africa; it has the same soft, hairy leaves and furry flowers set in whorls along the stem. Falling, the corollas leave behind a ring of spiky calyces after the manner of a *Phlomis*. Grown almost solely for its aluminium-white, comb-like foliage, *Senecio vira vira* (*S. leucostachys*) is a semi-scandent shrub which, if planted against a wall or tall support may reach 1·8 m/6 ft; among lower companions, it will weave sideways instead, reaching a mere 75 cm/2½ ft. It is one of those choice silvery plants with pale, not declamatory yellow flowers; the clustered, rayless heads are creamy white. Unlike most greys, it resents being cut hard back in spring.

Then there are the kniphofias of this pale flower colouring, as far removed from the old, coarse red hot poker as can be. 'Little Maid' is one of the most successful modern cultivars, the slender spikes growing to no more than 45 cm/18 in, of which at least half is set with creamy white florets, over fine grassy foliage. Because it is so small and slim, its charac-teristic outline is easily lost unless it is set among lower companions. I chose *Gazania* 'Cream Beauty', for its daisies are of the same creamy primrose, set on short stems above deeply lobed grey-felted leaves.

The older American *Kniphofia* 'Maid of Orléans' is of the same colouring as 'Little Maid', but makes a taller, stouter plant, similar to its offspring 'Mermaiden', though this last is greener in the bud, very like the big

(1·5 m/5 ft) 'Torchbearer', which we will encounter later. 'White Fairy' is somewhere between 'Little Maid' and 'Maid of Orléans', with slim 90 cm/3 ft spikes of pale primrose opening to ivory. Others are of soft biscuit, buff and pale apricot tones, assorting with the Californian musks: 'Apricot' is just the colour of the unripe fruit before the sun has touched it; 'Toffee Nosed' has light tan buds opening to cream. The slim, late flowering 'Underway' is a more uniform deep biscuit and amber. On the wall behind this cream and tan grouping, *Buddleja auriculata* displays its grey-toned foliage, smaller than the familiar butterfly bushes' leaves, dull green above and white beneath; it can be pruned hard back to a framework of branches in spring. The rounded clusters of cream, yellow-eyed flowers in grey-felted calyces are borne in autumn and winter and give off a sweet honey scent. The novelist Compton Mackenzie used to grow this, in Cornwall, with *Kniphofia multiflora*, which bore tall, narrow *Eremurus*-like spires of flower of the same ivory colouring at the same season; but I have never been able to find a source of this magnificent poker in Europe and fear that it will need to be reintroduced from the wild if we are to see it again. Yet between the world wars it was abundant enough to be offered wholesale.

Even among bold plantings there may be place for a few small treasures. In a little gap near the front of this border, one year, I planted some clumps of *Tulbaghia capensis*, a little 15 cm/6 in, grassy-leaved creature with nodding, cream and orange flowers. Another year it was corms of *Homeria collina*, which bears fragrant saucers of soft apricot or clear pale yellow on 45 cm/18 in stems. The primrose form cued in a group of soft pale yellows, echoed by *Canna glauca* nearer the *Beschorneria*. With these sulphur and primrose shades some pure blues were introduced; for as Miss Jekyll wrote, 'the pure blues always seem to demand peculiar and very careful treatment' in 'distinct but not garish contrasts, as of full blue with pale yellow'. One of the most appealing pale yellow-flowered plants I know is *Argyranthemum maderense*. The argyranthemums were until recently included in the genus *Chrysanthemum*; their most familiar manifestation is the white Paris daisy, *A. frutescens*. *A. maderense* is smaller, at 45 cm/18 in a front-line plant; it has finely cut blue-grey foliage and primrose yellow daisies. The bigger *A. frutescens* 'Jamaica Primrose' has similar wide pale daisies, but green foliage less feathery in texture; 'Brontes' is just a little deeper in colour; 'Levada Cream' paler, like clotted cream. There is also, now, a dwarf form of 'Jamaica Primrose', growing to about 60 cm/2 ft instead of 90 cm/3 ft.

By way of foliage contrast, *Hedychium gardnerianum* has broad green blades; the spidery flowers are intensely fragrant and come in two shades, pale primrose (chosen for this grouping) and a warmer yellow. The hardiest of the ginger lilies is probably *H. spicatum*, its fragrant, white butterfly-like blooms in loose spikes often marked with yellow or orange. When you come to divide your hedychiums – if suited, they increase fast – you will discover that the stout rhizomes smell very like fresh ginger, to which they are related.

Either form of *Salvia patens* looks well with primrose-yellow; I chose the less common 'Cambridge Blue' variety, which comes true from seed or can be raised from cuttings. In mild areas its tuberous roots can safely be left in the ground over winter. In my experience *S. cacaliifolia* is not quite so hardy; it is a low, sprawling plant with heart-shaped green leaves, and flowers of the same intense ultramarine as the common form of *S. patens*, but smaller and more numerous along the stems. Taller blue salvias include indigo *S. concolor*, *S. azurea* which carries its sky-blue flowers on long, slender spikes reaching 1·8 m/6 ft over greyish, narrow foliage, and *S. guaranitica*. This species is now considered to include the two distinct clones formerly known as *S. caerulea* and *S. ambigens*, both flowering in late summer and autumn. The taller is the erstwhile *S. caerulea*, now named *S. guaranitica* 'Black and Blue' on account of its vivid blue flowers in black calyces. 'Blue Enigma' is shorter at 1·8 m/6 ft, with smaller, paler flowers in green calyces, and smoother light green leaves where 'Black and Blue' has rough textured foliage.

There has been too much green foliage in the last paragraphs for a border that is supposedly pale with greys and silvers and glaucous blues; it is time to get back on course. *Coronilla glauca* takes us at least part of the way, for its pinnate foliage, composed of small blunt-ended leaflets, has a distinctly glaucous cast. The type has canary-yellow flowers appearing from winter onwards; much more desirable is the pale form 'Citrina', which is my choice in this grouping. If the emphasis is to be on pale colouring, you might prefer to choose the cream and glaucous 'Variegata', and accept that in their season the yellow flowers are too bright and fussy.

Several acacias have blue-grey foliage, and one, *Acacia baileyana*, was chosen for an angle in the house walls where there would be room for it to develop, as it will, into a small graceful tree. The leaves are doubly pinnate, with many tiny leaflets of bright glaucous-blue, setting off canary yellow, fluffy mimosa bobbles early in the year. In the border itself, the lower-growing *A. podalyriifolia* is of more appropriate stature, rarely growing taller than 3 m/10 ft. It is as silvery-glaucous as *A. baileyana*, but with entirely different foliage, composed of downy, obliquely ovate phyllodes 3–4 cm/1–1½ in long. The fragrant yellow blossom appears in winter and early spring, held in long racemes; by summer, when the border is in full swing, the acacia makes a pale and gleaming backdrop for the pure blues, whites and soft yellows of this section.

Bridging the gap between spring and summer is *Olearia* × *scilloniensis*, its greyish foliage obscured by massed white daisies. If pruned after flowering it will quickly refurnish itself with foliage to form a mound of grey throughout the border's main season. *Chiliotrichon diffusum* (*C. amelloides*) from South America is, in its broad-leaved forms, very like the olearia, with the same clouds of white daisies; in the needle-leaved variants also known as *C. rosmarinifolium* it is equally appealing, silvery when flowerless as though a rosemary had been dipped in platinum. More foliage contrast comes from *Aristea ecklonii*, a South African irid with evergreen, stiff and narrow leaves topped by branching stems of small, ultramarine flowers in early summer. *A. major* is taller, at perhaps 90 cm/3 ft, but otherwise similar. Both species need rich soil and a sheltered position to save the foliage from blackening in winter frosts. They resent disturbance, so are better increased from seed than by division of the rhizomatous roots. *Orthrosanthus* is a genus of southern hemisphere irids of similar colouring. The South American *O. chimboracensis* has leaves characterized by an off-centre midrib, and bright blue flowers on 30 cm/1 ft stems in late summer; the Australian *O. multiflorus* is paler and earlier. Yet another genus which takes the place of *Iris* in the southern hemisphere is *Dietes*. The flowers of *D. iridioides* (*Moraea iridioides*) are more like those of a true iris, wide and fragrant over stiff, grassy leaves; they may be white or glacier blue, with a lavender crest. The first flower to open is the terminal bloom; as it fades the flowering stem branches and more blooms open in succession during early summer. Far more splendid is *D. robin-soniana*, from New South Wales and Lord Howe Island, which grows to $2 \text{ m}/6\frac{1}{2}$ ft in flower, the sword leaves almost as long. Each flowering stem may bear hundreds of great white iris blooms, as noted by Compton Mackenzie the British novelist, who was also an experimental gardener succeeding, in his Cornish garden, with many challenging plants such as the Oncocyclus and Regelia irises, kniphofias now lost including *K. leichtlinii* and *K. comosa*, and the *Eremurus*-like *K. multiflora* with 3 m/10 ft spires of milk-white flowers.

There are several low, frontal plants that could joint this group: long-flowering South African composites prominent among them. Both *Felicia amelloides* and *F. amoena* (*F. pappei*) have pure, clear blue flowers; the second has neater foliage, needle-fine, of bright fresh green. But *F. amelloides* comes in two choice forms, the large-flowered 'Santa Anita', and 'Variegata' with leaves heavily cream-marked. This is a plant that causes exclamations of admiration, but it palls – on me at least – as fast as would a diet of Cornish cream alone. Give me rather the innocent sky-blue daisies of 'Santa Anita'. And then there is *Osteospermum ecklonis* 'Prostratum', in which the glistening white ray florets, pale inky-blue on the reverse, surround the indigo-blue disk. Again, if you like variegations, you could choose 'Silver Sparkler', not so prostrate, with similar flowers among leaves margined with cream-white, making a pale and fresh effect according well with the grey and silver theme we are supposedly pursuing. 'Weetwood' is similar but green of leaf. There are at least two upright cultivars of like colouring: 'Blue Streak', and the bizarre 'Whirligig', in which each ray floret is pinched at the centre to give a spoonbill effect. This is striking, if not beautiful, when the crimping develops uniformly to give a symmetrical flower; monstrous when the florets are part crimped, part normal.

The big *Agapanthus umbellatus*, so called (which may belong in *A. praecox*, rather than in *A. africanus*, the first of the genus to be introduced to western gardens), is almost too bulky for a border of this scale. In mild gardens it is readily naturalized, even in grass, where its deep or pale blue or white globes of lily-like flowers appear in high to late summer. But I would hesitate to consign the choicer agapanthus to the rough, and might be tempted to fit some in here. Though among the hardiest, *A. campanulatus patens* earns a place on account of its greyish green, narrow leaves; the widely flared flowers of soft Spode-blue form a dense but not large, rounded head on 1·2 m/4 ft stems. If one could find it, *A. campanulatus mooreanus* would be desirable for its clear blue colouring and dwarf habit. Also deciduous and hardy is *A. inapertus*, of which some forms have glaucous foliage; for the finest flowers, narrow tubes hanging down in a mophead, *A. inapertus pendulus* has no equal in its royal blue colouring. As well as these there are all the named and unnamed Headbourne hybrids in every shade from opalescent pale blue, grey and warm white through Spode and Wedgwood blues to ultramarine and navy, as well as pure white.

In a different context they might have been used as a unifying theme in this border, in clumps disposed at regular intervals; for their colouring assorts well with pale yellow and apricot to tangerine, as much as with pure pink and crimson and among grey-leaved shrubs. Only among the mauves and lilacs will you need to take care, confining yourself to the white and grey-opal forms, some of which are touched in the bud and the fading flower with purple. 'Ardernei Hybrid' has this characteristic. A larger, purer white is 'Albatross', perhaps a form of *A. praecox*. Of similar size is a plant I introduced, a seedling from among a bed of mixed 'A. umbellatus': opaline pale, it was named 'Phantom'.

Penstemon heterophyllus is a low, shrubby species for the front of the border, usually seen in opalescent tones of lavender flushed with pink, more suited to the further end of this border. But it comes, too, in gentian blue, its slender trumpets borne in sprays above narrow glaucous or purple-flushed foliage which adds a deeper, but still apt, note to the greys and silvers. By whatever name you acquire them − 'True Blue', 'Blue Gem', or 'Blue Springs' are all names I have encountered − they are annoyingly temperamental, rather than tender, and you should propagate them yearly from cuttings to ensure their survival, even in mild gardens.

There are shrubs, many unrelated to each other but all with shared characteristics, that I think of as quintessentially mixed border shrubs. They may be grown for their flowers above all, or for their foliage. Whichever it may be, they have in common a certain formlessness. If flowers are the reason for their inclusion, it will often be that they flower from high summer onwards, on the growths of the current year, and are habitually cut hard back in spring to a low, woody framework or even to ground level. Many foliage shrubs, among which we can count several of the silvers, are also hard-pruned in spring; the resulting new growths will normally bear larger or brighter foliage than old, outworn stems.

Typical of the former is *Caryopteris* × *clandonensis*, which now comes in deeper colours than the just off pure blue of the original hybrid. All have the aromatic foliage, hinting at turpentine but with an agreeable sharpness, of the original, but 'Kew Blue' and 'Ferndown' have deeper, violet-blue flowers of the same hazy outline, borne in late summer, and leaves not quite so grey. 'Heavenly Blue' is similar to the original clone, 'Arthur Simmonds', with paler flowers. Cuttings grow fast, and can be used as bedding, flowering in their first summer. These tones assort equally well with pale yellow, as of *Gladiolus natalensis* (*G. primulinus*), or with warm or pale silvery pink, enabling us to bridge the potentially tricky transition between warm and cool colours. In the borders of which I write, this was achieved painlessly by the presence of a rectangular pool, the full depth of the border and wide enough to separate warring colours. Such a contrivance is not always within one's grasp, so in most plantings the living components themselves must perform this task.

With the greys and silvers, purer blues and primrose yellows we can introduce pale clear pink as the first step towards the stronger or bluer pinks. Before the silver and pale candy-pinks, there comes a range of peach and salmon shades, which I like to use in a narrow span of soft harmonies. From among the sprawling stems, set with grey-green lobed leaves, of *Sphaeralcea munroana* arise the 45 cm/18 in spikes of *Kniphofia* 'Modesta', its pale coral buds echoing the satiny cups of the little mallow. As the buds open, 'Modesta' pales to cream. The taller 'Timothy' retains its coppery-pink shades to the end; the buds are deeper toned, echoing the tan-pink flowering stem. Of similar peach and cream colouring as 'Modesta', but as tall as 'Timothy', are 'Jenny Bloom' and 'Enchantress'. 'Dawn Sunkiss' and Beth Chatto's 'Strawberries and Cream' have extra-long, slender spikes. Their colouring is picked up by *Phygelius* × *rectus* 'Pink Elf', a dwarf hybrid cultivar bearing its narrow trumpets all around the stem; they are pale pink with deeper striations, the lobes crimson around a yellow throat.

The pinkest poker I ever grew came to me as 'Green Magic', and I never discovered its true name, if indeed it had ever had one: for kniphofias are very ease to raise from seed and the seedlings, often as good as any named cultivar, may be distributed without a name. The unknown one was set among a carpet of *Epilobium canum* (*Zauschneria californica*) 'Solidarity Pink', which forsakes the usual vivid orange-scarlet of the genus to adopt gentle shell-pink colouring according delightfully with the pale grey-green foliage. There is a mallow that in a larger, greener-based border could take the place of this and the *Sphaeralcea: Malvastrum lateritium* (*Modiolastrum lateritium*). A rampant spreader, it has wider mallow saucers of pale terracotta with deeper, brick-red eyes. I have seen on the show bench a variegated form of this, which looks like a plant fit for the bonfire: the cream margin is too narrow to make any impact, and serves only to distort and crumple the leaf.

We have been a bit short of bold foliage lately: though do please remember that all the plants I describe are not actually growing all at once in the border, for many are cited as alternatives. For all that, this is the place to introduce one of the noblest foliage plants I know, *Melianthus major*. This South African plant has woody stems, but even in comparatively cold areas is willing to compromise with the weather and, once established, behave as if it were herbaceous. The finest leaves, indeed, come on plants that have been cut back in spring, so you may care to perform with the secateurs what the winter frosts have failed to do for you. Each large, pinnate leaf is divided into saw-edged leaflets of glaucous-blue, the whole arrangement invariably reminding me of the plumes of *Archeopterix*, the prototype, fossil bird. I actually rather like the flowers, and am always tempted to leave a few stems to bloom, which they do in spring, the maroon spikes complementing a harmony of unfurling, palest jade foliage and deeper grey-green developed leaves.

By way of complete contrast in size, you could set the *Melianthus* about with *Plecostachys serpyllifolia*, more familiar as *Helichrysum microphyllum*. This latter name, though now considered invalid, is quite aptly descriptive, suggesting as it does a tiny-leaved version of the white-felted *H. petiolare*. The little *Plecostachys* has the same sprawly habit, and is as silver-white, but each leaf is a fraction of the size, though not perhaps so very minute as either specific epithet implies. Another year I used *Helichrysum populifolium*, with larger leaves, as white-felted as *H. petiolare* but pointed like an aspen leaf. The foliage of *Canna iridiflora* is as splendid as any other canna's, broad green paddles, but in this species the flowers are what we grow it for. Rich, deep pink, wide-winged, they open from early summer onwards, starting later in cool gardens than in very mild ones.

Among all this foliage, the purer pinks now come into their own, and lead felicitously to the tones of lilac, lavender and mauve, which with deeper notes of magenta and crimson will conclude the border. The genus *Diascia* includes a number of pink-flowered species with almost all the virtues needed in a mixed border flowering plant: a long season of flower, ease of cultivation and of propagation, and that indefinable quality which we call charm, though not, it must be admitted, much substance or form. Of the dozen or so species available, *D. vigilis* has the gentlest colouring, palest pink with a satin finish and a discreet purple eye. The *Nemesia*-like flowers are borne on open spikes reaching 60 cm/2 ft during an extended early summer to late autumn season, and in my experience they do not need dead-heading to remain tidy and full of flower.

Diascias are beset with nomenclatural confusion, even though it is scarcely ten years since the larger species of a genus formerly known as a rock garden plant, in the shape of *D. barberae*, were introduced to the west. The first of the newcomers, and still perhaps the best-known, is *D. rigescens*, which so far as I am aware has escaped the difficulties with naming; no doubt because it is one of the most distinct, with densely packed tapering spires of rich coppery-pink flowers on sprawling growths. I find it needs dead-heading at intervals, or it runs out of steam before the end of summer. Of similar warm colouring, but with open spikes of larger flowers more akin to those of *D. vigilis*, is the plant I have always grown as *D. elegans*. This appears to be correctly a synonym of *D. vigilis*, but the plants are clearly distinct. I must warn you, too, about *D. flanaganii*, which is a synonym of *D. stachyoides*, unknown to me; but the plant I received from a commercial source was like the pale *D. vigilis*. All these have more or less heart-shaped leaves, but *D. fetcaniensis* is distinct in its narrow, slightly greyed foliage, and flowers of much the same tone as *D. rigescens* but disposed in the airy style of *D. vigilis*, which it rivals in length of season. I am unsure of the accuracy of these names, which must be taken to describe the plants commercially available, and are not necessarily correctly ascribed.

Any of the deeper pink diascias can be paired with the Atlantic Island geraniums. *Geranium canariense* and *G. palmatum* are similar, forming mounds of glossy, deeply cut leaves topped by wide heads of fuchsia-pink flowers reaching 90–120 cm/3–4 ft. *G. maderense* is larger, at up to 1·5 m/5 ft, with foliage as finely cut as a fern, aromatic and mossy; in its second year the great sprays of magenta-pink, dark-eyed flowers, hazy with glandular hairs, emerge at any time from late winter onwards when there has been no frost. At this stage of the border some richer, though not strident, colours can be welcomed, such as the velvety-purple of *Osteospermum* 'Tresco Purple' (also known as 'Nairobi Purple' or 'Peggii'), which has sprawling stems. The ray florets have the texture of fine corduroy, the disc is maroon-purple also. The prostrate, pale mauve-pink osteospermums such as *O. jucundum*, 'Hopley' or 'Langtrees', or the exquisite pale lilac 'Bloemhof Belle', make a softer harmony. I added to this group of geranium, purple osteospermum and diascia the variegated form of *Erysimum linifolium*, its narrow, cream and grey foliage topped by abundant pale lilac wallflowers. Also for this group are the coloured forms of *Eucomis comosa*, in which the leaves, stems and pineapple-like flowers are tinted with maroon and dusky pink.

Of similar low, spreading habit are the verbenas which are perpetuated by cuttings, rather than seed, and are thus well suited to my kind of in-and-out gardening. Some are fragrant, such as 'Pink Bouquet' and 'Silver Ann' in candy-pink, cherry-red 'Lawrence Johnston', which may be a little too near to scarlet for this border, the delicious, clear lavender-mauve 'Loveliness', and very vigorous, strong magenta-pink 'Sissinghurst'. There are white verbenas too, including the albino form of *Verbena peruviana*, a smaller plant than the cultivars just proposed. The advantage of these is their tendency to grow sideways with considerable vigour – I have had a single plant of 'Sissinghurst' cover over a metre square of soil in one season – so that you need fewer plants than of the seed strains, which have been bred for compactness.

In complete contrast are the spear leaves of gladioli; not the gross florists' creations, but the South African species from which they were derived. One of the original parents of the Nanus hybrids, which if you must have hybrids are much to be preferred to the large-flowered kinds, is *Gladiolus cardinalis*, which bears hooded crimson flowers with pale flashes. Lighter and brighter is *G. carmineus*, in carmine with a pale splash, margined with deeper red, on the lower segments. Of the Nanus hybrids themselves, sometimes listed under *G. × colvillei* from the first cross between *G. cardinalis* and *G. tristis*, 'The Bride' is an exquisite pure white, while both 'Nymph' and 'Blushing Bride' are white faintly flushed with pink stains that are edged with carmine. The colour range deepens through all the shades of pink from peach to cherry, and leans both to lilac and to a difficult orange-salmon.

Watsonias are closely related to gladioli, but have almost wholly escaped the hybridizer's craft. As well as the sunset shades already adumbrated, they can be had in rosy-pink to lilac – *Watsonia knuysnana*, the fragrant *W. marginata*, tall *W. pyramidata* and *W. wilmaniae* among them – or white, as in the exquisite *W. ardernei*. Though now considered by the botanists to fall within the variable *W. meriana*, which may be cream or pink, orange-red, scarlet, purple or mauve in flower, this last is a very distinct plant to the gardener's eye, with large pure white flowers with rounded, widely-flared lobes. Dead white is an assertive colour – or non-colour – in the border, and I feel more comfortable using it in small quantities: just a few spikes of the watsonia, or a leafy clump of *Impatiens tinctoria*. This tall, tuberous perennial from eastern Africa has stout, succulent stems swollen into knuckles at each node; large, fragrant white flowers with a deep crimson central blotch and long, slender spur appear in autumn.

The crimson is echoed by the dahlia-like flowers of *Cosmos atrosanguineus*, which has a warm aroma of cocoa to match its rich chocolate-crimson colouring. Even in mild gardens this cosmos is very slow to show itself above ground in spring, and I believe that this at least in part accounts for its reputation for tenderness. Seeing, as late as the end of spring or early summer, an apparent gap in the border, the forgetful gardener may plant something else there. The cosmos's tuberous roots may be damaged by the fork, or its growing stems, still underground, discouraged by the new incumbent above, so that it fails to reappear, although if left alone it would likely have made an appearance before long. Once above ground it quickly builds up into a clump of darkish foliage, neater than the average dahlia's, soon to be topped by the blooms which will go on until the frosts. I have found it, like the dahlias to which it is related, quite a thirsty plant, soon flopping in dry soil. Set among silvery foliage, it is dramatic, but I like it as much, if not more, with the silvery pink of *Diascia vigilis* or sugar-pink *Verbena* 'Silver Ann'. As always, I like to change some of the components from time to time, pairing the verbena and diascia, in another season, with *Lobelia* 'Dark Crusader', which has plum-dark foliage and flowers of deep velvety crimson. Lobelias of this type, incidentally – 'Queen Victoria' is the best-known – move very well when about to flower if given a thorough soaking before and after transplanting. Later in the season *Gladiolus callianthus* (*Acidanthera mureliae*, *A. bicolor*) echoes, in its hooded flowers poised with elegance on arching stems, the pure white of the impatiens and its dark maroon central stain.

The cool pinks assort well also with clear lavender and violet. In early summer I like to match *Olearia* 'Comber's Blue' or 'Master Michael', which belong to the Splendens group of *O. phlogopappa*, with *Prostanthera rotundifolia*: the flowers are entirely different in shape but almost identical in colour, not as pure a tone as the olearia's name suggests but an appealing lavender-blue. Like the white-flowered types, *Olearia* 'Comber's Blue' has greyish foliage; that of the prostanthera is small, green, neat and aromatic, earning the genus its vernacular name of Australian mint bush. *P. melissifolia* var. *parvifolia* (*P. sieberi*) has larger flowers, nearer to mauve, and there is a near-pink form of *P. rotundifolia*, 'Rosea', which matches the lilac-pink flower of *Olearia* 'Comber's Pink'. *Prostanthera* 'Chelsea Pink' is also nearer to mauve than its name suggests. Their flowering season should, in mild areas, overlap with the first blooms of *Argyranthemum frutescens* 'Vancouver', which has double, anemone-centred pale pink daisies shading to deeper pink. The old 'Mary Wootton' has still paler flowers of the same shape, and there are single pink forms also: 'Wellwood

Park', deeper mauve 'Surprise', 'Pink Beauty', and the crushed-raspberry 'Rollason's Red'. The colouring of this last varies – at its brightest it is as cerise as the tight double 'Crimson Pompon', but sometimes it looks quite bleached and wan. Later in the season, if you seek to combine them with the same lavender-blue as the olearia, then a good form of *Aster albescens* (*Microglossa albescens*) will give you small but copious daisies on a greener shrub – but do see the plant you buy or acquire in flower, for some forms are skimmed-milk pale.

From high summer onwards, *Buddleja crispa* will add its own soft blending of white-felted stems and foliage, and lilac pink flowers in short panicles; like many buddleias, it is sweetly scented. The same colouring belongs to *Phlomis italica*, a low suckering shrub with narrow, woolly leaves on felted stems, set with whorls of pale mauve-pink flowers. Given space, I would want to add also *Dorycnium hirsutum*, a low-growing subshrub with tiny, fingered leaves fuzzy with silvery hairs, topped by little clusters of pink and white pea flowers in summer; and set at the front of the group, running back among the shrubs, a carpet of *Geranium traversii* elegans. This Chatham Islander has rounded, scallop-edged silvery grey leaves and opaque, pale pink flowers over a long summer season.

In another border, edged by a low retaining wall, I mixed this geranium and *Convolvulus sabatius*, which may or may not be the same as the Moroccan plant I used to know as *C. mauretanicus*. Both have the same non-invasive, sprawling habit and satiny saucers, but I have lately seen the older name attached to the form with more intense lilac-blue flowers, growing beside the paler one which was firmly labelled *C. sabatius*. Whatever the truth of their (or its) naming, *C. sabatius* likes to get its roots beneath a stone and, being of flopping habit, is well suited to softening stone edges.

Of similar colouring, but very different habit, is *Parahebe perfoliata*, an Australian subshrubby plant of surprising hardiness which, until it flowers, looks like a cluster of eucalyptus branchlets, the stem-clasping, blue-grey leaves tinged with plum-purple on first unfolding. Even if the old stems survive the winter, it is well to cut them out so that these new growths can emerge uncluttered. Later the stems are topped by open sprays of veronica flowers in tender lilac-blue. *P. perfoliata* creeps mildly below ground to make a clump about 75 cm/2½ ft high and wide.

Much more invasive than either the *Parahebe* or the Moroccan bind-weeds, but entirely in keeping with the colours of this part of the border, are *Convolvulus althaeoides* and *C. a. tenuissimus* (*C. elegantissimus*), both of them silvery of leaf and pale chalky-pink of flower, the latter with more finely cut foliage. They tiller and twine in a manner which clearly hints at their bindweed affiliations. Were it not for this, I should like to set them with *Erysimum* 'Bowles's Mauve', a stout perennial wallflower (perennial, that is, until it flowers itself to death) with slate-grey foliage and tall spikes of bright mauve flowers. Almost as pewter-pale in leaf as the bindweeds are the forms of *Argyranthemum foeniculaceum*, its name suggesting the finely cut, thread-like foliage but not its steely blue colouring, most marked in the cultivar 'Royal Haze', which has the usual smallish, pure white daisies; 'Chelsea Girl' is similar. There are double white argyranthemums too, old full double 'Mrs Sanders' and quilled 'Snowflake'.

The genus *Salvia* is one of the few that spans the spectrum, with flowers of yellow and scarlet and rust as well as pure blue, lavender, crimson and magenta. One of the most appealing, though hard to keep through damp chilly winters, is *S. leucantha*, a shrub with narrow, grey-green leaves and arching spikes, velvety-soft, of white and lilac. Its gentle colouring echoes the little clear lavender, *Agapanthus*-like heads of *Tulbaghia violacea*, and the taller *Dahlia merckii*. Only single-minded devotees of massive cactus dahlias can fail to enjoy the branching, airy heads of many small, single flowers of this Central American species, their subtly varying shades of lilac and lavender often dark-eyed and touched on the reverse with maroon, while others are paler of petal and yellow of disk, above finely cut foliage, green or maroon-flushed. The variations arise in seed-raised stocks, and I have had *D. merckii* seed itself for me; if you find a form you especially like then you can root cuttings as easily as of any other, grosser dahlia.

By comparison, *Salvia involucrata* 'Bethellii' is a large and muscular plant, with ample green leafage and stout spikes of bright magenta-pink flowers, characteristically fat in bud. *S. involucrata* itself is a slighter plant, and there are other named cultivars falling somewhere between the two in vigour: 'Mrs Pope', 'Boutin' and 'Hadspen'. They lack the smelly foliage of the more decidedly woody species of which *S. microphylla* is the most familiar manifestation. The leaves of the form *neurepia* (*S. grahamii*) are larger, paler green and as smelly, not far from the sweaty smell of the Vatican sage. The flowers of *S. microphylla* ssp. *microphylla* are deep maroon in dark calyces, *S. neurepia* is bright carmine-scarlet and var. *wislezenii* is paler carmine with flowers in dense spikes over foliage smelling of blackcurrant. 'Oxford Var' is pinkish-carmine. Similar is *S. greggii* with small leaves and magenta-carmine flowers; it has a pretty pale form aptly named 'Peach'. In all of these the balance of flower and leaf is quite different from the basal foliage and terminal flower spikes of *S. involucrata*; here flowers and leaves are more evenly dispersed. Even so, the near-scarlet *S. neurepia* is too vivid for this border. Another that I have grown, magenta *S. dorisiana*, is less satisfactory on account of its reluctance to flower freely.

The range of colour of the cestrums is similar to the salvias; I was fortunate in inheriting one of the purple-leaved, deepest crimson-purple flowered forms of the usually brighter, paler *Cestrum elegans*. Equally appropriate in this section would be one of the softer-toned forms, pale pink *C. elegans* var *smithii*, *C. roseum* or its cultivar 'Ilnacullin', which has rose-pink flowers on reddish stems. They appreciate the extra shelter of a wall at their backs, except in wholly frost-free gardens.

Dieramas are scarcely tender, but they thrive in mild, moist climates. Variously known as angel's fishing rods or wand flower, on account of their slender but tough stems, arching with the weight of flared bell-shaped flowers and swaying in the lightest breeze, they look best when grown in uncluttered surroundings. In this garden many are self-sown between paving stones in the terrace floor, where their soft lilac-pink or richer crimson-purple colouring accords well with the grey stone of the paving and the house behind, and they can move freely in the wind without catching on neighbouring plants. At one time a range of named cultivars was introduced, varying in colour from white to violet-purple, and in height from the 90 cm/3 ft of *Dierama pumilum* to the 1·8–2·4 m/6–8 ft of *D. pulcherrimum*. Coming from the Slieve Donard nursery, many had bird names – midnight-purple 'Blackbird', 'Windhover' in lilac-rose, and 'Plover' with lilac bells. If dieramas are to be set among other plants, then it could be some low spreader like *Salvia buchananii* (also listed as *S. bacheriana*), dark of stem and leaf and magenta of plush-textured flower.

The spreading or prostrate forms of osteospermum also answer well, and as their colour range is much that of the dieramas, matches or close harmonies can be contrived using *Osteospermum barberae* which has mauve-pink ray florets, bronzed on their lower side, but an overlarge yellow disk, *O. jucundum* which is of procumbent growth with daisies varying from mauve to rich purple, or the cultivars which derive from them, with infusion perhaps of the blood of white *O. ecklonis* 'Prostratum'. Among these, 'Bloemhof Belle', 'Langtrees' and 'Hopley', already mentioned in another context, could well be used again. Another is 'Lady Leitrim', with the same yellow disk as 'Langtrees' and 'Hopley', but with much paler petals earning it the synonym of 'Pale Face'. 'Cannington Roy' is a curious, very prostrate cultivar in which the ray florets open white with purple tips, but age to mauve-pink around a purple disk; the reverse is purple. Unlike 'Lady Leitrim', which is almost as tough as *O. barberae*, 'Cannington Roy' is about as frost-resistant as the crimped-petal cultivars, 'Whirligig' which we have already met, and its counterpart 'Pink Whirls' – which is to say, not very hardy at all. Other cultivars which have the same upright and rather leggy habit as 'Pink Whirls', reaching 60 cm/2 ft or a little more, are soft lilac-pink 'La Mortola' and 'Brickell's Hybrid', which has pink-mauve ray florets white at the base, around a blue disk. I have always wanted to pair this cultivar with *Lavatera maritima* (*L. bicolor*), its mallow flowers palest icy-mauve with a crimson madder central blotch, set among velvety grey foliage, making it one of these precious plants that have their own self-contained and perfectly balanced colour scheme. I like, too, to set near it Mr Bowles's mauve wallflower, which is an ideal in-and-out plant because of the imperative need to propagate it whenever you can find an unflowered shoot to take as a cutting, to frustrate its determination to flower itself to death. This means that you should always have young plants coming on, ready to slot into the border in new places to make new combinations.

In another garden, I saw a combination of plants that I wished I had thought of myself, centring around *Lavatera maritima*. At its feet were *Nierembergia frutescens*, with narrow greyish leaves and five-cornered saucers of clear pale lilac, deeper at the centre; *Tulbaghia violacea* with lilac flowers and glaucous leaves; *Convolvulus tenuissimus*, exquisite in finely-cut silvered foliage and shell-pink saucers, but so invasive that it would need very careful management so close to the tulbaghia; *Ceratostigma abyssinicum* which appears to have larger leaves, ciliate at the edges, than the common *C. willmottianum*, and larger flowers, set in the same reddish calyces, but of a paler sky-blue like *Plumbago auriculata*; the turquoise, grey-leaved *Oxypetalum caeruleum*; *Osteospermum* 'Silver Sparkler'; *Salvia patens* 'Cambridge Blue'; *Convolvulus mauretanicus*; and, running about the feet of all these choice things, *Polygonum capitatum*, of which the foliage, in full sun, takes on crimson tones half masking the dark V bisecting each leaf, to make a deep setting for massed spherical heads, $1 \text{ cm}/\frac{1}{2}$ in across, of pale candy-pink. Near enough to be in the same field of vision were the tender, shrubby Australian mallow *Alyogyne huegellii* 'Santa Cruz', with large violet-mauve flowers, a form of *Cestrum elegans* with purple tubes and green foliage, and *Solanum laciniatum* with potato flowers of much the same rich violet as the mallow. Not a bad plant among them, and beautifully combined.

Olearia frostii is another self-contained shrub. This Australian species has a reputation for tenderness which I believe to be entirely unfounded, for it has survived, undamaged, frosts of $-22°C$ with me. It is a small shrub with neat, rather blunt, grey woolly foliage and improbably large, solitary flower heads of many clear pale lilac ray florets around a yellow disk. I like to grow it within sight of the silvery, satin-finished *Convolvulus cneorum*, a smallish shrub itself, with fluted wide trumpets opening white from blush-pink, scrolled buds, successively throughout summer. Nearby, too, *Salvia discolor* finds a place, on account of its white-felted leaves and stems and the deeper note of small indigo-black flowers.

Unless you garden in a completely frost-free environment you will need to take cuttings each autumn, as insurance against loss, of this salvia. So, too, with *Senecio heritieri* and *S. maderense* (now respectively *Pericallis lanata* and *P. aurita*), which both have heart-shaped leaves somewhat lobed at the margins; the leaf backs and stems are white with a close felting, setting off flower heads wholly magenta-pink in the Madeiran plant. The Canary Islander, *S. heritieri*, has white rays tipped with magenta around a maroon-pink disk. Both are extremely fetching, lowly plants (75 cm/$2\frac{1}{2}$ ft or so) for near the front of silver and mauve schemes. You might add to this group the temperamental *Calceolaria arachnoidea*, from Chile. This is a creeping plant with leaves of the same texture as *Salvia argentea*, though smaller: a surface apparently composed of countless silvery cobwebs closely interwoven. Over this soft mat arise little clusters of pouched flowers, of typical *Calceolaria* shape but coloured in sombre mourning-purple. The recipe for success, which I have never wholly achieved, appears to be abundant moisture in summer and a dry winter: a combination not easy to achieve, especially in maritime areas where the atmosphere is ever charged with moisture.

In the actual borders I planted, as I went, I repeated certain elements, most notably using the interweavers such as *Senecio vira-vira* and *Helichrysum petiolare* both to link neighbouring groups of plants or soften spiky outlines and to provide a sense of coherence through the length of the border. I felt the need, in the end of the border dominated by the big *Buddleja colvilei*, for some stronger colours; for, blues and mauves being recessive, they could appear outweighed by even the gentle coral, primrose and buff of the opposite end, all colours that come to meet the eye. The silvery interweavers successfully linked the more insistent pinks and purples to the paler groups. A very dominant pairing, too strong for this border, that has been used at Great Dixter, where Christopher Lloyd practises his art and craft of gardening, served as inspiration: *Caryopteris* × *clandonensis* and *Lobelia* 'Queen Victoria'. I settled instead for *Salvia farinacea* 'Victoria', *Heliotropium* 'Princess Marina' (deepest of the named cultivars with a good perfume) and *Penstemon* 'Garnet' (which regrettably we are now instructed to call 'Andenken an Friedrich Hahn'), or the slightly brighter 'Rich Ruby'. The heliotrope cultivars 'Lord Roberts' and 'Chatsworth' are richer still in their almondy perfume than 'Princess Marina', but being paler in colour can form the link back to gentler tones. They are a little trouble, it is true, for they need renewing each year from cuttings unless grown entirely free of frost. So too, though for different reasons, do many penstemons: ideally, at least. Young penstemons form compact plants full of flower over a long summer to autumn season; old plants, grown woody, give one burst of colour at midsummer only.

There is also the question of hardiness. The larger the flowers borne by a penstemon, the more tender it will be, in general; and old plants too, whatever their flower size, are often less resistant to frost than youngsters of the same kind. The cultivars such as 'Evelyn', forming a good clump of narrow basal foliage topped by small flowers – pale pink in this case – are hardier than the larger-leaved, bare-stemmed varieties which have fewer but very large bells, typified by 'Rubicunda', with widely flared trumpets of cherry-red and white. Other pinks that belong in this section are 'Hidcote Pink', of clear colouring with deeper markings in the throat, and taller, pale 'Pennington Gem', its pure colouring assorting delightfully with lilac and mauve. 'Apple Blossom' is paler still in creamy blush tipped with rose-pink. With the deeper-toned group just adumbrated the purple penstemons would assort well, 'Purple Bedder', 'Burgundy' or 'Port Wine'. Lighter than these, with an iridescent bloomy finish to its purple-blue bells, is the penstemon correctly called 'Sour Grapes'; but this name has lately become attached to a paler cultivar still, rightly known as 'Stapleford Gem' – and indeed no grape that I have ever seen could match its opalescent cream and blue-lilac colouring.

Penstemons, salvias, diascias, osteospermums: all flower for weeks and months on end (with the qualification already noted in regard to aging penstemons). This is all very nice, and helps to keep the border looking colourful for a long season. For all that, by autumn something fresh is welcome; and few flowers are less autumnal in spirit than the nerines, with their crimpled, sheeny petals. The familiar *Nerine bowdenii* is bright candy pink; 'Fenwick's Var.' is a fine vigorous form with larger flowers, well known and widely available. If you find the colour too assertive, 'Blush Beauty' may appeal more, or the palest blush *N. bowdenii manina*, with long narrow petals. The hybrids 'Hera' and 'Aurora' are both of richer colouring, but 'Hera' at least is badly infected with virus and should be avoided until stocks can be cleaned up using modern techniques. Of the same parentage, the newer 'Rushmere Star' has large flowers of deep rosy-mauve. 'Quinton Wells', collected in the wild in South Africa, has been said to be of deeper colouring; the plant I obtained under this name matched the wild collected stock, with flower stems almost twice as tall, at 90 cm/3 ft, and small, very frilled flowers of rose-pink with paler centres. A hybrid of great vigour, 'Paula Knight', has much smoother segments of deep rosy-pink, each marked with a central stripe of silvery mauve. There is also a white *N. bowdenii*.

It is a constant surprise to find how pink the garden in autumn can be. The late flowers of *Salvia involucrata* and diascias, together with these nerines, are joined by the surprising, brilliant magenta daisies of *Senecio pulcher* and, if you can find them, pink cultivars of *Lobelia* such as 'Mrs Humbert' or 'Russian Princess'. Callicarpas are much too coarse as shrubs to be permitted in this border, but in a vase their vivid violet-magenta berries, clustered like beads, add just the right, slightly dotty note to an arrangement picked from these autumn flowers. The silver foliage which is a recurring theme assorts as well with sugar-pink and cerise as with the softer mauve and lilac tones that earlier in the season dominate the border.

More ephemeral than the nerines, but as lovely to behold, and even more valued on account of their fragrance of ripe apricots, *Amaryllis belladonna* and its cultivars and hybrids flower in autumn, following late summer rains or a substitute hosepipe flooding. The stout, often purplish flowering stems push up with startling suddenness from leafless bulbs; the strap-like foliage follows, in winter. There are several named cultivars, all with narrow buds opening to heads of up to eight trumpet flowers; for a fuller list, I refer you to my *Kew Gardening Guide: Tender Perennials*. The most reliable for flowers is said to be 'Rubra', with up to eighteen deep pink blooms on each reddish stem; 'Elata' is much paler, and especially fragrant. The lovely 'Hathor' is white with primrose throat; 'Beacon' is crimson. The pink-flowered varieties tend to flush deeper with age.

Among the hybrids of the belladonna lily with other, closely related genera is *Amarygia* × *parkeri*, with the blood of *Brunsvigia josephinae*. It has flowers of rich pink flushed at the throat with apricot; 'Tubergen's Variety' has smaller, deeper rose-pink flowers, and foliage that seems more resistant to frost. Loveliest, and frailest, is × *A. parkeri* 'Alba', tall and pure white, shading to cream in the throat. It is their habit of leafing in winter that imposes a sheltered position, as also their preference, shared with nerines, for growing near the soil surface with the bulb snouts exposed. Deep planting is no answer; they will simply sulk, flowerless, until they have worked their way to the surface. Both the belladonna lilies and nerines may also take a few years to settle down to flowering; nerines, especially, will simply make leaves until they have almost exhausted the nutrients in the soil about them, so you should not be kind to your flowerless nerines and attempt to encourage them with extra feeding.

The cross between *Nerine bowdenii* and *Amaryllis belladonna* has produced × *Amarine tubergenii*, in which the soft to deep pink flowers more closely resemble nerines; the selection 'Zwanenburg' is a richer crimson-pink. In × *Amarcrinum memoria-corsii* and × *A. howardii* the other parent is *Crinum moorei*, the influence of which is clearly visible in the pink flowers. All contribute most beautifully to the early autumn border.

The crinums themselves, characterized by huge, deep-rooting bulbs and coarse untidy leafage, flower earlier than the amaryllis and nerines, most appearing in high summer; they prefer moist soil and thrive on the rich feeding that would indefinitely defer the flowering of nerines. So moisture-loving are they, indeed, that my sister grows them very successfully in her bog garden in Wales. All have large, fragrant trumpet flowers, and need setting among some concealing foliage. I have seen *Crinum* × *powellii* growing and flowering freely among rhododendrons of the 'Fragrantissimum' persuasion, in a clearing where the sun's rays shaft down.

With the caveat about masking all that floppy foliage, however, they are also worthy of a place in a flower border. *C. moorei*, the parent of the amarcrinums, comes in pink or white and flowers less freely than its hybrid with *C. bulbispermum*, the more familiar *C. × powellii*. It is worth seeking out the beautiful white 'Album', or named pink cultivars such as deep 'Krelagei', paler 'Haarlemense' or rosy 'Ellen Bosanquet', the only one other than the white that I have personally grown. Their fragrance is delectable.

These crinums have somewhat diverted me from my line of thought, which was to discuss some of the flowers of autumn. Very much of this season are the Kaffir lilies, *Schizostylis coccinea*: yet another example of the misuse of the word lily, for these are gladiolus relatives in the family Iridaceae, and the belladonna lilies are, of course, in Amaryllidaceae. The Kaffir lilies are as moisture-loving as crinums, and prefer a damp atmosphere too; the moisture-laden air of maritime gardens suits them well, and I have grown them as often with their feet virtually in running water as in a more conventional border. The crimson-scarlet type, and selected clones of similar colouring, are too bright for the border I am still, theoretically at least, describing; they will be given due acknowledgement later in this chapter. But among the pinks and mauves and lilacs, adding their own note to the general pinkness of autumn in this section of the border, the several pink-flowered cultivars are valuable, extending the season well into winter.

The earliest to flower, I believe, in late summer, is rose-pink 'Tambara', followed by the paler 'Mrs Hegarty'. 'Pallida' is even more ethereal, nearly white, and flowers over a very long season. There is also a pure white, rather small in flower, but appealing at close quarters on account of the apple-green tint at the heart of the petals. 'Sunrise' is a large-flowered pink now widely grown; a newer cultivar is 'Jennifer'. For a deeper, duskier pink, there is 'Professor Barnard'; 'Zeal Salmon' is a clear, clean colour not at all suggestive of the flesh of the fish whether raw or cooked. 'November Cheer' indicates in its name its northern hemisphere flowering season, late into autumn; the older 'Viscountess Byng' is of this season also. All have silky, saucer-shaped blooms and narrow grassy foliage; all increase rapidly in the moist soil that they prefer and can be split almost as often as you desire to make larger, or new, clumps.

Several of the brightly-coloured hebes with the blood of *Hebe speciosa* in them, which are such excellent wind-resisters that they found their place in Chapter II, could also be used in this border. Hebes do not enjoy a wet soil, but neither do they relish drought and starvation. Their preference for well-nourished soil means that you could pair them with fuchsias, also – indeed even more so – greedy plants. In the main their colouring assorts well, though fuchsias also run slightly to coral and salmon

pink cultivars which belong further along in the border towards the
beschorneria. There are so many fuchsias available, and in mild gardens
there is so little need to worry that any of the named hybrids will not
survive the winter, that it hardly seems worth giving mention to any
particular cultivar. Later I shall certainly mention some fuchsia species
with scarlet, coral or orange flowers; and a choice handful of species with
flowers of appropriate colouring for this part of the border, but which
are very tender, will get due mention in Chapter V with other shrubs
needing wall protection even in mild gardens.

And so here we are at the foot of the large old *Buddleja colvilei* 'Kewensis',
sturdy enough to host a not too vigorous climber. Many climbers belong
in other chapters, but here seems an appropriate place to mention the
maurandyas, soft-wooded scramblers which can be raised annually from
seed to produce their flowers of crushed strawberry or foxglove pink,
shaped indeed like wide foxgloves, among soft-textured, heart-shaped
leaves. There is a certain piquancy in finding, among the flowers of a
shrub, the quite differently shaped but similarly coloured flowers of the
climber it is supporting. *Maurandya erubescens* (*Lophospermum erubescens*)
has rose-pink flowers; those of *M. barclaiana* are nearer to purple, though
white and pink forms also exist.

The hot colours

The walled garden within which I chose to isolate the hotter colours,
scarlet and copper and orange, canary and citron-yellow, slopes to the
south and is bisected by a Lutyens-style, stone-bound rill, the water
splashing musically over a succession of low falls from a tank at the top
of the garden, and temporarily stilled by a circular pool at the centre
before falling several feet to the stream and grassy banks below the outer,
lower walls. Here, in geometrically-shaped beds echoing the narrowing
rectangle of the walls, were groups of the choicer kniphofias, scarlet
and flame watsonias, hedychiums and cannas, *Calceolaria integrifolia* and
Epilobium canum, and all the tribe of scarlet, plush-textured salvias. The
original purpose was to display the National Collection of kniphofias, so
that many lowly plants had the dual role of decoratively clothing the
ground around the pokers and of separating clumps of similar cultivars.
Thus, for example, yellow kniphofias of medium height such as 'Gold
Else', 'Sunningdale Yellow', *Kniphofia citrina* and its seedling 'Chrysantha',
the Slieve Donard cultivars 'Yellow Hammer' and 'Canary Bird', 'Green
Lemon', and 'Wrexham Buttercup', were grouped in adjacent but distinct
clumps, with *Epilobium canum* 'Dublin' running around and between them
and blending into the taller *Lobelia laxiflora* (*L. cavanillesii*), which has very

narrow leaves and curving tubular flowers of scarlet and yellow echoing the vermilion trumpets of the epilobium. Another group of later-flowering yellow pokers, including 'Brimstone', 'Bees' Lemon', and the canary-coloured 'Limelight', were threaded about by *Salvia blepharophylla*, which has creeping roots and short stems set with abundant vivid scarlet flowers, contrasting with the massed canary-yellow pouches of the annual, self-sowing *Calceolaria mexicana*.

On the wall behind, *Salvia fulgens* and *S. gesneriiflora*, both with fiery scarlet flowers, are set with the alluring *Kniphofia ichopensis*, a species from Natal with foliage more like that of a Spanish iris than a poker, and spaced florets of lime-yellow just touched with orange in the bud. Here too grow some of the choicer hedychiums, including tangerine-scarlet *Hedychium coccineum* 'Tara' and *H. greenei* with maroon-backed foliage. In the open beds *H. densiflorum* 'Assam Orange', with narrow tangerine spikes, and the slightly pinker form of the same species which is known only by its collectors' number, L S & H 79313, are perfectly hardy. But *H. densiflorum* 'Stephen', with wide spidery heads of primrose-cream enlivened by scarlet stamens, was given a choicer, wall position near a large plant of *Abutilon* 'Golden Fleece', which – with others of its kind – is described in Chapter V.

In another bed the green and creamy-green pokers are grouped with *Galtonia viridiflora*, *Nicotiana langsdorfii* – perennial in mild climates – and two interweavers, *Helichrysum petiolare* 'Limelight' mingling its butter-yellow to lime, heart-shaped leaves with the ferny foliage and vivid yellow lazy daisies of *Bidens ferulaefolia*. The tobacco has the usual clammy green basal leaves, topped by tall open sprays of many small, clear lime-green tubular flowers with small lobes flaring around the sky blue anthers. They are not so different in colour from the nodding, fragrant bells of the galtonia, which is a slighter plant than the more familiar Cape hyacinth, *G. candicans*.

The pokers are the tough and hardy 'Green Jade', still the best of the green cultivars despite a tendency to turn tatty at the base of the spike before the topmost buds have fully opened, and 'Chartreuse', very similar though just touched in the bud with bronze. 'Green Magic' and the larger 'Torchbearer' both open from acid-green buds to cream and lemon-white. The newer 'Mermaiden' is very similar, and indeed is of the same parentage as 'Torchbearer': 'Prince Igor' crossed with the old, pale primrose 'Maid of Orléans'. Their creamy primrose, just touched with lime, is picked up by the curving tubes of *Phygelius aequalis* 'Yellow Trumpet', a crassly named newish cultivar which is said to come true from seed; though as it is very easy from cuttings, there is no need to put this to the test unless you want to. 'Yellow Trumpet' was introduced from the wild: like the more familiar *P. capensis*, *P. aequalis* is a native of South Africa, though

with a more northerly distribution, growing on rocky stream banks.
Lately a range of cultivars has been raised by crossing the two species:
'Moonraker' is pale yellow, differing from 'Yellow Trumpet' in bearing its
straighter bugles all around the stem instead of in a one-sided spray. These
cape fuchsias look well also with primrose kniphofias: 'Zeal Primrose'
with well-spaced florets, 'Tubergeniana', 'Vanilla', and 'Primrose Beauty'.

One of the beds holds pokers of maize and saffron yellow, buff and
honey-gold, clear pale tangerine, biscuit and bronze. The palest of the
pokers in this bed include 'Toffee Nosed' and 'Apricot', already used in
the main border outside the walls of this garden, 'Comet' in pale coral
and honey-cream, Slieve Donard's amber-yellow 'Goldfinch', 'July Glow'
in buttercup-yellow overlaid with apricot, and biscuity 'Bees' Sunset'.
They were joined, one year, by *Hibiscus trionum*, a tender perennial which
can be grown as an annual to produce, in high summer, its creamy
flowers with darkest burnt-umber eye. Another year, it was *Osteospermum*
'Buttermilk', chosen for its soft yellow ray florets backed with tan around
a bluish-tan disk. A more permanent companion is *Malvastrum lateritium*,
already alluded to as too rampant for the border of soft colours.

The pokers that approach more nearly to orange, big 'Painted Lady',
the colour of maize opening from amber-orange buds, and smaller
'Redstart', a Slieve Donard cultivar of clear pure orange, tawny-gold
'Ada' and The Plantsmen's Buckshaw Hybrids in amber and apricot, pale
tangerine and flame, followed later in the season by Norman Hadden's
lovely 'Underway' which in autumn pushes up slender spikes of creamy
orange opening from dusky amber buds: these were joined by *Tropaeolum*
tuberosum used as ground cover. If you set the tubers beside peasticks half
snapped and laid at right angles to the soil and about 15 cm/6 in above it,
very quickly the leafy stems of this climbing nasturtium clothe their
supports, allowing the red and yellow flowers to appear above the foliage.
One of the precocious flowering forms is to be preferred, such as 'Ken
Aslet', to be sure of a long season of flower before the frosts of winter cut
the top growth. Here too belong the brighter forms of *Argyranthemum*
frutescens: canary-yellow, single-flowered 'Overbecks' and a double form
of like colouring.

In autumn, silvery foliage takes on a tender luminosity that calls, not
only for the harmonizing mauves and lilacs and pinks of the main border,
but also – in separate groupings, of course – cinnabar and scarlet and
vermilion, mandarin and poppy and orient red. *Lotus berthelotii* will already
have made its own scheme in these colours, earlier in the year, when its
claw-shaped coppery-crimson flowers appear among the cascading stems
set with silvery needles; now, it can make a backdrop. A sprawler, it is
best planted where it can fall downwards over a rock face or retaining
wall. If you enjoy planting tubs or urns with fresh combinations each

year, this and its paler, tawny yellow counterpart *L. maculatus* are certain to be among the plants you will want to return to again and again, mingling them perhaps with the little double, trailing nasturtium 'Hermione Grashof'.

In autumn come several kniphofias deriving from *Kniphofia triangularis* ssp. *triangularis* and its near kin – *K. galpinii* of gardens. They share a tendency to grassy foliage and slim spikes on stems usually not more than 75 cm/2½ ft in height. The species itself is the slenderest of all, I believe, in flame-scarlet from green buds. Not much more robust in appearance is 'Little Elf'. The Bressingham set – 'Comet', 'Flame', 'Gleam', 'Glow' and 'Torch', all prefixed with the nursery's name – are stouter, and vary in height from 50 cm/20 in to 75 cm/2½ ft. *K. rufa* is allied to *K. triangularis* subsp. *triangularis*; it has fairly long yellow florets, widely spaced and opening from red buds, on 50 cm/20 in stems. From Kenya and Uganda comes the species *K. thomsonii* subsp. *snowdenii* (*K. snowdenii* of gardens), in soft coral-scarlet with a long, loose spike of curving, widely separated florets; despite its origins it is not that tender, and increases fast by runners. It is energetic enough to pair off with the interweaving *Senecio vira-vira* or *Helichrysum petiolare*, or the shrubby, feathery-fine *Artemisia arborescens* which in mild gardens may reach 1·8 m/6 ft, especially if it has a wall at its back. A hardier form, 'Faith Raven', has the same silky, divided foliage.

The smaller pokers, however, would be better matched with plants of equally finely cut silver foliage but more stay-at-home disposition. More compact than *Artemisia arborescens* is its hybrid 'Powis Castle', a rounded bush of 75 cm/2½ ft, with silver-grey filigree foliage and no inclination to flower, a positive asset in a genus where flowers, in the main, only detract from the lovely leaves. The silvery white *Senecio cineraria* forms are well-known and much used, grown from seed, in bedding schemes. In mild gardens they are permanencies, needing rigorous spring pruning to remain neat all summer. Most people seem to prefer the cut-leaved forms such as 'White Diamond', but I have a weakness for 'Cirrus', with broader lobes, a fetching thing and very effective in a mass. For the same reason I am attached to *Centaurea rutifolia* (*C. candidissima* of gardens), which is one of the whitest silvers I know, growing to 30 cm/1 ft or so with broad-lobed leaves. *C. cineraria* (*C. gymnocarpa*) is fine and feathery, the leaves bipinnatifid – divided, that is, and again subdivided into lacy segments; each up to 30 cm/1 ft long, they are assembled into loose rosettes about 60 cm/2 ft high and wide. Raised from seed, it has the maddening habit of trying to make yet more seed by producing its boring little mauve flowers, which you must keep severing to bring it to heel. If you acquire the form 'Colchester White', you will have a plant that is not only still more lacy, still paler platinum-white, but also one that has been raised from cuttings and should be correspondingly less apt to run to flower.

Almost as pale, but quite different in texture, is *Calocephalus brownii* (*Leucophyta brownii*), a very tender Australian composite, its thin stems furnished with tiny appressed leaves, giving it the appearance of a tangle of silver wire about 60 cm/2 ft high and wide. As well as with the flames and scarlets already proposed, I have seen it used to good effect in a cool combination with the centaurea just described and the china blue daisies and needle-fine fresh green foliage of *Felicia amoena* (*F. pappei*).

The white form of *Leonotis leonurus*, already mentioned, is less often seen than the bright orange type, in which grey woolly foliage forms the setting for the whorls of clawed flowers. And although they have green foliage not grey, other hybrid phygelius that I have not yet mentioned could join this flame, scarlet and silver planting, for in the main they have a long season. 'Devil's Tears' is deep pinkish-scarlet with orange red lobes, 'African Queen' clear red with brighter lobes. They are hardy enough in mild gardens not to need wall shelter, but I find it advisable to give some protection to the triphylla fuchsias, which also have hanging trumpet flowers, though differently disposed and rather differently shaped, straight-tubed and with more pointed lobes. They come in several shades of scarlet or coral: 'Fanfare', 'Koralle', and pinkish-salmon 'Billy Green' fit here, and I used others in a different context.

Fuchsia splendens, with velvety soft, corrugated foliage and scarlet and green flattened trumpets, and the plant for long known as *F. cordifolia*, are hardier than the triphylla hybrids, though still apt to be cut back by frost. *F. cordifolia* is now considered to be a name with no botanical standing. The plant gained an Award of Merit when I showed it to the Royal Horticultural Society in June 1984, whereupon it needed a recognized cultivar name: for it is now considered to be a form of *F. splendens*. Both were introduced from Central America; my award plant, common in south-western English gardens, was named 'Karl Hartweg' for the plant collector who first discovered it. It has larger, paler green leaves than the type, less markedly veined, white-dusted when young, and paler coral, longer-tubed flowers similarly flattened in one plane as though pinched between finger and thumb. The oblong, dark maroon fruits that follow are pleasantly tart with a peppery after-taste. *Fuchsia fulgens* is another species of the same style, with bright orange, green-tipped tubular flowers, and a tuberous rootstock.

Here too would be the place to grow *Penstemon isophyllus*, a lanky shrub from California with brilliant coral-scarlet, narrow-tubed flowers. A plant I received as *P.* 'Taosensis' may or may not belong here: it is extremely free-flowering, with a mass of coral flowers on 75 cm/2½ ft stems over distinctly glaucous foliage. *P. cordifolius* is leafier and can be grown through a neighbouring shrub to show off its glowing scarlet, tubular flowers clustered at the branch tips.

A genus that I have scarcely mentioned yet is *Gazania*. Yet these South African daisies are every bit as valuable as the osteospermums and felicias, coming in a wide range of colours, with sizeable flowerheads often enlivened by green or black zoning at or near the base of the rays. 'Silver Beauty' is a low, spreading plant with leaves as silvery, if not as finely cut, as the centaureas, and vivid yellow daisies with a greenish black basal ring. This works well as the setting for *Kniphofia* 'Royal Standard', a 90 cm/3 ft bicolor, its acid-yellow and clear vermilion colouring giving it considerable allure – unlike most red and yellow pokers.

As well as all these kniphofias, which few gardeners other than an addict like myself would wish to collect in one place, there are several fine watsonias to give you sword-like foliage with flowers resembling miniature gladioli but much more refined, in orange and scarlet. I chose to grow a number of them here. The easy and familiar *Watsonia beatricis* varies from coral to scarlet, with densely-flowered 90 cm/3 ft spikes in summer. *W. fulgens* is now considered to include the plant I first knew as *W. angusta*, with looser spikes of vivid vermilion-scarlet in early summer; the bright scarlet 'Stanfords' is similar. An unnamed kind came to me as a gift; it has sharp orange flowers. Here, too, I planted the rather more tender *Chasmanthe aethiopica*, which resembles a *Curtonus* of extra magnificence, and needs shelter to protect the evergreen, bold sword leaves from winter damage. Slim 90 cm/3 ft spikes of orange-scarlet open in summer. The flowers of *Chasmanthe floribunda* are larger; var. *duckitii* has yellow flowers in place of the vermilion of the type. The related crocosmias are hardier, even the largest-flowered cultivars which derive their size from the tender, amber-yellow *Crocosmia aurea*. Burnt-orange and wallflower-red 'Emily McKenzie' is still offered; the wide nodding flowers appear on 60 cm/2 ft stems in autumn, after the paler 'His Majesty'. The shades of rust and tan assort well with the brown-flowered cultivars of *Calceolaria integrifolia*, deep sienna 'Campden Hero' and the paler 'Kentish Hero', once popular and much used in bedding and now cherished to be passed around between collectors. Other crocosmias are of similar colouring: 'James Coey' is very dark orange-red, paler within, with sienna splashes; 'Queen of Spain' is taller at 90 cm/3 ft, opening from dark rust-red buds to clear orange with paler throat. The largest of all in flower is 'Star of the East', in soft apricot-yellow flushed with red at the tips and on the outer segments; it flowers in early autumn. There are a few others still in cultivation, out of well over one hundred cultivars raised over the years by Lemoine and others, but these are the only large-flowered kinds I have managed to obtain. In complete contrast is 'Jackanapes', barely 60 cm/2 ft tall, with small flowers of alternating scarlet and yellow segments. 'Carmin Brillant' has medium-sized flowers of bright scarlet, fading towards carmine, a colour which I have seen in no other crocosmia;

it is a good doer, as willing to increase as 'Citronella', and I would not be without it.

Mention the genus *Hippeastrum*, and most people would first think of the gross flowers sold as houseplants. But there are virtually hardy members of this bulbous family, less monstrous in flower. *Hippeastrum* 'Acramanii' has pointed, flared segments of brilliant pure scarlet, contrasting beautifully with the green throat, on 45 cm/18 in stems in summer. *H. aulicum* is slightly larger in flower; the segments are of similar colouring, a touch less brilliant, striated with paler and deeper shades of scarlet-crimson around the same green throat.

I kept out of the walled garden some of the more massive pokers which would have been out of scale, as also most of the red and yellow bicolors. Of these, only one or two are worthy of mention here. 'Red Admiral', for example, has stout spikes on 1·2 m/4 ft stems, very beautiful when still wholly scarlet but spoiled when the lower florets fade to off-yellow. The noble 'Samuel's Sensation' ages more gracefully, its very long coral-red spikes on 1·5 m/5 ft stems shading to creamy yellow at the base. And despite its colouring, I cannot overlook *Kniphofia rooperi*, which flowers in autumn, when its stout stems are topped by goose-egg-shaped heads of orange and yellow. I have on occasion paired it with *Salvia uliginosa*, a herbaceous species with running roots and tall, slender, lolling stems bearing many sky-blue flowers. The combination works best if the poker is seen outlined against sky or sea. Emulating an association seen in another garden, I have also grown it with the hardy, lime yellow-leaved *Fuchsia* 'Genii' and *Lobelia laxiflora* in a late summer and autumn border in which orange and tan were set among sharp citrus colours of leaf and flower. Here were the indispensable *Helichrysum petiolare* 'Limelight' and *Nicotiana langsdorfii*, orange crocosmias, and the hardy *Philadelphus coronarius* 'Aureus'. The coral tree, *Erythrina crista-galli*, belongs here for its large, vivid scarlet pea flowers borne on leafy stems. In very mild areas it will form woody stems, but it is perfectly willing to settle down to a herbaceous existence and regenerate from the roots each spring. So too will the Mexican *Amicia zygomeris*, a legume again, with lush green leaves characteristically notched at the apex, and tawny-yellow flowers in late summer to autumn. The Argentine *Grindelia chiloensis* is a mixed border shrub that is surprisingly undervalued, for it has narrow, toothed, grey-green leaves and cheery yellow daisies appearing over a three to four month summer season. Each part-opened flower head is topped by a white sticky substance, with the texture of uncooked meringue.

A wholly red border can make a stunning impact, not always agreeable; I recall that when I first saw the red borders at Hidcote I felt as though I were walking through an abattoir. But on a later visit I felt less uncomfortable, and I was quite won over to all-red plantings by the smaller red border in Peter Healing's garden at The Priory, Kemerton. Both demonstrate, the latter with more concentrated impact, the use of strong scarlets and crimsons with coppery and purple foliage. Here there is no room for faintheartedness: you must go all out for intensity of colour in a range from vermilion to garnet and blood red, using only fully saturated tones. The keynote can be the bold, maroon-purple paddles of *Canna indica* hybrids such as 'Le Roi Humbert' or 'The President', which have gross red flowers, more appropriate in this context than apricot 'Wyoming'. I prefer the more restrained *C. indica* 'Purpurea', with neat little scarlet flowers among narrower leaves of the same rich colouring. The purple-backed leaves of *Hedychium greenei*, already several times mentioned, are of similar shape but smaller; they point upwards to show their glossy, dark reverse.

The old, virus-infected but still vigorous *Dahlia* 'Bishop of Llandaff' earns a place here for its finely laciniated metallic black-purple foliage as much as for its glowing scarlet flowers. It has vigour enough to grow lustily despite the debilitating virus, but should not be accompanied by other, less robust dahlias which, once infected, will succumb. Much the same colouring belongs to *Lobelia* 'Queen Victoria' and 'Bees' Flame': spikes of scarlet over beetroot-purple leaves. Newer cultivars from Canada have been introduced, in which fuller, richer spikes of larger flowers are combined with greater hardiness, as in 'Cherry Ripe', garnet-crimson 'Dark Crusader' and the vermilion-scarlet, green leaved 'Brightness' and 'Will Scarlet'. Some classic bedding plants have metallic purple foliage: *Iresine herbstii* and nettle-leaved *Perilla* 'Nankinensis', annual ruby chard which has crimson midribs to its purple, spinach-like leaves, and purple castor oil (*Ricinus communis* 'Gibsonii') for its wide palmate leaves on tall stems. The castor oil, in particular, needs growing well; nothing is more wretched than a half-starved, half-sized specimen probably emerging in the dubious role of dot plant from above some equally unhappy scarlet salvias or French marigolds.

If so much bedding worries you, there are hardy purple-leaved plants to fill out this border, alone or in combination with the tenders. *Sedum maximum* 'Atropurpureum' has beetroot-maroon foliage and stems, and Miss Jekyll's *S. telephium* 'Munstead Red' is cloudy purple with flat heads of muted maroon flowers. Of similar succulence, but decidedly tender, is *Aeonium arboreum* 'Atropurpureum' (the clone 'Schwarzkopf' is perhaps a superior selection), taller at 90 cm/3 ft than the sedums, composed of rosettes of stubby, fat, burnished metallic purple leaves. The yellow cones of flower should be cut out unless the colour scheme is to become unbalanced. At a lower level *Tradescantia pallida* 'Purpurea' (*Setcreasea purpurea*) creeps about, below crimson nicotianas that add flowers of appropriate colour, if not scent: for these coloured, day-awake tobaccos are virtually or wholly without perfume. For scent, plant *Verbena* 'Lawrence Johnston', in cherry-red, the nearest to scarlet of the fragrant verbenas. The very bright scarlet 'Huntsman' derives its colouring from *V. peruviana* and is scentless. Both, however, have a relaxed, widespreading habit, knitting together neighbouring groups of plants. Penstemons add long-lasting colour on taller plants, for there are many in scarlet or crimson: 'Garnet' and 'Rich Ruby' have already made an appearance. One of the best purer reds is 'Firebird' ('Ruby' or 'Schoenholzeri' appear synony-mous), with medium-sized soft scarlet bells. 'Southgate Gem' is brighter, and more untidy; 'Newbury Gem' dwarfer, in crimson-red etched with deeper markings in the throat. The white throated 'Castle Forbes' and 'George Home' both have fat scarlet bells, though even these are restrained compared with the triumphantly gross, scarlet and white 'Rubicunda'. 'King George' is claret-scarlet with speckled throat, 'Chester Scarlet' a good, sizeable pure red.

The few kniphofias which are red enough to admit are nearer to vermilion, and of these any that fade quickly at the base to yellow are excluded. One that entirely escapes this tendency is 'Erecta', of beautiful coral-scarlet colouring. Some people loathe it for its bizarre habit of abandoning the accepted, down-pointing poise of the florets: as the spike matures the florets turn skywards, at first protruding horizontally before ending their days clasping the stems upside down. This does at least ensure that the spike remains clean, without any fading or decaying florets at the base, for a long period. The best forms of 'Corallina' and 'Pfitzeri' are of similar colouring without the upside-down stance; they have long, slim spikes and flower quite early, around midsummer. They are followed in later summer by 'Lord Roberts' and 'John Benary', both of sealing-wax red with elegantly tapering spires. None is as large as the massive pokers of 'Prince Igor' in cherry-red. The foliage of kniphofias contributes nothing to the purple and red theme, and to help conceal it, you might set in front of them some of the triphylla fuchsias with dark, velvety leaves and narrow scarlet hanging trumpets: 'Thalia', 'Gartenmeister Bonstedt', and 'Mary'.

In colder gardens the shrubby backbone of a purple patch like this will have to be composed of deciduous shrubs: *Cotinus coggygria* 'Royal Purple', *Berberis* × *ottawensis* 'Superba' and the like. In mild areas, though, we can turn to evergreens such as *Pittosporum tenuifolium* 'Tom Thumb' and the taller 'Purpureum', or the purple form of *Dodonaea viscosa*. This New Zealand shrub has oblanceolate leaves of maroon-purple on slender stems, and winged seed capsules of the same colouring from which more, like-coloured plants can be raised. It is extremely wind-hardy but not very resistant to frost. Also from New Zealand, but hardier, are the hebes, of which two cultivars with purplish foliage, already proposed for exposed gardens (see p. 38) might be admitted, given their reluctance to flower: 'Mrs Winder' and 'Waikiki'. Both grow to 75 cm/2½ ft or so, but unfortunately fade towards dark green as summer advances. More constant in colouring are the bronze-purple forms of *Corokia* × *virgata*: 'Bronze King', 'Bronze Lady', 'Bronze Knight'. They are worthwhile variants on the greyish-leaved type, all with a burnished metallic finish to the upper surface of the leaf, tempered by the grey-felted reverse. *Coprosma* 'Coppershine' is alleged to be a hybrid of the very tender *C. repens*: it makes a narrow, compact shrub of 2 m/6½ ft or so, the rounded dark green leaves suffused with copper, enhanced by the highly polished sheen of *C. repens* itself.

The purple-leaved forms of *Cordyline australis* add a spikily alien outline. I used to think that there were simply the seed-raised forms known as 'Atropurpurea' or 'Purpurea' to be had; as they are variable, some milk-chocolate brown and others nearer to the metallic purple tones we are seeking here, it is wise to select your plants in the nursery. Lately, I have seen a good named cultivar – good on the show bench, at least – called 'Torbay Red'. Torquay, like other mild western coastal areas of the British Isles, has appropriated *Cordyline australis* to itself as the Torbay palm (further north it becomes, for example, the Manx palm); it is neither a palm nor a Devonian native, though so happily settled in the area as to become a characteristic feature of the sea-front. As the plants mature, they develop trunks; in this red border, they would be better when still forming a stemless, bold rosette.

At the end of the season the scarlet-crimson *Schizostylis coccinea* forms begin to flower. The old 'Major' is still a good thing, but you might prefer deep crimson-red 'Cardinal'; both have satin-petalled flowers over grassy foliage. In a mild garden I have had them flowering into winter, long after much of this border has gone to sleep and the shrubs and trees of the garden hold the eye free from colourful distractions.

IV

Shrubs and Trees

In this chapter, I propose to deal with the shrubs that can form the backbone of your plantings. I do not mean that I will only be describing evergreen, structural shrubs: indeed, the flowering shrubs, whether deciduous or evergreen, look certain to dominate here. But certain categories of woody plants, horticulturally speaking, have later chapters reserved for them, as we have seen: those so tender that wall shelter is more or less imperative even in the climate I am presupposing; the Mediterranean and Californian natives that thrive in hot, dry soils, and the imports from other lands that join them to make the Riviera atmosphere in warm sunny gardens; the shrubs (and trees) of the temperate rain forest margins, that need, or at least greatly prefer, the kind of maturing woodland garden where shade and shelter and moisture help to mimic their native habitats; and shrubs that by virtue of their foliage, or their general deportment, can help to create a tropical look in a garden where yet there is a risk of frost, however slight. Plants are, it is true, remarkably adaptable, and you may therefore disagree with my choice of headings or with the chapter to which I ascribe a given species. My decisions are based as much upon visual as upon cultural congruity, and are entirely subjective.

Many of the shrubs that I consider to belong in this chapter, whether species or garden cultivars, have a domesticated or even sophisticated appearance, so that they fit into a gardened environment, near the house or among garden architecture; others, such as heath-like shrubs, are better suited to a less formal setting among other untamed species. The mixed border has already claimed its share of shrubs, especially those of rather formless outline where the floraison is all that counts. Many of the flowering shrubs in this chapter will possess a more decided structure, though many could equally find their way into a mixed planting; and many a border could benefit from an infusion of some of the shrubs of dominant presence, to rescue it from any charge of flimsiness. It is, indeed, with these more dominant shrubs that I want to begin.

Like its hardier relative *Griselinia littoralis*, *G. lucida* has foliage of spring-fresh, peridot-green all year; but the rounded, thick-textured leaves are larger, up to 15 cm/6 in long, markedly oblique at the base and even more highly polished. This species does not grow as large as *G. littoralis*, which I have seen at 12 m/40 ft high and as much across, in a mild coastal garden. The deeply veined leaves of *Eriobotrya japonica* are much longer in relation to their width than those of the griselinias, up to 30 cm/12 in long, deep green and rough-textured on the upper surface and buff-woolly beneath. The loquat is usually seen as a large shrub in all but the mildest gardens, where it may form a tree. Where the summers are long and hot, but only in exceptional years in temperate maritime climates, it bears pear-shaped, yellow fruits, which have an agreeable taste and are now quite widely offered for sale, even on street-corner fruit stalls in London. But a fruiting specimen will not bear the most handsome foliage, and the loquat is in any case a rather coarse thing.

Not so the finest of the osmanthuses. The ones most often seen, in British gardens at least, are *Osmanthus delavayi* and *O. heterophyllus*, the first treasured for its deliciously fragrant white flowers in spring, the second autumn-flowering, very fragrant also, and apt (like holly which it so resembles) to sport to variegated forms. In leaf, neither can compare with *O. armatus* or *O. yunnanensis*. Both have mid-green but not highly glossed, somewhat holly-like leaves with many short sharp teeth along the margins, and fragrant waxy cream-white flowers in autumn and winter; *O. yunnanensis* is fast-growing and ultimately larger. Less splendid, but still fine evergreens, are *O. × fortunei* (*O. fragrans × O. heterophyllus*) and the smaller-growing *O. serrulatus*, both with gleaming, dark green, holly-like leaves. *O. serrulatus* differs from the others in flowering in spring, but none of the holly-leaved species can be called showy in flower, though all are fragrant. *O. fragrans* itself is much less hardy, and I feel inclined therefore to bring it to your notice again later, at a more appropriate moment.

Viburnums are usually thought of as flowering shrubs, but some are in the first rank as evergreen foliage plants. I do not intend to extol the virtues of *Viburnum davidii*, for I can somehow never love it and would never waste garden space on it where less hardy evergreens will thrive. *V. cinnamomifolium* is something else again. Its large, dark green, lustrous leaves are similar to those of *V. davidii*, though of thinner texture; but they are borne on a larger shrub with none of the dumpiness of its near relation. The large, leathery leaves of *V. japonicum* are more highly polished, and not marked with the three deep longitudinal veins of *V. cinnamomifolium*; they may be as much as 15 cm/6 in long. Older plants bear rounded clusters of white, fragrant flowers at midsummer, but I should be perfectly content if my *V. japonicum* never flowered. But the most exciting of the three viburnums I am prepared to admit in this essentially foliage context is *V. odoratissimum*, a larger shrub with larger leaves still than *V. japonicum*, of gleaming dark green, often at maturity turning scarlet in winter and early spring. Again, you should not expect flowers on young plants; when they finally appear, they are held in large conical panicles in late summer and are as fragrant as the specific name suggests. Despite its origins – it is a native of Malaya – *V. odoratissimum* is hardy enough for the open border in climates equivalent to that of coastal Devon and Cornwall and will thrive in colder gardens against a sheltered wall.

Most shrubs of dominant nature grow slowly, taking their time to form a sturdy, enduring framework. It can be hard to believe, when you see the young shrub apparently barely moving, that in not so many years it will be an imposing adult. *Trochodendron aralioides* can reach 20m/66 ft, but is more often seen as a spreading shrub, much sought after for its handsome foliage and its green, ivy-like flower panicles appearing in early summer. The leaves, held on stalks as much as $7\,cm/2\frac{1}{2}$ in long, are fresh bright green with a yellowish tinge, and have scalloped edges. *Citronella mucronata*, scarcely better known as *Villaresia mucronata*, has no particular floral beauty, though the little off-white clusters are fragrant in their midsummer season; but it forms a fine glittering, dark green shrub with leaves as hard and polished as holly and, like those of holly, variable in shape from spiny on young plants to entire on the flowering shoots of mature trees.

Since I am describing some holly-leaved shrubs, this is as good a moment as any to mention a few superior *Ilex* species, true hollies. The leaves of *I. latifolia* are almost sweet chestnut-like, though thick-textured and evergreen; glossy green above, they have toothed but unarmed margins. The little berries, not far removed in colour from the artist's pigment known as light red, are clustered closely to the branches. *I. kingiana* is another large-leaved species, thriving best in shelter; the matt green blades, up to 20cm/8 in long, are set with small, fierce teeth. Young plants have smaller leaves, with wavy margins and undisciplined teeth pointing in every direction.

There are many shrubs with leaves like holly, as testified by the frequency with which specific epithets such as *ilicifolius* or *aquifolium* are encountered. But the only shrub I know with leaves remarkably like a rhododendron's is *Daphniphyllum macropodum*. Its purple-red petioles reinforce the impression of something akin to *Rhododendron fortunei*, but the daphniphyllum cannot offer any worthwhile flowers. For all that, it is a handsome shrub, the long leaves glaucous beneath. The rather tender privet, *Ligustrum confusum*, is not wholeheartedly evergreen, but when full of pale, polished green, lance-shaped leaves it is a fine thing, especially striking when bearing its clean white flower sprays.

Like the privets, the genus *Euonymus* has its share of rather pedestrian shrubs, but also some species of great beauty. I want particularly to draw to your attention three evergreen species needing a mild climate to give of their best. *E. wilsonii* is a large, lax shrub up to 6 m/20 ft tall, with slender stems bearing pointed, narrow leaves up to 15 cm/6 in long. *E. frigidus* is of stiffer habit, not at all inclined as is *E. wilsonii* to sprawl into any adjacent tree; the slender pointed leaves are scarcely smaller, lustrous dark green above and heavily veined. Finest of the trio is *E. lucidus*, a large shrub to 7·5 m/25 ft or even tree-like in sheltered woodland. The long pointed leaves, glossy green above, are a rich shining red when first unfolding, as fine as any *Pieris*.

The photinias are also known for the colour of their new spring growths. The hybrid photinias, *Photinia × fraseri* 'Robusta', 'Red Robin', and others, are familiar in quite cold gardens and are especially valuable in limy soils. The more tree-like parent of this hybrid group is *P. serrulata*, a fine evergreen with large, gleaming foliage, brilliantly coppery-red when unfolding in spring. Rather less hardy is the *Stranvaesia*-like *P. davidsoniae*, a small thorny tree with red young shoots, and leaves a little smaller, but similarly polished green. *P. glabra* is the other parent of the *P. × fraseri* group; in its cultivar 'Rubens' it is even more brilliant in young growths than they, but it is also less hardy. Stranvaesias are now included in the genus *Photinia*, and most are hardy; but *S. nussia* does best in mild areas, where it forms a large evergreen shrub with leathery, narrow leaves, neatly toothed, polished green on the upper surface and, at first, white with woolly felt beneath. More tender still, but well able to thrive and form a large, imposing tree-like shrub in mild localities, *Cinnamomum camphora* is as aromatic as its generic name suggests, with long-pointed, rather thin-textured leaves with a smooth and lustrous finish. On emerging they are coppery-red.

Aromatic also, but less frost-tender than the cinnamons, *Illicium anisatum* is an evergreen shrub related to the species that produces star anise, *I. verum*. The starry, fleshy fruits are similar in shape, indeed, to the spice used by oriental cooks; they follow many-petalled, pale yellow or greenish-cream flowers. The pointed, bright green leaves are thick-textured and gleaming, and congregate at the branch tips. Two other species can be grown in humusy soil with some shelter, even in gardens where *Cinnamomum* would perish. *Illicium floridanum* bears flowers of similar shape to *I. anisatum*, but of deep maroon-purple; those of *I. henryi* are pink to crimson. Both shrubs are agreeably aromatic also. Some people, on the other hand, find the bay laurel-like *Umbellularia californica* uncomfortable to be near, for its medicinal aroma is strong and carries on the air. A whiff or two leaves the head feeling clearer, but if you breathe it for long it is alleged to cause headaches.

Many pittosporums have fragrant flowers, but none, that I am aware of, aromatic foliage. Some are among the finest wind resisters we have for coastal gardens, others (the cultivars of *Pittosporum tenuifolium* especially) are artificial-looking confections belonging firmly in a domesticated setting. They have been described in Chapters II and III respectively. That still leaves a good many members of this versatile genus, including some which, with their handsome foliage and firm structure, qualify as dominant where the climate allows them to thrive. The plain green-leaved *P. tobira* slowly builds up to a large shrub, with bright shining green leaves in whorls, and creamy-white flowers scented like orange blossom in late spring. It is remarkably tolerant of drought and neglect, and dusty hedges of it can be seen in Mediterranean towns, flowering valiantly; but it deserves better. Far less frequently seen, at least in Europe, is *P. adaphniphylloides* (*P. daphniphylloides*), another Chinese species with the largest leaves of any that is hardy in cool temperate areas; each dark green, narrow blade is up to 25 cm/10 in long. The fragrant flowers are greenish-yellow. The New Zealand *P. dallii* is usually seen as a spreading shrub with long, pointed, toothed leaves. It has fragrant white flowers, but needs a good summer baking to bloom. Also from New Zealand are two species with wavy-edged leaves, larger than the blunt and crinkly foliage of *P. tenuifolium*. *P. undulatum* and *P. eugenoides* both, like *P. adaphniphylloides* and many other shrubs that I regard as dominant, can develop into small trees if the climate suits them. The fragrant flowers of *P. undulatum* are creamy-white, those of *P. eugenoides*, with a distinctive and far-reaching honey perfume, are pale yellow. The Australian *P. phillyraeoides* has very narrow leaves, and is at its most striking when hung with strings of pea-sized, orange fruits. The leaves of *P. revolutum* are slightly broader, dark green above and brown-felted beneath. And, of course, *P. tenuifolium* itself can become very tall, with a distinct, black-barked trunk; the maroon-purple, honey or chocolate scented flowers are borne in spring.

The provenance of *Drimys winteri*, as well as the climatic conditions which you can offer it, may partly determine whether you will ultimately have on your hands a tree or a shrub. The Andean var. *andina* is invariably shrubby, wider than high and ultimately only about 1–1·5 m/3¼–5 ft tall, with obovate, rather matt-green leaves and ivory-white flowers borne even on quite tiny plants. There seems to be some dispute among the authorities I have consulted as to whether var. *latifolia* is shrubby or tree-like. Interestingly, the taller, tree-like forms of *D. winteri* come from the southernmost ranges of its South American distribution, where it grows among forest vegetation; further north it grows in moist soil and is more shrubby. Neither extreme suggests that it will, as in fact it does, stand much wind. The most attractive forms are those with leaves distinctly glaucous-white beneath, evident even on seedlings. The starry, fragrant cream flowers are borne in late spring. The aromatic *D. lanceolata* from Tasmania and south-eastern Australia makes a tidy, large shrub with much smaller, pointed dark green leaves on red petioles; the young growths are coppery-red also. White flowers in spring are followed, on female plants if a male is about, by surprisingly showy black fruits.

Similar conditions, with shade and moisture at the roots but their heads in the light, suit the eucryphias, white-flowered shrubs and trees from South America and Australasia. In the wild *Eucryphia cordifolia* makes a dense columnar evergreen of considerable height – up to 30 m/100 ft – but I have not seen it over 12 m/40 ft in cultivation. The matt dark green leaves are, as the specific epithet suggests, somewhat heart-shaped, with toothed and wavy margins; they are pink-tinged and hairy while unfolding, when their upright stance reveals greyish undersides. In late summer appear the white flowers, wide-cupped around the dense brush of russet-tipped stamens; they are very alluring to bees. The other Chilean species is the deciduous and hardy *E. glutinosa*, a branching shrub with pinnate leaves turning orange and scarlet in autumn. The Tasmanian *E. lucida* is a beautiful species from the high-rainfall south and west of the island, where it grows with *Nothofagus cunninghamii* and *Atherosperma moschatum*, or as an understorey to eucalypts. It forms a large and fast-growing columnar shrub in captivity. The resinous, oblong leaves are intensely white-glaucous beneath; the fragrant white flowers, much frequented by bees, nod in the leaf axils at midsummer, their translucent delicacy enhanced by pink anthers. Pink-petalled forms have been found in the wild, and one – a tree as large as any white-flowered form at 21 m/70 ft, with a trunk of 60 cm/2 ft diameter – has been propagated and introduced to cultivation under the name 'Pink Cloud'. It is identical but for its colour, palest pink deepening to near-crimson at the centre and just blushing deeper at the edges of the petals; the stamens are white.

Eucryphia milliganii is a miniature of *E. lucida*, forming a little tree with tiny shining leaves and white cups opening from sticky buds. As a native of New South Wales, Australia, *E. moorei* is probably the most tender of the genus; it has elegant pinnate leaves, glaucous beneath, and white flowers smaller than those of *E. glutinosa*. Several eucryphia hybrids have been raised, the most familiar *E.* × *nymansensis* which unites the two South American species. A narrowly columnar shrub or tree, it is rather variable: the clone 'Mount Usher' resembles *E. cordifolia*, with simple leaves predominating, and flowers often double (a fault found also in seedlings of *E. glutinosa,* all too commonly); 'Nymansay' has wide white flowers in great abundance in late summer. *E.* × *hillieri* has two Australasian parents, *lucida* and *moorei*, and is generally represented by the clone 'Winton', with pinnate or trifoliolate leaves and cupped flowers like those of *E. lucida*. The same cross arose in a Cornish garden, Trengwainton; this clone is named 'Penwith'. In hybrids with *E. glutinosa* the evergreen character of the other parent predominates, whether *E. cordifolia* or, as in *E. × intermedia* 'Rostrevor', *E. lucida*. The leaves of this fast-growing hybrid, in which a Chilean and a Tasmanian species are joined, are glaucous beneath, and either simple or trifoliolate on the same plant. Its broad column of greenery is smothered in late summer with fragrant white, yellow-centred flowers. The only other hybrid which to my knowledge has arisen, or at least is in cultivation, has no name of its own. It is simply identified as *E. cordifolia × lucida*, from which you may deduce that it is a vigorous and fast-growing evergreen. The leaves are midway between the two parents', large, leathery and oblong, pointed and wavy-edged, glaucous beneath; the flowers are like those of *E. lucida* but larger.

The crinodendrons are Chilean trees which are, like *Drimys winteri*, unexpectedly wind-tolerant, though they can look rather bruised if too much exposed. The more familiar is *Crinodendron hookerianum* (*Tricuspidaria lanceolata*), a large, multi-stemmed shrub with narrow, pointed, hard-textured deep green leaves and bright crimson, lantern-shaped flowers hanging on long stalks in late spring, beautiful always but especially when lit by a lowering sun. *C. patagua* (*Tricuspidaria dependens*) is more tree-like, with broader blunter leaves of dark, rather greyed green, and fringed white bell-shaped flowers in late summer. The soap bark tree, *Quillaea saponaria*, is a large shrub unless in the mildest localities or its native Chile, where it makes an 18 m/60 ft tree, with leathery-thick, gleaming dark green oval leaves toothed at the margins, and sizeable white, purple-eyed flowers in spring.

Of lesser size, and very different in character, are the Asiatic mahonias with bold pinnate leaves, typified by *Mahonia lomariifolia*. This, indeed, may reach 9 m/30 ft in height, with several stems, when the leaves are borne only towards the branch tips, giving it a gauntly imposing presence rather than the dominance of bulk. Each leaf is composed of up to twenty pairs of narrow, spiny leaflets of stiff, hard texture; together, the leaves form a beautifully patterned ruff upon which sit, during winter, the erect, candle-like spikes of yellow flowers. In its youth, before the tall bare stems have developed, you can look into and down upon the foliage and flowers; but their decorative outline is no less clearly revealed when you are able to stand beneath them. *M. napaulensis* is shorter-growing and has glossy green leaves with fewer leaflets; its near ally *M. acanthifolia* is very fine, with leaflets almost as numerous as those of *M. lomariifolia*, and dense spreading spikes of pale yellow flowers from late autumn. I have not seen the clone 'Maharajah', attributed to *M. napaulensis*, but it sounds good, the flowers apparently deeper yellow. Nor have I yet seen anything but a small specimen of *M. siamensis*, said to be very uncommon in cultivation but the most handsome of the genus, with long leaves composed of up to seventeen widely spaced, asymmetrical leaflets, toothed and often waved at the margins like holly, and very fragrant, clear yellow flowers in bundles of six to ten 25 cm/10 in candles in winter. Its provenance suggests that it will need a very mild climate.

With age, meaning two gardeners' lifetimes or more, *Arbutus unedo* develops into a tree with a definite trunk, revealing dark red, shreddy bark. But for long it forms a bulky shrub with very dark green foliage, and clusters of pitcher-shaped white or pinkish flowers in autumn and winter among the strawberry-like fruits of the previous season. F. *rubra* has deep pink flowers. *Viburnum tinus*, laurustinus, is a shrub about which I cannot get excited, though there is no doubt it is a useful evergreen (what a damning word 'useful' can be) for maritime gardens as well as relatively cold inland areas. It forms a large, brooding dark presence with flowers, borne in winter, that are pink in bud but open to a rather dirty white. The more tender var. *hirtum* has larger, hairy leaves; var. *lucidum* is more glossy in leaf. The Canary Island *V. rigidum* is like a magnified *V. tinus*, with large hairy leaves and white flowers from early spring; it makes a loose, rounded shrub less densely leafy than laurustinus. I would be less reluctant to give room to *V. suspensum*, a shrub reaching 3 m/10 ft or so, with lacquered green rounded leaves and wide panicles of fragrant, pink-flushed flowers in spring. It needs maximum summer sun to flower freely, and is sometimes grown with the backing of a wall to help the shoots to ripen throughly. The large *V. cylindricum* flowers later in the year, from summer to early autumn, the tubular white flowers with protruding lilac anthers assembled into wide, flattened heads. The leaves are dull green in colour with a curious waxy coating that cracks and turns grey when the leaf is rubbed or bent or scratched.

Balance of flower, foliage and form

The dividing line between dominant shrubs and those that I think of as endowed with the quality of balance is a fine one, shifted by scale or emphasis. By balance, I mean that the plant – be it tree, shrub, perennial or even conceivably annual – is valued for its form and its foliage, its flowers, or even its own self-contained colour scheme, in roughly equal proportions. Thus a mophead hydrangea, for example, will not qualify, for it is grown solely for its mass of floral colour; but *Hydrangea sargentiana* or *H. villosa* may. And this immediately suggests one way in which at least some of these shrubs differ from those that I consider to be dominant:

they may shed their leaves in autumn. A shrub that is bare stemmed for
half the year cannot legitimately, I believe, be regarded as dominant;
though, by virtue of its stature and line, a deciduous tree may impose as
much without its leaves as with. This chapter, however, is only incidentally
concerned with trees: only, that is, in as much as many of the species we
can grow in the milder garden may, if thoroughly suited, develop into
something more tree-like than shrubby.

Sometimes it seems as though every Chilean shrub has either red or
white flowers; but all the azaras are yellow. The tiny scraps of stamens
that make up the flowers of *Azara microphylla* are hidden beneath the
elegant sprays of little dark green leaves in winter, betraying their presence
only by their strong vanilla perfume. Usually seen as a shrub, it will make
a small tree, as – in mild areas – will its variegated form, in which each
tiny leaf is edged with cream, giving a light and airy effect just avoiding
fussiness. The other species have more showy flowers, puffs of yellow
stamens mostly appearing in spring. In *A. lanceolata* they are set among
narrow, polished leaves of the same fresh green on both surfaces. Like
most azaras it is happiest in a humus-rich soil. *A. dentata* is quite drought-
resistant, however; it is often confused with *A. serrata*, which has larger,
toothed leaves not felted beneath, though with the same glossy finish to
the upper surface. Both are more restrained in growth than the potentially
tree-like *A. microphylla* and *A. lanceolata*, reaching perhaps 3 m/10 ft. In *A.
integrifolia* we have another tall species, as much as 9 m/30 ft, showing to
a marked degree the azara tendency to bear one large leaf and two smaller
leaf-like stipules at each node. The finest in flower is *A. petiolaris*,
with holly-like leaves, toothed though not ferociously armed, and
fragrant mimosa-like clusters of long, creamy-yellow stamens in early
spring.

The yellow-flowered forms of *Embothrium coccineum* have only lately
been introduced to cultivation, and one cultivar has been named 'Eliot
Hodgkin'; it was raised in the UK from seed of a narrow-leaved, deciduous
parent with flowers as bright as *Jasminum nudiflorum*. They may not be as
striking as the vermilion-scarlet, honeysuckle-like blooms of the embothriums familiar in our garden, but the yellow is likely to be an easier colour
to place. The scarlet embothriums need careful siting where no pink or
blue-red flowers can jar; the ample greenery of late spring, in which
sharper tones often dominate over the bluer greens, forms the most
appropriate setting for what W. Arnold-Forster aptly called the embothriums' 'acid scarlet . . . a most jealous colour'. Embothriums vary in habit and
hardiness, from the suckering, narrow-leaved, deciduous forms grouped as
var. *lanceolatum* to the tree-like 'Longifolium' with long, narrow, oblong,
persistent leaves and flowers borne all along the branches rather than
clustered towards the tips. 'Norquinco Valley' is a selection of var. *lan-*

ceolatum with abundant flowers. All embothriums need moist, lime-free soil, but do not flower freely unless in full light.

The requirements of the genus *Telopea* are more difficult to satisfy: a moist but well-drained soil, low not only in pH but also in phosphates, and more sun than the embothriums. This may be why they are so seldom seen in cultivation, despite their spectacular flowers. The Tasmanian waratah, *T. truncata*, should be the easiest to satisfy, for it has to contend with strong winds on its native mountain slopes. The thick leaves are often curiously truncated and notched at the ends; the young shoots are clad in silky, rust-red fur. The rich crimson flowers are crowded in a wide terminal head at midsummer; yellow forms are known in the wild. Even more spectacular is the Australian *T. speciosissima*, with prominently veined leaves sharply toothed towards the apex and flowers in dense, rounded heads with crimson involucral bracts. It needs heat and abundant moisture during the growing season, but a dry spell while dormant: not easy to organize in gardens where the rain falls chiefly in winter. The other two species, *T. oreades* and *T. mongaensis*, are much less familiar, if indeed any members of a genus so little known in European gardens can be called familiar at all; some authors consider both to be the same species under the name *T. oreades*. It grows in moist upland eucalyptus forests in Australia, where it reaches as much as 12 m/40 ft, and on the dry ridge tops where it may be no more than 1·2 m/4 ft tall, so that one might expect it to be more adaptable, but for the particular soil requirements. The flowers are arranged spirally in pairs, surrounded by inconspicuous pinkish bracts.

The myrtles are both South American and Australasian; the European *Myrtus communis* will receive due acknowledgement with other Mediterranean shrubs, later. They shuffle in and out of different genera, according to the state of taxonomic knowledge at any given time, and I will give the name which I believe to be current, followed by the more familiar *Myrtus* name in brackets. They are less particular about soil than the mostly lime-hating embothriums and much easier to satisfy than the waratahs, but appreciate similar climatic conditions, though some species are reasonably wind-tolerant. The cinnamon-stemmed *Luma apiculata* (*M. luma*) makes a bare-trunked tree in mild areas and will be described later, but most of the other species are essentially shrubby. *Luma chequen* (*M. chequen*) is one of those most inclined to grow towards tree stature; it inhabits, in its native Chile, wet places. The small, rich green leaves, thickly clothing the stems, are aromatic; the flowers are the usual fuzz of white, with unusually long stamens, in late summer. Even when developed to a tree-like state *Amomyrtus luma* (*M. lechleriana*) is apt to bear its neat, glossy, pointed leaves on branches right down to ground level; its season is spring, when the young foliage is bright coppery-purple or golden-tan, and the fragrant white flowers are borne in clusters at the leaf axils. The

black berries are edible. So, too, are those of *Ugni molinae* (*M. ugni*), which
has the English name of Chilean guava; though this suggests something
much more ample than the small, amber brown, aromatic fruits, which
are borne even on young plants. It is much smaller, even at maturity, a
branchy shrub of 1·5 m/5 ft or so with dark polished green foliage, and
flowers of a different style from the usual white puffs: for they are waxy,
pale pink bells on long stalks, opening in spring.

The New Zealand species are sufficiently different in character to have
earned their own genus, *Lophomyrtus*, though they too have also been
ascribed to *Myrtus*. *L. obcordata* is a twiggy, graceful shrub of medium size
with leaves conspicuously notched at the apex, dark green above and paler
beneath; the dull white flowers have the usual abundance of stamens; the
fruits are deep crimson or violet. The rounded leaves of *L. bullata* are
characterized by the curious puckering between the veins, as though large
blisters were raised on the surface; in full light the leaf colour is a metallic
red-purple or copper, fading towards green in shade. White flowers are
followed by maroon berries. *L. × ralphii* is a natural hybrid between the
two New Zealand species, close to *L. bullata*, but that the leaves are barely
puckered; it has given rise to a number of garden cultivars ranging from
the large-leaved 'Kathryn', which inherits both the blistering and the
coppery colouring of *L. bullata*, to tiny 'Lilliput' and 'Pixie', with bright
green leaves overlaid wine-red, on purple stems. Variegated cultivars such
as 'Variegata', 'Versicolor', 'Sundae' and 'Gloriosa' should have been
mentioned in the preceding chapter; 'Pinkalina', though repellently
named, is quite appealing with pale bronze foliage, coral-pink at the tips
of the growths.

Of the two *Weinmannia* species familiar to me, the New Zealander is
the less striking, but a desirable plant nonetheless. *W. racemosa* is variable
in foliage, from the three- to five-lobed or parted, toothed leaves of young
plants to the unlobed but still coarsely toothed blades of older trees, which
are graceful in habit, and pretty when bearing their narrow spikes of white
or pale pink flowers in early summer. *W. sylvicola*, which I have never
seen, is said to differ in having more numerous leaflets, up to eleven at the
young stage and three on adult trees. Neither species can compare, though,
with *W. trichosperma*, in which the pinnate leaves are decorated by small
triangular wings set along the rachis between each of the small, sessile,
toothed leaflets, which number between eleven and nineteen. The result
is an intricately patterned blade that looks as though it were fashioned
from dark, burnished metal. The dense spikes of white flowers in late
spring are followed by tawny red capsules.

Sometimes it is hard to know whether to mention a particular shrub
here, or to keep it for a later chapter where plants needing sheltered
woodland conditions are to be grouped. Thus with *Acradenia frankliniae*,

which I first saw as a slender, open shrub under a tall tree canopy in the subtropical gardens of Abbotsbury on the English Channel coast. But it will also grow in more open conditions, forming a compact shrub to 3 m/10 ft. Its trifoliolate leaves, the oblong leaflets shallow-toothed, are stiff-textured, forming in spring a dark green setting for the white flowers which slightly suggest those of *Choisya ternata* – as well they might, for both the Mexican and the Tasmanian are in Rutaceae, the citrus family.

The proteaceous *Persoonia toru*, though not very frost-resistant, needs an open site in full light, its roots in well-nourished but free-draining soil. It forms a small much-branched tree of symmetrical habit, with elegant, narrow lanceolate leaves highly polished on both surfaces; the young growths, buds and flower stalks are clad in rusty felt. The pale tawny flowers, borne in summer, are very fragrant with a far-carrying honey perfume. Also in Proteaceae are the lomatias, some South American, some Australasian. *Lomatia ferruginea* is a native of the Chilean rain forest, where it forms a sparsely branched shrub or tree with a few huge, fern-like leaves at each branch tip; grown in a more exposed position, which it tolerates remarkably well, it stays more compact and full of leaf, each much-divided frond uncurling in a fuzz of rusty velvet. Though primarily a foliage plant, in flower it is handsome also, the tawny buff claws opening in summer. The other Chilean species I know, *L. dentata*, is extremely rare, a most desirable shrub with leaves like holly and handsome green-white flowers. I have not seen *L. hirsuta*, a tree-like species with a wider range in South America; its shining green leaves, tan-felted at first, are toothed but not divided, its flowers pale greenish primrose. The Australasian species tend to have longer, looser spikes of creamy-white flowers, often very fragrant. Both *L. fraxinifolia* and *L. silaefolia*, found in Queensland, have divided leaves, those of the former with stalked segments, while *L. silaefolia* has frond-like foliage, once, twice or even thrice pinnate; it is a small spreading shrub, whereas the ash-leaved lomatia grows to form a small tree. *L. ilicifolia* is rare in cultivation, a low growing species from Victoria and New South Wales with toothed, somewhat holly-like leaves on stiff, erect branches, and loose sprays of cream flowers in late summer. The leaves of *L. myricoides*, also an Australian species, are long and narrow, and coarsely toothed; the grevillea-like flowers are cream to primrose yellow and very fragrant. It is said to prefer damp semi-shade, but I have found it happy enough in a more open position provided the soil is well nourished. From Tasmania comes the sprawling, often suckering *L. tinctoria*, very variable in leaf from entire to twice or thrice pinnate, the lobes long and slender. In heliotrope-scented flower it is also very elegant, with racemes of green buds opening to cream or sulphur flowers on long, pale pink stalks, in summer.

There is a Californian shrub, native of Santa Catalina Island, that has something of the air of a fern-leaved lomatia and is every bit as desirable. *Lyonothamnus floribundus aspleniifolius*, though, is in the rose family, an affinity betrayed in spring or early summer when it bears its creamy white, slim spiraea-like panicles of flower. The glossy evergreen foliage is pinnate, the leaflets divided to the base into oblong lobes and grey hairy beneath. Something so desirable might be expected to grow painfully slowly, but in fact it will soon form a graceful, slender little tree displaying its shredding, tan and grey bark.

Although, in the wild, it is often bathed in sea fog, the *Lyonothamnus* grows most often on steep rocky cliffs; it can stand a good deal of drought, and prefers a well drained soil. Drained soils and full sun also suit the brachyglottis of New Zealand, as we have seen; here I want to describe some that are less common than the admirable wind-resisters of Chapter II. They may well be every bit as unmoved by salt spray and gales, but until I have stock to spare I prefer to keep them more closely under my eye in less testing conditions. One that, from its parentage, should have no difficulty coping with the fiercest ocean gales is 'Leonard Cockayne', which is *Brachyglottis greyi × B. rotundifolia*. The hybrid forms a much-branched shrub to as much as 3 m/10 ft tall, with the young shoots, and the underside of the leaves at all times, white-felted. The upper side of the leaves later becomes shining green; the flower heads are borne in large terminal sprays. The very tender *B. perdicioides*, a native of North Island, is less tall; it forms a bushy shrub with small oblong, much-toothed leaves, and small yellow flowers in summer. Its cross with the Dunedin hybrids is taller, with finely-toothed rather yellow-green leaves and larger flower heads of the same bright yellow.

Although one of the features that distinguishes *Olearia* from *Brachyglottis* is that no olearia has yellow flowers, there are brachyglottis with white flowers. *B. hectoris* forms, in the wild, a tall, semi-evergreen shrub, sparsely branched, with a loose wool covering the young growths and a 'grey, cottony down' the undersides of the big, coarsely toothed leaves. These, unlike those of any other *Brachyglottis* species, are pinnatisect towards the base. The white flower heads, with the typical bright yellow disk, are borne in wide heads in summer. A cross between this and *B. perdicioides* is named 'Alfred Atkinson' for the owner of the garden in New Zealand where it arose. It is fully evergreen, and forms a bushy shrub like the yellow-flowered parent, but has from *B. hectoris* its large leaves, at first buff-felted beneath and later pale almond-green on both surfaces, and its white flowers. Its colouring is very effective among both greys and darker greens, a relief for the eye from what might become monotonous, yet avoiding the abrupt contrasts that come from the introduction of 'gold' foliage. *B. kirkii*, from low altitudes of North Island, is probably more tender than *B. hectoris*, which is a South Island species. It is a tall, erect evergreen, with small but very variable leaves, and large flower heads up to 5 cm/2 ins wide, pure white with a yellow disk, borne in great abundance.

A Chatham Island species, *B. huntii*, looks until it flowers more like a spurge than a brachyglottis. It forms a shrub or small rounded tree up to 6 m/20 ft tall, with narrow, pale shining green leaves clustered at the ends of the branches; the downy felt that covers the undersides of the young foliage is not something found in the genus *Euphorbia*, however. The yellow flower-heads are borne with great freedom in rounded or pyramidal panicles. The true spurges themselves are like nothing else in flower. The Mediterranean *Euphorbia characias* is now considered by taxonomists to include, at subspecific rank, what we used to class as separate species under the names *E. wulfenii* and *E. sibthorpii*. As garden plants, they remain distinct. *E. characias* ssp. *characias*, from the western end of the Mediterranean region, has the usual thickish stems and narrow, darkly glaucous leaves; the inflorescences are narrowly cylindrical, with green bracts and chocolate-brown glands, a combination which earned it the nickname 'frogspawn bush', bestowed upon it by one of the boys who worked for Mr E. A. Bowles at Myddelton House. Ssp. *wulfenii*, with a more easterly distribution, has broader, more open columns of brighter, chartreuse to acid-yellow bracts without the dark eye. 'Lambrook Gold' is an especially fine form. What I have grown, admittedly from seed of garden origin, as *E. characias* ssp. *wulfenii* var *sibthorpii*, is even more handsome, with wide airy heads of sharp yellow, and very glaucous foliage; it seems less hardy than the others. All of them tend to flush with purple in winter. From late winter onwards, the stems that will flower turn their heads down like shepherds' crooks, before turning upwards again as the flowers open; as soon as they begin to look untidy (not too soon, if you want to save seed) these flowered stems should be cut right out at the base to make way for next year's flowering shoots. This attention is also cosmetic, for the shrubby euphorbias are handsome foliage plants at all times if kept groomed. This is truer still of the Canary Island *E. mellifera*, which is more tender even than *sibthorpii*; a shrub of up to 3 m/10 ft, it has abundant dark green, lanceolate leaves earning it a place in the garden even if it never flowered. The inflorescences are borne in late spring; tawny-red in colour, they are less showy than those of *E. characias*, but their honey fragrance more than compensates.

Though I allowed myself willingly to be seduced away from the Antipodes with the mention of the spurge-like *Brachyglottis huntii*, Australia and New Zealand have more good things to offer. Among several more *Olearia* species which are in cultivation, I cannot resist introducing two, one with a warning, the other with a recommendation. The dud is *O. speciosa*; with a name like that, it should be good, but is in fact disappointing; though Ernest Lord, an Australian author, refers to 'hand-some broad glossy leaves . . . often pink veined in the woolly undersurface', so perhaps better forms remain to be introduced. The recommendation is that you should seek out O. *rotundifolia*, which W. Arnold-Forster calls O. *dentata*; even the usually restrained Bean calls this 'one of the most beautiful of the olearias, for few of them have flower-heads combining size, pretty colour and number to such an extent'. You may also, Bean tells us, find it – if find it you can, for it is very rare – as O. *tomentosa*. The 'pretty colour', usually lilac, may also be white, with the usual yellow disk.

There remain, too, some pittosporums which seem to me neither to have the character of dominant shrubs, nor to be so wind-tolerant as to deserve mention with the admirable *Pittosporum crassifolium* and others; yet which have much allure, so that I should not like to be without them. The genus is both polymorphic and widespread geographically; I will take first one of the antipodeans. P. *cornifolium* is unusual in that it is often, in the wild, found as an epiphyte on large forest trees; in cultivation, though slightly frost-tender, it adapts well enough to ordinary soil to become a neat evergreen shrub of 1·5 m/5 ft, with clustered, whorled leaves and musk-scented, dull red flowers in early spring. The South African P. *viridiflorum* is taller, and perhaps more tender; the foliage is dark glossy green, the jasmine-scented flowers are yellow-green. From China comes P. *heterophyllum*, a dense, compact shrub of 1·5 m/5 ft, or occasionally taller, with large panicles of clear yellow flowers in late spring.

The genus *Berberis* is another that is widespread, found in Europe, Asia and South America. The large-leaved species, though less popular than the coloured-leaved, deciduous kinds, are imposing shrubs when well grown, with handsome foliage. The gleaming dark green leaves of B. *valdiviana* are almost spineless, and set off handsome flowers of saffron orange held in pendulous racemes. It is one of the largest, making a dome of 4·5 m/15 ft when suited. At 1·5 m/5 ft or so, B. *insignis* is easier to fit into small gardens. Its leaves are up to 15 cm/6 in long, elliptic in outline, with many small spiny teeth along the margins; they are glossy on both surfaces, paler beneath. The flowers are yellow. B. *hypokerina* is even smaller in stature, a wide spreading shrub nicknamed 'silver holly' by its discoverer, Frank Kingdon Ward, on account of its leaves, among the most beautiful in the genus. Up to 15 cm/6 in long, spine-toothed in the manner of some exceptionally fine holly, they are dark sea-green above and silvery-white beneath, held on purple stems.

In my pursuit of the quieter shrubs in which all attributes are in unemphatic balance, I find that many other shrubs with leaves like holly have this quality. Thus *Itea ilicifolia*, a Chinese shrub growing to 3 m/10 ft or so, which in late summer decks itself in slender catkin-like racemes of pale green among the glossy dark toothed foliage. *I. yunnanensis* is less attractive, with narrower leaves and dull white arching catkins in early summer.

It is not until the Californian *Prunus ilicifolia* bears its creamy, fragrant flower spikes that it reveals its true affinities; until then it looks very like a neat holly, with glossy spine edged leaves, their dark green just hazed with a greyer tone than common holly. *Prunus lyonii* is much larger in leaf, and has longer spikes of whiter flowers borne earlier, in spring.

There is a form of *Olearia erubescens* which, in recognition of the leaf shape, is known as var. *ilicifolia*. Both this and the type are low evergreen shrubs treaching 1·5 m/5 ft at maturity, with stiff, leathery, toothed, leaves; those of var. *ilicifolia* are larger, and despite the epithet they are less spiny. In flower it is handsome, the clean whiteness of the branching inflorescences contrasting with the polished dark green of the leaves. The type, with its smaller leaves, is sometimes miscalled *O. myrsinoides*, a distinct species forming a low, densely branched or straggly bush, with very small, glossy green leaves resembling those of *Myrsine africana*; but the olearia has small white daisy flower-heads whereas the insignificant, brownish flowers of the myrsine are followed by blue-lilac fruits. The much taller, even tree-like *Myrsine chathamica*, which grows in the wild with *Olearia* 'Henry Travers', has larger leaves, notched at the apex, and small purple-blue fruits.

It is chiefly for its royal blue fruits that *Rhaphithamnus spinosus* is valued. A member of the verbena family, this Chilean shrub is of medium height in cultivation but may reach 6 m/20 ft in the wild. The small, glossy dark green leaves, in opposite pairs of clusters, are accompanied at each node by needle-sharp spines; the tubular light-blue flowers are borne in pairs at the leaf axils in spring. A humusy soil and a sunny position suit it best.

The larger-leaved forms of *Quercus coccifera*, the Kermes oak of the Mediterranean *maquis*, are very like holly in all but the disposition of the leaves. Here, too, I want to call to mind two other oaks, one Himalayan, the other from Cyprus. *Q. incana* forms a large shrub or small tree with slender oval, pointed and toothed leaves, dark green above and white-felted beneath, like *Rhododendron arboreum* which it accompanies in its native Himalaya. The Cypriot, *Q. alnifolia*, is very slow growing – indeed I have never seen it larger than small shrub size, though it is said to form a small tree in time – and very distinct, with rounded or broadly obovate, hard-textured leaves, dark polished green above and clad in old-gold felt beneath.

The velvety fur that clothes the flower buds of *Michelia doltsopa* is golden-brown; the sheaths part to reveal milk-white, very fragrant flowers, green-washed at the base, cupped like little magnolias: to which the michelias are related. 'Silver Cloud' is a selection with bright golden buds and larger, cream flowers. The long, leathery leaves, glaucous beneath, are semi-persistent in mild climates. Both *M. compressa*, a hardier species, and the tender *M. figo* are more wholeheartedly evergreen. The first is a slow growing shrub, ultimately a small tree, with glossy leaves and powerfully fragrant, pale yellow flowers, purplish at their hearts, opening in late spring. The small, brown-purple flowers of *M. figo* (*M. fuscata*) are strongly scented of pear drops or ripe bananas in their long spring and summer season; the small, gleaming, dark green leaves are comely all year.

Shrubs with leaves that unfurl in suede or velvet texture, though usually less bright in the landscape than those that flare into crimson and scarlet at leaf fall, have the quality of appealing to more than our visual sense. I shall not soon forget my first sight, and touch, of the rare *Neolitsea sericea*, an aromatic relative of bay laurel with leaves unfolding as soft as chamois leather, pale golden brown above and silken white beneath; as they mature, the upper surface becomes dark shining green while the underside retains a burnished metallic silver or pale bronze finish. The long-pointed leaves of the related *Persea ichangensis* (*Machilus ichangensis*) are copper coloured at first, aging to leathery, glossy green; the short spikes of white flowers are followed by pea-sized black fruits. Not entirely evergreen in Britain and similar climates, it is more inclined than the shrubby *Neolitsea sericea* to make a small tree. The young foliage of *Myrsine australis*, also with the potential to make a small tree of up to 6 m/20 ft, is almost as showy as that of *Photinia × fraseri*, bright coppery-red; the leaves are different in shape, however, with very wavy margins.

Mainly about flowers

Much less uncommon than these members of Lauraceae, the species and hybrids of *Rhaphiolepis* can serve to introduce the variety of shrubs that are grown primarily for their flowers. Many of them will sit equally at ease among the more domesticated plants of the mixed border or in less contrived settings where shrubs and trees dominate, in groupings where the gardener's concern is to satisfy the cultural needs of his plants before his own aesthetic demands. With their neat, rounded habit, glossy foliage and pretty flowers, and their preference for warm sunny positions, the various *Rhaphiolepis* are admirable shrubs to grow as part of the foundation planting around a house, against a wall or by a patio, for they are never shabby. The least hardy is probably *R. indica*, a shrub of 1 m/3¼ ft or so with narrow, toothed leaves and loose racemes of pink-flushed flowers borne intermittently all spring and summer. 'Springtime' is an American selection with tawny young growths and intensely pink flowers. In the wild *R. umbellata* is taller, but in cultivation it is usually seen at about 1·2 m/4 ft. The thick, leathery leaves are broader and barely toothed, the lightly scented white flowers are borne in upright clusters in early summer. The hybrid between the two, *R.* × *delacourii*, is in many ways the most satisfactory in gardens, a rounded 2 m/6½ ft shrub with broad obovate, shining leathery leaves and conical spikes of rose pink flowers in spring or summer. 'Coates' Crimson' is a selection with deeper coloured flowers. A newer cultivar of unspecified parentage is 'Enchantress', of compact rounded habit up to 1·2 m/4 ft high and wide, with polished leaves and showy clusters of rich pink flowers. It is said to flower equally well in New Zealand in sun or part shade, but it may be that in the maritime gardens of Britain, at least, it will, like the others, need full sun to ripen the wood if it is to flower adequately.

A quiet little shrub for which I have great affection is *Abelia schumannii*. Semi-evergreen, it grows to around 1·5 m/5 ft, with arching stems bearing flowers like little lilac-pink foxgloves from midsummer to late autumn. It is one of a number of shrubs which would fit comfortably into a mixed border of more shrubby emphasis than those I have described in the previous chapter. *Sphacele chamadryoides* is also easily accommodated in a flowery, shrubby border. A Chilean labiate, flowering in summer, it grows to 60–65 cm/2–2½ ft, with wrinkled leaves and loose sprays of tubular, pale blue flowers. Several of the prostantheras, labiates too but from Australia and Tasmania, flower at midsummer or before. Their colouring, typically, is lavender or lilac, as in *Prostanthera rotundifolia* and *P. melissifolia* var *parvifolia* already mentioned, with excursions into pink. *P. cuneata* is a dwarf, aromatic shrub with tiny, shining green, rounded leaves and short spikes of white flowers flushed with pale violet. The flowers of *P. lasianthos* are similar, but this is a larger shrub, of upright habit, its long, narrow, dark green leaves toothed at the margins. The large flowers of *P. nivea* are pure white or just blue-tinged like skimmed milk, the throat spotted with brown or greenish yellow; they open from spring onwards. This is a tall, slender shrub, up to 3 m/10 ft, with linear, dark green leaves. Also tall, ultimately, is the curious *P. walteri*, which I have seen only as a young specimen. The leaves are narrow, the flowers large for the genus, with a long upper lip; their colouring is a subdued but fetching greyish-green with purplish veining. The little, pale lilac helmets, spotted within, of *Jovellana violacea* are scarcely brighter, but they are borne in abundance on a twiggy, 90 cm/3 ft bush with small lobed leaves, slightly bronzed where touched by the sun if the soil is not too rich.

All the indigoferas make good mixed border shrubs, with pinnate leaves and pea flowers of pink or rosy purple borne over a long season. Most

are frost-hardy, even if their top growths may be cut by severe winters.
In an almost frost-free climate, *Indigofera pulchella* should survive to
produce its long racemes of red-purple flowers. As amenable as the indigos
to hard spring pruning, and as well suited to mixed border life, the summer
flowering buddlejas have much more to offer than the ubiquitous butterfly
bush. 'Lochinch', that fine, fragrant hybrid between *Buddleja davidii* and
B. fallowiana, needs no introduction, for its luminous grey foliage and
broad, lavender blue spikes have won it acclaim in many gardens. The
second-named parent, again, is scarcely less well known; its milk-white
form is preferred, each little fragrant floret enlivened by the same orange
eye as those of 'Lochinch'. Of similar hardiness – that is, effectively frost
resistant in the British Isles – is *B. × weyeriana*, which unites *B. davidii* and
B. globosa, and reveals both parents in its soft buff-orange flowers,
assembled into rounded clusters diminishing in size towards the apex of
the panicle. The type of the cross is of unappealing colouring, mauve and
orange combined; but 'Moonlight' is a lovely pale creamy buff with so
faint a hint of lilac as to be scarcely noticeable, while 'Sungold' is a uniform
warm orange and 'Elstead Hybrid' is soft apricot with tawny throat. In
another of my gardens I used this as a backdrop to buff, apricot and tan
shades, with some of the kniphofias already noted, and creamy apricot tea
roses.

Of more typical buddleia colouring is *B. candida*, so named for the
dense white flannel which envelops the narrow leaves and stems alike.
The violet flowers, opening at the normal summer to autumn season,
are borne in long, loose, arching spikes. The curving spikes of *B. lindleyana* are purple-violet, but the flowers seldom open enough together
to make a reasonable show, though individually they are very beautiful.
The cylindrical racemes of *B. forrestii* are of more subdued colouring,
at first pinkish lilac, fading to pale tawny-yellow, but for the tips of the
florets, which retain a lilac flush. *B. pterocaulis* is similar, but stouter in
the spike.

I always think of *Buddleja crispa* as a fairly modest shrub, though if
unpruned it can grow large. The toothed, ovate leaves are white woolly,
the fragrant lilac flowers borne in cylindrical panicles appear in summer
and autumn. I have already proposed the combination of this buddleia
with *Phlomis cashmeriana* and *Dorycnium hirsutum*, to which I would be
tempted to add *Lavatera maritima*. *B. caryopteridifolia* is in the same mould
but flowers in spring on the previous year's wood, as does *B. farreri*, a
tall and imposing, velvet-leaved species in which the flowers are rather
incidental to the foliage. The flowering time of *B. salviifolia* seems variable,
according perhaps to season or cultivation, between summer and late
autumn to early winter. The crinkled leaves are only slightly sage-like;
the strongly scented flowers are borne in terminal clusters, creamy-white

with a purple or mauve tinge and darker orange centre, not showy, but curiously fetching at close quarters.

Like the summer flowering buddlejas, tamarisks that flower on the season's growths can be hard pruned each spring, to make shrubs of manageable size with fine feathery plumes of pink flowers. The clone known as *Tamarix pentandra* 'Rubra', of rich pink colouring, is, it seems, a selection of the species correctly called *T. ramosissima*. *T. ramosissima* 'Rosea', then, is presumably the correct name for the paler *T. pentandra*. Perhaps one should stick to 'Pink Cascade', a good bright pink of which the cultivar name is both easy and descriptive. In all, the tiny leaves are glaucous green, contributing to the cloudy effect of the great plumes of flower. The more compact *T. hispida* needs a continental summer baking to flower well, but is very handsome in its pale glaucous colouring and bright pink flowers.

Much later in the season, *Eupatorium ligustrinum* (*E. micranthum*, *E. weinmannianum*) bears its large, flat heads of hazy, blush-white flowers, with a curious, almost acrid but not unpleasant fragrance. The evergreen foliage is dark shining green, but the shrub has not much substance and is often cut back by frosts. For all that, there is nothing quite like it and I persevere with it, greeting its characteristic aroma gladly each year as the first flower heads open.

It is tempting to build a little more on the pink, lilac and lavender theme that links the tamarisks, buddlejas and prostantheras. At a lowly level are *Hebe hulkeana* and its allies, very different in their airy grace from the spiked *H. speciosa* cultivars. *H. hulkeana* itself grows in the wild on sunny rock ledges with *Olearia insignis*, but in gardens seems more adaptable than the daisy-bush to a variety of soils and situations, so long as it is reasonably sheltered and not shaded, nor with its feet in poorly drained, cold soil. A loose, rather lax shrub, it has small toothed leaves with reddish margins, and soft lilac veronica flowers in 45 cm/18 in branching sprays in early summer. 'Fairfieldii', which may have the blood of the dwarfer, pinker *Hebe lavaudiana* in it, is a sturdier plant with lilac flowers in shorter, broader panicles, while 'Hagley Park' may derive its pink-mauve flowers and dwarf but open habit from the more or less creeping *H. raoulii*.

The more tender solanums must wait their turn until the next chapter, but in mild gardens in the open border *Solanum crispum* will survive to form a large, sprawling shrub if hard pruned in spring. The lilac-blue potato flowers are borne in wide clusters in summer; the form to choose is 'Glasnevin', which flowers early and late, even into winter. I like to see it combined with the wide, icy lavender saucers of *Abutilon vitifolium*, their seasons overlapping at midsummer. The mallow may reach 4·5 m/15 ft or more, when the solanum can scramble into its lower branches. 'Veronica

Tennant' is a selected cultivar, very free with its large, lavender-mauve
flowers; like the type, this too has an exquisite, translucent white form. A
Chilean species, *A. vitifolium* is surprisingly wind-hardy, but needs firm
staking, for it grows very rapidly, and is apt to blow over. *A. ochsenii* is
greener of leaf and deeper violet in flower; it is still sometimes seen under
the name 'Margharita Manns', the name of the lady who collected the
plant in its native Valdivia. The two species have united in the fine
A. × suntense, with cupped flowers sharing the richer violet colouring but
not the dark central markings of *A. ochsenii*. Again, named cultivars have
already been introduced: 'Violetta', greyer in leaf than the type; 'Jermyns';
and 'White Charm'. If you have the space to allow them to self-sow,
which they do freely, you can soon have a grove of mauve, lilac and
white abutilons. I fancy that they would assort well with *Philadelphus
mexicanus* 'Rose Syringa' (*P. coulteri* of gardens), a tender mock-orange
with rose-perfumed, thick-petalled creamy white flowers, stained purple
at the heart.

The lilac and mauve of the abutilons and solanum also look well with
yellow, especially the soft, primrose to buff shades of the double Banksian
rose, *Rosa banksiae* 'Lutea'; this, like *Solanum crispum*, can be hard pruned
after its spring flowering to grow into a large, lax, wide-spreading bush,
especially in Mediterranean climates. A brighter but still gentle contrast
can be had if you pair the solanum or abutilon with *Cytisus battandieri*, a
large Moroccan broom with laburnum-like foliage, silvery-silky with a
coating of fine hairs, and cylindrical or cone-shaped clusters of densely
packed yellow pea-flowers smelling of pineapple. And where its soft-
wooded stems survive the winter so that it can flower at midsummer,
Cestrum parqui adds its tall plumes of pale yellow flowers, which are
deliciously fragrant: but only at night, which in Britain means scarcely
before bedtime. During the day, all that you will get from it is the sour,
solanaceous smell of the leaves, if you crush one. In common with many
of the shrubs already described, it will settle down to a virtually herbaceous
existence if the topgrowth is slaughtered by winter frosts; but it will then
flower a month or two later, or even into autumn.

The Himalayan *Colquhounia coccinea* has a fruity smell, but in this case
it is the whole plant that smells of green apples. At a casual glance, this
rather soft-wooded shrub could be taken for a buddleja with orange-
scarlet flowers; yet it is a labiate, as a closer look at its flowers immediately
reveals; and the flowers are borne in whorls which together form a long
panicle. The large leaves are softly woolly, especially in the form *mollis*
(*vestita*), which has lighter orange flowers. It can be hard pruned in spring
in the same way as the later summer-flowering buddlejas.

Cassia corymbosa (of gardens) also flowers in late summer and can be cut
down in spring if winter's frosts have not done the job for you. The

clusters of rich yellow flowers are borne most freely after hot summers, on 1·5 m/5 ft stems set with pinnate leaves. Many plants cultivated as *C. corymbosa* are probably *C. candolleana*, also known as *C. obtusa*; the true *C. corymbosa* is less robust and paler in flower. If you enjoy the rather assertive contrast of pure blue with bright yellow, you could set your cassias in a sweep of *Ceratostigma griffithii*. Though not everyone agrees with me, I prefer this to the better known, and rather hardier, *C. willmottianum*; for it has neater foliage, rounded and bristly, readily flushing crimson-red in autumn, and flowers of deep indigo-blue, on spreading stems with more substance than those of the brighter, bluer *C. willmottianum*.

Many of the hypericums also lend themselves to hard pruning in spring, to remain neat without loss of flower. In mild gardens 'Rowallane' can be grown in the open border; it is cherished for its large, bowl shaped flowers, formed of firm-textured, overlapping petals, borne all summer along on 1·8 m/6 ft stems clad with sea-green leaves. One of its parents is the more tender *Hypericum leschenaultii*, an evergreen shrub of lax habit with similar rich yellow flowers, once considered a variety of *H. hookerianum*; the other parent of 'Rowallane' is *H. hookerianum* 'Rogersii', which imparts its greater hardiness to the hybrid. Dwarfer than these, at about 1 m/3¼ ft, is *H. monogynum* (*H. chinense*), a pretty and rather tender shrub with large flowers, filled with a brush of stamens after the style of the invasive *H. calycinum*. In very warm gardens the Canary Island *H. grandiflorum* could be tried; it grows in the wild in dry laurel forests and among conifers, where it bears its bright yellow flowers in loose clusters in spring.

I have hesitated for longer than the wretched shrub deserves over whether, and if so where, to mention *Aristotelia chilensis* (*A. macqui*) 'Variegata'. In its plain form it is damned by the word 'interesting' in *Hilliers' Manual of Trees & Shrubs*; in its variegated form, it appeals greatly to some (not to me) on account of its bright yellow leaf markings. You can cut it hard back in spring to ensure the largest and most obtrusive leaves. Other *Aristotelia* species are genuinely interesting or beautiful or both, but belong in a later chapter.

If the shrub borders contained nothing but these soft-wooded shrubs that may, or must, be hard pruned in spring, the winter would present a scene of dereliction. There are the evergreen shrubs already considered, which mitigate this by their dominating presence. Then, too, there are shrubs which, grown chiefly for their flowers, yet look respectable all year, at least in climates where the frosts of winter are so slight that the evergreen leaves remain unscorched.

Take, for example, the bottlebrushes, species of *Callistemon* and *Melaleuca*; and one might include the allied *Acca sellowiana* (*Feijoa sellowiana*).

Indeed, this Brazilian shrub is more substantial than many of the bottle-brushes themselves, forming a large, bulky shrub with elliptic dark green leaves, grey-white felted beneath. The flowers, borne singly in the leaf axils, are formed of four thick-textured, edible crimson and blush-white petals cupped around the brush of red stamens. In good seasons, and if you have a good fruiting clone, you may have a crop of egg-shaped fruits, which are delicious: indeed seeds were offered a few years ago by one of the British seed houses under the name 'fruit salad bush', with the promise of fruits tasting in themselves of several different fruit flavours.

The true bottlebrushes, *Callistemon* species, are Australian and Tas-manian natives, the showy part of their flowers the long stamens assembled into the cylindrical spikes which give the shrubs their vernacular name. The hardiest species are not necessarily the brightest in flower: *C. sieberi*, for example, has narrow short spikes of yellow flowers in high summer, and thick linear leaves densely arranged on the branches. The willow-leaved *C. salignus* is of like hardiness; the flowers, borne in longer bottle-brushes, are commonly pale creamy-yellow, sometimes pale pink (though red and white forms are known in cultivation) and appear at midsummer. The young growths are clad in silky hairs casting a soft pink haze over the new leaves. The Tasmanian *C. salignus* var. *viridiflora* (*C. viridiflora*) has lime-yellow flowers; the closely related *C. pallidus*, also Tasmanian, has cream bottlebrushes and young, greyed-pink leaves cobwebbed with silky hairs. One of the hardiest of the crimson-red species is *C. subulatus*, less than half the height of the potentially tree-like *C. salignus*, with glossy green foliage and long crimson spikes. *C. linearis* is scarcely taller, at 1·8 m/6 ft, the dense bottlebrushes of crimson-carmine longer still, up to 12·5 cm/5 ins, appearing in summer. For earlier flower, there is *C. ridigus*, named for the stiff texture of its sharp-pointed leaves. The dense, dark red spikes of flower open from spring onwards. The tree-like *C. speciosus* flowers at much the same season, but only with freedom when mature; the stamens are bright carmine-red with yellow anthers. *C. viminalis* is very similar, but with pendulous, not stiff branches; the related *C. phoeniceus* is a much smaller plant, with slender branches and leaves. One of the most striking, though not very hardy, is *C. citrinus*, its name deriving from the lemony aroma of the leaves, released when they are crushed. A spreading shrub to 3 m/10 ft, it has looser spikes than many, composed of dark scarlet-red stamens, at midsummer. The old cultivar 'Splendens' has extra long filaments of bright crimson and flowers over a long season.

Callistemons are very easy to raise from their dust-fine seed, which is borne in woody capsules adhering in cylindrical clusters to the branches; they remain for several years, the branch growing on to produce another year's flowers and another until there is a string of successive years' capsules alternating with leaves. Named cultivars, on the other hand, must be grown from cuttings to be true to name. *C. citrinus* itself has given rise to several named cultivars: 'Burning Bush' is compact, with carmine-red flowers, 'Reeve's Pink' rosy-pink, and its seedling 'Mauve Mist' nearer to lilac. 'Hannah Ray', which is of semi-weeping habit with bright orange-red flowers, may be a selection of *C. viminalis*, as is 'Captain Cook', of low, spreading habit to 1·2 m/4 ft, with young growths red-pink and flowers of deep crimson in late summer. 'Perth Pink' is a soft carmine, taller at 3 m/10 ft.

The melaleucas are more variable in both leaf and flower than the callistemons. Some of them are so salt-tolerant as to be useful in exposed seaside gardens, among them the needle-leaved *Melaleuca armillaris*, a rounded spreading shrub of up to 4·5 m/15 ft or even a small tree, reasonably hardy when mature. The flowers are borne in bottlebrush spikes, white or rarely pink, in spring and summer. *M. ericifolia* is very salt-tolerant, but sensitive to wind; it grows to 3 m/10 ft, with the little needle leaves implied by the specific epithet, and stubby bottlebrushes of creamy-white flowers. The graceful *M. leucadendron*, with a more northerly distribution extending to Malaysia, makes a large tree with thick spongy brownish-white bark peeling in layers, tapering leaves, and cream flowers from early summer to autumn. It is not very frost-hardy, but extremely resistant to salt spray. I doubt if *M. styphelioides* would be very happy where salty winds could reach it; it used to grow in Tresco Abbey Gardens, where extensive shelter belts were planted before the garden proper was ever begun. A stately evergreen tree, it has light green foliage and thick, papery white bark; the fuzzy flowers are pure white. Smaller and hardier, but not especially noted for salt-tolerance, *M. squarrosa* makes a dense rounded 3 m/10 ft shrub with small sharp-pointed leaves in two pairs of opposite rows, and abundant cylindrical spikes of fragrant cream to pale yellow flowers in early summer. Growing in wet heaths in its native Tasmania, it prefers a soil not too dry in cultivation.

Also from Tasmania and southern Australia, both *M. gibbosa* and *M. squamea* have lilac-mauve or light purple flowers. The first is a wiry little shrub with small, crowded leaves, and short dense spikes of flower in summer; the rather taller *M. squamea* comes in cream as well as lilac-pink. *M. decussata* should be worth a try; it has small mauve spikes fading quickly to off-white, on pendulous branches set with greyish foliage. Also grey-green in leaf, but much brighter in flower, is *M. elliptica*, a bushy shrub of 1·8 m/6 ft with large pinkish-red bottlebrush spikes in spring, summer and autumn. The Western Australian *M. wilsonii* also has flowers of pink or red, borne in spring in loose small clusters along the shoots among narrow, blue-green leaves. Brighter still is *M. lateritea*, from the same regions. It is rather tender, and I suspect that like many western

Australian natives less adaptable than species from the east of the continent; but worth cherishing for its brilliant orange-vermilion flowers. One of the most distinct is *M. hypericifolia*, mimicking very exactly in leaf a hypericum, but the muted orange-red bottlebrushes give the game away from late spring to autumn.

While on the subject of shrubs from the southern hemisphere, which so often have a rather alien appearance among the more familiar vegetation of the north, I am inclined to write about some of the hardier members of the Proteaceae, a family of infinite fascination and variety (hence, indeed, its name). Some genera have already made an entry: *Persoonia*, *Lomatia*, *Embothrium*, *Telopea*. There are also the grevilleas, a very large Australian genus of which many species are far too tender for our purposes. Not so long ago, indeed, the only species at all well known in European gardens were the crimson-flowered *Grevillea rosmarinifolia*, *G. sulphurea* (*G. juniperina sulphurea*) and, as a greenhouse plant, *G. robusta*, valued for its much-divided, silky foliage and the ease with which it can be raised from seed to form in a season a plant big enough to bed out. *G. juniperina sulphurea* is remarkably hardy, a fresh green needle-leaved species varying from an upright 1·8 m/6 ft shrub to a semi-prostrate sprawler, set with spidery pale yellow flowers in early summer. The rosemary-leaved grevillea is represented in western gardens largely by material believed to be of hybrid origin, with the blood of *G. lanigera*, forming 2 m/6½ ft shrubs with dark green foliage. The cultivar 'Jenkinsii' is more compact and very free-flowering; smaller still is 'Canberra Gem', perhaps a hybrid, reaching 60 cm/2 ft or so, very appealing when full of its waxy crimson-pink flowers. *G. alpina* is of similar stature, with densely packed dark green leaves like broad needles; the flowers are variable in colour, often red, sometimes yellow or pink, and are borne over a long season. It is found in the mountains of New South Wales and Victoria, from both low and high elevations; the higher altitude collections should be hardy. One of the more tender species is *G. thelemanniana*, with thread-fine silky foliage like an artemisia's, and slender-clawed pink and yellow-green flowers. Crossed with *G. sulphurea*, it produced the delightful *G.* × *semperflorens*, a shrub of 1·8 m/6 ft or so, with the same soft, fine foliage and abundant warm buff flowers tipped with pinkish- and yellow-green.

Lately the plant breeders in New Zealand have turned their attentions to the genus, and some of their hybrids and selections are reaching European nurseries, such as 'Robyn Gordon', a compact spreading shrub to 1 m/3¼ ft, wider than high, with large spidery flowers of vivid red in showy arching sprays over a long season. 'Robin Hood' is a selection of *G. asplenifolia*, which as its name suggests has fern-like foliage; the crimson flowers are borne in long showy spikes on a bushy shrub of 2 m/6½ ft.

Although most of these proteaceous shrubs are natural species, and even

the cultivars have a look, still, of untamed species, their exotic appearance –
in the literal sense of something from outside, alien, non-native – means
that they can often comfortably take their place in the more intensively
gardened areas. Other genera may need different treatment. I always feel,
for example, that the double, and even the more brightly coloured single-
flowered, cultivars of *Leptospermum scoparium* belong in borders, but that
the wild form itself, together with other species in the same genus, belongs
among the less formal shrubs still to be considered. Cultivars such as the
old 'Chapmanii', which was in fact discovered in the wild, are quiet
enough to fit in where you wish; this one has bright pink flowers and
bronzed foliage, narrow and almost needle-like as always in *L. scoparium*.
Perhaps it is the colouring of 'Nicholsii' which makes me reluctant to mix
it with the greens and greys of undomesticated shrubs; for it has very dark
bronze-purple foliage, and crimson flowers. 'Nicholsii Grandiflorum' is
the same, only with larger flowers; 'Burgundy Queen' has bronzed foliage
and crimson-magenta flowers, black at the centre; 'Winter Cheer' has
bright red flowers and purple-bronze leaves. There are double-flowered
cultivars of the same colouring: 'Red Damask', very free-flowering, and
'Ruby Glow'. I suspect that one I saw labelled 'Burgundy Glow' was the
result of confusion in someone's mind between 'Burgundy Queen' and
'Ruby Glow'; it was a rather nasty, hard blue-crimson double with dark
foliage. Double pinks include 'Gaiety Girl', very pert and self-conscious
in salmony-pink, 'Fascination', and the semi-double 'Blossom', pink with
a darker eye over grey-green foliage. A double white leptospermum can
be pretty: 'Snow Flurry', 'Leonard Wilson'. Most of the other cultivars
that I want to mention at all can wait; but I think the dwarf kinds fit
better here than in the wilder parts of the garden. Some are so tiny that
they belong in the rock garden, not in this book at all; others are pleasant
little things for small borders. Often prefaced with the epithet *nanum*, they
derive from the original of that name, which grows to about 30 cm/12 ins
and has rose-pink flowers over rather bronze-green leaves. 'Huia' is deep
pink, 'Tui' white and blush, 'Kiwi' twice as tall with reddish foliage and
red flowers. 'Cherry Brandy' is semi-dwarf, with rich deep red foliage;
'Pink Champagne', green in leaf and pale pink in flower.

Before finally coming to the shrubs which seem to me virtually to
demand informal treatment, I must consider two groups of highly bred
woody plants that each, in their way, impose themselves on their surroundings as less assertive shrubs do not: the mophead hydrangeas, and
the tea roses. They have in common a framework of no beauty at all,
serving – to the garden maker, at least – merely to support the flowers
which are the reason for their being. Yet those flowers are each, in their
way, of such formal or artificial nature that we cannot banish the shrubs
to the outer reaches of the garden, there to lose themselves decently among

surrounding evergreens until their season of bloom comes round again. A vague sense of this individuality may be what impels some people to herd their roses together in ghettos: it is easier than trying to think how to integrate them. Massing works better with hydrangeas, although it is less often practised, than with roses; for the essence of a mophead hydrangea is that it should form a mass of flower colour, and this being so, five or ten or fifty bushes will make five or ten or fifty times the impact. The billows of hydrangeas near the sea in south-western Britain, where the acid soils turn them brighter than the sea and sky in every shade of ice and turquoise and electric and marine blue, fading into verdigris and jade and malachite, cardinal-red and crimson and papal-purple: these are inseparable from coastal holidays. Pink or red hydrangeas somehow have not the same allure, at least in the mass, though individually they may charm. There is such a wide choice of mophead hydrangeas for mild gardens, where even the cultivars bred for indoor work should thrive, that I can do no more than pick out a few tested kinds which in the right soils should give you the colours you desire. In any case, I believe that most people acquire their hydrangeas by being given cuttings off a neighbour's or friend's bush rather than buying them by name. Of blues, needing an acid soil to stay that colour, the famous old 'Générale Vicomtesse de Vibraye' is a clear pale sky-blue, 'Maréchal Foch' deep marine, 'Mousseline' between the two. 'Hamburg' is a good blue on acid soils, bright pink on lime. 'Ami Pasquier' and 'Westfalen' both stick at wine or violet-purple on acid soils, but turn crimson or blood-red in neutral or alkaline conditions; 'Heinrich Seidel' is cherry-red. Other pinks for lime soils are tall 'Goliath', paler 'La Marne' and 'Oriental'. The splendid 'Mme Mouillère', with wide heads of flower, is white whatever soil you give her. 'Ayesha', pink or blue according to pH, is distinct in the shape of its thick, cupped florets, giving it the air of a lilac, almost. And little 'Preziosa' is popular for its pink flowers, deepening from blush to crimson among coppery-red foliage. Give it sun for the best colouring, and – as for all hydrangeas – a moist and well nourished soil. A limp hydrangea does nobody credit. If you like powerful contrasts of colour, the deeper true blues can be paired with yellow hypericums: but I think you need a strong stomach to live with intense colours that are fighting for supremacy.

The colours of the tea roses, the precursors of the modern hybrid teas or large-flowered roses, are gentle, with no hint of stridency even in the coppery-pinks which represent the brightest of the range. The tea roses are less hardy than the hybrid teas, deserving a sheltered sunny aspect, and a well nourished but perfectly drained soil. In the gardens of the Riviera they form great bushes, full of flower, with only brief rests to regain strength, from late spring to autumn; even in slightly colder gardens they should be pruned only lightly, so that you remove dead or damaged wood and old, weakened shoots, but otherwise encourage them to form a permanent woody framework renewing itself from the base as the oldest shoots are cut out.

One of the oldest surviving teas is 'Triomphe du Luxembourg', dating from 1840. Its soft colouring of skin-pink shaded with buff and rose is typical of the class, but the flowers open flat in the old style; the long high-centre bud appeared in later teas, such as 'Souvenir d'Elise Vardon' (1855), the first to display the conical petal formation – it is an exquisite rose with large, fragrant cream flowers shaded coppery-yellow – and shell-pink 'Catherine Mermet'. The cream and copper colouring appears again in 'Anna Olivier'. Saffron or maize yellows come in the famous 'Safrano' and deeper apricot 'Lady Hillingdon'. 'Perle des Jardins' is straw coloured, almost canary-yellow at times, and very fragrant, but easily spoiled by bad weather. Another typical tea colouring is that of 'Marie van Houtte', pale lemon or creamy-primrose edged or shaded with soft carmine-pink: also of this type is the American-raised 'William R Smith'. Of purer pinks, 'Duchesse de Brabant', with cupped, very sweetly scented blooms, is one of the prettiest; 'Maman Cochet' is pale pink with deeper centre, and the classic 'Mme Bravy' is paler still, with outer petals creamy-white and only the centre flushed with pink. A more muscular tea rose is 'Baronne Henriette de Snoy', its colouring soft peach-pink. Then there is the delightful 'Mme Berkeley', which forms a bush of more character than most, the arching branches set with mahogany young foliage, the ideal foil to small, high-pointed scrolled buds of peach-pink, deeper at the centre, nodding gracefully on slender stalks. But perhaps the teas that have the strongest hold on my heart are those of coppery-pink or terracotta shades. 'Général Schablikine', 'Archiduc Joseph', the paler 'Dr Grill', 'Monsieur Tillier' in carmine and brick-red shaded with copper, 'Freiherr von Marschall' and – nearest to crimson of this group – 'Papa Gontier'. I cannot think of any modern rose in which this colouring has been reproduced: it has nothing in common with the fluorescent vermilion of 'Super Star'. I like to set the tawny pink teas among grey and glaucous foliage, and the blues of agapanthus and *Felicia amelloides*; indeed, all the soft colours of the teas look well with grey and blue. Despite their air of semi-dereliction when not flowering, the tea roses also look well in formal settings near the house, or near garden masonry. Their ancestry – they derive in part from the tender, climbing *Rosa gigantea* – means that they are very well adapted to hot dry summers such as regularly occur on the Riviera and occasionally in the maritime regions of southern Britain, but dislike cold winters. They have survived, to be reintroduced into cultivation in Britain and parts of North America, in gardens in Bermuda and New Zealand.

Shrubs that flower in winter, especially if at other seasons they do not look shabby, are also welcome near the house. And if they are fragrant also, like *Freylinia lanceolata* or *Buddleja officinalis*, that is even better. There is nothing unusual about this buddleja except its flowering season: it has leaves shaped much like the common butterfly bush, dark green above and softly buff to grey felted beneath, and the honey scented flowers are borne in tapering panicles of pale lilac mauve. I believe *B. asiatica* to be rather more tender, and will describe it with other wall shrubs. The South African *Freylinia* is an evergreen shrub which is said to reach 3 m/10 ft, though with me it never grew beyond 1·2 m/4 ft or so. The rather angular branches are well clothed with narrowly lanceolate, dark green, rather hard-textured leaves; in winter the very fragrant, creamy or nankeen-yellow flowers are borne in terminal panicles. Although *Freylinia* is in Scrophulariaceae its flowers are sufficiently like the tubular blooms of the solanaceous *Cestrum* to have earned it the alternative specific epithet of *cestroides*.

Their fragrance is one of the most endearing qualities of the daphnes, too. Most are hardy; but the evergreen forms of *Daphne bholua*, collected at lower altitudes in the Himalayas than the deciduous variants, and the plain green leaved form of *D. odora*, both deserve some shelter, especially the former. The allied *Edgeworthia chrysantha* (*E. papyrifera*) is fairly hardy also. The fragrant nankeen-yellow flowers, packed into rounded terminal heads, are white with silky hairs on the outside and open in late winter; f. *rubra* is as white outside, but pale orange deepening to near-red within. Unfortunately the only *Sarcococca* which is not fully hardy, *S. saligna*, which might earn a place for its long, tapering, glossy leaves as year-round furnishing, has insignificant greenish-white flowers that do not have the delicious fragrance of other members of the genus.

The informal shrub garden

From this point, I ask you finally to imagine that we are moving away from the house, the usual focal point of such formality as you may allow in your garden, towards the parts where a more natural style of planting, and of plants, seems appropriate. First, some shrubs that, though certainly not ugly in leaf in the manner of many highly-bred border plants, would scarcely be grown if they did not flower.

Curiously enough, the first time I saw a hoheria in flower, many years ago, was in a tiny garden otherwise devoted entirely to old roses, which suggests that these members of the mallow family will fit as well with domesticated flowers as with wild species. I am not sure if my faint recollection of unease at seeing *Hoheria glabrata* among the damasks and cabbage roses and gallicas, all flowering with it, is retrospective or genuinely remembered. Certainly the hoheria was by far the most beautiful thing there. A tall, shrubby tree with clear almond-green leaves, each drawn out to a slender point, it was bowed with the weight of innumerable fragrant, creamy-white flowers, massed like cherry blossom. What I did not then know is that the young leaves of *H. glabrata* unfurl in 'a subtle mixture of pale cream, yellow and silver-grey-green' and that in autumn they slowly change to 'a pale honey or straw yellow or to lemon-white in the shade' (David Wright, in *The Plantsman*, Vol. 5 pt. 3, December 1983). Arnold-Forster found that it flowered freely in a draughty, shady northern aspect. The closely allied *H. lyallii* is worth growing also, for its leaves are grey downy and its flowers follow those of *H. glabrata* a fortnight later. It prefers a drier soil than its cousin, which is found in watercourses in its native New Zealand.

Both these species are deciduous, but *H. sexstylosa* has persistent leaves, differing in shape on juvenile and adult plants, as so often with antipodeans. The fragrant, pure white flowers, borne in abundance in high summer, have six pink styles to distinguish them from other species. They open from pearly buds, and are beloved of bees. Seedlings often appear in great numbers beneath flowering specimens; the young plants form tangled shrublets with small, roundish, toothed leaves. *H. sexstylosa* and *H. glabrata* are joined in the hybrid 'Glory of Amlwch', a small, virtually evergreen tree with pale green, slender-pointed leaves and densely massed white flowers in summer. Less hardy than all these is the elegant *H. populnea*, a small evergreen tree with pure white, very fragrant flowers in clusters in early autumn. The species has given rise to a number of cultivars, of which 'Foleis Purpureis' is desirable for the maroon-purple reverse to the leaves, and 'Albo Variegata' appeals to those who like variegated foliage ('Variegata' has the reverse markings, yellow at the centre of the leaf). 'Osbornei' has leaves flushed purple on the undersides, less striking than 'Foleis Purpureis', and flowers with purple-blue stamens. *H. angustifolia* is elegant in its narrow leaves, but the least showy in bloom, for the white flowers are borne singly or in small clusters in late winter. The allied *Plagianthus betulinus* is graceful in habit, with toothed leaves on slender stems, but the white flowers are scarcely less inconspicuous, despite being borne in large panicles in late spring. Juvenile plants form dense tangled bushes of interlacing stems with much smaller leaves.

A large, white-flowered shrub of entirely different character is the Brazilian *Escallonia bifida* (*E. montevidensis*), one of the most tender of the genus. The large leaves of rather muted, polished green form the setting for tall panicles, as much as 25 cm/10 in long, of white flowers in late summer. Butterflies love it. At much the same season, or a little later, the long loose sprays of lilac flowers belonging to *Vitex negundo* begin to open, especially if the summer has been long and hot. This is a pretty tree, with five-parted or trifoliolate leaves, greyish beneath; the foliage of var. *heterophylla* is more elegant, with deeply cut leaflets. In common with many woody plants from areas where the summers are hot – in this case, southern China and India – *V. negundo* will survive quite low temperatures if the wood is well ripened by summer sun, but resents cold winters that follow upon cool, wet summers encouraging soft growth.

It would be rash to approach too closely to the colletias to inhale their sweet fragrance, for these are among the most ferociously armed of all shrubs. In *Colletia armata* and *C. infausta*, slender green spines do duty for the leaves, which are either missing altogether or so tiny as to be hardly worth having. A full-grown specimen of either, standing at 2·4 m/8 ft or so, full of white or blush flower, is worth seeing, at arm's length. The first, which is close to *C. spinosa* (a species perhaps not in cultivation) flowers in late summer to autumn, in either white or, in cv. 'Rosea', pale pink. *C. infausta* flowers from spring to midsummer. Both are much less bizarre to the eye than *C. paradoxa* (*C. cruciata*), a species from Uruguay growing up to 3 m/10 ft, with very stiff branches set with huge, rigid, triangular thorns. The almond-scented, creamy-white flowers open in autumn.

Most of the viburnums grown only for their flowers are hardy, and the evergreen species with handsome glossy foliage have already been described. So there is just one more species that I am reluctant to leave out: *Viburnum erubescens*, a tall deciduous shrub with fragrant, blush-white flowers in loose, hanging sprays at midsummer. Var. *gracilipes* has longer panicles, and is hardier. As all who see it admire it, I am puzzled that it is not more often grown.

It is a pity that *Leycesteria crocothyrsos* is not hardier; if it were, I am sure we should see it in every garden. It was discovered by F. Kingdon Ward in Assam as a low shrub growing on steep, sheltered cliffs, and nicknamed by him 'golden abelia' on account of its long, hanging racemes of yellow flowers. My own plant never fruited successfully, but Norman Hadden grew it in his west Somerset garden, where he found it 'nearly as attractive in autumn when bearing long racemes of jade-green gooseberry-like fruits, as it was in May with its lovely golden flowers'. The foliage is blue-green. I have found it easy to grow from seed, when seed is set. So too *Vestia foetida* (*V. lycioides*), a solanaceous shrub with typically sour-smelling leaves, and nodding, tubular flowers of primrose-yellow in spring and summer. There is something so appealing about a flower that hangs its head that I cannot understand why plant breeders always seem to be trying to make the blooms of their creations stare you in the eye.

Perhaps this is why the yellow-flowered sophoras are so alluring. The New Zealand and Chilean species are evergreen shrubs or trees with decoratively patterned pinnate foliage, composed of a large number of very small leaflets, and rather tubular, drooping pea-flowers in shades of green-tinged to mustard or tawny yellow, followed by curious seed pods like strings of winged beads. The Chilean species, *Sophora macrocarpa*, has leaves of thirteen to twenty five leaflets, tan-silky beneath, and flowers in clusters of up to twelve in late spring, and wingless seed pods. It is likely to grow taller than the New Zealand *S. tetraptera*, which on mature plants has up to forty-one leaflets to each leaf, and rich yellow flowers in spring. There is a curious cultivar, 'Gnome', which grows slowly to about half the height of the type, reaching perhaps 1·8 m/6 ft, with stiff, erect branches; it flowers when still very small. *S. microphylla* is similar to *S. tetraptera*, but with even more numerous leaflets, up to forty pairs on each gracefully drooping leaf. When young it forms a shrub with zigzag stems and fewer leaflets, beginning to take on its tree-like character from about 3 m/10 ft in height. *S. prostrata*, which has densely interlacing stems, may be no more than a permanently juvenile form of this with fertile flowers.

Most *Stachyurus* species are yellow-flowered: in mild gardens the coastal form of *S. praecox,* var. *matzusakii* (*S. lancifolius*), should succeed; the stiff catkin-like racemes are borne in early spring. *S. himalaicus* flowers at much the same season, usually in wine-purple to pinkish-red, occasionally in yellow; it is a vigorous shrub where suited in a sheltered position, with long-pointed leaves held on red petioles. Though it is more frost resistant, *Clethra delavayi* also reaches its fullest beauty in a sheltered site. It is, I think, the finest of the deciduous clethras, a large shrub growing to well over 4·5 m/15 ft, with softly downy leaves and fragrant flowers, each like a tiny, creamy-white lily-of-the-valley bell with brown anthers, held in grey-felt calyces and assembled into long, one-sided horizontal racemes in summer. As the flowers fall the calyces turn pink, contributing to a colour scheme of great subtlety.

The Andean *Vallea stipularis* is another shrub, uncommon and rather sensitive to frost, which is very charming in its gentle colouring of cup-shaped pink petals held in paler, rose-red veined sepals. It belongs in the same family, Elaeocarpaceae, as *Crinodendron*, but the relationship scarcely jumps to the eye. There is little doubt about the affinity of *Dichroa febrifuga* with the genus *Hydrangea*, however. This virtually evergreen, almost hardy 1·2 m/4 ft shrub has glossy, toothed leaves on purple petioles, and large, loose, terminal clusters of clear blue flowers with rather thick petals.

Dichroa febrifuga was found by F. Kingdon Ward in Upper Burma, which adjoins Yunnan, the home of *Leptodermis pilosa* (*Hamiltonia pilosa*). This deciduous shrub, growing to about 1·5 m/5 ft, has dark grey-green leaves, and sprays of flowers like lilac, with a daphne fragrance, in summer to early autumn. From the other end of the Himalayan range comes *L. kumaonensis*, a smaller shrub with larger, downy leaves and clusters of small tubular flowers opening white or blush and fading to lilac or mauve-pink, in summer. Both need a reasonably sheltered position, in sun. Two other species that I have not seen are said to be hardier: *L. oblonga* with flowers like a small Persian lilac, and *L. purdomii* with pink flowers in panicles on arching stems.

Sun, some shelter, and a drained soil also suit *Osteomeles*, a small Chinese genus of evergreen shrubs characterized by dainty greyish pinnate leaves composed of many tiny leaflets. *O. schweriniae* is the taller of the two species I have grown, at 3 m/10 ft; the slender branchlets arch gracefully. *O. subrotunda* is slower growing and stiffer in habit. Both have hawthorn-like white flowers at midsummer.

I have decided, rather arbitrarily perhaps, to describe most *Ceanothus* species in a later chapter, with other shrubs – Californian and Mediterranean, chiefly – that thrive in hot and dry soils. Not all ceanothuses grow on the hot slopes as part of the chaparral, however; some are found in open places in the moist redwood belt, or are mountain species preferring slightly cooler, leafy soils, so long as the drainage is good. Reading Mrs Lester Rowntree's descriptions, I wish that my visits to California had been made earlier in the year, when *C. megacarpus* is 'making a light gray-white cloud on hill and mountain sides'. At midsummer, when I was there, even *C. integerrimus* was over; it bears loose, frothy panicles, sweetly (even sickly-sweet) scented, varying from white to sky-blue, lavender-pink or even a pure pink opening from salmon buds. It is a tall shrub, up to 3 m/10 ft, not wholeheartedly evergreen. Both *C. incanus* and *C. velutinus* are almost as tall, and retain their leaves all winter. The first, a thorny shrub which grows in the redwood belt, has very large leaves for a ceanothus, shining green above and blue-grey on the reverse; at flowering time the young leaves are pale grey-green, so the effect is very grey with the white-bloomed stems and stiff, pearly white flower spikes. *C. velutinus* is usually seen as a rounded, very wide shrub, with cinnamon-scented, glossy leaves – Mrs Rowntree writes 'even a quite Coprosma-like glitter on well-grown shrubs, looking as though they had been shellacked' – and large stiff panicles of white flowers.

If the flowers of some *Ceanothus* species are just sufficiently like lilac for the whole genus to have acquired the vernacular name Californian lilac, individually the flowers of leptospermums are a little like hawthorn, though they are unrelated: hawthorn (and *Osteomeles*) are in the rose family, *Leptospermum* in Myrtaceae. The familiar *L. scoparium*, when not producing aberrant double flowers or dwarfed forms, can grow to tree size; I had one which was 10 m/33 ft tall, with a leaning, peeling trunk and a crown of dense aromatic foliage, half hidden in its late spring season by the white flowers. Several of its seedlings were pale to rose-pink. A recognized botanical variant, *incanum*, has large blush flowers and leaves that are silky below, but some of the named cultivars are even finer.

'Boscawenii' was raised from New Zealand seed by Canon Boscawen of Ludgvan Rectory, where so many New Zealand plants grew to greater perfection than ever in their native habitat; it has deep pink buds opening to large white flowers with a pink eye, and forms a bush of compact habit. The rather tender 'Keatleyi' bears its large, waxy, soft pink flowers in winter; the young growths are crimson-pink and silky, the foliage grey-green. 'Martinii' has particularly large flowers, up to 2 cm (a little under an inch) wide, opening blush white and aging to deep pink; 'Pink Cascade' has weeping stems. New cultivars are being introduced, many of them dwarfed, some selected for hardiness rather than flower size; as leptospermums are so easy to grow from seed, you can have fun making your own, and indeed where they are suited they will sow themselves.

So far as I know, only white forms of *Leptospermum ericoides* are offered commercially, though I believe it may vary to pale pink in the wild. It is an aromatic shrub or even a spreading tree of up to 15 m/50 ft, with heath-like leaves, and abundant small flowers in late spring. *L. liversidgei* is aromatic also, with a faint scent of lemon, and slender twigs closely set with many tiny leaves. The white flowers are borne at midsummer in graceful sprays. It is one of the hardiest species, though it did succumb to − 22°C in one of my gardens, where it grew quite out in the open without protection. *L. stellatum*, with small bright green leaves, is also quite hardy; the flowers are white. Another hardy species is *L. flavescens* var. *obovatum*, which has obovate leaves and small but very abundant white flowers. Those of the Tasmanian *L. sericeum* are pink, the leaves silvery-grey. But greyest of all is the form of *L. lanigerum* which was originally introduced and described as *L. cunninghamii*, in which the leaves are silvery-silky, and the young growths pinkish-brown, on red stems. It flowers several weeks later than typical *L. lanigerum*, which has longer, narrower glossy leaves, purple-tinged when young. Sometimes the silvery form is listed as *L. lanigerum* 'Cunninghamii' to distinguish it, and there is also a cultivar called 'Silver Sheen' with large white flowers, which may or may not be distinct.

The largest flowers in the genus belong to *L. rodwayanum* (*L. grandiflorum*), a spreading shrub with grey-green leaves and white flowers each 3 cm or more wide (over one inch) in late summer. Those of *L. nitidum* may be no more than half as wide; they are closely packed in the axils of the pointed, shining green leaves. This species varies greatly in height, according perhaps to the altitude at which it grows in Tasmania; three of Comber's collections were from plants of 1–2 ft, 10–20 ft, and 8–12 ft respectively (30–60 cm, 3–6 m, and 2·4–3·6 m). An Australian author, Ernest Lord, refers to the form 'Macrocarpum', which sounds good: 'deep bronze-purple glossy leaves; young stems red. Flowers greenish yellow with deeper centre'. The same author describes the leaves of *L. laevigatum* as greyish, rounded-oval, and thickish; but the form I know, which agrees with other descriptions by English authors, has glossy leaves, larger than most.

In a garden blessed with a benign climate, I would not want to waste space on the European heaths and heathers, except for the tree heaths which fill the air, in their late winter or early spring season, with a honeyed fragrance. There are, however, a number of shrubs of heath-like character which are worth planting. A couple of them, indeed, have already found their way into these pages, for both *Cassinia leptophylla fulvida* and *Olearia solanderi* are valuable wind-resisters for coastal areas. Very likely the other cassinias, grey-white *C. leptophylla* and the very silvery *C. vauvilliersii albida*, and stubby, greyish *C. retorta*, should do as well; the last, indeed, inhabits sand dunes in its native New Zealand. I have grown them all in colder but less windy situations, where they thrived. But I have found the other heath-like olearias more tricky, and more tender, than the cassinias. Indeed, I have never even been successful in propagating *Olearia floribunda*, let alone growing it for long; but when its succeeds, which it certainly does with others more competent than myself, it is very fine in flower, with great plumes of tiny white daisies over bright green foliage. The very tender *O. ramulosa* is similar, very graceful with arching slender branches, a mass of white when in flower. It inhabits dry open pastures in full sun in its native Tasmania. *O. algida* differs, as I know it, in its glaucous-grey foliage, which gives it a slight resemblance to *Cassinia vauvilliersii albida*. The most distinct is *O. pinifolia*, a stiffly erect shrub with thick shoots, often branched only at the shoots tips, and narrow, stiff, prickly-tipped leaves with margins so tightly involuted that they appear cylindrical. The low and humpy *O. ledifolia* has narrow leaves, less extremely revolute, green above and silvery or rusty-felted beneath, which as W. Arnold-Forster justly pointed out make it look, when not in flower, 'rather like a dark, wind-beaten rosemary'. Wind-beaten in the wild it certainly is, growing, as its collector Harold Comber tells us in his field notes, 'in most exposed places on moors, rocky forests or hillsides' in Tasmania. The flowers are the expected white daisies.

The genus *Ozothamnus* is also in Compositae; it has moved in and out of *Helichrysum* and is, I believe, at present correctly residing in that genus. I will however retain the name *Ozothamnus* for the sake of differentiating the several species that I have grown from the curry plants and my favourite *H. petiolare*. Those that I regard as ozothamnuses are much less variable than *Helichrysum* taken as an all-embracing whole. The least heath-like is *Ozothamnus antennaria*, a rather dull shrub, frankly, densely branched and upright in habit, with oblanceolate, leathery light green leaves and dense terminal clusters of white flowers at midsummer. Much more appealing is the aromatic *O. ledifolius*, which gives off a smell very like stewed plums. It is a low-growing and hummocky shrub with crowded, somewhat sticky narrow leaves, shining green above and yellow with resin beneath, held so the undersides are visible. The dense clusters of white flowers open from long-lasting, coppery-red buds, so that in its different seasons the shrub passes from a cheerful yellow-green to tan to white and back to yellow-green. *O. ericifolius* is similar, but taller and of more upright habit, with flowers in both terminal and lateral clusters combining into long flowery sprays. Then there are three species which are often confused. The most tender and the least ornamental – though all are handsome – is *O. purpurascens*, a sharply aromatic, upright shrub with linear leaves and dense terminal and lateral shoots of white flowers opening from purple-pink buds. The wide clusters of flower of *O. thyrsoideus*, often miscalled *O. rosmarinifolius*, are almost everlasting, remaining clean white for months over narrow deep green leaves. But *O. rosmarinifolius* itself is the most appealing of the three rosemary-leaved species, for its white flowers open from bright crimson-red buds which hold their colour for two weeks or more. The selection 'Silver Jubilee' is similar in flower, but much more silvered in leaf. Another that I have seen only on the show bench is 'Sussex Silver'; it is said to be hardier, and looks to have a rather more open habit.

Many antipodean shrubs, though not so like heaths and heathers as to deceive, have evolved small leaves and a habit of growth that suggest the wild wide open spaces. I think especially of the genus *Coprosma*; not the glossy-leaved species and their garden cultivars that we have already met, but those such as *C. acerosa*, a low shrub small enough for the rock garden, or *C. rotundifolia* which may reach tree stature. *C. acerosa* and the allied *C. brunnea*, and the mat-forming *C. petriei*, are virtually hardy; they are valued especially for their translucent berries, borne on female plants. The colour of these abundant fruits may vary from white to many shades of blue or pink. The taxonomic status of *C. kirkii* seems uncertain; I have seen it listed as a species, but also as a natural hybrid between *C. acerosa* and *C. repens*. It is a trailing shrub, with small narrow green leaves; there is a variegated form, quite pretty with very pale, slender leaves.

I once raised a large batch of *C. rugosa* from wild-collected seed. As infants they were enchanting, with narrow leaves on slender, divaricate branches; they varied in colour from pale bronze to deep chocolate-brown, and some were more compact than others. As they grew to their ultimate height of 3 m/10 ft or so, some turned green, but others retained the pale coppery tones. Female plants bear translucent pale blue fruits. Another species that I grew and enjoyed for its foliage colour was *C. rotundifolia*, a little tree with tiny circular, bronze-brown leaves and flaking bark. The fruits are bright red. It is harder to describe *C. rhamnoides*, for it is a very variable species; my plant was about 1·5 m/5 ft tall, with little rounded leaves. *C. propinqua*, which has pale to indigo-blue fruits, is another that may reach tree size, though not with me; it has an angular branch structure, and very narrow leaves clustered at the nodes. Its hybrid with *C. robusta*, which I have not grown, is *C. × cunninghamii*, with somewhat wider leaves and pale yellow fruits.

The genus *Pittosporum* is widespread and polymorphic, which accounts for its frequent appearance in these pages in very different contexts. *P. anomalum* is a small shrub of 1 m/3¼ ft or so, very densely branched, with small-toothed or divided juvenile leaves and aromatic, linear-oblong mature foliage. The little honey-scented flowers are yellow. The change from juvenile to mature foliage occurs in *P. divaricatum* also; it is a curious, tangled shrub resembling *Corokia cotoneaster*, except that the flowers are so deep maroon as to be almost black. *P. rigidum* differs in the branching structure, dense but not interlacing, and blunter leaves. Although it forms a small, upright tree, *P. patulum* also displays differently shaped leaves on young and on mature plants; they are prettiest when young, long and very narrow and neatly lobed along their entire length. Later they become lanceolate, with smooth or sparsely toothed margins. The dark red flowers, borne in spring, are extremely fragrant. The divaricate habit and different juvenile and mature stages occur in a great many New Zealand plants whether related or not – *Coprosma* is in Rubiaceae, *Pittosporum* in Pittosporaceae. We even find it in Malvaceae, in the shape of *Plagianthus divaricatus*, a densely branched shrub of up to 1·8 m/6 ft, with linear or spathulate juvenile foliage.

Although they are in the citrus family, Rutaceae, the South African adenandras and barosmas are heath-like in growth. *Adenandra uniflora* (*Diosma uniflora*) is a small evergreen shrub with dense aromatic foliage and pretty, flax-like flowers opening from bright red buds to show their white, pink-striped petals in spring and early summer. Other species that should be worth trying are *A. umbellata*, and the pink-flowered *A. fragrans*. *Barosma pulchella* (*Diosma pulchella*) is also aromatic; the flowers are mauve. *Eriostemon* and the closely allied *Crowea* are in Rutaceae too, but are natives of Australia. All seem happiest in sandy soils but with some shade for their roots, even if it is just a large stone. *E. buxifolius*, as its name implies, has rounded leaves on a shrub of hummocky outline; the starry white, waxy flowers, opening in spring from pink buds, are crowded along the length of the branches. The willow-leaved *E. lanceolatus*, despite its very different foliage of much greyer cast, is often cultivated under the name *E. buxifolius*; it is very pretty in flower, the larger pink or white stars very abundant along arching stems. It may grow as tall as 2 m/6½ ft. Another species, rather variable in leaf, is *E. neriifolius*, an aromatic shrub flowering from midwinter onwards; the small white stars, opening from pink buds, are clustered along the stems. Willow-like leaves characterize *Crowea exalata*

(*Eriostemon crowei*), which grows low and spreading in sandy soils exposed to the sun, but up to 1·2 m/4 ft in cool shade. It bears its bright pink, waxy flowers over an exceptionally long season from summer to winter.

Again and again little byways of information add to the fascination of the plants we grow in our gardens. The phenomenon of parallel evolution is one I find particularly interesting. Is it the pressure of similar climatic and edaphic conditions that acts upon plants that are separated by oceans or continents, so that they evolve apparently independently towards a similar conclusion? In the southern hemisphere, for example, the family Epacridaceae to a great extent fills the same ecological niches as Ericaceae (a not solely northern hemisphere family) in the north. Most, if not all, species in the genus *Epacris* itself are too tender for the open garden in the climatic range I am discussing, but at least two species of *Cyathodes* are reasonably hardy, and assort well both visually and culturally with heathy plants. I do not include *C. colensoi*, a tough little rock garden shrub with glaucous foliage; it would be swamped by most of the shrubs I am prepared to admit. But both *C. juniperina* and *C. robusta* can grow quite tall; usually 1–2 m/3¼–6½ ft in height, they may reach as much as 4.5 m/15 ft. Both have leathery, linear leaves, glaucous beneath, and modest white pitcher-shaped flowers followed by the more showy fruits, white or carmine or claret in colour.

The daphne family, Thymelaeaceae, is represented in both hemispheres, but *Daphne* itself is confined to the north, while *Pimelea* occurs only in Australasia. *P. drupacea* is a pleasant little evergreen with narrow leaves and terminal clusters of white flowers in summer; but it is overshadowed by *P. ferruginea,* a neat rounded shrub of 90 cm/3 ft high and wide, with polished green leaves precisely arranged in rows, and very abundant, peach or deep pink flowers in terminal heads in spring.

Another instance of parallelism is found in the broom tribe. *Cytisus* and *Genista* are northern hemisphere plants; in Australasia their place is taken by *Carmichaelia, Notospartium* and *Chordospartium*; This last is no longer able to reproduce itself in the wild, and in gardens is far from common. This may be because anyone growing it from seed, unless forewarned, risks throwing out the young seedlings in the mistaken belief that they are dead; for, during their first two years or more, they look quite brown and lifeless, like wisps of straw. If they survive infanticide, they will in time form almost leafless shrubs of weeping habit, up to 3 m/10 ft tall, bearing in late spring or early summer dense spikelets of pale lilac-mauve pea-flowers with deeper stripes on the standard. In bud they are green; at first the racemes are as triangular as kittens' tails, drooping elegantly as all the flowers open.

Notospartium carmichaeliae also has pendulous, almost leafless stems, but it is rather small in growth. The pea-flowers are lilac-pink, in short spikes in summer. It grew well at Ludgvan, according to W. Arnold-Forster, 'hanging out over a hollow floored with the vivid magenta creeper, *Heeria elegans*'. It needs sun and a drained soil, and is hardy once it has formed wood. The much taller *N. glabrescens* is probably less frost resistant. It makes a round-headed tree of 4.5 m/15 ft or more, with flattened stems, leaves so small as to be almost invisible, and white, purple blotched pea-flowers in racemes in late spring. The cultivar 'Woodside' has mauve flowers with deeper veining and a deep maroon-purple stain on the standard.

Some of the carmichaelias have flattened stems also. *Carmichaelia australis* makes an upright shrub of 1–3 m/3¼–10 ft, with flat leafless twigs and lilac flowers in small racemes at midsummer. The grooved, drooping branchlets of *C. glabrata* bear leaves in spring and summer; the flowers are white, with both standard and wings blotched and veined with purple. It is close to *C. odorata*, which has very abundant lilac-pink, fragrant flowers. In the wild it apparently grows on shady banks, beside streams and at forest margins, yet in cultivation it seems to do better in sun, sheltered from cold winds. The red-purple flowers of *C. flagelliformis* are very small and grouped in few-flowered racemes, at midsummer; nor are those of *C. grandiflora* as large as the name implies; they are very fragrant, and prettily coloured in lilac with violet veining. The large flowers of *C. williamsii*, each up to 2·5 cm/1 in long, depart from the usual colouring, for they are creamy-yellow tinged with green, only the standard just stained with red-purple; they are borne in spring, in small clusters. Though rated Z8, this species seems less hardy than the others.

Instead of parallel evolution, quite the reverse phenomenon is manifested in the family Violaceae. We in the northern hemisphere are so accustomed to our sweet violets and pansies that we scarcely expect the family to include woody plants. To the ordinary gardener, the relationship between *Hymenanthera* and *Melicytus*, from the Antipodes, and *Viola* is not discernible. *Hymenanthera* is a genus of angular, rigid, fat-stemmed semi-evergreen shrubs with small leaves, extremely insignificant flowers, and curious white and dull purple berries. The three species I have grown do not differ greatly one from the other: *H. crassifolia* is low and wide-spreading, with blunt leaves; *H. angustifolia* is narrower in leaf and more upright in habit; and *H. obovata* has larger leaves which are occasionally toothed at the margins. The one species of *Melicytus* I have grown is a large shrub, much larger than the hymenantheras: *M. ramiflorus* has lanceolate, toothed leaves and tiny, greenish flowers turning to violet or dark indigo berries.

There are always some shrubs too individualistic to be corralled into the categories an author has arbitrarily decided upon, and so I will now round them up, to conclude this chapter. By a quirk of botanical naming three genera that have so far eluded my pen begin with the letter M, and I sometimes have to think for a moment to be sure I am not confusing *Melicytus* and *Melicope*. It is only the similarity of name that trips me; they are quite different to look upon, and are in entirely different botanical families, *Melicope* being in Rutaceae. The large, semi-persistent leaves of *Melicope ternata* are trifoliolate, the flowers greenish-white, in autumn. Most of the species of *Meliosma*, natives of the Far East, are handsome in leaf and have spiraea-like plumes of white flowers. Most, too, are hardy, and I shall not enumerate them. *M. veitchiorum* earns a mention for its striking appearance both in leaf and when bare in winter, for the stout, rigid branches form a decorative pattern, and the pinnate leaves are very large. The creamy-white, fragrant flowers ('meliosma' means smelling of honey) are followed by violet fruits. The more tender *M. myriantha* has simple, sharply toothed leaves, and broad panicles of many small, greenish-yellow, sweetly scented flowers at midsummer, followed by little round, red fruits. *Mallotus japonicus*, though widespread in the Far East, is also rather tender; it is a handsome foliage plant in the spurge family, with large, rounded leaves and large sprays of small flowers.

Another very fine foliage tree from the milder parts of the Far East, extending as far south as Malaysia, is *Rhus succedanea*. Like others of its kind it has large, pinnate leaves, deep green above, colouring brilliantly in autumn, an attribute more associated with woody plants from colder areas. The wax yielded by the fruits of the female tree was once used for making candles in Japan, much as the fragrant wax from the berries of the North American and Caribbean *Myrica cerifera* is used.

Most gardeners will be painfully familiar with the rubus tribe which, in the shape of seedling brambles, can be a menacing weed among shrubs where it can grow large enough to form deep, tenacious roots before its thorny tops are noticed. Familiarity with the New Zealand brambles is painfully earned too; yet the almost leafless species, with their white or cream prickles and tangled, scrambling stems, have a bizarre fascination. They are changeable creatures, depending on their habitat, and I have never fully got to grips with their nomenclature; but I will describe as best I can those I have grown. The most distinct in my mind is *Rubus squarrosus* (*R. cissoides pauperatus*), which is apparently a tall climber with foliage in its native forests, but, if growing in the open, forms the low, spreading, skeletonized shrub which I know, without flowers but with masses of creamy-yellow prickles. *R. cissoides* itself is easily confused with *R. australis*; both are as prickly as *R. squarrosus* but not leafless, and the flowers may be followed by orange-red fruits like wan blackberries. The berries of *R. schmidelioides* are edible, but this is a potentially rampant and very prickly climber, so there seems little justification for substituting it for the native bramble unless in a spirit of enquiry. It has crossed with *R.*

parvus to produce *R.* × *barkeri*, which has pretty saw-toothed foliage, narrowly arrowhead-shaped, of a rather bronzed green, brick-red when young in full sun; like *R. parvus* itself it forms a more modest, procumbent shrub with small prickles. To admire the Himalayan *R. lineatus* there is no need to have a perverse fondness for thorns, for this beautiful foliage shrub has none. It is semi-evergreen, losing its leaves in cold winters, and needs shelter except in very mild gardens, where it forms a graceful shrub with slender silky-hairy stems up to 3 m/10 ft long, set with leaves each composed of five palmately disposed leaflets. Each leaflet has up to fifty parallel, impressed vein pairs; the undersurface is silvery-white, with a glossy silken sheen.

V

Using Walls

WALLS represent opportunities. Apart from considerations of garden design, they extend the range of plants that you can grow, whatever your climate, their shelter helping some to survive, others to reach their potential; they retain and reverberate the heat of the sun, so that plants not necessarily frost-tender, but demanding a thorough summer ripening, can be induced to flower abundantly when in the open garden they might simply run to leaf. But they may also represent problems. In a windy garden there may be eddies and down-draughts on the leeward of a wall that are almost as destructive as the wind you are seeking to escape. The soil at the foot of a wall, especially house walls, is often very dry, and may be contaminated with builders' rubble, which may raise the pH of the soil to unacceptably high levels or contain undesirable chemicals from the materials used in construction. And some walls are difficult to fit with the trellis or wires that you need to support your chosen climbers. But gardeners who are determined to make the most of their garden will always contrive ways of getting round such obstacles.

Foundation planting

Virtually every house has some wall space that could be used to give shelter to a tender shrub or support to a climber. With house walls, more than with any others you may have in your garden (boundary walls, walls of sheds and outhouses, the enclosing walls of gardens within gardens . . .), you need to consider whether you will use them as a congenial home for all sorts of plants too tender to risk in the open garden, or decide that aesthetics must triumph. If the second, then you will seek to create what has aptly been called foundation planting. You will be looking for shrubs and climbers that will decoratively clothe the walls, and will reject any plant that does not look respectable all year. You will not welcome the prospect of starting all over again if a severe winter wipes out an established shrub, so you will avoid anything likely to be tender, however that may be defined in your own garden climate. Your house will never be clad in the untidy stems of something that cannot be cut back until spring is well advanced, lest a late frost kill it, nor with a shrub or climber that in four years out of five hardly flowers at all. But you may miss a lot of fun, and you will not know the thrill, in the one year out of five, of seeing what that climber can do if sun and wind and weather all combine in just the right proportions. Compromise is called for, in gardening as in life: some of your plants can be chosen for reliability, some in the spirit of adventure.

Many of the shrubs described in the previous chapter as dominant, and some of those with the quality of balance, can be grown as wall shrubs; they would not disgrace any house. Most houses, indeed, are the better for some concealing foliage; few of us live in mansions so elegant or so architecturally important that they are best left unadorned. To these shrubs we can add climbers with the same quality of looking well all year. Evergreen climbers with good foliage, and preferably with good flowers too in their season, should be the first choice for the walls either side of a front door; the wrong choice for this important position may haunt you for years. Any of the trachelospermums, if your wall is sunny or only half shaded, would be a good choice. These jasmine-like climbers are related to periwinkle, and have the propellor-shaped flowers common to the genus. They are twining and self-clinging, though some are more efficient self-stickers than others. The species best able to cling to the wall by its aerial roots is *Trachelospermum asiaticum* (*T. divaricatum*, *T. crocostemon*), which has polished, abundant dark green foliage, quite small and neat, as the setting for very sweetly scented, creamy-white flowers aging to Naples yellow in late summer. It is tidier in growth than *T. jasminoides*, which has larger leaves of shining dark green, and larger, whiter flowers with the same strong, sweet perfume. Its form 'Variegatum' has foliage bordered and splashed with cream often turning to crimson-pink in winter. The plant known as *T. majus* in gardens is of obscure origin; the name correctly belongs to a variant of *T. asiaticum*, but the gardener's *T. majus* is a vigorous, tall climber, larger in leaf even than *T. jasminoides*, frequently turning blood-red in winter.

In the mainly tropical family Lardizabalaceae are some genera of vigorous twining evergreens suitable for mild areas. In time, and if neglected, they may become untidy, with a mass of tangled stems and dead foliage; but well-cared-for they are handsome in leaf and deliciously fragrant, though not showy, in flower. *Stauntonia hexaphylla* and the holboellias are very alike, with large, leathery, dark green compound leaves; the flowers are whitish, flushed with mauve or brown. The first to flower is *Holboellia latifolia*, in early spring; the male flowers are greenish white, the female purple-flushed. *H. coriacea* and the stauntonia follow in mid-spring; again, the holboellia's flowers differ in colour between male and female, while those of the stauntonia, also differentiated sexually, are of the same mauve-flushed white whether male or female. In sunny summers, and especially if the flowers are hand-pollinated, the fleshy, purple sausage-shaped fruits may form; they are said to be edible. *Lardizabala biternata* is more tender, needing a Mediterranean climate to do well; the chocolate-purple and white flowers open in winter, the male flowers held in long, hanging spikes and the female solitary. Again, in long hot summers they may be followed by edible, purple pods. The glossy, persistent leaves are composed of from three to nine oblong leaflets.

Gelsemium sempervirens is so like a jasmine that it is a surprise to learn it is related to *Buddleja*. It is a twining evergreen climber, with narrow, shining green leaves, and clusters of fragrant, yellow, trumpet-shaped flowers in late spring or early summer. The appeal of *Kadsura japonica*, a more slender, smaller-growing climber than this, lies as much in the scarlet fruits borne on female plants as in the fragrant cream flowers that open in summer. The lanceolate leaves are shining green and may turn red in autumn. By contrast *Cissus striata* is grown solely for its luxuriant, polished green, deeply cut leaves borne on zigzag stems; the fruits are like bunches of red currants. It needs a very warm, sheltered wall. Also from South America is the hardier *Ercilla volubilis* (*Bridgesia spicata*), a pleasant self-clinging evergreen with rich green, rounded leaves and dense spikes of small purple-flushed flowers in spring. It is suprisingly wind-tolerant, and can be grown in half shade. *Elytropus chilensis* needs a sheltered wall and prefers semi-shade; it is a vigorous, twining evergreen, with small white, lilac-flushed flowers in spring among the bristly, fringed leaves. Even deep shade will suit *Ficus pumila*, a self-sticker with small, two-ranked, heart-shaped leaves in the juvenile stage, and much larger (up to 10cm/4in long) mature foliage, of rich dark green. A garden form, 'Minima', has very small juvenile leaves. When suited, this little fig makes intricately patterned dense cover.

The portmanteau family Liliaceae has been reviewed lately by botanists, and broken down into more manageable parts, so that no longer do *Agapanthus* and *Kniphofia* rub shoulders with *Ruscus* and *Lapageria*. Though a climber, the last is not so easy that you can expect it to make ample evergreen cover unless in just the right conditions, and it must therefore wait until a later chapter. But *Ruscus* has a close relative from the Canary Islands, *Semele androgyna*, which is like a luxuriant climbing butcher's broom with evergreen stems and handsome large cladodes like polished green leaves. Also formerly in Liliaceae, and now in its own family Smilacaceae, the genus *Smilax* has some members with attractive evergreen foliage; but they have prickly stems, apt to grow into a tangle. With that caveat, you might want to try *S. aspera*, from the Mediterranean area and the Canary Islands, for its glossy, leathery leaves, which vary in shape from lanceolate to cordate; or *S. excelsa*, which is hardier, and has handsome pointed leaves.

The foliage of *Clematis armandii* is often cited as an asset, for it is evergreen, and the large, oblong leaflets are glossy and leathery in texture; but it does need grooming to remain respectable. If you are prepared to give it this regular attention, then by all means grow it in an important position, especially if you can obtain one of the named forms such as 'Snowdrift' or pink-budded 'Apple Blossom'. These can be relied upon to give you good, vanilla-scented blossom in spring; seedlings may turn out very dowdy in flower.

It is sad that the evergreen climbing hydrangeas with pink flowers are probably too tender for any garden where frosts occur, no matter how slight. But the Mexican *Hydrangea seemannii* appears suprisingly hardy, and makes a valuable addition to the range of evergreen, self-clinging climbers with good foliage. The white flowers, set off by its bold leaves, follow the usual hydrangea system of large sterile florets among the small, fertile ones.

Flowering Climbers

When it comes to adorning your walls with climbers selected chiefly for their flowers, then the choice is very wide. You will be able to select from the best of the honeysuckles, jasmines and roses, clematis and passion flowers and the trumpet-flowered climbers in Bignoniaceae, as well as many lesser genera. As to roses, I will refer you to Chapter VI where the Banksian and tea roses are described, and to Chapter VIII for some synstylae roses needing shelter and more space than the average house wall can offer. That leaves me just a few to deal with here. The Macartney rose, *Rosa bracteata*, is a slightly tender Chinese species, very beautiful with its dark, gleaming evergreen foliage and white, lemon-scented flowers with saffron-yellow stamens, set in conspicuous leafy bracts. Also Chinese is *R. laevigata*, which has so established itself in the United States that it is known as the Cherokee rose. Less wholeheartedly evergreen, it has glossy dark foliage and large, single, creamy-white flowers with a delicious perfume, borne early in the season. Its hybrid with, apparently, *R. gigantea* is known as 'Cooper's Burmese Rose'; this has much of the vigour of the second-named parent, but resembles *R. laevigata* in leaf, with large pure white flowers that are only slightly fragrant. Also descended from *R. laevigata* are two exquisite pink roses, *R.* 'Anemona' which is very like *R.*

laevigata itself except that the wide single flowers, borne over a long season, are clear pink with a pale silvery reverse; and the deeper sport 'Ramona', its rich carmine petals backed with silvery buff.

The most magnificent of all honeysuckles is *Lonicera hildebrandiana*, a tall species from Burma, Thailand and south-western China with large, evergreen leaves and hand's-length, fragrant, creamy-white flowers aging to warm yellow. Of more manageable size, the Spanish *L. splendida* is beautiful in bright glaucous blue leaf; the fragant flowers are purplish-red and appear in summer. Although it is nothing much in flower, I have a fondness for *L. giraldii*, on account of its softly furry evergreen leaves, which form a dense covering to the twining stems.

In a mild garden *Clematis paniculata* (often still called *C. indivisa*) is as free with its pure white flowers as *C. montana* in colder areas. It is a fine evergreen New Zealand species flowering in late spring. Other New Zealand species are less showy, but very appealing at close quarters. The finely cut evergreen foliage of *C. australis* sets off fragrant, creamy-green starry flowers in spring; *C. fosteri* is much the same in colour, with a fragrance of lemon verbena, and the foliage is fresh apple-green. The Himalayan *C. napaulensis* is applied to *C. cirrhosa*, and like that species flowers in winter; the blooms are creamy-yellow bells with purple stamens. Also from Nepal is *C. phlebantha*, a summer-flowering, trailing species with silvery-silky stems and leaves; the flowers are creamy-white with red veining. The South African *C. brachiata* has green-tinted white flowers with a prominent brush of sharp yellow stamens, borne in autumn; they are sweetly scented.

The scented jasmines, whether tender or not, need sun to flower freely. One of the most familiar of the frost-sensitive species is *Jasminum polyanthum*, sold as young flowering pot plants by every florist in winter. Outside, in a sheltered position, the dark evergreen pinnate leaves set off bright pink buds, opening, from spring until summer, into powerfully fragrant white flowers. Other tender species need even more protection from frost, but where they do well, they will fill the air with their perfume. The genus is cosmopolitan: *J. dispermum* is a Himalayan species with white or blush flowers, *J. simplicifolium* ssp. *suavissimum* (*J. suavissimum*, *J. lineatum*), which flowers in late summer and has long narrow leaves, is Australian. From South Africa comes *J. angulare*, a species with dark evergreen trifoliolate leaves and large panicles of white flowers in late summer. The foliage of *J. azoricum*, a Madeiran species, is similar; the white flowers open from purple-flushed buds in summer and on into winter. More tender even than these is the Indian *J. sambac*, an evergreen species with glossy, unlobed leaves and intensely fragrant flowers, opening white and blushing pink as they age, borne almost continuously where the climate permits. 'Grand Duke' is a double-flowered form. In mild gardens, the familiar, showy but scentless *Jasminum nudiflorum* can be replaced by *J. mesnyi* (*J. primulinum*), the primrose jasmine, which has larger, semi-double flowers borne in spring among evergreen, trifoliolate leaves. *J. floridum* flowers in late summer; its yellow flowers are small but abundant.

The passion flower most familiar to gardeners in cool climates is *Passiflora caerulea*, a very vigorous climber with much divided, dark green leaves and flowers composed of white tepals surrounding the blue, purple and white corona. The blooms open over a long season, though only in bright weather, and in hot summers are followed by orange, egg-shaped fruits. The curious structure, said to have reminded Spanish priests in South America of the instruments of Christ's passion, is very clearly seen in this, the hardiest of passion flowers: the ten tepals represent ten apostles, the corona – the ring of filaments within the tepals – the crown of thorns, the five stamens the five wounds, and the three stigmas the three nails. 'Constance Elliott' is a white-flowered cultivar of the blue passion flower; its hybrid with *P. quadrangularis*, *P.* 'Allardii', more nearly resembles the hardier parent and has inherited much of its frost resistance; the flowers are larger, white or blush pink with a blue and white corona, and open in late summer and autumn. They are subtly fragrant in the warm still air. *P. quadrangularis* itself is the giant granadilla, so called because of the size of its fruits; the large flowers are white or pink, with a blue, white and purple corona. *P.* × *caerulea-racemosa* is another hybrid of the blue passion flower, vigorous and fairly frost-hardy; the flowers composed of lilac tepals and purple corona open over a long summer season. *P. racemosa*, the other half of this hybrid, is very vigorous indeed, though not very frost-resistant, and bears its flowers in terminal racemes, not singly. They are rich scarlet, starry confections with purple, white-tipped filaments. *P. quadrangularis* and *P. racemosa* are united in the fine hybrid *P.* × *caponii* 'John Innes', which has large claret-purple and white flowers. Somewhere between this and the blue passion flower in hardiness is *P. edulis*, the granadilla, which produces the passion fruits sold by greengrocers. The flowers are white with a green reverse, the corona composed of curly white, purple-banded filaments. In hot summers it freely produces fruit, and even in a mild maritime garden I have had a ripe crop from it. Depending on the variety, the fruits may be the brownish purple of those you see in greengrocers, or larger and yellow.

The passifloras with long-tubed flowers were formerly classed as *Tacsonia*; they come from the warmer areas of Central rather than South America, and are correspondingly less able to resist frost. One of the hardiest is *P. umbilicata*, with amethyst-purple flowers; it is vigorous and fast-growing, and flourished in Norman Hadden's garden at Porlock on the north Somerset coast of western England. The pink-flowered *P. mollissima* is so vigorous as to have become a pest in warm countries, but even a light frost will knock it back. But on a very warm and sheltered wall it may well survive to produce its large hanging flowers, opening in succession from midsummer until late in autumn. One of the most beautiful species of the *Tacsonia* type is *P. antioquiensis* (*Tacsonia vanvolxemii*), which has large, rich, rose-carmine flowers with a small violet corona, hanging singly on long stalks in late summer and autumn. This species is characterized by foliage of two types, unlobed leaves, and leaves composed of three long, slender, pointed lobes. A hybrid between *P. mollissima* and *P. antioquiensis* was raised by Messrs Veitch of Exeter in 1870 and bears the name *P. × exoniensis*; it is vigorous, free-flowering and beautiful, with rose pink flowers and downy, three-lobed leaves.

Several climbers in the bignonia family are not so much tender as sun-loving, needing a long hot summer to flower freely. Such are the species and hybrids of *Campsis*, never so spectacular in oceanic climates where the summer skies are grey as in more southerly gardens. The Chinese *C. grandiflora* has, as its name suggests, the largest flowers, orange in the throat, with flared, orange-apricot lobes; it is not a very efficient self-sticker. *C. radicans*, a North American species, is much better at clinging to a wall without assistance; in the type, the flowers are scarlet-lobed, and there is a beautiful soft yellow form *flava*. The hybrid between the two has justly become popular for its good temper and willingness to produce plenty of its salmon-orange trumpets even under the grey skies of England; it is only a shame it bears the cumbersome name of *C. × tagliabuana* 'Madame Galen'. *Bignonia capreolata*, the only species left in the genus which gave its name to the whole family, is an evergreen tendril climber from the south-eastern United States, very splendid when it has enough sun to produce plenty of its vermilion-orange, flared trumpets.

The Brazilian *Pyrostegia venusta* is more tender, needing shelter as well as sun. It is a vigorous tendril climber, the rich orange, tubular flowers opening in late winter and spring. *Tecomaria capensis*, from South Africa, is perhaps a little hardier, though still needing a warm sunny wall; its vivid scarlet trumpets are produced in late summer and autumn on self-clinging, twining stems. Colour forms have been named 'Apricot', vivid red 'Coccinea', deep yellow 'Lutea' and 'Salmonea' with pale coral flowers. The cat's-claw vine, *Doxantha capreolata*, climbs by means of hooked tendrils; its bright yellow funnels open in late spring and summer. The Australian *Pandorea jasminoides* departs from the usual bright colouring, for its flared trumpets are white or blush-pink, with a crimson stain at the heart. It is much less vigorous, indeed barely a climber at all. New Zealand also has its own species, *Tecomanthe speciosa*, a beautiful twining climber with glossy, leathery leaves and many-flowered clusters of cream corollas shaded with green in velvety calyces, from late spring to high summer.

The easiest of the bignonia family is *Eccremocarpus scaber*, often grown as an annual but well able to survive year after year in warm gardens. As well as the type, which has hanging clusters of narrow, curved tubes of tawny orange lipped with yellow, there are available the coppery-crimson var. *carmineus* and amber-yellow var. *aureus*; new seed strains are said to include cherry-red, pink and cream as well.

Wall shrubs and climbers in association

It is time, I think, to have a break from climbers, and to consider instead some of the tender shrubs that can be used, with these or other climbers of lesser genera, in the shelter of your walls. With the blues and lilacs and rosy purples of the passion flowers, toning shades of rose and magenta and lavender, with grey foliage, are needed. A shrub which fulfils both requirements is *Desmodium praestans*; on a wall it may grow to 3m/10ft, its stems set with leaves usually of one single, large, rounded leaflet, occasionally trifoliate with two much smaller side leaflets. Whichever style it adopts, the leaves are grey-felted. The purple-pink pea-flowers are borne in long dense panicles from autumn until discouraged by the frosts of winter.

The potato flowers of most solanums are nearer to pure violet in colour. *Solanum aviculare* and *S. laciniatum* are closely allied (the latter is sometimes said to be a tetraploid form of *S. aviculare*), both forming deciduous, thornless shrubs growing to about 2·4m/8ft, with lanceolate or lobed leaves and abundant violet-blue flowers, up to 5cm/2in wide in *S. laciniatum*, during summer and autumn. Orange-yellow egg-shaped fruits follow; new plants can be raised from the seeds they contain, and often appear spontaneously. *S. rantonettii* is smaller, at 1–1·5,/3¼–5ft, and like these two may behave almost herbaceously if its soft-wooded stems are cut by frost, though it is less hardy than they. The leaves have wavy margins, and are drawn out to a long point; the flowers are violet with the usual yellow pointel at the centre, and the showy fruits are bright red. The deciduous, suckering *S. valdiviense* is twice as tall as this, with clusters of small, fragrant lilac to white flowers all along the stems in summer followed by pea-sized green fruits. Palest of all is *Solanum jasminoides*, a milky or slate blue in the type and white in 'Album', in which the bright yellow central cone of stamens is especially showy by contrast. It is a climbing species which fails to compete with the jasmines that it superficially resembles only because it is scentless: indeed, all you will get from it is the sour solanaceous smell if you bruise the leaves. But perhaps the finest of the solanums that can be attempted outside in a mild oceanic climate, with all the shelter that can be contrived, is the climbing *S.*

wendlandii, which has branching clusters of large, lilac-blue flowers in late summer.

In hot, dry climates, *Mackaya bella* (*Asystasia bella*) is recommended for shade, but as a South African native it is likely to need plenty of sun in gardens with an oceanic climate; though it does like a stiff, loamy soil and resents summer drought. The 5cm/2in flowers, in loose terminal sprays, are shaped a little like the trumpets of a *Campsis*, but they are quite different in colour, pale lilac veined with purple. Also from South Africa is a shrubby senecio, *Senecio glastifolius*, which, unlike the New Zealand species, has lilac-pink daisy flowers in summer; it grows to about 1·5m/5ft and is surprisingly hardy.

By comparison with all this exuberance, the flowers of *Abelia floribunda* and of *Cantua buxifolia* are small. They are not for anyone who is shy of magenta; for both are vividly coloured, and the cantua even adds a splash of orange to the tips of its sheeny tubular flowers, which open in late spring. It is virtually evergreen, with neat, finely toothed foliage, and the flowers hang gracefully from horizontal shoots. *Abelia floribunda* flowers later, from midsummer, its bright cherry-magenta tubular flowers, shaped like a triphylla fuchsia's, nodding among glossy pointed leaves. I like to see this assertive colour set among the pure pale blue of *Plumbago auriculata* (*P. capensis*), a scrambling shrub which flowers freely from late spring to autumn and can be trained to a wall, or encouraged to form a little standard tree in the manner of a fuchsia. When it is allowed to scramble over supporting wires on a wall, then I like to plant *Rhodochiton atrosanguineum* to twine through it. This Mexican climber can be raised annually from seed to flower in its first year, but in mild climates should survive the winters. The heart-shaped leaves are tinted with purple, but it is the flowers that catch the eye, despite their muted colouring. Each papery, pale, red-purple calyx is shaped like an umbrella, from the centre of which hangs a long-tubed, almost black, five-lobed corolla. Their season is long, and they are followed by balloon-like seed capsules filled with little flat seeds.

Another twining climber that can be raised each year from seed is *Oxypetalum coeruleum* (*Tweedia caerulea*) from South America. It is more modest in growth, and entirely charming with its grey, soft, heart-shaped leaves and fleshy, sky-blue flowers that as they fade are tinged with pink. It is in the same family, Asclepiadeaceae, as *Araujia sericofera*, called the cruel plant because of the way night-flying moths, seeking nectar, are trapped by the tongue in its white or mauve-pink flowers. This too can be quickly and easily raised from seed, but is reasonably hardy on a sheltered wall, and much finer once established. The twining stems bear persistent, grey-green leaves; the saucer-shaped flowers are slightly fragrant. The name *Wattakaka* might suggest that this is an antipodean genus;

but the specific epithet of *W. sinensis* (*Dregea sinensis*) tells us that this asclepiad is a Chinese native. A twining climber needing a sheltered wall, it has downy umbels of fragrant white hoya-like flowers, each with a central zone of red freckles, in summer, and leaves which are grey-downy on the undersides. In the same soft-coloured theme is *Alstroemeria pelegrina*, which opens its lilac-pink or white, freckled flowers in early summer. Here too you might find a place for some of the frail and lovely *Gladiolus* species: *G. carinatus* perhaps, the mauve Afrikana, which has fragrant, chartreuse and lilac flowers; or *G. undulatus*, with green-washed, white, cream or soft pink flowers stained with deep pink on the lower segments.

The twining pink bindweeds, *Convolvulus althaeoides* and *C. elegantissimus*, found their way into Chapter III, and are in any case not really wall plants. But the Japanese *Calystegia pubescens* is a beautiful, rather tender herbaceous climber that could well twine through a wall shrub to display its double, rose-pink flowers. Beth Chatto has allowed it to mingle with *Clematis florida* 'Sieboldii', which has creamy-white flowers filled with a central boss of purple stamens. The Chilean *Lathyrus pubescens* also needs some shelter; a perennial pea, it has lilac or lavender-blue flowers.

With these pretty climbers, shrubs that might be overshadowed by the dramatic passion flowers can find congenial companions. From South Africa comes *Sutera grandiflora*, which is related to penstemons and foxgloves, but has flowers that are more phlox-like, clear mauve over greygreen foliage in summer. It grows to about 90cm/3ft. Also South African, *Bowkeria gerardiana* is an evergreen with small, white flowers pouched like little calceolarias, dotted about the bush in summer. It has an unpleasant smell. The Australian boronias, on the other hand, are grown for their fragrance; W. Arnold-Forster goes so far as to say that 'no shrub has a sweeter, more memorable smell' than *Boronia megastigma*. The little chocolate cups hanging on thread-like stalks are not showy; the clear citronyellow waxy bells of the form 'Lutea' stand out better among the fresh green needle leaves. 'Heaven Scent' may be a form or a hybrid of *B. megastigma*; it has chocolate bells, shaded yellow inside, and a delicious fragrance. If you cannot catch the perfume, it may be that you are one of the people who are, it seems, genetically incapable of smelling it; if you can, you will surely want to collect other boronias, such as *B. heterophylla* which has shiny, pinnate leaves and carmine-pink bells closed at the mouth. In the same family as the boronias, Rutaceae – in which are many species with aromatic foliage – the South African coleonemas need a warm sheltered position. *Coleonema album* is a pretty, aromatic shrublet with abundant starry white flowers in spring; the taller, less compact *C. pulchrum*, which may grow to 1·8m/6ft, has pink flowers borne in late spring and early summer with great freedom. The Cape heaths themselves were once extremely popular as conservatory plants; now that conservatories are again becoming common, the Cape heaths may once again be taken up by nurserymen. Meanwhile, gardeners in mild areas have continued to grow not only the hardiest of them, *Erica canaliculata*, which is described in the next chapter, but also *E. pageana*, which bears its bright yellow, faintly scented flowers in cylindrical spikes at the branch tips in spring. There are many others that may be worth trying; they extend the colour-range to scarlet, crimson and green, as well as yellow.

In Australia, as already noted, the family Epacridaceae fills the niche that Ericaceae occupies in the northern hemisphere. Like the Cape heaths, the genus *Epacris* was at one time much grown in conservatories, and early gardening literature lists a great many with Latin names that seem in fact to be hybrids or cultivars, as well as some with vernacular names such as 'Diadem' in rosy-pink and 'Mont Blanc' in white. Most *Epacris* hybrids apparently derive from *E. impressa*, an upright, heath-like shrub of 90cm/3ft or so, with nodding tubular bells of pure white, cream, pink or deep red in a one-sided spike during winter and early spring. Another, perhaps worth trying in a hot sunny position against a wall, is *E. longiflora*, which bears its tubular, scarlet flowers, each tipped with white, in spring; its hardiness rating is Z9–10, which is better than the outright Z10 of some of the shrubs I have succeeded with in a mild coastal garden. The same rating is ascribed to *E. purpurascens*, which has white flowers aging to purple-pink in spring; a double form is described by W. Arnold-Forster as 'very long flowering and reliable'.

The myrtle family is widely represented in Australasia; I have already described not only the shrubs recognizable as myrtles, but also the bottle brushes and *Metrosideros*. *Calytrix sullivanii*, which I believe may now have been absorbed into *C. tetragona*, is a heath-like shrub betraying its affinities in the myrtle fragrance of the leaves; the starry white or pink flowers are borne in abundance in spring, and after they fall the reddish calyces remain to add colour to the bush for weeks. *C. alpestris* (*Lhotskya alpestris*) is a little taller at 1·5m/5ft, with star-like white flowers in spring, very bright against the heathy dark green foliage.

It is slightly unexpected to find a member of the myrtle family with leaves smelling like peppermint, but so it is with *Agonis flexuosa*, a graceful little tree with long and very slender, pointed leaves on half-weeping branches. The small, fragrant white flowers, gathered into globular heads, are borne in spring. *A. marginata*, which flowers in winter, has broader leaves and clusters of small white flowers with dark red centres.

The small, heath-like *Pomaderris phylicifolia* has woolly shoots and linear leaves, almost hidden in spring by the wide clusters of many tiny, creamy-yellow flowers. The brightest of the genus is *P. kumeraho*, a shrub or small tree of 2–3m/6½–10ft, with oval leaves, blue-green above and pale felted below; the bright yellow flowers form fuzzy rounded clusters up to

10cm/4in wide. Taller again, *P. apetala* has toothed leaves that are wrinkled above and felted below; the large panicles of creamy- to mustard-yellow flowers appear in summer. Another worth trying in the poor soil and sun that suits the genus is *P. elliptica*, a shrub of 1–2m/3¼–6½ft with leaves densely white felted beneath, and flat clusters of pale yellow flowers. I should like to see the later-flowering pomaderrises paired, in the hope that their seasons would coincide, with the bluebell creepers, Australian climbers with slender, twining stems. *Sollya heterophylla* (*S. fusiformis*) has sky-blue bells in summer and autumn; *S. parviflora* (*S. drummondii*), with very narrow leaves, has smaller, royal-blue flowers. They are easy to raise from seed and will stand a few degrees of frost. The related billardieras are also twining climbers of restrained growth; the flared bells are lime-green, but it is the fruits of *Billardiera longiflora* that catch the eye, gleaming oblong dark blue (or sometimes red, purple or white) fleshy-seeming capsules that are in fact dry, the seeds rattling audibly inside. *B. scandens* has green and yellow fruits. Among these dainty things I like to set *Gladiolus tristis*, of all the species I have grown perhaps the most appealing on account of its delectable clove perfume, strongest at night. It comes in two colour-forms: clotted cream flushed with green on the lower segments and feathered with tan on the buds and the upper segments; or unmarked cream faintly flushed with green. It has given rise to many hybrids, including the Nanus hybrids briefly described in Chapter III, and the entirely lovely, pale 'Christabel'. *G. citrinus* is brighter, a decided yellow with sombre purple-brown marks in the throat.

Slender climbers that will not smother or choke the smaller wall shrubs are always welcome. One that is scarcely a climber, and needs ample frost protection, is *Sandersonia aurantiaca*. Related to the gloriosa lilies, and of similar growth, it has clear tangerine Chinese-lantern flowers. The frail stems of *Tropaeolum tricolor* are set with small, trefoil leaves and scarlet, snub-nosed flowers tipped with black, opening from late winter onwards. The bomareas, which are in effect climbing alstroemerias, are more vigorous, but the twining stems die back to tuberous roots each winter. Their flowers are narrow tubes, less flared at the lobes than the alstroemerias', but like those, freckled with contrasting colours. The most colourful of those I have grown is *Bomerea kalbreyeri*; my plant had vivid orange flowers in large, open clusters. The closely related *B. caldasii* has yellow flowers flushed with orange, or wholly orange-red, the inner petals flecked with greenish-brown. The frost-resistant hybrid *B. × cantabrigiensis* is of quieter colouring, inviting you to peer closely but making no show at a distance. Another herbaceous climber of great charm is the Californian *Dicentra chrysantha*, which has palely glaucous, ferny foliage and bright yellow lockets in upright clusters in summer. It pulls itself up through its supporting host by leaf-tip tendrils. Also Californian is *Dichelostemma volubile*, which is a cormous relative of *Brodiaea*. Its colouring does not fit well here, for it has nodding pink flowers on long twining stems.

There are plenty of wall shrubs that will not clash with these hot-coloured climbers. *Abutilon megapotamicum* is a shrub with slender, lax stems and dark evergreen arrowhead leaves; the waisted, hanging flowers have deep red calyces and narrow yellow skirts from which emerge the club-shaped purple cluster of stamens and stigma. Its hybrid with *A. pictum*, *A.* × *milleri*, is more graceful in flower, the amber, red-veined flowers more widely flared. Very similar to this are two cultivars between which I find it impossible to distinguish, 'Kentish Belle' and 'Cynthia Pike'; both have longer, more widely flared skirts than *A.* × *milleri*, in amber-orange with crimson stamens, and decent green foliage. 'Patrick Synge' has larger burnt-orange lanterns than *A. megapotamicum*. The bell-flowered hybrid abutilons come in yellow ('Golden Fleece' and the softer butter-yellow 'Canary Bird'), deep red as in splendid, maroon-crimson 'Nabob', white ('Boule de Neige'), and the crushed strawberry or warm brick-red of 'Ashford Red'. 'Cerise Queen' has more blue in it, and 'Louise Marignac' is clear pink. All are large shrubs which if hard-pruned in spring to keep them within bounds bear enormous light green leaves overwhelming the flowers. In the same mallow family are the hibiscuses. The tropical species, with their wide bright flowers, are beyond us, but in mild gardens *Hibiscus hamabo* (which is not the same as the cultivar of *H. syriacus* which has taken the same specific name as its pet name) should survive to produce its creamy-yellow, maroon-eyed flowers in high summer.

One of the most spectacular of the caesalpinias is the rather tender *Caesalpina gilliesii* (*Poinciana gilliesii*), the South American 'bird of paradise', a large shrub not fiercely armed like the hardy *C. japonica*, but with even more elegant bipinnate foliage, and long erect racemes of as many as forty flowers, each with cupped, bright yellow petals and a conspicuous cluster of scarlet stamens up to 8cm/3¼in long. The Australian *Chorizema ilicifolium*, by contrast, belongs to the section of the Leguminosae with pea-flowers; it is a much smaller shrub with slender shoots up to 90cm/3ft long, flopping weakly onto neighbouring plants, and long trails of small flowers with terracotta standards and magenta wings. The leaves are heart-shaped and lightly toothed – or smooth-margined in the forms once described as a separate species, *C. cordatum*. The bottlebrush beaufortias are also from western Australia. *Beaufortia sparsa* grows in swampy soils in the wild, but in cultivation does much better in well-drained soils in full sun; it has small oval leaves neatly arranged in two opposite rows, and brilliant orange-scarlet flower heads in late summer. Another worth trying is *B. decussata*, a stiff shrub of 1·2m/4ft or so with pale green leaves and bright vermilion-scarlet clawed stamens. Still in this vivid colour range,

Sutherlandia frutescens is a South African shrub of upright habit, with greyish pinnate leaves to set off its large, terracotta-scarlet pea-flowers in summer. It is fast growing and easily raised from seed, always an asset if you are of an adventurous nature.

The Mexican *Bouvardia ternifolia* (*B. triphylla*) grows to about 90cm/3ft and bears showy scarlet, tubular flowers in summer and autumn. From South America comes *Fuchsia boliviana*, which has large hanging clusters of blood-red tubular flowers with reflexed sepals among greyish-green, downy leaves. Of much the same rich cinnabar-scarlet are the flowers of the Jacobean lily, *Sprekelia formosissima*, composed of slender recurved segments forming a striking pattern. *Vallota speciosa* (*Cyrtanthus purpureus*), the Scarborough lily (why such a tender exotic should be ascribed to a coldly bracing North Sea resort, I do not know) has more conventionally shaped flowers, flaring funnels of soft scarlet in early autumn; with a wall at its back it should survive and flower outside. Neither of these is a true lily, for they are not even in the lily family let alone the genus *Lilium*; both reside in Armaryllidaceae. The blandfordias or Christmas bells are lily relatives from Australia and Tasmania, slow to grow and to flower but worth the wait for their waxy, hanging flowers, 2·5cm/1in long bells of terracotta, coppery-red or warm yellow held several together on 45cm/18in stems. *Blandfordia grandiflora* is one of the most popular, but perhaps less hardy than *B. nobilis*, or the Tasmanian *B. punicea*, with waxy bells of coppery-red outside, yellow within, borne in dense racemes on 90cm/3ft stems.

I have found *Datura sanguinea* much more resistant to frost than its reputation suggests. The sinuate, light green leaves are soft to the touch, but the shrub is grown for the long, tubular, hanging, brick-red trumpets which open over a long summer season. Even if cut to the ground by frost, it will usually regenerate so long as the roots themselves are not frosted. The flowers are smaller than, and lack the powerful night fragrance of, the angel's trumpet datura, *D. suaveolens*. Here is a shrub which is so valued for the beauty of its long hanging white flowers with long-pointed, recurving lobes, that many gardeners grow it in tubs so that it can stand outside during the summer and be kept protected from frost in winter; it also does very well in a cool or unheated greenhouse, planted out in a bed. A double-flowered form is listed. *D. versicolor* has its specific name from its tendency to age from white to creamy-peach; the form 'Grand Marnier' is of a subtle pale apricot, as though the liqueur had been stirred into double cream. Others no less desirable are *D. arborea* with long, perfumed white flowers borne even in the first year from seed, yellow *D. chlorantha*, the exquisite *D. meteloides* with palest ice-lilac flowers and perhaps the most powerful fragrance of all, and *D. cornigera*, of which the double white form 'Knightii' differs from the double form of *D. suaveolens* in the much longer-drawn-out points to the lobes. If you choose to grow them from seed, give *D. stramonium* a miss; it is the thorn apple or jimson weed, with little beauty and extremely poisonous prickly fruits.

The daturas are so splendid that I am always inclined to keep them away from other shrubs that they might overshadow, or to set them near shrubs that flower at quite another season. The winter-flowering buddlejas might answer, for in their season they too are very fragrant. *Buddleja asiatica* is not brightly coloured, but its long cylindrical tassels of white flowers have as sweet a perfume as any; the long narrow leaves are white on the reverse. The more tender *B. madagascariensis* is a tall, lax evergreen with terminal panicles of yolk-yellow flowers deepening to orange, contrasting with the white stems and buds and the silvery-white reverse of the leaves. It has been known as *Nicodemia madagascariensis*, and to confuse us still further its hybrid with *B. asiatica* is sometimes called 'Nicodemus'. The accepted name is *B.* × *lewisiana* 'Margaret Pike'. By whatever name you meet it, it is a desirable addition to the range of winter-flowering shrubs, a tall shrub with long white-woolly stems and dense terminal panicles of honey-scented flowers opening palest cream and slowly aging to deep saffron-yellow.

The small genus *Luculia* includes one species which flowers in late autumn or winter. *L. gratissima* is a semi-evergreen shrub with large clusters of very fragrant, five-lobed, soft pink flowers looking almost phlox-like. *L. pinceana*, from the Khasia hills of Assam, flowers from late spring to autumn and has narrower leaves and larger flowers, opening cream and aging to pink. Perhaps the hardiest of all in this tender genus is *L. grandifolia*, a deciduous shrub which often colours vividly in autumn. The pure white, fragrant flowers are borne in very large terminal corymbs in summer. On the wall above the luculias one might try to establish one of the Chinese species of *Bauhinia*, which are seldom seen in gardens with oceanic climates despite their Z8 hardiness rating. Perhaps one reason is that *B. densiflora* is described as 'without garden merit', though its kidney-shaped leaves and white flowers are pleasing if not exciting. *B. yunnanensis* is more colourful, with blue-green leaves and longer, hanging racemes of blush-pink, purple-striped flowers. A far more appealing member of the pea family is the tender, South African *Podalyria calyptrata*, a shrub of 1–2m/$3\frac{1}{4}$–$6\frac{1}{2}$ft with silky, silvery stems and leaves, and powerfully fragrant, pale pink pea-flowers in velvety calyces in late spring and early summer. As its name implies, *P. sericea* is also silky with fine hairs, so that the leaves are like burnished silver. The fragrant mauve flowers are followed by large silvered pods.

In the same colour range, but with green leaves, are two fuchsias which look more like lilacs in flower. Both *Fuchsia paniculata* and *F. arborescens* are Mexican species with erect panicles of small magenta-pink or lilac flowers; the second is the brighter, flowering over a shorter period but with more flowers open at once. The softer pink cestrums, already described in Chapter III, could join this group also.

The hardenbergias are Australian climbers in the pea family, sometimes called native wisteria because of their sprays of violet-blue pea-flowers in spring. *Hardenbergia comptoniana* also has a pink form, 'Rosea', while *H. violacea* comes in violet, pink and white, always with a yellow blotch; the leaves are formed of a single leaflet, where *H. comptoniana* has three or five. They are well suited to trailing through other climbers, and might occupy the same stretch of sunny, sheltered wall as the passifloras, to carry the same colour theme through from spring to autumn. Most of the kennedias, by contrast, have flowers in the opposite half of the spectrum, from the scarlet of the spring-flowering coral pea, *Kennedia coccinea*, to the dusky red of *K. rubicunda*, its drooping racemes borne in early summer. In this species the young foliage is covered with soft tawny down. *K. macrophylla* has red flowers in summer among large, light green leaves, and the running postman, *K. prostrata*, has bright scarlet flowers with a yellow splash on the standard. In a warm garden it can be encouraged to cover the ground like ivy in colder areas; in bloom it becomes a sheet of vermilion. Another species that will as happily spread across the ground as climb upwards is *K. eximia*, red again. The most sombre of the genus is *K. nigricans*, with chocolate-violet and lemon flowers.

The easy way to raise these leguminous climbers is from seed. The Chilean jasmine, *Mandevilla suaveolens*, which is neither Chilean (it comes in fact from Argentina) nor a jasmine, being a member of the periwinkle family, can also be grown from seed, but this is not the way to be sure of a fine specimen: some seedlings are very reluctant to flower even when they should be fully mature, while others have poor squinny blooms. Someone should select and name a clone with good, broad-petalled flowers and propagate it from cuttings. The pure white blooms open from narrow, pointed, creamy buds during summer, and are followed by those seductive, twinned pods, filled with the seeds, reclining in their silky fluff, from which you can so easily make a whole forest of mandevillas. The foliage is pretty, the long, narrowly heart-shaped leaves of a dark, bronzed green that makes the glistening flowers all the whiter by contrast. Despite its origins it is a surprisingly hardy plant, more so than *M. splendens* (*Dipladenia splendens*) which has luxuriant pink or carmine flowers: 'Alice du Pont' is a named hybrid which is said to be fragrant, though I cannot catch the scent, although I have no difficulty detecting the faint sweet perfume of *M. suaveolens*. The New Zealand *Parsonsia heterophylla* is another climber in the periwinkle family with fragrant white flowers; they are small, but borne in large clusters among leaves which alter from the juvenile state, when they are long and narrow, to the shorter, elliptical mature foliage. Warm shade seems to suit it better than baking sun, although in the wild it is found in coastal scrub as well as at forest margins.

Lemon verbena, *Aloysia triphylla (Lippia citriodora)* is such a familiar plant that it seems always to have been with us; and indeed it was introduced from Chile as long ago as 1784. Its appeal lies solely in the sharp-sweet lemon fragrance of the leaves; the airy sprays of little lilac flowers are, at best, quite pretty. Plant it, if you can, where you will brush against it, or can easily reach for a leaf to crush, to inhale that aroma. Because its looks are so understated, it can be paired with something quite bold, as it might be the bigeneric hybrid × *Halimiocistus wintonensis*. This rather pernickety shrub is worth cosseting for its large white sunrose flowers, which are marked with a crimson-maroon zone and a bright yellow basal blotch on each petal, making a three-banded effect. Even more beautiful is the sport 'Merrist Wood Cream', identical but that the ground colour of the petals is that of clotted cream, set off by the same soft grey-green foliage.

Another companion for the halimiocistus might be *Psoralea pinnata*, a small shrub with very pretty pinnate leaves and blue pea-flowers striped with white, very freely borne in clusters among the leaves at midsummer. This species is South African; the taller *P. glandulosa*, from South America, is said to have both tender and hardier forms. The trifoliolate leaves are not so elegant, but the blue and white pea-flowers are crowded into a spike as much as 12·5cm/5in long. Blue and yellow, so long as neither is too insistent, is always a popular combination, and the yellow might come from one of the hibbertias. These evergreens from Australia, if well protected at the root, will often grow away from ground level even if the top growth is cut by frost. *Hibbertia cuneiformis (Candollea cuneiformis)* is shrubby, growing to 1·8m/6ft, with wedge-shaped leaves and clear yellow five-petalled flowers; it is very tolerant of the dry soils that often are found at the foot of a wall. The climbing *H. scandens (H. volubilis)* will grow tall on a sunny wall where it has a supporting shrub to twine through; the young foliage is bronzed, the bright yellow flowers are borne over a long summer season. The other species I have grown, *H. dentata*, is a less determined climber with attractive foliage of coppery-green, softly downy. The flowers are a deeper yellow and open in spring and summer.

A nodding, tubular flower is always seductive in contrast to the flaunting wide-open style of bloom. This must be why the correas have such a hold on my heart. Evergreen shrubs of modest, or at least manageable, size, often with thick, felted foliage, they come in a range of colours to fit any scheme you may contrive, and flower as the spirit moves them from winter through to summer. *Correa alba* is creamy-white, the narrow bells with widely reflexed lobes firm-textured and downy among almost circular, white-felted leaves. Several species have flowers of soft greenish-primrose or lemon-white: narrow-leaved *C. lawrenciana*, the taller *C. calycina* and *C. backhousiana*, which has rounded leaves buff-felted beneath, and thick, creamy green funnels in spring. *C. reflexa* is an allied species which, to judge from catalogues and older gardening literature, is very variable. W. Arnold-Forster lists several tantalizing kinds, variously described as species or hybrids, which seem to have been variants or derivatives of this: *C. virens*, 'nearly always carrying some of its pale green-tinted flowers ... an attractive glittering evergreen ... able to thrive in windy exposures'; '*C. magnifica*, with greenish-cream well-shaped flowers, is another good hybrid.' What he takes to be *C. reflexa* itself has 'vermilion flowers tipped with pale green, and ... small dark leaves ... [a] distinguished looking plant'. To confuse matters still further, it seems to have been called *C. speciosa*, and many acknowledged hybrids are said to have *C. speciosa* as one parent.

Other *Correa* species with red flowers include bright crimson, green-tipped *C. ventricosa* which has a long season in bloom, and the low-growing *C. decumbens*, which has narrow grey-green leaves and crimson tubes tipped with green. The hardy *C. schlechtendalii* is very low and spreading, with narrow dark grey-green leaves and cinnabar-red, green-lobed flowers in winter. The rosy red *C.* 'Harrisii' is very free-flowering in its spring season; it is brighter than *C.* 'Dusky Bells'. 'Mannii' is perhaps the same as 'Harrisii', with dusty-pink flowers; palest of all is *C. pulchella*, perhaps a variant of *C. reflexa* and very pretty with its almond-pink flowers borne in winter. I should like to see it paired with *Bauera rubioides*, a Tasmanian like many of the correas, forming a shrubby undergrowth of wiry stems in the more open parts of the forest and seldom without its white or pink flowers set off by crimson calyces.

The cestrums, like the correas, come in both pink and scarlet. *Cestrum fasciculatum* is nearer to pure red than *C. elegans*, with more robust stems, and flowers much constricted at the mouth; they open during late winter to spring, or are delayed until summer in cooler gardens. 'Newellii' may be a form of this, or a hybrid between it and *C. elegans*; it is the brightest of all, in scarlet with a hint of orange. The night-blooming jessamine, *Cestrum nocturnum*, is probably just too tender for any garden where even the lightest frosts may occur; but it is very easy to raise from cuttings or seed, so you may want to experiment, for the sake of the delicious night perfume of its greenish-yellow flowers. Even the buff-ochre *C. aurantiacum*, already proposed as a component of a tawny and cream scheme in Chapter III, really needs a very warm wall to survive light winter frosts. With it I like to see the Atlantic Island foxgloves, *Isoplexis canariensis* or *I. sceptrum*. Both are subshrubs growing to 1m/3¼ft, with long glossy leaves, and tapering spires, shorter and broader at the base than the true foxgloves', of tawny yellow flowers; of the two, *L. sceptrum* is the brighter tan-orange. You could add, for the summer if not as a permanent component of your planting, the marmalade bush, *Streptosolen jamesonii*, which does well in a pot and is very free with its bright orange flared trumpets in rounded clusters in summer. Contrasting sword-shaped, pleated foliage comes from *Wachendorfia paniculata*, which bears starry yellow flowers in early summer, or the more striking *W. thyrsiflora*, much taller at 1·8m/6ft, with rich yolk-yellow flowers on short side shoots. It grows fast from seed, and a young plant, waiting to reach a size to plant out in a sunny, warm border, will quickly fill its pot with fluorescent orange roots.

Some climbers, whether grown on a wall or not, are happier with their stems threading through a supporting shrub, their roots shaded. Such are the mutisias, spectacular but temperamental climbing daisies from South America, clambering to the light by leaf tendrils, preferring a rich soil for their roots and their heads in the sun. If you were planting one near the coppery *Isoplexis* species, it would need to be *Mutisia clematis*, one of the most showy when its orange-scarlet nodding daisies open in summer and early autumn. It is less hardy than *M. decurrens*, but this species, which seems happier in warm shade than in full sun, is one of the most difficult to establish. The daisy-flowers are of much the same vermilion-orange. Of the pink-flowered mutisias, the holly-leaved *M. ilicifolia* is all too often spoiled by trails of dead brown leaves; but the mauve or pink daisies are pretty. The flowerheads of *M. oligodon* are a clearer pink, with a satin finish to the ray florets. Mutisias often sucker at the root, leading one to imagine that here is an easy way to increase them; but they deeply resent any attempt to sever the new stems, and at worst both the parent and the potential offspring may simply die on you. You must also be sure to protect the suckers against accidental damage, as their loss may leave the plant with only aging stems that sooner or later will die, leaving you with nothing at all.

Perhaps the most alien-looking shrubs that can be grown on a sheltered wall in a mild maritime climate are the banksias, an Australian genus in Proteaceae with cylindrical or barrel-shaped, many-flowered clusters and, often, handsome foliage toothed at the margins with geometric precision. The leaves of *Banksia serrata* are long and narrow, deeply toothed, and squared at the tips; they are white beneath. The flowers are described by W. Arnold-Forster, with his artist's vision, as 'light yellow overlaid with small lilac-blue dabs – the unopened perianths'; most people see them simply as silvery or bluish-grey. One of the hardiest is *B. marginata*, its leaves toothed and rather spiny, dark green above and ice-white beneath, with the same bitten-off ends; the stubby flower-cones of acid-yellow may open at almost any time of the year. The first banksia I grew was *B. canei*, which finally succumbed to −22°C of frost; its narrow pointed leaves are sometimes toothed like holly, setting off cylindrical primrose flower spikes. The narrow toothed leaves of *B. verticillata* are borne in the distinct whorls which give the shrub its specific name; the long spikes of pale yellow flowers are as handsome as any. The foliage of *B. grandis* is especially striking, each leaf up to 30cm/12in long and cut to the midrib in triangular sections, bright yellow-green above and silvery beneath. The huge sulphur-yellow cylinders of flower sit proudly on these leafy crowns. The paler, greenish-white to icy-lemon *B. integrifolia* has more sombre foliage, with entire or coarsely toothed margins, dark green above and white beneath. These last two stand a surprising amount of wind. Brightest in flower of those that could be tried with a reasonable expectation of success in a maritime climate is *B. coccinea*, which has squat, ribbed cones of brilliant scarlet flowers among greyish foliage.

VI

Hot and Dry

YOUR choice of plants will be very much restricted if you have to garden on hot and hungry soil. Maybe your garden is entirely made on sand, or on thin soil over chalk; maybe you have a cliff face or quarry to plant, with no more than a film of soil over rock. Or perhaps you simply have one hot, dry area – a dry-wall top, a steep bank facing into the midday sun – within a garden otherwise blessed with a kinder soil. I have had to contend with all these variants on the hot and dry theme with the exception of a chalky soil, and well recall the sense of achievement with which I contemplated the transformation of a once barren rock face, in which only opportunistic brambles thrived, or the tapestry of foliage and flower that covers a steep bank where once, at my weekly peril, I had to swing a hovermover on a rope to keep the grass from running to thin, sunburnt hay.

The transition from grassed bank to a complete covering of shrubs is not an entirely simple one. A steep bank, especially where the soil is loose or sandy, will quickly crumble and erode once its stabilizing turf is stripped off. And whatever the soil, each time you dig a planting hole, clods and stones will escape down the slope. On one large, very steep bank that I planted, I broke the slope with a path, cut into the hillside, leading diagonally from bottom to top. Then, because this garden was in a region of rocky outcrops and there was plenty of stone about, I built a low retaining wall on the uphill side of the path, and constructed rock-edged pockets for the larger shrubs. If stone is inappropriate or unavailable, you can still ensure that your planting holes are cut back level into the hillside, and erect a temporary barrier of metal strip (the kind used for lawn edging, perhaps) or even a corset of wire netting, to retain the soil, any mulch you apply and, of course, water. For even the most determined xerophyte needs water from time to time during its existence, especially when newly planted; and it is no good sloshing a can of water over the poor thing, if

149

ninety percent of it simply disappears downhill taking most of your loosened soil with it. Remember, too, that you may need to shore up the soil on the uphill side of your planting hole, to stop it slipping down over the occupant and stifling it.

Of course, this does not answer the question what to do about the soil between the shrubs, while waiting for them to grow together. One possible answer, if you do not object too strongly to the sight of the dead grass meanwhile, is to plant in prepared pockets after you have killed the grass with herbicide but not stripped the turf. Even dead turf retains the soil with its mat of roots; as your shrubs grow they will spread over the browned grass, which will in time rot to improve the texture of the soil, helped by the fallen leaves trapped in the stems of the growing shrubs.

It is almost impossible to mulch on a steep slope; most of your mulch will finish at the bottom of the bank. Some people peg down over the bank a covering of chicken wire: wire netting with a mesh size of around 2·5 cm/1 in; this helps to retain the soil itself and can act as a brake on your mulch. Another possibility is a stone mulch, appropriate only if you are in an area where the soil is naturally stony. The stones must be large enough to stay put on the slope; whether they are angular or rounded will depend on what is available and what will fit with the natural landscape. It is all too easy, if you attempt this, to finish up with a bank that looks like a Dundee cake studded with almonds. The effect to aim for should be more as though a natural stone-fall had tumbled down the slope, and the shrubs had self-sown into the resulting scree and rubble. Concentrated around the roots of your shrubs, the stones will help to keep the soil cool until the shrubs' own topgrowth makes a cool canopy of shade for the roots.

Many Mediterranean shrubs, components of the vegetation known as *maquis* or *macchia* and *garrigue*, are ideally adapted to growing on dry, sunny slopes. *Maquis* is the shrubby growth which was once the understorey of the evergreen forest: cistuses, rosemary, lavender, *Spartium junceum* and tree heaths. In *maquis*, a few surviving, unfelled pines and evergreen oaks may remain of the forest itself. *Garrigue* is the name given to the much sparser growth on the hottest, driest slopes among rock and rubble, where no trees remain. Here sage, *Phlomis* species, rue and many bulbous plants grow. Virtually all the woody plants are evergreen, and many are aromatic; some have beautiful flowers.

All three attributes belong to a number of *Cistus* species and hybrids, which have the further merit of growing fast, the quicker to clothe your bank, and of developing by throwing out new layers of growth over the old, remaining comely and knitting together into an interlacing thicket of stems. The flattest of all cistuses is *Cistus salvifolius* 'Prostratus', which has all the qualities just noted except that of aromatic foliage; it is well adapted to draping over a dry wall, or flowing down over the retaining rocks of one of your planting pockets. On trailing stems that mound up to about 30 cm/1 ft, set with sage-like foliage, it bears creamy-white sun roses stained with yellow at the centre. It looks well in company with another trailing plant, the North African *Convolvulus mauretanicus*, which bears its satiny, lavender-blue flared trumpets over a long season. The two are well matched in vigour. If you were growing *C. salvifolius* itself, you would need more assertive companions than the convolvulus; for it makes a shrub of 60 cm/2 ft high and much more in width, and also increases by self sowing. Somewhere between *C. salvifolius* and its prostrate form in vigour are two pink-flowered cistuses which avoid the family tendency to magenta: *C. parviflorus* and its hybrid *c.* × *skanbergii*. Both have flowers of dog-rose pink, and pale grey-green foliage. The parent has broader leaves and larger flowers, but the tiny sunroses of *c.* × *skanbergii* are very pretty, and freely borne enough to make an impact by their quantity. Both form low, wide mounds. Their gentle colouring suggests as companions the silvery foliage of lavenders, with *Dorycnium hirsutum* for its little pink and white, clustered pea-flowers and silky trifoliolate leaves, feathery *Artemisia* 'Powis Castle', santolinas, and the soft, grey-purple *Salvia officinalis* 'Purpurascens'. Also suited to this group is the shrubby *Convolvulus cneorum*, with slender leaves of silver satin, and white cups opening from pink buds all summer.

Of similar habit to *Cistus parviflorus*, but with much more assertive flowers of magenta-pink, is *C. crispus*, which has greyish, wavy-edged leaves. Paler still, indeed almost white in leaf, is the woolly *C. albidus*, with flowers more lilac than pink; while the hybrid between the two, 'Sunset', has blooms of the most superbly insistent magenta of the whole *Cistus* tribe. Again, if you want this bluer pink in a vigorous and spreading species that will also increase by self sowing, you can choose the gummily aromatic *C. creticus* (*C. villosus*, *C. incanus*), which if allowed to naturalize in this way forms a colony of variable offspring, greyer or greener in leaf and paler rose-pink to near magenta in flower. Beware of the old hybrid 'Silver Pink'; once justifiably popular, it seems to have lost its vigour through over-propagation. At one time I thought its failure to do well was my fault, and certainly it seems to need a better soil than most; but I hear reports of problems with 'Silver Pink' from other gardeners. Better by far, though not so hardy as a thriving 'Silver Pink', is 'Anne Palmer', a clear pink hybrid of *C. crispus*. 'Peggy Sammons' is tougher, and tall at 1·8 m/6 ft, with grey-green foliage and clear pink flowers; it should become as popular as 'Silver Pink', but its name has not the sales impact of that cultivar. And there are the blotched pink cistuses too: *C.* × *purpureus*, with large rosy-purple flowers marked with chocolate-maroon at the base of each petal, and narrow greyish leaves; and its even more gaudy cultivar

'Betty Taudevin'. Theirs is none too easy a colour to place; it works well with the muted green of rosemary bushes, and if the flowering season overlaps no harm is done. Even the brightest rosemaries are quiet enough, thanks to the balance between flower and leaf, to pose no threat to the cistuses. *Teucrium fruticans* is another near blue shrub from the Mediterranean regions which assorts well with strong pink; it has neat foliage, white felted beneath, on white, spreading stems making a shrub of less dense habit than the sun-roses. 'Azureum' is a deeper blue in flower, and more tender.

As well as *Cistus salvifolius*, from which I was led astray by the pure pinks, a great many other sun-roses have white flowers. Least exciting are the species such as *C. hirsutus*, which bear their small flowers in clusters. *C. × florentinus* is a good workhorse for covering banks, of spreading habit, with narrow, dull green leaves and medium-sized flowers with a yellow basal stain. But of the wide-mounded, white-flowered cistuses best adapted to banks, two stand out: *C. × lusitanicus* 'Decumbens' with clammy, sub-glossy leaves and large flowers, each crimped silken petal bearing a crimson basal spot; and *C. × corbariensis*, which holds its creamy flowers, opening from deep pink buds, over wide hummocks of foliage which in poor soils and full sun turns from dark green to bronze in autumn and winter.

This by no means exhausts the cistuses that are worth growing; but on the whole I find the lower, widespreading kinds better suited to dry banks than the taller or more upright ones, which I will return to later. Another typical, and familiar, Mediterranean evergreen shrub is *Phlomis*, a member of the labiate family like rosemary, *Teucrium* and many of the aromatic shrublets used as flavourings in dishes of Mediterranean origin – thyme, oregano, savory. Two of the less familiar *Phlomis* species are *P. purpurea*, with rather narrow, greyish foliage, whiter beneath, and whorls of purple-pink flowers; and the prettier, suckering *P. italica*, woollier-white in leaf and clearer pink in flower. Their colouring qualifies them to join groupings of pink cistuses and grey foliage, as it might be in the group already adumbrated. From much further east comes *P. cashmeriana*, very pretty in lilac-pink and grey-green. Much better known is *P. fruticosa*, the Jerusalem sage, a widespreading shrub up to 90 cm/3 ft, with grey foliage – a grey with a characteristic yellowish cast – and whorls of bright mustard-yellow flowers borne in the spiky frills typical of the genus. 'Edward Bowles' is a good, low-growing selection, with broad, heart-shaped grey leaves and sulphur-yellow flowers. I prefer *P. chrysophylla*, yellower still of complexion, with clearer yellow flowers in widely spaced whorls, and broader leaves. It looks well with the low, wide mound of *Hebe rakaiensis* (*H. subalpina* of gardens), which has small, close-packed leaves of fresh apple-green, and with some silvery foliage, or with the variegated sage,

Crocosmia 'Lady Hamilton', with *Helichrysum petiolare* in the foreground: Coleton
Fishacre, Kingswear, Devon

Beschorneria yuccoides (*above*) and *Fuchsia splendens* 'Karl Hartweg' (*below*): Coleton Fishacre

Isoplexis sceptrum: The Strybing Arboretum, San Francisco

Watsonia fulgens: Coleton Fishacre

Alstroemeria pulchella growing through *Helichrysum petiolare*: Coleton Fishacre

Osteospermum 'Whirligig' (*above*): RHS Garden, Wisley; *Convolvulus sabatius* (*below*): Coleton Fishacre

Salvia involucrata 'Bethelli': Coleton Fishacre

Senecio scandens (*above*) and *Tropaeolum tuberosum* (*below*): Coleton Fishacre

Dianella sp.: Coleton Fishacre

Penstemon 'Taosensis': Coleton Fishacre

Clematis paniculata: The Garden House, Buckland Monachorum, Devon

Rhododendron eximium: courtesy of Major Walter Magor OBE, Lamellan, St Tudy, Bodmin, Cornwall

Rhododendron 'Lady Chamberlain': Coleton Fishacre

Senecio candicans: Coleton Fishacre

RIGHT *Pseudopanax crassifolius*: Castlewellan, Northern Ireland

Plumeria alba (Frangipani): private garden, Florida (*above*); Tea Rose 'Mme Berkeley': The Level, Pillowell, Glos (*below*)

Salvia officinalis 'Icterina', a form of the common or culinary sage in which the habitual greyish-green of the leaf is marked with olive and yellow.

Grey foliage and flowers of an especially appealing clear yellow combine in several of the halimiums, close relatives of the cistuses with the same tolerance of sun and drought. One of the smaller species is *Halimium ocymoides*, in which spreading main branches are set with upright, slender branchlets. The small leaves are pale pewter-grey; the flowers, borne in clusters, open from coppery-red buds to reveal a black blotch at the base of each little canary-yellow petal. Larger in leaf and more spreading, *H. lasianthum* comes in two forms: *formosum* with a bitter-chocolate blotch, and *concolor* in plain pure yellow. This is especially appealing in its simplicity and I love it. Either form is finer than *H. halimifolium*, a greyish shrub with narrow leaves and yellow flowers marked with a little black spot at the base. Another species is the slender, needle-leaved *H. libanotis*, with yellow flowers in small clusters. The little bigeneric hybrid × *Halimiocistus sahucii* is hardier; its squarish white flowers are set off by narrow, very deep shining green leaves. × *H. revolii* is greyer, with silky white, yellow-based or sometimes creamy-yellow flowers; × *H.* 'Ingwersenii' is grey-green hairy, with showy white flowers.

The arching green stems of *Cytisus* × *praecox*, or the smaller, flatter *C.* × *kewensis*, also fit well with the phlomis; both are transformed in spring into a billow of cream pea-flowers, those of the larger Warminster broom heavily fragrant. The brooms also look well with the smoky or near-true blues of *Ceanothus*. This Californian genus includes many species adapted to dry, poor soils; they form part of the chaparral, the brush of Californian foothills, colonizing exposed banks of gravelly, rocky soil. For fast cover *C. thyrsiflorus repens* is hard to better, provided you get the clone I first acquired by that name; it rapidly reaches sideways to cover 3 m/10 ft of soil, with stiffly arching stems, mounding up to 1·2 m/4 ft, densely clad with glossy dark green leaves among which the powder-blue flowers appear in abundance each spring. Other clones offered as this are slower and more compact, so if possible you should ask to see a mature specimen of what you propose to plant before buying a youngster. 'Yankee Point' is more consistent, growing to about the same height but less wide, with brighter blue flowers. It is believed to be a form of *C. griseus* var. *horizontalis*, a near relation of *C. thyrsiflorus*, collected from the coastal area of the Monterey peninsula known as Yankee Point. Also coastal is the ground-hugging *C. gloriosus*, which inland grows taller; so if you have a shoreside bank to cover, this might be a good one to try, for it has honey-scented, smoky blue flowers on creeping stems set with dark green, holly-like toothed leaves.

Shrubs with grey-felted leaves which withstand sea winds are also, very often, adapted to cope with hot sun and poor soil: here, the sturdy,

spreading *Brachyglottis* 'Sunshine' and smaller *B. monroi* would assort well
with the brooms and ceanothus. A useful little shrub for hot sunny slopes,
with insignificant flowers but pleasant, woolly, heather-like foliage that
is camphor-scented, is *Camphorosma monspeliaca*.

In the first chapter of this book I suggested that the more important a
given plant or planting, whether considered as shelter or as an element of
design, the more certain you should be that it will be able to survive the
worst winters it is likely to suffer in your garden. Now if planting a steep
bank has special difficulties that call for special remedies, removing the
carcases of plants that have died is even more difficult. It makes particular
sense, therefore, to garden within your climate on the steepest banks, and
experiment only where you can easily replace the plants that do not
survive. If a plant grows extremely quickly and can be easily removed
once dead, then by all means take a chance.

Cliffs and quarries

Plants that meet these requirements are the Hottentot fig, *Carpobrotus
edulis*, and its near ally *C. aciniciformis*, both from Cape Province, South
Africa. They bear thick succulent leaves, triangular in cross section, and
many-rayed daisy-like flowers in summer. The first is bright magenta-
lilac in colour; the other runs also to orange-buff, lemon, and soft yellow.
They can be seen falling in curtains over the cliffs at Dawlish and elsewhere
in south Devon and along the south Wales coast, where they receive full
measure of the salt-laden winds and sea spray with equanimity. They are
much used in California to cover the wide embankment along the free-
ways; they have great vigour, quickly covering the soil. In Greece, they
drape the rocks of the Acropolis, undaunted by the fierce sun. I used them
in planting a quarry face in a garden in south Devon, confident that they
would quickly settle into the meagre pockets of soil I was able to contrive.
The shrubby mesembryanthemums, species and hybrids of *Lampranthus*,
also thrive in the hottest spots. *L. zeyheri* is one of the flattest, its prostrate
stems set with magenta-pink flowers. *L. spectabilis* is crimson-scarlet, *L.
blandus* palest pink, and *L. roseus* a deeper but still not strong or bright
pink. In the other half of the spectrum, *L. aureus* is a cheerful orange-
yellow, *L. aurantiacus* closer to red, *L. coccineus* scarlet, and the appealing
L. glaucus has lemon-yellow flowers. They are one of the features of the
garden at Tresco Abbey on the Isles of Scilly, and several forms or hybrids
of *L. spectabilis* have been named from there: 'Tresco Red', 'Tresco
Brilliant', a vivid magenta, and 'T. Apricot'.

From South Africa also, like the species of *Carpobrotus* and *Lampranthus*,
comes a group of genuine daisies for hot, dry soils. *Venidium*, *Arctotis* and

Ursinia are often grown as annuals in cooler areas, but there are true perennials among them and they offer the usual range of brilliant, pure colours as well as the softer tones often called art shades: buff and straw, pale tangerine and apricot and wine. Especially fetching are the Venidio-arctotis hybrids, with ruffled grey-green foliage and large daisies. They are commonly offered by colour: apricot, flame, wine. I wonder how many of those that are ordered on impulse from the Chelsea Show stands that feature them will survive their first winter; but in the right place, hot and dry and unthreatened by more than a degree or two of frost, they are sound and vigorous perennials.

W. Arnold-Forster tells us that *Olearia insignis*, better known as *Pachystegia insignis*, grows in its native New Zealand 'in clefts and ledges of sun-baked schistose rocks'. This makes it an obvious candidate for a quarry or cliff-face garden, to which its thick-textured leaves and stout stems will add a greyish tone. It is variable from seed; some forms have dark green leaves quite white woolly beneath, others are bronzed above and buff-felted below; it varies in size also from a stout, widespreading bush up to 1·8 m/6 ft in height to a compact, small-leaved form, var. *minor*. All have large, solitary, marguerite-like white flowerheads on long stems. In the wild it is apparently accompanied by *Hebe hulkeana*, and I have no doubt that the slender hebe, with its wide open panicles of starry lilac-blue veronica flowers, would contrast as well in the garden with the uncompromising solidity of the olearia's foliage.

It may be that on your quarry or cliff face you will want some more restrained plants, those that will fill a pocket of soil but not spill out. In the quarry I planted, steps had been cut at a diagonal across the rock face from bottom to top: they were hazardous enough, the shaly rock crumbling and breaking away in places, without the extra threat of concealing foliage; so on the uphill side, only the most stay-at-home plants were admissible. A very mealy white *Dudleya*, *D. farinosa* I believe, settled in well, reminded perhaps of its native Californian cliffs. Dudleyas were until recently included in the genus *Echeveria*, and have similar succulent rosettes, topped, in *D. farinosa*, by lemon-yellow flowers. *Echeveria secunda* var. *glauca* is a high-altitude, rock-clinging Mexican species with a purplish flush to its glaucous leaves, and rose-pink or red flowers.

In keeping with these bloomy colourings is the North African *Othonnopsis cheirifolia*, a subshrubby composite with spoon-shaped glaucous blue leaves packed in close fans on trailing stems. The short-rayed yellow daisies would be a disappointment, but that they are apt to open in winter. The narrow, pointed leaves of *Euphorbia rigida* (*E. biglandulosa*) are of similar colouring; they are borne spirally along the procumbent stems, which in early spring are topped with bracts of the typical spurge colouring, sharp lime-yellow. In summer, if the soil is as dry as on my quarry or the spurge's native Peloponnese, the leaves are flushed with red. The much larger *E. dendroides*, a shrubby species reaching 2 m/6½ ft, makes a dome of yellowish stems with narrow, grey-blue leaves on the upper portion only, and the expected yellow-green flower heads. Its natural habitat is dry, rocky places in sight of the sea.

We have all seen how wallflowers may become perennial if planted, or self-sown, in old mortared walls; they are just as ready to live long in rock crevices. *Erysimum linifolium* is often grown as a biennial; in a cliff face its clear lilac flowers in spring look well against silvery-grey rock. Brighter than this is the sterile hybrid 'Bowles's Mauve', already proposed as a mixed border ingredient; it has slate-grey foliage on rounded bushes topped by an unending succession of vivid mauve spires. Always inclined to flower itself to death, it should be longer lived in a rock face where the drainage is impeccable; but you should, even so, look out for every available unflowered shoot to pull off and root, so as to ensure the next generation. Even more appealing, *E. capitatum* makes a low mound with flowers of the tenderest creamy-green, endowed with a delicious clove perfume.

Planting a cliff or quarry is a hazardous business, and you should never try it alone in case you fall. I well recall hanging head downwards from the quarry summit, with a helper clinging to my ankles, in order to plant as far down the face as I could reach. Before the planting could begin, we had to remove brambles that had been left to grow unchallenged for years and had thick woody stems, with roots reaching into the living rock. In the course of their removal, much shaly rock and some soil fell to the foot of the quarry or was caught on a wide ledge part way down. This open, fast-draining, stony soil made an ideal medium for xerophytes that needed more space; the rock wall at their backs retained the sun's warmth, and the curve of the quarry deflected any wind that filtered through the great shelter belts of *Pinus radiata*.

On the wide ledge *Furcraea longaeva* was planted to expand its massive, *Beschorneria*-like rosettes and, in time, its towering fountains of bloom. These can reach 6 m/20 ft or more, the drooping side branches bearing bell-shaped, creamy-white flowers touched with pale green; as they fade, bulbils form which drop to the ground, there with luck to root and make new rosettes. The huge effort needed for the mature rosette to ensure its own succession is also its death sentence; the carcass is a horrid sight and needs rooting out, a disruptive and exhausting process. Just as well, then, that furcraeas do not flower each year, or even every few years. There are other species, of which *F. bedinghausii* is in cultivation; it has fragrant, waxy pale green flowers on 7·5 m/25 ft stems, over similar rosettes of broadsword-shaped leaves.

The desert atmosphere

Almost as imposing as a maturing rosette of *Furcraea* is a good-sized specimen of *Agave americana*. Despite its name this armed succulent is, like *Beschorneria* and *Furcraea*, a Mexican native. The broad-based, pointed, grey-blue leaves are up to 1·5 m/5 ft long and form wide rosettes; each leaf is marked with the imprint of its precursor's toothed margins. In bloom it is dramatic rather than handsome, the pale yellow flowers borne in flattish clusters on short side branches on a 6 m/20 ft main stem. There are variegated forms which look more appropriate in pots, or in sight of the house, than in a less formal part of the garden. But as you may more likely have a hot, dry, gravelly area by your patio than in a quarry – for quarries are hardly common in gardens – they may as well get a mention here. 'Marginata' has creamy-yellow marginal markings, while 'Medio-picta' has a broad central stripe of yellow on each leaf blade. Although the rosettes, even of the variegated forms, become very bulky in time, they can be accommodated in a large pot for many years; and offsets are formed which you can detach and grow on against the day when your original rosette outgrows its station. In a small garden in south Devon, facing down towards the Dart estuary, the variegated agaves are grown in the open border, among the rocks that restrain the soil from slipping down the slope; they increase, and are spread about by the owner of the garden, as happily if not as fast as the far smaller rosettes of hardy sedums cover the ground in colder areas. If *Agave americana* is too large, or too tender, for your garden, then *A. parryi* may be your choice. It has broad, spine-edged dark green leaves, forming the usual armed rosette.

Like the agaves, yuccas are plants of the deserts of south western USA and Mexico. Some of the tender or more tricky species should thrive in the driest, hottest places you can give them, on poor, free-draining soil. *Yucca glauca* is rated as one of the hardiest, yet it seems unaccountably reluctant to submit to captivity unless in such desert-mimicking conditions. Where it can be persuaded to thrive it is most handsome, with numerous rapier-fine, blue-grey, white-edged leaves assembled into a hemispherical rosette up to 1·2 m/4 ft across. The flowers, if they appear at all, are white tinted with green, borne on a narrow scarcely-branched spike. But the marvel of the genus is *Y. whipplei*, once thought sufficiently distinct to merit a genus of its own, *Hesperoyucca*. It demands just such free-draining, stony soil as I am presupposing here, and the sunniest spot you can give it; a rock face, or a wall at its back, will help to trap and reverberate yet more heat to encourage it to flower. Even before it reaches this stage it is beautiful, with as many as two hundred stiletto-like glaucous grey leaves packed into a dense rosette. Like the massive rosettes of the furcraeas, this is monocarpic, dying after the effort of producing its 3–4 m/10–13¼ ft spire bearing hundreds of cream-white, lemon-scented bells.

There are, of course, other yuccas you could grow in your evocation of a Mexican desert; but many are hardy enough for the ordinary border and have already received mention. One of the stemless species that has not is *Y. baccata*, which has stiff, sword-like leaves of very thick texture, conspicuously blue-green, and short (1 m/3¼ ft) flower spikes bearing very large white flowers in late summer. Mr E. A. Bowles found that in his dry garden at Myddelton House it existed only 'in a state of summer convalescence'; but that garden lies north of London, and despite its free-draining gravelly soil has not what I would consider a mild climate. The allied *Hesperaloe parviflora* (*Yucca parviflora*) is a Texan plant forming a dense clump of very narrow rapier leaves of bright green with white threads along the margins. In flower it resembles an aloe, the slender panicles bearing many nodding, soft orange-scarlet flowers marked with yellow within, in summer.

In South Africa it is the genus *Aloe* that has adapted to hot, dry conditions. The soothing properties of *Aloe vera* are now well known, for the gel is widely used in cosmetics. In gardens, among the species most likely to be grown are *A. arborescens*, with glaucous rosettes topped by scarlet flower spikes reminiscent of red hot pokers, and *A. aristata*, its dark green, pointed leaves marked with white, below slender 60 cm/2 ft orange pokers. It is a huge genus with several hardy species: one I grow, with toothed green leaves on short stems, bears flower spikes of scarlet-orange and yellow remarkably like those of *Kniphofia* 'Royal Standard'. As yet, I have not put a name to it. Aloes will grow happily with their rosettes set vertically in a wall or rock crevice, their flowering stems arching outwards.

The bromeliads that can be successfully grown out of doors in mild but not wholly frost-free gardens come from South America. *Billbergia nutans* is familiar as a houseplant that will survive much neglect; but it is scarcely one of the most exciting of hardy bromeliads, with its open rosettes of long, narrow, rather untidy toothed leaves and unbranched flowering stems set with hanging blue, green and pink flowers in bright pink bracts. The fascicularias form good ground cover in dry, poor soils, spreading to form colonies of rosettes composed of viciously spiny grey, white-backed leaves; the spines are set pointing backwards, so that it is easy to put your hand in among the leaves but nearly impossible to withdraw it without painful lacerations. In the centre of these rosettes the round clusters of china-blue flowers nestle, stemless; as they form, the leaf bases around them turn brilliant scarlet, to fade with the flowers' dying. As I know them, *Fascicularia bicolor* is the more reliable in flower, with narrower leaves; *F. pitcairniifolia* the larger, with rosettes up to 75 cm/2½ ft wide. The leaf rosettes formed by *Ochagavea lindleyana* are very similar, but the pink flowers are borne in rounded clusters on a short stem of 30–45 cm/1–1½ ft, arising from the heart of the silvery rosettes.

The puyas are even more alien in appearance than these. Their huge rosettes are not so comparatively flat as those of the fascicularias; each narrow, prickly leaf may be as much as 1·2 m/4 ft long in *Puya chilensis*, forming great hostile clumps in the Chilean landscape. The flowering stems may be as long as 3 m/10 ft, the inflorescence itself up to 90 cm/3 ft long forming a huge cone of greenish-yellow and orange flowers. *P. alpestris* has rosettes of grey-green arching leaves, like the top of a giant pineapple. After some years a 90 cm/3 ft spike appears, densely set with three-petalled flowers of metallic turquoise and sea-green in bright red bracts. *P. berteroniana* is similar, with taller spikes; the sea-blue flowers have vivid orange anthers. Should you become capitivated by the bizarre strangeness of these plants you will no doubt seek out the rare, and smaller, *P. caerulea*, with turquoise flowers, the Andean species *P. mirabilis*, with yellowish flowers, and the colossal *P. raimondii*, whose unbranched flowering stems may reach 10 m/33 ft.

It seems entirely natural for such plants to be surrounded by bare, stony soil; if you want to suppress weeds or have a tidy mind you could set them in a thick gravel mulch. It will not stop the weeds growing, of course, but should make them much easier to extract. And into this warm and welcoming rubble you may introduce plants more desirable than groundsel, hoping they may make themselves as much at home. The prickly poppies, species of *Argemone*, are plants of mild regions, with glaucous, thistle-like leaves, often milk spotted, and silken poppy flowers. Clear lemon to tangerine *A. mexicana* is a familiar annual, and the white *A. grandiflora* and *A. platyceras*, both around 90 cm/3 ft in height, have *Romneya*-like flowers with a central boss of yellow stamens. I suspect that *Hunnemannia fumariifolia* might settle to become perennial in hot and stony soil. Even if it did not, it is worth raising new plants each year for their finely cut, blue-grey leaves and yellow flowers which agree, in their successive phases, with both elements of their English name 'tulip poppy', for the petals have the high gloss of tulips and are at first held with tulip-like poise. The horned poppies are European in origin, but relish the same conditions as the prickly poppies. *Glaucium flavum* is clear yellow in flower, the one I know as *G. phoenicium* is a rich burnt-orange, and *G. grandiflorum* is scarlet to tangerine. The first two have intensely blue, deeply crinkled leaves which in their first winter form rosettes; from these, in the second summer, arise the stiff, leaning flower stems; the flowers are followed by the long, slender, curved seed pods which give the glauciums their English name. The hot-coloured horned poppies need to be kept well away from *Calandrinia umbellata*, a compact little plant with grey-green leaves hidden by incandescent magenta cups all summer. You could set either among the twisted and tangled, silver wire stems of *Leucophyta brownii* (*Calocephalus brownii*), a native of sandy Australian beaches and thus quite at home in the hottest soil we can offer it. The little annual *Omphalodes linifolia* seeds itself freely in hot and gravelly soils, contributing its own colour scheme of glaucous blue foliage and skimmed-milk white flowers.

Grey, glaucous or silver foliage looks especially appropriate in the hottest corners of the garden, for often the leaves of plants adapted to withstand baking sun are covered with fine hairs or a waxy bloom which protects against excessive transpiration and gives them their characteristic colouring. But there are green-leaved succulents also, such as *Sedum dendroideum*, which with its yellow flowers looks like an enlarged version of the hardy, rock garden sedums; its spoon-shaped, flesh leaves are held in loose rosettes on 60 cm/2 ft stems. Much more striking is *Aeonium arboreum*, from Morocco. Its fleshy, blunt-ended leaves are held in rosettes like some great houseleek on 90 cm/3 ft stems, topped with conical heads of yellow flowers. The form 'Atropurpureum' is a handsome deep maroon-black form with a metallic gloss. By contrast the lance-shaped leaves of *Tradescantia pallida* 'Purpurea' have only a faint sheen. This is the plant I used to know as *Setcreasea purpurea*; its updated name rightly evokes the houseplants to which it is related and which it resembles. In dry conditions it is remarkably hardy, springing from below ground if its topgrowth is killed by frost.

Mediterranean gardens

It may be that the atmosphere you wish to evoke is not so much the desert as the Mediterranean: not just the *maquis* or *garrigue* of cistuses, Jerusalem sage, rosemary and lavender and myrtle, lentisk and arbutus, but the gardened Mediterranean. This is the landscape of acacias seen against a backdrop of umbrella pines, of olive groves and orange blossom and the dark spires of cypress, of climbing tea roses and bougainvillea in all its clashing colours, tamed by the white heat of the sun. Parts of California share a similar climate of hot dry summers and cool – but not cold – wet winters; and California too, as we shall see, has its own characteristic vegetation, the chaparral, of *Ceanothus* and manzanita, dwarf evergreen oaks and species of *Rhus*, with its own unmistakable fragrance and aroma.

Of course, many of the plants that now seem so much part of the Midi, the acacias most especially, are imports, from Australia, or New Zealand or South Africa. However, since the climate I am writing for is not truly Mediterranean, but rather mild oceanic, you must not be misled by the 'hot and dry' heading of this chapter to suppose that, except in very unusual summers, I expect your garden to be as hot, as dry, as the Riviera, let alone southern California; nor will your winters be as temperate. But although some of the most alluring plants of Mediterranean gardens may be denied you, by selection it is certainly within your reach to create something of its atmosphere. And who knows, if the much talked of greenhouse effect really is altering our climate, many of us at present condemned to growing only the hardiest of plants may find that our conservatory and cool greenhouse plants become the commonplace ingredients of our gardens.

Before I embark upon the acacias, which do so much to make that ambiance on the acid-soiled areas of the south of France, let us first consider the typical gymnosperms of the Mediterranean that will form the dark counterpoise to the airy grace and fluffy lemon blossom of mimosa. On the mainland of Africa, on the Iberian peninsula and eastwards to Italy, the maritime pine, *Pinus pinaster*, is widespread. Old trees have a long, bare trunk, branched only for the upper one third or quarter of their height, the branches forming a flat-domed crown with greyish needles clustered at the tips. It has been much planted in areas such as Les Landes of south-western France, where it grows successfully in poor, dry, sandy soils. The characteristic pine of the Riviera is the stone pine, *P. pinea*, also called umbrella pine on account of its broad, dense, flat-topped crown. The shadow cast by these spreading trees is greatly valued in the scorching heat of summer. The Aleppo pine, *P. halepensis*, also thrives in warm, dry regions and is tolerant of poor, chalky soils; it forms a medium-sized tree with fresh green needles. Another equally typical conifer of southern Europe is *Cupressus sempervirens* 'Stricta', which forms the dark, slender spires punctuating the Tuscan landscape. It is not particularly sensitive to frost except when young.

The mimosa of southern France is not just one species of *Acacia*, but several. The Australian and Tasmanian acacias, with which we are concerned here, fall into three main groups: those which retain feathery, much-divided juvenile foliage; those with entire, often willow-like foliage; and the spiny species. In acacias, it is a solecism to speak invariably of leaves: some acacias as they mature develop phyllodes, leaf-like structures which perform the functions normally carried out by true leaves. Of the feathery kinds, *A. dealbata* is the most familiar, a tall tree (up to 30 m/100 ft) which if cut down, by frost or the axe, will form a thicket of slender stems. The white-powdered leaves are doubly pinnate, each of the twenty or so divisions bearing thirty to fifty tiny leaflets; the fragrant, yellow mimosa bobbles are borne in panicles which start to show colour in late winter. *A. baileyana*, which has already found its way into Chapter III, is even brighter in leaf, pale glaucous blue contrasting with the bright yellow blossom at the turn of the year. The blackwood, *A. melanoxylon*, displays both bipinnate leaves and mature, scimitar-shaped phyllodes even on young trees; in blossom it is less decorative than many, the little fluffy globes few and washy pale. It is allied to *A. longifolia*, a willow-leaved species differing from those so far described in its slim, cylindrical spikes of bright yellow flower. It is a very much smaller tree than the blackwood, reaching only 5–10 m/16–33 ft, and tolerant of wind and of sandy soils. Of similar size is *A. pycnantha*, almost eucalyptus-like in aspect with glossy green, sickle-shaped phyllodes; the abundant yellow mimosa balls open in spring. As its specific name implies, *A. cyanophylla* has very blue-glaucous foliage, oblong or curved, on weeping branchlets wreathed all along their length with bright yellow blossom. Scarcely less blue is the very fetching *A. pravissima*, a graceful small tree with slender branchlets, on which the small, triangular phyllodes are densely set edgeways. The little rounded yellow flower heads are grouped into long compound racemes and open in spring. *A. cultriformis* is in effect a silvery grey-leaved version of this, the phyllodes each with a little hooked point. Those of *A. podalyriifolia* are larger; they and the shoots are silvery-glaucous and downy. Long racemes of fragrant flowers open in late winter. Its hybrid with *A. baileyana* is *A. × hanburyana*, named for the creator of that once great garden at Mentone, La Mortola. Both the blue, feathered leaves of the one and the flat phyllodes of the other parent are present in this beautiful mimosa, which has large fluffy yellow balls of flower in panicles up to 60 cm/2 ft long. Both *A. verticillata*, with dark green needle leaves in whorls, and the allied *A. juniperina*, are familiarly known as prickly Moses. They bear lemon-yellow flowers in bottlebrush spikes in spring, on a densely branched framework of stems up to 10 m/33 ft in height. *Albizia lophantha* is closely related to the acacias and was at one time classed with them; it has feathery bipinnate leaves, each of the fourteen to twenty four pinnae set with up to 60 slender, silky leaflets. The flowers are soft creamy-primrose, green-tinged bottlebrushes, appearing in summer.

Almost as tall in favoured climates as many of the acacias, the scented brooms of the Atlantic isles, typified by the florists' 'Genista fragrans', thrive in the Mediterranean climate. The more I attempt to unravel their nomenclature the more confused I become, so I will merely suggest some of the names that are encountered, with the observation that they make tall, leafy shrubs or small trees, with spikes of rich yellow, fragrant flowers in early summer. This generalized description could apply to *Cytisus stenopetalus*, or to *C. maderensis*; the luxuriant var. *magnifoliosus* has been variously attributed to both by the authorities I consulted, as has the allegedly distinguishing colour of the silky hairs that cover the shoots, which may be silvery-grey or rusty-brown. The florists' genista, *Cytisus × spachianus*, is said to be *C. stenopetalus × C. canariensis*, but the latter is also offered as *Genista fragrans*; and *Cytisus racemosus* is another name you may meet. Buy what you see and like seems to be the safest advice. Even with the hybrid 'Porlock' our trials are not at an end, for this very free-flowering shrub, growing to around 1·8 m/6 ft, seeds itself, and the progeny are sometimes offered as though they were the original.

With the hardier, and almost completely leafless, *Genista aetnensis*, there is no difficulty of naming that I am aware of. It flowers in high summer, preceded by its smaller near ally, *G. ephedroides*. This is valued for the delicious fragrance of its large and abundant yellow flowers, held in loose racemes on thin, arching stems. With *G. cinerea* and *G. tenera* we come to another confusing pair of brooms, tall shrubs of graceful habit with cascades of fragrant yellow pea-flowers. *Cytisus proliferus* is from Tenerife, a graceful small, half-drooping tree, of greyish cast, the stems wreathed with milky-white flowers in spring. The pretty Tenerife broom, so-called, *Spartocytisus nubigenus*, bears its fragrant ivory white flowers, blushed with rose, on *Spartium*-like stems later in spring, thriving in hot, dry soils. Also white-flowered is the frail *Genista monosperma*, a little shrub of 1 m/3¼ ft or so, which bears its sweetly scented flowers in early spring.

Though I dismissed in a few words the plants of the *maquis* in my haste to describe some of the great genus *Acacia*, with *Genista monosperma* I have come full circle to a native of the Mediterranean region itself. Nor is this pretty thing the only indigenous species deserving of garden space, whether you garden actually in the Mediterranean region, or in an area with a sufficiently similar climate for them to thrive. Some we have met in earlier chapters, such as *Coronilla glauca* – though I think I forgot the more compact *C. valentina*, with similar cheerful yellow flowers fragrant of ripe peaches, appearing in early summer, and pinnate foliage, glaucous beneath, composed of seven to eleven blunt-ended leaflets. For very hot corners there are many other members of the pea family: the gorse-like *Genista falcata*, *Anagyris foetida* which has its specific epithet from the evil smell of the leaves when crushed (the French call it, more bluntly, *bois puant* – stinkwood) and bears yellow flowers with a brown patch on the standard very early in spring; and the species of *Adenocarpus*. In contrast to the almost bare stems of most Mediterranean genistas, these are leafy evergreen shrubs with bright yellow flowers. The foliage of *A. anagyrifolius* is slightly glaucous, that of *A. foliolosus* is greyish, contrasting with the dense spikes of orange-yellow flowers. *A. decorticans* is of rather gaunt habit, with long branches full of leaf, and gorse-like flowers. One of the most attractive members of the pea family from these regions is *Anthyllis barba-jovis*, an upright evergreen shrub reaching 3 m/10 ft, entirely silvery-grey in stem and pinnate leaf, with creamy primrose flowers in clusters in late spring.

Building on the grey and yellow theme, you might try in your hot border an amusing shrubby crucifer, *Vella pseudocytisus*, with blunt, rounded, bristly leaves of fingernail size, and sprays of little yellow, four-petalled flowers. At much the same modest height, 45 cm/18 in or so, *Linum arboreum* has vividly glaucous, narrowly spathulate leaves, rather thick-textured and often clustered in dense rosettes, below a long succession of bright lemon-yellow flowers in upright panicles. It is short-lived, so that you need to take cuttings every year to be sure of keeping it. I have a deep affection, too, for *Halimium atriplicifolium*, too precious to risk on a bank, on account of its silver-felted, almost rhomboidal leaves and wide, bright yellow sun-rose flowers held on hairy stems in summer.

There are several *Cistus* species and hybrids, natural or manmade, which I also excluded from my bank plantings because their height made them less suitable than the spreading kinds. Of the numerous natural hybrids I have an especial weakness for *C. × aguilari*, which has long leaves of cheerful green with very wavy edges, and sizeable pure white flowers. Its form 'Maculatus', with petals crimson-blotched, is more gummy and no more beautiful. The flowers of *C. × cyprius* are wide and white with a carmine spot; like *C. × aguilari*, this is a natural hybrid reaching 1–2 m/3¼ ft–6½ ft, with gummily aromatic foliage that turns cold, leaden green in winter. Both have as one parent the gum cistus itself, *C. ladanifer*, which has almost the largest flowers of the genus borne singly on slender branchlets, the white petals each with a bold oxblood-red blotch. A comparatively recent introduction to gardens is the lovely *C. palhinhae*, with pure white flowers as large as the gum cistus's, and rich green foliage that is glossy with resinous gum. Its discoverer, Captain Collingwood Ingram, united *C. palhinhae* and *C. ladanifer* in the very fine hybrid 'Paladin', which has blotched flowers on a bushy shrub less inclined to blow over than the rather thin-habited gum cistus. 'Blanche' is of the same parentage but unblotched, 'Pat' is more like 'Paladin', while 'Elma', which is *C. laurifolius × C. palhinhae*, inherits the first-named parent's clustered flowers. They all flower in summer, and all have the family habit of shedding their crumpled silk petals after only one day, so that by evening the ground beneath is carpeted with white. The following morning, over a long period, more buds open to whiten the bush again. The less exciting kinds, *C. × cyprius* or even *C. laurifolius*, can be used when not in bloom as an evergreen backdrop to other flowers; but I should be sorry to relegate the best of the cistuses to such a purely supportive role.

The familiar oleander, *Nerium oleander* to give it its full botanical name, is native of the Mediterranean region also, and in its various colour forms is much planted. It is less hardy than most cistuses, but is very tolerant of heat and drought and should be worth trying where frosts are not too severe or prolonged. You would need the climate of Florida or southern California to achieve those massive hedges of oleander, standing 3 m/10 ft high and more, massed with white, pink or crimson flowers. The colour range is extended to include some subtle apricot and peach tones, purple, sulphur-yellow and scarlet, in single or double forms.

Many shrubs native of the Mediterranean region are aromatic: some of the cistuses, rosemary, lavender, myrtle. *Rosmarinus officinalis* is variable in habit, and, to a lesser degree, in the colour of its lipped flowers. I cannot warm to the pink, so-called, actually a rather unpleasing mauve; nor do I have much enthusiasm for the white form. But some of the named blues are fine things, varying from upright, clear cobalt 'Tuscan Blue' and very narrow-leaved, semi-erect 'Benenden Blue', which is lapis-lazuli coloured, to the spreading 'Severn Sea' and richly coloured 'McConnell's Blue'. Flattest of all is *R. officinalis* 'Prostratus', with long trailing branches and light blue flowers; it is often labelled *R. lavandulaceus*, which is apparently a distinct species lacking the glandular calyx of *R. officinalis*. Although it is not aromatic, *Lithodora rosmarinifolia* is one of the prettiest blue-flowered shrubs for Mediterranean climates, with narrow persistent leaves on upright stems – it grows to 45 cm/18 ins or so – and clear bright blue flowers in terminal clusters in winter.

In mild climates you can grow the finest of the lavenders, including the French lavender, *Lavandula stoechas*, with its intensely aromatic foliage and bizarre, cockaded purple flower heads. More attractive in leaf are the Iberian *L. dentata*, with grey, finely toothed leaves, and white woolly *L. lanata*, which is strongly perfumed. The common myrtle, *Myrtus communis*, makes a good aromatic hedge, or can be allowed to grow freely to form a glittering evergreen of 3–5 m/10–18 ft. The flowers, a brush of creamy-white stamens emerging from rounded buds, are fragrant also. There is a double-flowered form, and the tiny-leaved var. *tarentina*, which stands a good deal of wind. There is also a cream-edged form, prettier than many variegated shrubs.

I have never heard of a variegated bay, but as well as the plain green leaved type there is *Laurus nobilis* 'Aurea', quite handsome with its lime-yellow foliage. Var. *angustifolia* has elegant, long, narrow, wavy-edged leaves, paler green than the type. Like bay, the carob, *Ceratonia siliqua*, is essentially a foliage plant, from the gardener's point of view; though from its dark brown pods, ripening in autumn, is extracted the substance now increasingly used as a substitute for chocolate. It is supposedly the locust tree which enabled John the Baptist to survive in the wilderness. As a large shrub or round-headed tree it is often seen in the Mediterranean region, for example in Jordan, where its handsome dark green, pinnate leaves contrast with the silver shimmer of olives or the blue-grey of introduced acacias. Hardier than this, if you seek such a contrasting note in a garden where the carob is tender, are the Kermes oak, *Quercus coccifera*, and *Rhamnus alaternus*, of which var. *angustifolia* is a most appealing, gleaming evergreen with elegant, narrow, toothed foliage.

Several species of tree heath are native to the Mediterranean region or the Iberian peninsula. *Erica mediterranea* itself, now correctly *E. erigena*, extends into Ireland; it is more compact than many, with rose-red or white flowers. Then there are the two invariably white tree heaths, *E. arborea* with globular ashen white, fragrant flowers in early spring, and *E. lusitanica* which has tubular flowers, in the best forms opening from bright pink buds. It is even more fragrant, with a free-floating, honeyed perfume. The hybrid between the two is *E.* × *veitchii* 'Exeter', fragrant also, with bright green foliage. *E. australis*, the Spanish heath, flowers later and is very showy in rose-purple, a difficult colour that must be kept well away from the fresh yellows of spring; its white cultivar 'Mr Robert' is easier to accommodate. But none of these can compare with the South African *E. canaliculata*, which can grow to 5 m/18 ft, gracefully branched, the lilac-pink cup-shaped flowers borne in large cylindrical panicles. Under glass they come white, when the chocolate-brown anthers show up in stronger contrast. Latest to flower, apart from the greenish *E. scoparia*, is *E. umbellata*, grey-green in foliage and rosy-pink and white in long-lasting flower.

Most evocative of the Mediterranean regions is the olive, which though perhaps originally native of the Near East has been so long cultivated that it is an integral part of the landscape. Gnarled old trees in oil-producing groves, younger trees in villa gardens, new plantations on the hillsides, all add their note of silvery-green as the narrow leaves reveal their glaucous reverse. All the bulbous plants of the Mediterranean that grow with the winter rains, flower in spring and retreat again to their underground storage organs can be naturalized beneath olives: many-coloured *Anemone pavonina* and other anemones of the region, the sweetly scented *Narcissus tazetta* 'Grand Soleil d'Or' and 'Paper White', pale 'Scilly White' and 'Grand Primo', and the great, leafy 'Avalanche' and 'Grand Monarque'; mauve-pink *Tulipa saxatilis* which increases by stolons and flowers well only if sun-baked; and Roman hyacinths. The South African *Freesia lactea* (*F. refracta* var. *alba*) should naturalize here also to spread a carpet of its powerfully fragrant, cream to buff yellow, sometimes green-washed flowers. Multi-coloured *Sparaxis* hybrids and the metallic green *Ixia viridiflora* should also do well. During late winter the Algerian, fibrous-rooted *Iris unguicularis* in all its variants, from white through mauve and lavender to violet-purple, flowers freely if well ripened in summer. Another import which may naturalize, spreading freely where suited, is *Amaryllis belladonna*. And if you seek bright colour above your head as well as at your feet, in spring the hillsides are decked with vivid splashes of magenta-pink as the Judas trees, *Cercis siliquastrum*, come into bloom, the abundant pea-flowers bursting out even from the trunk and main branches.

With their glaucous foliage and often marbled trunks, eucalypts suggest a climate where the summer heat quickly reduces the lushness of spring to a sun-bleached landscape. Yet with the introduction of seed on the one hand from areas where species formerly considered tender are at or near the limits of their cold tolerance, and on the other from successive generations grown to maturity in cool climates, more and more species are becoming available which can be regarded as hardy. You may still need a genuinely Mediterranean climate to succeed with the spectacular, cinnabar red *Eucalyptus ficifolia*: the most northerly oceanic-zone garden where it grows and flowers is probably Tresco Abbey on the Isles of Scilly; though a tree did survive and even flower on the mainland of Cornwall, at Penzance, for some years. Another that survived in sheltering woodland at Tresco is *E. calophylla rosea*; while at La Mortola on the Riviera *E. leucoxylon rosea*, which comes in pink, crimson or scarlet, was used in preference to *E. ficifolia* for its greater hardiness.

Many of the species with cream or milky-white flowers are quite hardy. *E. gunnii*, the lovely python-barked *E. niphophila*, and tough and wind-hardy *E. coccifera* (one of the few that will stand coastal winds without resentment) are too well known to be allowed more space here. Scarcely less familiar, and virtually as frost-hardy, *E. dalrympleana* is very fast-growing, soon developing a trunk with a patchwork bark of cream, buff-pink and tan; more colour comes from the young growths of coppery-pink or scarlet. Its near relation *E. viminalis* is less hardy; it differs also in its tapered dark green juvenile foliage and bark peeling in strips, not in flakes. The young adult foliage of *E. glaucescens*, another fast-growing species which is potentially very hardy if of the right provenance, is glaucous or pink-flushed; the juvenile foliage is entirely glaucous white. As the trunk develops the bark matures from green to white. *E. urnigera* is tough and quick-growing, with glossy green adult leaves; it seems to be more wind-fast than *E. gunnii*. All the eucalypts, especially those that grow very rapidly, risk tipping over as their top hamper outgrows the roots' ability to anchor the tree. By pruning them hard back – reducing by half their height at 3 m/10 ft and again when that height is reached once more – you can help the roots to establish themselves more securely and the stem to thicken so that the top-heavy head no longer flops groundward.

The spinning gum, *E. perriniana*, gets its nickname from the way the semi-circular juvenile foliage, each pair united at the base to appear as one single round leaf threaded onto the stem, works loose and spins around the stem in the wind. The mature leaves, like the juvenile, are glaucous, but they share the common eucalypt tendency to change to a narrower outline, lanceolate or somewhat sickle-shaped. As its name suggests, *E. pulverulenta* has very silvery-glaucous juvenile foliage, heart-shaped and stem-clasping; it is slower growing than the spinning gum and less hardy.

R. C. Barnard, who did much to popularize the gums in the United Kingdom, described its foliage as 'fluorescent bedewed in the sunlight' (RHS Journal vol. 91 [1966] p. 300). It is very like *E. cordata*, which although rather frost-tender is remarkably resistant to sea winds; the bark is white to greenish. For its bright silver foliage it has been often used in bedding, in common with *E. globulus*, a species with larger, blue-green leaves, white glaucous beneath. This is one of the fastest growing species, reaching, in California, 12–13 m/40–43 ft in little over three years from sowing the seed; older trees, if cut down, regenerate to make 30 m/100 ft giants in six to eight years. The lemon-scented *E. citriodora* is also very fast-growing and very tender. Specialist nurseries list an increasing number of species that are proving hardy, or else are so beautiful as to be worth attempting in mild areas where they can be enjoyed at least for a few years until an exceptionally cold winter proves too much for them. Here I want to mention just one more, the elegant *E. nicholii*, a weeping tree with very slender, willow-like juvenile foliage hanging gracefully, glaucous blue bloomed with purple in spring, and shreddy bark.

A little evergreen tree that is much seen in countries bordering the Mediterranean is the South American pepper tree, *Schinus molle*. It has an elegant, graceful semi-weeping outline and pretty pinnate foliage; the creamy flowers are followed, on female trees, by clusters of carmine-pink, pea-sized fruits. It is a little tender, thriving in the hottest, driest positions. *S. dependens* is more shrubby, with spiny shoots, small obovate leaves, and purple 'peppercorns'. The lentisk, *Pistacia lentiscus*, and the deciduous, terebenthine-yielding *P. terebinthus*, which extends from the Mediterranean countries across into Asia Minor, are related to the pepper trees. They have pinnate leaves; the first, a characteristic *maquis* shrub, produces the resinous substance known as mastic.

The hakeas, a protaceous genus that can be grown in mild but not entirely frost-free climates, are chiefly shrubby. One of the most tree-like is *Hakea laurina*, much cultivated on the French and Italian Rivieras but not well suited to growing further north, which is sad, as it is a most beautiful tree, with eucalyptus-like foliage and pincushion heads of carmine or crimson, studded with the creamy 'pins' of the exserted styles. Much hardier, and quite wind-tolerant, is *H. lissosperma*, which is remarkably like a conifer in aspect except when bearing its white or cream flowers. Though more slender in leaf, *H. sericea* is otherwise similar; the flowers are usually white, sometimes pink. At least as hardy, *H. microcarpa* is rather smaller in growth, up to 2·4 m/8 ft, of dense habit with sharp needle leaves and clusters of fragrant, white or cream flowers in late spring. The pale grey-green, willow-leaved *H. saligna*, quickly forming a sturdy, erect bush, has white flowers in dense clusters. Both *H. gibbosa* and *H. epiglottis* have prickly needle leaves and cream flowers in axillary clusters;

the first has a distinctly glaucous cast and flowers from winter onwards. Even more prickly, *H. suaveolens* bears its fragrant white flowers in summer.

The Atlantic Island echiums are spectacular shrubby perennials or biennials to associate with the soft yellows of mimosa or the milky brooms of the Mediterranean spring. Where the winters are mild enough they will also do well in oceanic climates; I know of several coastal or estuary gardens in south western Britain where the towering *Echium pininiana* flowers and self-sows to perpetuate itself as easily as foxgloves in an English wood. This biennial species from the Canaries forms a wide rosette of green, rough-hairy leaves from which, in its second year, immense tapering spires of tightly packed lavender-blue flowers reach up to 3 m/10 ft or more. Its sheer size commands respect, but it is scarcely so beautiful in flower as some of the shrubby species with narrow, grey, hairy leaves on branching stems, topped by dense cylindrical spikes of pure or violet-blue: *E. fastuosum* from the Canaries, the paler *E. nervosum* from Madeira, and the beautiful, white-hairy *E. candicans*, known as the pride of Madeira. Hybrids from Tresco Abbey gardens are known as *E.* × *scilloniensis*: 'Tresco Blue' is a fine selection with deep ultramarine spikes. A named hybrid, of course, must be perpetuated by cuttings, whereas the species are easy and quick from seed. The Canary Island *E. wildprettii* departs from the habitual blue or occasional white of most species to astound when, over rosettes of hairy, soft, narrow leaves, it opens a stout pyramidal spike of rich red flowers, as tall as *E. pininiana*. Among the blues of the echiums, the yellow of mimosa is reinforced by yellow Banksian roses, which in warm gardens may be grown away from sheltering walls, either to fling their long, supple, green, unarmed wands into dark pines, or – pruned hard after flowering – grown as a big loose shrub. The double yellow is the prettiest, its massed clusters of little pale flowers contrasting with the fresh green foliage; but the double white, and the two single-flowered kinds in white or soft yellow, are much more fragrant, with that haunting, violet scent so unlike most roses.

The tea roses, which do so well in the south of France, have already found a place in an earlier chapter, and it is worth mentioning that several also exist in climbing form; but there are other roses too for Mediterranean climates. In early to mid-summer, 'Fortune's Double Yellow' opens its loose, semi-double flowers of warm yellow flushed with coppery-scarlet. The Banksian hybrid *Rosa* × *fortuneana*, with large, solitary, creamy white flowers among light green glossy foliage, also flowers at this time. Then there are the tenderish climbers such as rose-pink and coppery-salmon 'La Follette', the paler, creamy peach 'Belle Portugaise' with its delicious tea scent, and 'Climbing Devoniensis', with creamy flowers, touched with apricot at their hearts on just opening to a camellia-like perfection.

The tea fragrance of 'Devoniensis' and others may derive from *Rosa gigantea*, a tall and vigorous climber reaching 10 m/33 ft or more in mild climates. Frank Kingdon Ward, in *Plant Hunter in Manipur* (1952) pp. 45–6, describes how in the wild the limp, soft leaves were deep red, the 'slim, pointed flower buds a pale daffodil yellow; but when the enormous flowers opened they were ivory-white, borne singly all along the arching sprays, each petal faintly engraved with a network of veins like a watermark'. 'Belle Portugaise' is half *R. gigantea*, the other parent a hybrid tea. Of less certain parentage is 'Maréchal Niel', a rather tender climber with nodding flowers of long, elegant tea rose shape and exquisite soft, buttery-yellow colouring. 'Niphetos' is of similar quality but paler lemon-white. When, over a quarter of a century ago, I discovered that there was more to gardening than hoping to earn sixpences weeding my parents' herbaceous borders, it was 'Maréchal Niel' who was directly responsible. Six cut blooms from a river bailiff's greenhouse, their silky petals fallen, were stuck by my inexperienced and ignorant fingers in a corner of the little plot of red Cornish earth that I called a garden: every one of them grew roots. This early success carried me triumphantly past successive failures; perhaps the most important lesson learned was that the right time to take a cutting is when someone gives it to you. It is thanks to this naïve belief, and the immense generosity of fellow gardeners, that I have been able to grow so many of the plants I describe in these pages.

The wood of *Rosa hemisphaerica* is not frost-tender, for it comes from western Asia where the winters can be harsh. But the globular, sulphur-yellow blooms, tightly packed with petals, need a hot season to open; even a drop of rain will discourage the buds and turn them to a mildewed mess. When they do succeed in opening fully, the contrast of their clear colouring with the glaucous-blue foliage is in perfect balance.

As the season advances, bougainvillea makes its declamatory statements; the common type is magenta, unashamedly flamboyant, but you can also see scarlet and tangerine and warm yellow, coral and shell-pink, white and crimson. Pomegranate, *Punica granatum*, in scarlet or white, single or double, and the crape myrtle, *Lagerstroemia indica*, are winter-hardy in even quite cold areas if their wood is sufficiently ripened by summer sun and heat, which also encourages flowers. The *Lagerstroemia* in particular is valued for its late summer season, when the crimpled flowers in pink, white or purple are borne in 20 cm/8 in panicles. The shiny deciduous leaves and peeling, cinnamon-pink bark are attractive, but not enough to compensate for the shrub's reluctance to flower in climates where the summers are grey.

The South African polygalas flower almost continuously in warm, sunny gardens. No matter how I try, I cannot sort out in my mind whether *Polygala* 'Dalmaisiana' and *P. myrtifolia* 'Grandiflora' are the same or not; there are so many conflicting views. The same or not, they are branching evergreen shrubs reaching about 1·5 m/5 ft, with rather pea-like flowers of brilliant purple; I have seen the name 'Dalmaisiana' attached to a more magenta-rose version, whether correctly I know not. *P. virgata* is distinct, being almost deciduous, taller and willowy with slender shoots terminating in many-flowered spires of bright purple. All the polygalas will grow in the driest and most arid parts of Mediterranean gardens.

Also from South Africa are the species of *Euryops*, daisy-flowered shrubs that run to bright, clear yellow, a colour to keep away from the polygalas. *E. pectinatus* is hairy in leaf, especially in hot, dry soils, when the yellow daisies contrast most satisfactorily with the finely cut grey foliage. *E. chrysanthemoides* is green of leaf; *E. abrotanifolius* has, as its name suggests, thread-fine foliage, very like that of southernwood except that it is green not grey. All the osteospermums and gazanias and gerberas, and the brilliant annual daisies of South Africa, some of which we have met in earlier chapters, thrive in the Mediterranean heat. So too, to the point of naturalizing itself, does the South American *Nicotiana glauca*, a tall shrubby tobacco with large, smooth, bright glaucous leaves and stems, and loose sprays of tubular yellow flowers. It assorts handsomely with *Ipomoea acuminata* (*I. learii*, *Pharbitis learii*), the blue dawn-flower from tropical America with rich purple-blue, wide convolvulus-like saucers, marred only by their tendency to fade towards red-purple.

There is much else that can contribute to a Riviera atmosphere if your garden is hot and dry; for example, some of the shrubs and climbers described in Chapter V. But if any one genus is more evocative of the Mediterranean than *Olea europaea*, the olive, and the mimosas, it is the citrus tribe, oranges and lemons and tangerines. Hardiest are the oranges; indeed, a Seville orange tree survived for over two hundred years at Salcombe on the south Devon coast of south-western England, and over shorter periods 'oranges, citrons, lemons and limes come to perfection in the open air and are equal, if not superior, to any brought from abroad' (*Illustrated London News*, March 1, 1856). The hybrid 'Meyer's Lemon' is surprisingly hardy, with the same powerfully fragrant, creamy flowers at almost any season, and juicy, aromatic lemons ripening fast.

The Californian chaparral

Just as, for several centuries now, the Mediterranean flora has enriched gardens in cooler climates, so, more recently, the plants of California have come to be valued, often for similar qualities: fragrance of flower or foliage, evergreen leaves, and a willingness to grow and flower in hot, sunny gardens. Many are plants of the chaparral, that close-knit community of shrubs, the Californian equivalent of the *maquis* which, like the *maquis*, has its own special aroma. The precise components vary from region to region, differing also with aspect and altitude: but the most common genera are *Ceanothus* and *Arctostaphylos*, dwarf evergreen oaks, some *Salvia* species, *Rhus*, *Cercocarpus*, and *Photinia arbutifolia*. In our gardens, *Ceanothus* are the most widely grown and, as many are both evergreen and blue-flowered, greatly valued. The simple word 'blue' scarcely suggests their variety, from skimmed milk and pale china-blue to the deep ultramarine of *C. impressus*, pale smoky blues and indigo, and excursions into clear lavender, mauve-pink and white. Almost all are at their happiest in dry, free-draining soils: they can be found colonizing the gravelly scars left by road builders, or covering hot, stony slopes. For rapid cover of hot banks in our gardens it is hard to better *C. thyrsiflorus repens*, as noted. In their native land *C. dentatus* and its var. *floribundus* grow low and wide, covering stony banks; the variety has tiny leaves densely packed in clusters, and smothering masses of brilliant blue flowers. In catalogues, however, there is great confusion between these and the natural hybrids *C.* × *veitchianus* and *C.* × *lobbianus*, both introduced from California by William Lobb in the 1850s. (Ceanothuses, it may be said here, are extremely promiscuous and with rare exceptions will cross-breed with any other species that finds itself in their neighbourhood.) The confusion is unfortunate, for *C.* × *veitchianus* is a tall shrub of 3 m/10 ft or so, against 30 cm/1 ft in height with a spread of up to 4 m/13½ ft for *C. dentatus floribundus*. The same William Lobb collected a plant known as *C. floribundus* (which is perhaps, or perhaps not, *C. dentatus floribundus*) now believed to be lost from European gardens; it had very fine, rich blue flowers. Any of these names, in nurseries, should be attached to a good shrub; but whether tall, or low and wide, is not predictable, as nurserymen seem to have regarded the specific epithets as freely inter-changeable.

The name *Ceanothus prostratus* sounds promising as suggesting a shrub to cover sunny banks; but this low, spreading shrub, which makes prickly carpets marching over any low obstacle in the wild, resents captivity, refusing all too often to live long enough to produce its clusters of bright lavender blossom. The near-related *C. divergens* is more accommodating, making wide bumpy carpets of toothed leaves. *C. foliosus* varies from a low shrub to a spreading, semi-prostrate mat of glossy, minutely toothed leaves; the fragrant flowers vary from lavender-tinted cobalt to a much purer, brighter gentian-blue. It is not so keen on blazing sun as some, though free drainage is still important and under the grey skies of maritime gardens it should still be given a position in full sun. Var. *austromontanus* is lower and wider than the type and seems to grow well in heavy soil. E. B. Anderson's seedling of *C. foliosus*, named 'Italian Skies', is a splendid, vigorous, spreading shrub with brilliant blue flowers in dense conical clusters.

Aloof little *C. rigidus*, which seems never to hybridize in the wild though it has been a parent of some good garden hybrids, is another coastal species growing on exposed bluffs on Monterey County, where it forms low, wide mounds with wedge-shaped, prickly leaves and fragrant flowers in broad clusters, varying in colour from lilac and lavender and violet to pure blue, or white, as in the cultivar 'Snowball'. If given too much shelter it grows tall and gangly, but it is a rather tender species needing a warm climate to thrive without the backing of a wall. *C. ramulosus* is similar, with paler flowers of powder-blue or white; var. *fascicularis* has lavender-blue blossom with a strong honey perfume.

Though ceanothuses are valued especially for their blue blossom, some species are less pure in tone, yet not to be despised for all that. *C. purpureus* admits to the colour of its flowers, which open from silvery-pink buds to rich bright purple, fading to nearer lavender; the leathery leaves are holly-like, the branches widespreading. Its near relation *C. jepsonii* is less satisfactory in cultivation; its colour is more variable and includes a good blue as well as white.

Gardeners in cool climates are accustomed to growing *Ceanothus impressus* with wall protection, where it can reach $2\,\mathrm{m}/6\frac{1}{2}\,\mathrm{ft}$. In the wild, it remains low and spreading, with branches that grow up and out before arching downwards where sheltered from the wind, or reach out horizontally in open, blowy places. The little dark green leaves are marked by the deep grooves of the veins on the upper surface. Again, as known in cultivation it has deep pure blue flowers, but in the wild may vary from a pinkish-lavender or woodsmoke-blue all the way to ultramarine. The cultivar 'Puget Blue' grows naturally more erect, and may usefully lead us to some of the taller ceanothuses. One of the most appealing is *C. papillosus*, a spreading shrub up to $3\,\mathrm{m}/10\,\mathrm{ft}$ in cultivation, though often lower and wider in the wild on exposed hillsides. The foliage is very distinct, narrowly oblong, varnished dark green, with little bumpy warts on the upper surface; var. *roweanus* has even narrower leaves. The best forms of both the type and its compact variety have fragrant, lapis-lazuli blue flowers. 'Concha' is a good cornflower blue, flowering later than *C. papillosus*, perhaps under the influence of its other parent, *C. impressus*. Low-growing 'La Purissima' is of the same parentage; it was named for the Mission which was landscaped by Edward Rowe who gave his name to *C. papillosus* var. *roweanus*. 'Delight' and 'Dignity' are old hybrids of *C. papillosus* with *C. rigidus*, hardy and tough with glossy leaves and rich blue flowers in long spikes. Another, newer hybrid of *C. papillosus* var. *roweanus* is 'Cynthia Postan', which has stout arching stems forming a $2\cdot4\,\mathrm{m}/8\,\mathrm{ft}$ mound clothed to the ground with glossy, narrowly oblong, deeply-veined leaves and, in its late spring season, with massed clusters of rich blue flowers.

Ceanothus sorediatus is a species of unusually airy appearance, which it owes in part to the rather sparse, shining leafage, grey on the undersides, and in part – in their late spring season – to the foamy, smoke or powder-blue blossom, each little flower held on a thread-like pedicel. It makes a wide shrub of up to 2·4 m/8 ft and sometimes flowers again in autumn. This dual season it shares with three well established old hybrids, intense blue 'A. T. Johnson', the densely leafy, rich blue 'Burkwoodii' and paler 'Autumnal Blue'.

The season opens, in gardens, with *Ceanothus arboreus*, which in mild areas may flower as early as late winter; indeed, one of its cultivars is named 'Winter Cloud'. It is, as the specific epithet implies, a tree-like shrub reaching as much as 9 m/30 ft, with comparatively large, ovate leaves, of dull greyish-green, felted beneath, and large pyramidal panicles of pale sky-blue, fragrant flowers. If this weak colouring is too washed out for your taste, you could plant 'Trewithen Blue' or the hardier 'Ray Hartman'. The deep blue 'Theodore Payne' is a hybrid of *C. arboreus* with *C. spinosus*, a very drought-resistant tall shrub with palest grey-blue, almost white flowers in loose panicles. On its native hillsides *C. spinosus* looks, from a distance, like a drift of smoke or sea fog when in bloom. *C. thyrsiflorus*, of which we have already met the form *repens*, is a tall shrub or tree with sizeable dense panicles of azure flowers. It has been suggested as a probable parent of 'Burtonensis', which in fact greatly resembles the other putative parent, *C. impressus*, but that its glossy leaves are almost circular in outline. 'Cascade', on the other hand, is very like *C. thyrsiflorus*, a tall shrub with arching branches and powder-blue flowers in long, loose panicles. 'Treasure Island' unites *C. arboreus* and *C. thyrsiflorus*, making a 2·4 m/8 ft shrub with deep blue flowers.

Lastly, *Ceanothus cyaneus*, a beautiful species which needs warmth, free drainage, and shelter; for it is very sensitive to root disturbance and therefore dislikes wind. A large shrub or even a little tree, it has polished green leaves and very large, upright, branched panicles of marine-blue flowers opening from deeper buds and paling as they age.

Though many ceanothuses make good-looking shrubs with no off-season, thanks to their glossy foliage, they are grown essentially for their floraison. So, too, are the fremontodendrons, spectacular yellow-flowering shrubs which can be set among the deeper blue *Ceanothus*, with due regard to the season of flower, for a bright pairing of complementary colours. By contrast with the varied genus *Ceanothus*, there are just two *Fremontodendron* species: *F. californicum* and *F. mexicanum*. Both form shrubs as much as 4 m/13½ ft tall, the branches spreading widely if not crowded, especially in the Mexican species. The dull green, fig-shaped leaves are felted beneath with rusty or greyish hairs and the stems are also clothed in brown fur, which rubs off easily when the shrub is handled and can be a severe irritant. The flowers are satiny bowls of rich yellow with waxy centres, pure pale gold in the Californian species, larger and flatter and of a deeper yellow marked with red-gold on the exterior in the Mexican, which is more densely branched and leafy. The Mexican species is also more tender. Their hybrid, 'California Glory', has flowers with the broad petals of the Californian parent but the larger, flatter saucer shape and reddish exterior of the Mexican. All should have hot, free-draining, droughty soil; too much moisture and they grow fast, but die soon.

In the wild *Fremontodendron californicum* can be found on hot, gravelly slopes with *Dendromecon rigida*, the tree poppy, capricious in cultivation but beautiful when it succeeds, with blue-green, willow-like foliage and fragrant, silky, clear yellow poppies on a slender, 3 m/10 ft shrub with shredding bark. *D. harfordii* has green foliage; found wild on the islands of Santa Cruz and Santa Rosa off the Californian coast, it is rather more tender than the mainland species. By contrast *Carpenteria californica* is both hardy and easy, only proving obdurate in the matter of propagation; for seedlings are not invariably full-flowered, and cuttings, the preferred method of perpetuating good forms such as 'Ladhams' Variety', are hard to root. The fragrant flowers are held in clusters, and are reminiscent of single white camellias, set against narrow, dark blue-green leaves. Also related to *Philadelphus* is the pretty, and rather temperamental, *Fendlera rupicola* (*F. wrightii*), a deciduous shrub with white, blush-tinted fragrant flowers in late spring.

Although it grows, in its native California, in the hottest and stoniest soils among rocks, on mountain slopes overlooking the desert, *Romneya coulteri* is surprisingly adaptable to the relatively damp western European soil and atmosphere. But if you have a hot garden with gravelly or sandy soil, it should feel entirely at home. A root-traveller, it has many stems set with divided, smooth, blue-grey leaves and topped by huge, silky-petalled white poppies with a conspicuous central boss of yellow stamens. The rounded buds are encased in blue-grey calyces which, in *R. trichocalyx*, differ in being hairy. This species is also shorter and tidier, earlier in flower, and even more apt to run at the root. Both are best cut right down to ground level in winter; you can plant small bulbs among them to fill the bare patch in early spring.

The Californian mahonias, natives of the same hot, desert-facing slopes as *Romneya*, are as blue as they in leaf; but the foliage is stiff and spiny, forming intricate patterns. It is hardly necessary, unless you are a collector of the genus, to grow every one; you can choose from *Mahonia trifoliolata glauca*, a Texan and Mexican species as is *M. haematocarpa*, *M. nevinii*, Texan *M. swaseyi*, or the pick of them all, *M. fremontii*, with narrow, spine-edged, twisted leaves of bright grey-blue colouring. The flowers, if you feel you need them despite such lovely leaves, are of the expected yellow but cannot compete with the candle-like spikes of the Asiatic mahonias.

California is also the home of several species of lupin. The tree lupin has already been mentioned, for it is an easy and quick, wind-resistant shrub. Far more beautiful, and correspondingly less accommodating in cultivation, are the silvery-leaved *Lupinus albifrons*, a coastal and yet reasonably hardy species, and the exquisite *L. chamissonis*. This low, branching shrub has small, silvery, silky palmate leaves and short, open spikes of cloudy lilac-blue flowers, each little pea-flower with a brighter mauve-blue keel and palest lavender standard, in early summer.

By contrast with all these Californian and Texan shrubs with striking flowers, the genus *Arctostaphylos* is modest in bloom. Yet many are among the most beautiful shrubs we can grow. I do not have in mind the likes of *A. uva-ursi* or *A. nevadensis*, but the taller species of the chaparral which are, in the main, so hard to propagate from cuttings that we seldom see them in gardens. If one had space and patience, and a sunny garden where the soil is an acid sand with some humus, then it would be a worthwhile thing to grow all the species that could be acquired. As it is, the memory of those that I have seen in other gardens, and the impressionistic word-pictures of Mrs Lester Rowntree, impel me to write these final paragraphs in a spirit of encouragement to try even one or two. *A. manzanita* (*A. pungens* ssp. *manzanita*), one of the most obdurate in the matter of cuttings, and resentful of transplanting, is also one of the finest, tall and erect with a 'circumspect, prideful look', chocolate-brown bark catching the eye at a distance, and grey-green leaves. The waxy, urn-shaped flowers are white or blush, and are grouped in larger, more graceful sprays than those of other species. It comes from open stony places and is reasonably wind-hardy.

The foliage of *A. canescens* is greyer still, especially in spring when the young growths are almost white with a dense coating of down and the new leaves are velvety grey with a pink flush. It is a smaller, dense and gnarled shrub with dark red bark on the older stems, pink flowers borne very early in the season, and flattened, rose-pink berries aging to russet-brown. The smooth grey-green leaves of *A. glauca* are almost round in outline, and the shredding bark is mahogany-red; the flowers are white, and are followed by 'heavy drooping bunches hang[ing] like clusters of dull red-brown cherries'. *A. tomentosa* is more consistently shrubby, up to 2·4 m/8 ft, with peeling russet bark and grey-green leaves thickly felted on the undersides. It grows at the edge of *Pinus radiata* forests and on windy coastal bluffs, and has the ability to regenerate after forest fires from the woody burl that forms at the base of the stem in the manner of the mallee eucalypts of Australia. *A. patula* shares this characteristic; it is a much greener shrub, with chocolate-brown bark and honey-scented pink flowers among the broad leaves, which are held edgeways to the stems. The young foliage of *A. mariposa* is bright, light green, but as it matures it becomes uniformly glaucous-grey, beautiful against the dark mahogany, polished bark; the little tight-lipped flowers are lavender-pink. It is close to *A. viscida*, which has bright deep red bark and pale glaucous-white leaves, with a lavender flush to the margins when young; its quite large, bright pink flowers are held on red stems. Like *A. bicolor*, which has leaves of very dark burnished green on the upper surface and pale grey felted beneath, it grows on hot slopes. Gravelly slopes form the habitat of *A. andersonii*, an upright shrub of up to 3·6 m/12 ft, with rich tan bark and bright yellow-green, stem-clasping leaves; the flowers appear early in the season and the fruits that follow are very sticky. The foliage of *A. stanfordiana* is also a bright, light green; the pink flowers are held in graceful, open panicles and 'the distinctively long loose clusters of berries which follow them are like narrow, very loose bunches of little grapes'. The shrub that used to be known as *A. diversifolia* is now *Comarostaphylis diversifolia*; here the bark is grey rather than the usual chocolate- or mahogany-brown, and the white flowers in long hanging racemes are held by red berries 'which look as though covered with minute translucent red-glass beads'.

VII

The Mature Milder Garden

SOONER or later in the development of the milder garden – sooner in areas of high atmospheric humidity and moderate winds, later where salt gales or burning sun scorch your young plants – there comes a time when you can stand among your sheltering trees in the awareness that, imperceptibly, they have formed a canopy. Above your head, perhaps, they are whipped by a fierce sou'westerly, and you can hear the plaint of the branches, the song of the windswept leaves, each different from species to species. But at ground level, all is tranquil, and the silence among the tree trunks is the more poignant for the commotion above. Or perhaps it is one of those cloudless, windless days when the sun for weeks has beaten down unrelentingly and only the greys and silvers, in the open garden, are brighter and whiter than ever; all else looks bleached and crumpled in the heat. Then you can step from the furnace into the coolness of your trees, beneath which the foliage of shrubs and ferns is fresh and beautiful still.

Trees for flower and foliage

Here, I want to consider some of the trees, many of them evergreen, that can be grown within the shelter of trees that withstand gales and salt spray, or in gardens where there is no threat from wind. They will include some species that, in less favoured climates, are more often seen as large shrubs. *Cornus capitata* is one such; in a mild garden it forms an evergreen tree of 9m/30ft or more, with a clean trunk and an elegant umbrella-shaped canopy of matt green foliage. In early summer the leaves are almost hidden by the flowers, or rather by the primrose-yellow bracts that surround the insignificant flowers themselves. Strawberry-red, knobbly fruits follow, composed of many seeds set in a pulp which is edible, tasting like an insipid and overripe banana. These fruits are very popular with squirrels, and scattered seedlings may result. *Cornus chinensis* (not to be confused with *C. kousa* var. *chinensis*) is tender also; it is allied to, and resembles, the yellow, winter-flowering *C. mas* but has much finer foliage, large and deeply veined, to follow the showy clusters of blossom on bare green branches. Its collector, Frank Kingdon Ward, thought very highly of this tree, describing, in 'Plant Hunting in Assam' (RHS Journal, Vol. 77, p. 207 [1952]), how it forms 'a straight slender trunk crowned with sulphur yellow flowers in great numbers'. It was, he considered, 'from the horticultural point of view perhaps the most striking plant we found'.

Also more usually seen in a shrubby state is *Magnolia delavayi*. Whether as a wall shrub, or an imposing free-standing tree in warmer gardens, this Asiatic magnolia is valued for its bold, handsome foliage, something like that of a rubber plant, with a fragile, bloomy finish enhancing the deep sea-green colouring. Beneath a large *M. delavayi*, nothing will grow, for the tree makes its own cover of downsweeping branches, trapping the litter of hard and leathery, chocolate and tan-brown fallen leaves. Many people are dismissive of the flowers, and it is true that they will not transform the tree as will the chalices of a *M.* × *soulangiana*, or even the more sparsely borne, wide bowls of *M. grandiflora*. But if you take the trouble to look closely, climbing the tree if need be to reach them, you will see that each evanescent bloom is formed of tepals with the texture of primrose-yellow suede, and deliciously scented too. Within hours of opening, which they are apt to do towards evening, the creamy tones turn to brown and the tepals fall. But there can be reward in such fleeting blooms, the more valued because there is no opportunity to take them for granted, still less to tire of them.

The North American *M. grandiflora* is a good deal hardier, and is familiar even in quite cold areas, sheltered by a wall. In the open it can be allowed to form a fine spreading tree; it needs a sunny clearing, both for the glinting reflection off its highly polished foliage and to ensure a succession of creamy, lemon-scented flowers. In very warm climates such as that of southern California the bull bay will flower from late spring onwards; where less fiercely ripened by the sun, mid- or even late summer will be its starting time, with odd flowers appearing until the frosts. Seed-raised bull bays take many years to reach flowering size, unless you should by rare good fortune come upon a precocious form. Safer by far to invest in a named clone known for its flowering qualities, such as 'Exmouth', which makes an upright tree with narrow leaves, tan-felted beneath when young. If the rusty undersides appeal, you could choose 'Ferruginea', its shorter leaves coated below with a more lasting tawny felt. 'Goliath' was selected for its large flowers, not for its foliage, which is green underneath, with the usual glossy upper surface. Hybrids with the smaller-flowered *M.*

virginiana, the sweet bay, are so like *M. grandiflora* in leaf that I wonder where the often deciduous parent's influence is to be seen; perhaps in the very slightly smaller flowers, though in 'Maryland' they are as fine as any *M. grandiflora*.

Another hybrid of *M. virginiana*, *M.* × *thompsoniana*, resulted from a cross with *M. tripetala*, from which it inherits the umbrella-like arrangement of its large leaves, with a suggestion of the glaucous undersurface of the sweet bay. Although one parent is deciduous, and the other not determinedly evergreen, the hybrid retains many of its leaves through winter in mild areas. The wide creamy flowers are sweetly scented and appear over a long season. The same cannot be said for *M. tripetala* itself, the umbrella tree, which is a smelly beast in flower and wood alike, and brittle too, suffering wind damage unless thoroughly sheltered. But the large leaves in parasol whorls at the ends of the shoots are handsome, and the flowers are followed by showy rose-red fruits filled with scarlet seeds. In the matter of foliage, however, it comes a poor second to *M. macrophylla*, which has immense leaves of flimsy texture, up to 80cm/32in long, absurdly large for a tree of only about 10m/33ft; they are light green above and blue-white beneath. The fragrant, cupped, ivory flowers, borne at midsummer, fade fast to buff and parchment. It goes without saying that to protect these great leaves from being bruised and torn, the tree must be given all possible shelter from wind; it appreciates more even than most magnolias a deep, cool, moist soil. The variety *ashei* needs both shelter and sun; being slightly tender, it does better in a more continental climate where summer ripening compensates for cooler winters, provided always that it does not suffer from dryness at the roots.

Other magnolias with the umbrella-like disposition of the leaves are Asiatic, where those I have so far described are American. The hardiest is *M. hypoleuca* (*M. obovata*), named for the striking white undersides to the large leaves; it forms a rather open tree with large, very fragrant, ivory-buff, suede-textured flowers with a central boss of crimson stamens. The related *M. officinalis* is even more fragrant. Shelter is essential for *M. rostrata*, which has stout shoots, the young leaves and buds thickly coated with coppery fawn fur; expanded, the leaves are as large as those of its kin, up to 50cm/20in long, half hiding the white, melon-scented flowers. It is easily wind-damaged, and none too hardy either. I believe it to be less frost-tender than *M. nitida*, however. Here is a tree with evergreen leaves smaller than those of the umbrella trees; they have a high gloss finish, with metallic bronze colouring when young. The small, scented flowers appear in late spring.

All the magnolias of the summer-flowering group which includes *M. sieboldii* and *M. sinensis* are essentially shrubby, and hardy too. For all that, I want to mention just three, atypical of the group. *M. globosa* is uncommon, perhaps because it is less appealing in flower than most, the little nodding, fragrant blooms easily browned by rain, or even dew; but the foliage of this large, spreading shrub or small tree is bold and handsome, glossy green above and at first covered with a blue-white bloom, later retaining a silvery-brown tint on the underside. The most showy *M. sieboldii* has produced two hybrid offspring, *M.* × *wiesneri* (*M.* × *watsonii*) and 'Charles Coates'. Both have as the other parent a species of the umbrella-leaved group. *M.* × *wiesneri* is *M. sieboldii* × *M. hypoleuca*; it forms a small tree of spreading habit, almost indeed a large, open shrub, with quite large leaves glaucous beneath. But the flowers, and especially their fragrance, are the thing, creamy-fawn chalices fashioned as if out of fine suede, with a large central boss of crimson stamens, and the most amazing, far-reaching, rich, fruity perfume. 'Charles Coates', of which the umbrella-tree parent is *M. tripetala*, flowers earlier, in late spring; it has leaves of *tripetala* style but smaller, and flowers shaped like those of *M. sieboldii* but held erect, cream with crimson-red stamens and a rich fragrance.

The great Asiatic tree magnolias, many of them pink-flowered, are among the most beautiful flowering trees that can be grown in temperate climates. Their wood is resistant to frost, but as they flower very early the blooms are apt to be spoiled by frost in cold or inland areas. In gardens where spring frosts are rare, or where an established tree canopy and free air drainage combine to create a favourable microclimate, they can be breathtaking. *M. campbellii* is a Himalayan species now considered to include, as a subspecies, *M. mollicomata*; but as so often, what the botanists lump together, gardeners will persist in regarding as wholly distinct, on account of certain qualities which make one or the other more desirable. In the case of these two, *M. campbellii*, growing among oaks and tree rhododendrons in the wild, has the lovelier flowers, of a clear, warm pink where those of ssp. *mollicomata*, with a more easterly range in the wild among open forests of fir, has blooms of a rather chilly, blued pink. However, it has one immense advantage, horticulturally speaking. Whereas *M. campbellii* will seldom flower until well past its teens, even at twenty-five years of age or more, ssp. *mollicomata* reaches maturity much more rapidly. The two appear to need rather different conditions in the garden also; *M. campbellii*, a taller, multi-stemmed tree, is a sun seeker whereas the more spreading and bushy ssp. *mollicomata* thrives in cooler, woodland conditions. Happily, the most satisfactory setting for *M. campbellii* is an uncluttered backdrop of sea or sky, whereas the shade-loving spp. *mollicomata* can be set against the dark, rather blue-green of pines, for example, in sympathy with its mauvish tones.

The choice is not just between *M. campbellii* and its subspecies *mollicomata* as such; there are various clones available, including some resulting from crosses between the two. Apart from the pink *M. campbellii* usually seen in cultivation there is a white form, f. *alba*, apparently more common in the wild; and deeper rose-pink cultivars, such as 'Darjeeling', from the Darjeeling Botanic Garden in India, or its near-crimson seedling 'Betty Jessel'. This last, later flowering than most, could be a safer choice for gardens where spring frosts are a hazard. Also very richly coloured, almost violet-red fading to lilac-purple, is 'Lanarth', raised from seed of *mollicomata* collected by George Forrest; its habit is upright, quite unlike the usual *mollicomata* sprawl, making it easier to fit into a small garden. Crosses between *M. campbellii* and ssp. *mollicomata* have given rise to 'Charles Raffill', a precocious flowering clone with large blooms of intense pink only just a shade off the clear tones of *M. campbellii* itself, and 'Kew's Surprise', with even larger crimson-pink flowers, white within the pink veins.

The *M. × veitchii* hybrids, which are *M. campbellii × M. denudata*, are tall, vigorous and free-flowering, but unfortunately very brittle, needing all possible shelter from wind. The two named clones of the original cross are 'Peter Veitch' in pink, and 'Isca', white; a later cultivar with deep claret-red flowers is 'Veitchii Rubra'. All have chalice-shaped flowers, whereas *M. campbellii* and its subspecies are of the cup and saucer outline, the outer tepals reflexing to form the saucer.

M. sargentiana, and more especially its variety *robusta*, are much more wind-tolerant than *M. × veitchii*, and even the flowers, with thick-textured tepals, are surprisingly weatherproof. A large *M. sargentiana*, after taking at least twenty-five years to reach the flowering stage, can be superb, its slender, upright branches decked with huge, wide-open pink blooms. But I have also known it, even after forty or fifty years, to be very costive, producing a parsimonious half-dozen flowers a year. Var. *robusta* takes less time to come to maturity, its big almost shrubby framework covered with untidy, loose, almost one-sided flowers, white flushed with mauve-pink; they have a spicy perfume.

Also ragged in flower is *M. dawsoniana*, a twiggy tree which first flowers after twenty years or so, taking many more to fill with blooms; which it does from the top downwards, so that for several more years after the first flowers appear you have to crane to see them in the upper branches. At least they nod, so you can see inside them; but this conceals the richer colouring of the exterior, so all you perceive is the near-white inner surface. Better than the type, on this account, is 'Chyverton', in which the crimson exterior of the tepals is intense enough to suffuse the inner surface, enhanced by a tuft of rich crimson-red stamens.

Flowering as much as two months after the earliest forms of *M. campbellii*, *M. sprengeri* has, like that species, both pink and white forms. The latter, *M. sprengeri* var. *elongata*, has ivory or pure white flowers more like the yulan, *M. denudata*, with a purple flush at the heart. *M. sprengeri diva*, the pink form, resembles in flower a smaller, richer carmine *M. campbellii*, the blooms held erect on the branches. Its seedlings include 'Claret Cup', clear pink 'Copeland Court' and rosy-purple 'Burncoose'. A cross between *diva* and *M. sargentiana robusta* produced the very fine 'Caerhays Belle', which has immense, saucer-shaped, warm pink flowers of solid texture.

The genus *Manglietia* is related to the magnolias; the two species I shall describe are more tender than all but *Magnolia nitida*, unless we start to venture into the low-altitude magnolias such as *M. coco*. Both *Manglietia insignis* and *M. hookeri* form evergreen trees of perhaps 12m/40ft, with stout shoots and dark, glossy green leaves paler or glaucous-green beneath. The fragrant flowers open in spring; those of *M. hookeri* are creamy-white, while *M. insignis* may bear white, pink or deep red blooms like small magnolias.

With the few exceptions I have described, magnolias are chosen above all for their flowers, though none has unattractive leaves. But there is a very different pleasure to be had from trees which form characteristic and beautiful patterns of foliage. One of the most desirable trees I know, not for flower or even especially for foliage as such, but simply for its personality, is *Emmenopterys henryi*. Though introduced as long ago as 1907 by E. H. Wilson, it has yet to flower in Europe with sufficient enthusiasm to match its discoverer's descriptions as 'one of the most strikingly beautiful trees of the Chinese forests, with its flattish to pyramidal corymbs of white, rather large flowers and still larger white bracts'. Though hardy, it prefers a sheltered position in moist, deep loam; and who, having once seen it, would deny it such a special position? Though of no striking shape, being of the uncomplicated outline described as ovate, the leaves are large yet not coarse, and are held with grace and poise on the branches; in spring they unfold in tones of bronze and copper. Though it was many years ago, I shall not forget my first sight of the fine tree at Borde Hill in Sussex; rarely have I stood beneath a tree with such presence. At one time exceedingly rare in cultivation, *Emmenopterys henryi* is now beginning to be offered by the trade, grown either from imported seed or by tissue culture.

Many *Nothofagus* species are beautiful in the disposition of their very small leaves. This is especially so in some of the antipodean species of this genus which extends from South America to New Zealand, Tasmania and the Australian mainland, earning it the vernacular name of southern beech. The Chilean species are in the main deciduous and hardy, and I will skim past them. The impressive coastal species *N. betuloides*, very densely leafy, dislikes cold dry winds but should do well in coastal gardens where the winds are more often mild and moisture-laden; it grows in the wild with *Drimys winteri*. Mature specimens of *N. dombeyi*, another evergreen species from Chile and Argentina, are said to develop a cedar-like habit; its associates in the Chilean forests are *Eucryphia cordifolia* and *Desfontainea spinosa*.

The small evergreen leaves of the New Zealand *N. solanderi*, its near ally *N. cliffortioides* (*N. solanderi* var. *cliffortioides*) and *N. menziesii* are held in ferny sprays. Of the three, *N. cliffortioides* is the smallest, making a tree of up to 10m/33ft at best; a mountain species, it is often no more than a shrub at high altitude in its habitat, and seems to resent exposure to sea winds. *N. solanderi*, up to twice as tall, develops furrowed black bark on older trees; it is more wind hardy. Loveliest of the three is *N. menziesii*, with little triangular or near-circular leaves of leathery texture, with toothed margins; the trunk, often buttressed, is clad in silvery bark marked with horizontal bands. The larger-leaved *N. fusca* is very different, a tall evergreen tree characterized by the deep coppery-red colouring of the leaves in winter. From damp gullies in the mountains of Tasmania comes *N. cunninghamii*, a beautiful, large, evergreen tree with small, rhomboidal or triangular leaves. Beneath its sheltering branches, in its native habitat, tree ferns – *Dicksonia antarctica* – grow.

Nothofagus is a genus that has comparatively recently become familiar in gardens and as a plantation tree in the northern hemisphere. By contrast, both *Acer* and *Sorbus* have long been grown as ornamental trees, the first for its foliage above all, the second for fruit and foliage. Neither genus is associated specifically with mild climates, yet in both there are species that will thrive only in warm seas. *Sorbus insignis*, indeed, is far more suggestive of the rain forest than of the hills where most rowans grow. The forms with the fewest, largest leaflets, numbering five and nine, each up to 20cm/8in long, used to be considered as a separate species, *S. harrowiana*; but some authors make them one, on the grounds that the size and number of leaflets form an insufficient distinction, especially as these characteristics are not constant. As often, there is perhaps more reason from a horticultural point of view to consider them as distinct; for the first introduction, by George Forrest in 1912, was from Yunnan and has proved a great deal more tender than either F. Kingdon Ward's later reintroductions, or *S. insignis*, also introduced by Kingdon Ward. Both have pinnate leaves composed of toothed leaflets, shining dark green above and glaucous beneath; in *S. insignis* KW7746 from Assam they number up to fifteen, the whole forming a frond up to 25cm/10in long. Both species, or variants, grow into small trees with stout upright branches, bearing dingy white flowers in wide heads followed by small pink or blush fruits which last long on the bare branches into winter and beyond.

Despite their appearance of subtropical forest trees, these are still recognizably rowans. Many of the less hardy acers, on the other hand, are very distinct from the maple-leaf image of the genus. The semi-evergreen *Acer oblongum*, a Chinese and Himalayan species, forms a small tree with unlobed leaves up to 30cm/12in long, bright green above and glaucous-white beneath. Its close ally *A. lanceolatum*, from Hong Kong, is similar, while another related species, *A. paxii*, bears leaves either entire or three-lobed, even on the same shoot. Others, recently introduced, that I have not yet seen are *A. albopurpurascens* and *A. cinnamomifolium*, this last a promising name if it implies a resemblance to *Cinnamomum camphora*. *A. laevigatum* is described by Bean as 'the senior member of a small group that ranges from the central Himalayas to eastern China'; it has gleaming, sword-shaped leaves with conspicuous veins beneath. The rare *A. wardii*, discovered by and named for Kingdon Ward, but introduced by George Forrest, has similar leaves even more prominently veined, glossy yellow-green above and glaucous below. The young shoots of *A. hookeri* are red, setting off unlobed leaves which are heart-shaped at the base and drawn out at the apex to a long slender point. *A. sikkimense* is similar, with large leaves; despite growing to as much as 10m/33ft it is usually epiphytic in the wild, growing even on *Rhododendron arboreum*.

Another group of desirable maples suited to milder climates has lobed leaves more akin to the expected outline of a maple leaf. Both *Acer craibianum* and *A. campbellii* have crimson-red young foliage; the first has three blunt, forward-pointing lobes to each leaf, the second is five to seven lobed, each lobe drawn out into a slender, tail-like point. The allied *A. flabellatum*, with sharply serrate lobes, and its variety *yunnanense*, are hardier, though still unreliable in very cold areas. But of all the species best suited to milder areas perhaps *A. pentaphyllum* is the loveliest. A Chinese species, it forms a tree to 10m/33ft, with spreading branches and fingered leaves composed of from four to seven slender leaflets, glaucous beneath, on scarlet petioles. Even as a very young plant, it has great elegance.

Fashion plays its part in garden design, and in the choice of plants that we grow in them, as much as in other spheres of human activity. For a long time, trees such as *Phillyrea latifolia*, which have no bright or fragrant flowers to offer, were despised. Yet the Victorians valued them, and we are beginning to once again, for their elegant masses of dark, shining evergreen foliage. *P. latifolia* itself has many of the qualities of the holm oak; it is smaller in growth, with an attractive silhouette, and is a better neighbour. A *maquis* plant, it is nonetheless very tolerant of a wide variety of soils, and perfectly hardy. It is also, as we have seen in Chapter II, remarkably wind-tolerant. A related tree, much less common, is *Picconia excelsa* (*Notelaea excelsa*) from the Canary Islands; it is, as might be expected, less frost-hardy than its Mediterranean cousin, but is also surprisingly wind-tolerant. It forms a handsome evergreen with fragrant white flowers in little panicles from late winter onwards. The tree-like *Maytenus* species are rather similar in effect. *M. boaria* is of more graceful habit than the phillyrea, with lax branches; the lesser-known *M. magellanica* is of more upright, even narrow outline. Both have glossy dark green foliage, and both are light-loving species, not from the rainforest areas. In mild areas *Laurus nobilis*, the Mediterranean bay laurel, forms a sizeable shrub or even a tree; more tree-like still is the Canary Island laurel, *L. azorica*, with larger leaves equally aromatic, bright glittering green above. *Laurelia serrata* is known as the Chilean laurel, but despite the similarity of names both botanical and English, it is not even in the same family. The leathery, dark green leaves, however, are also strongly aromatic, somewhat like the true bay laurel; a big specimen makes a fine, imposing presence in the garden. A deal hardier than this uncommon tree is *Ligustrum lucidum*, a privet, but an extremely superior one, making a shapely tree with handsome, quite large, shining, pointed leaves, almost like those of *Camellia japonica*. Unlike the laurels true and false, it is striking in blossom also, with bold panicles of many small white flowers in late summer.

In the mildest gardens *Corynocarpus laevigatum* will form a handsome canopy tree as it will in its native New Zealand; the large, polished, leathery leaves are dark green. Not quite so tender, but still at their best only in sheltered woodland in deep humusy soil, are the species of *Lithocarpus*, a largely Asian genus related to the oaks. One of the most striking is *L. pachyphyllus*, a small, spreading tree with long, lance-shaped leaves drawn out to a long point at the tip, lustrous dark green above and metallic silver beneath; the thick spikes of stubby acorns, each almost hidden in its cup, have been likened variously to colonies of giant barnacles or to shillelahs.

All these trees are handsome, with their masses of dark glittering foliage. The genus *Arbutus*, of which the strawberry tree, *A. unedo*, is the best-known, includes other, tree-like species with similar sprays of white, pitcher-shaped flowers and showy, orange or red, grainy fruits. Despite all these qualities, they are most admired for their beautiful bark. *A. unedo* itself is the least handsome in this respect, even when grown past the shrubby state in which it is often seen to form a multi-stemmed tree with white or deep pink (f. *rubra*) flowers. Much rarer is the Greek *A. andrachne*, with flaking, tan bark. Plants so labelled are in fact often the hybrid between these two species, *A.* × *andrachnoides*, which has strikingly beautiful, cinnamon and russet bark inviting a caress. There is a fine specimen in Bodnant in N. Wales, of which Lord Aberconway wrote (RHS Journal Vol. 79, p. 184 – 1954) 'I know of no tree whose aspect alters more readily with the changing vagaries of light and shade, breeze and calm'. Of the species from the Pacific coast states of North America and southwards to Texas and Mexico, *A. menziesii* is a noble evergreen of the moist rich valleys and redwood forests. If you are not sure whether to pronounce the specific name menzeezy-eye or mingiz-eye, you could save face by calling it, as do the Californians, madrona. Its one defect is that it transplants very badly; the slightest shock to the roots can be fatal, and the most likely way to get it safely established is to acquire, or raise your own, seedling, which you will plant with the greatest care from its container into the lime-free soil it prefers. It develops, if successfully established, into a grand tree with bark like in colour to blood-oranges wearing sheer black silk stockings, burnished foliage, sprays of white flowers and clusters of small, yellow-orange fruits. Related species – *A. texana* with redder fruits, *A. xalapensis* from Mexico with ashy-grey bark and the narrow-leaved *A. arizonica*, also grey-barked – cannot compare with the madrona itself.

The Chilean *Luma apiculata* (*Myrtus luma*) is on a smaller scale, with neat dark green leaves, and abundant white, fuzzy flowers in late summer. Shrubby in cooler gardens, in warm areas it develops into a small tree with its trunk and main branches clothed in strokeable, cinnamon suede bark flaking off in patches to show the creamy inner surface. It self sows freely and you can make a little grove in quite a small space; before long you may find yourself having to compost the surplus seedlings. The uncommon *Persea ichangensis* (*Machilus ichangensis*), a Chinese native related to bay laurel, is valued not for coloured bark but for its long, narrow, deep green glossy leaves, coppery-red when unfolding in spring.

Fragrant flowers are borne by the two *Reevesia* species which could be attempted in mild areas. *R. pubescens* grows to 18m/60ft in its native eastern Himalayas; the one mature specimen known in the British Isles after the bitter winter of 1962/3, in a Cornish garden, was already 15m/50ft tall in 1979. The specific epithet derives from the bronze-pink felt which thickly coats the young growth and remains on the underside of the dark green, leathery mature foliage. The small flowers are creamy-white, with bright yellow stigmas, and are borne in large corymbs in summer. Rare also is *R. thyrsoidea* from further east, with white to cream flowers and narrower leaves.

Except for the acers, the two rowan species and some of the magnolias, every tree I have described so far in this chapter is evergreen. It is the preponderance of evergreens, indeed, that gives gardens in mild areas such a different character from those that are obliged to rely chiefly on deciduous broadleaved trees. But for mild gardens too, there are trees that shed their leaves, yet have special qualities commending them apart from their need of warmth and shelter. Some of them, even in the soft climates which do not usually induce good autumn colour, can sometimes perform well as the dying leaves turn to scarlet. The Chinese tallow tree, *Sapium sebiferum*, is so named from the waxy coating to its seeds; the rounded, abruptly pointed leaves often colour brilliantly in autumn. The aromatic *Sassafras albidum* has unusually shaped leaves, attractive when they adopt their characteristic, but not invariable, outline with three forward-pointing, blunt-ended lobes; even if they fail to colour well, this is a worthwhile tree. The more tender *S. tzumu*, in areas where its wood is insufficiently ripened in summer, makes great succulent annual growths with larger leaves, red-veined; slowly it builds up to form a woody framework.

There are two rather tender cherries, acclaimed solely for their beautiful blossom. Needing an open, sunny, sheltered position, both *Prunus campanulata* and *P. cerasoides rubea* have richly coloured flowers, deep rose-red to carmine, borne very early in spring. The second was discovered by Kingdon Ward, who described it (in *Plant Hunter's Paradise*, pp. 149–50) as 'the most significant hardy flowering tree I have ever seen . . . just a mass of blossom, stark crimson'. They are at their best against an uncluttered background, whether of sky and sea, or of dark conifers.

Conifers for the milder garden

To anyone whose sole encounter with conifers has been the relentless march of Sitka across Forestry Commission plantations, or the spruce-clad slopes of the Alps, it may be a surprise to learn that among the gymnosperms are species from much warmer climates, many of them of great beauty. The pines of Mexico and of the Himalayan slopes, the podocarps of New Zealand and southern China, are just two genera of many we could plant and enjoy in a mild garden. As already noted, *Pinus radiata* and *P. muricata*, from Californian coasts, are in the first rank as salt-tolerant trees to shelter the garden against sea spray and gales. The Mexican species would for preference be planted within this shelter; they vary in hardiness according to their natural habitat, but all do best in a warm and sheltered site, preferring a moist, well-drained loam. There are a great many of them, more are being, or to be, discovered, and it appears that the genus is still evolving in Mexico. Furthermore, related species hybridize freely, and many are inherently variable also. I cannot attempt to describe more than the few that are already familiar in cultivation. Of these, *P. montezumae* is a great, looming tree, with an immense, wide, domed crown; the long, blue-grey needles are held in big, sweep's-brush clusters. Its variety *lindleyi*, more tender still, has very long, apple green needles which droop gracefully. Other varieties are *hartwegii*, of narrower outline and certainly hardier, and *rudis*, a tender kind; these two are now regarded as species.

The first *Pinus patula* I ever saw grew in the Botanic Gardens at Geneva, suggesting that it is at least reasonably hardy; though only a young plant, it was already showing its graceful habit, with long, pendulous, bright green needles. The needles of *P. ayacahuite* are very slender, and of pale glaucous grey colouring, standing out brightly from among a dark background of Monterey pine or *Rhododendron ponticum*. Like certain Mexican species, some pines from the old world have large, edible seeds, the *pignons* of the Midi, or *chilghoze* (singular *chilghoza*) of the Indian subcontinent. The chilghoza pine itself, *P. gerardiana*, grows in dry areas of the north-west Himalaya and Afghanistan, and makes a small tree of which the chief attraction, apart from the seeds, is the beautiful bark, mushroom-pink flaking plane-like to reveal the citron and tan new bark. It is by no means so tender as *P. roxburghii*, a subtropical species from the monsoon belt of the outer Himalayas, at lower altitudes than the more familiar *P. wallichiana*. It needs full light, shelter, and a deep well-drained soil, and should be worth trying for its very long needles, to 30cm/12in or more, hanging gracefully. It is apparently closely allied to the geographically very distant *P. canariensis*, hopelessly tender except in very mild maritime areas, but enchanting as a youngster with silvery needles.

Some of the most graceful of all conifers are found in the genus *Cupressus*. The Chinese *C. duclouxiana* has thin branchlets dividing into thread-like, grey-green segments. Elegant though it is, it cannot compare with *C. cashmeriana*, a species long known only from temple gardens and recently discovered in the wild, in one locality in Bhutan. The basic outline of this tree is conical, with ascending branches; these are curtained with hanging sheets of branchlets clad in sprays of bright glaucous-blue foliage. It is distinctly tender, and easily spoiled by wind, but in a sheltered position, at all ages from babyhood on, the Kashmir cypress is one of the most beautiful of all conifers. Where the climate is just too severe for it, an alternative would be *C. lusitanica*, which despite its specific name is not from Portugal but from Mexico and Guatemala; it is the more surprising that it should be so relatively frost-resistant. It has good peeling bark, and pendulous branchlets with grey-green foliage, brighter and more glaucous-blue in 'Glauca' and the weeping 'Glauca Pendula'. The Tecate cypress, *C. guadelupensis*, is found on Guadelupe Island off the coast of Baja Californica (Mexico). Its bark is cherry-red to dark grey, peeling in thin flakes; the grey-green foliage is borne in ferny sprays on ascending branches.

It is to the southern hemisphere that we must turn for the remaining gymnosperms I propose to suggest to you: except, that is, for certain species of the mainly southern genus *Podocarpus*. Conifer buffs will no doubt protest that I have skimmed over the pines, and point out that I have entirely omitted any mention of the Mexican species of *Abies*, and much else besides: but I can only get just so excited about conifers, and by the time I have written about *Phyllocladus* and *Podocarpus* (which I love) and nodded in the direction of *Araucaria, Callitris, Agathis, Athrotaxis* and the graceful dacrydiums, I shall have reached the limit of both my knowledge and my tolerance.

Everyone knows the monkey puzzle, *Araucaria araucana*, a hardy tree not often seen in cultivation at its potentially noble best. It is, I should say in passing, a good wind-resister but intolerant of industrial pollution. Much less hardy is the Australian *A. bidwillii*, which in middle-age forms a fine dome-shaped tree with very dark green leaves spirally arranged, and cones like great pineapples. *A. cunninghamii* is probably even more tender, its range extending from New South Wales to New Guinea; on young trees the needles are spirally arranged, while on older trees, especially on coning branches, they are shorter and more densely packed, bunched towards the end of the branches. Sundry cultivars are known, including the silvery grey 'Glauca'. The glory of the genus, forming a noble tall tree with symmetrical horizontal branches piling up in tiers, is the Norfolk Island pine, *Araucaria heterophylla*: but it is very tender.

The genus *Agathis* is related to *Araucaria*. The kauri pine, *A. australis*, forms a large tree in its native North Island of New Zealand, with thick, whorled branches and needles varying with the maturity of the individual plant from lime-green on young plants, which are flushed with purple, to shorter and stouter, densely packed green leaves on older specimens. It must be a bad neighbour when mature, for the bark remains clean by constantly shedding in flakes, which build up to a mound as high as 2m/6½ft around the base of the trunk.

The most tender of the Tasmanian genus *Athrotaxis* is the temperate rainforest species *A. selaginoides*, which grows with *Nothofagus cunninghamii*. In appearance it is between the two hardier species, *A. cupressoides* with very closely imbricated, dark green, scale-like leaves, and *A. laxifolia* with leaves larger and slightly more spreading. Rare in the wild, this species is the commonest in cultivation. *Callitris oblonga* is also a Tasmanian native, symmetrically branched, with thread-like branchlets. Both this and *C. rhomboidea*, which occurs also in Australia, are best given sheltered woodland conditions in cultivation.

Shelter is needed, too, for the dacrydiums, of which *D. franklinii* is a Tasmanian species making a large shrub or small tree of graceful habit, with slender, widely spaced, drooping branches clad in rich green, scale-like leaves. Most dacrydiums are natives of New Zealand, where the wood of *D. intermedium* is used for boat building and telegraph poles. Other species are also valued for their timber: the wood of *D. biforme* is fragrant, close-grained and pinkish. *D. colensoi* makes an open-habited tree with long slender branchlets, the needle-like juvenile leaves giving way to scale-like adult foliage. Like this species, the delightful *D. cupressinum* needs shade and moisture to recall its native New Zealand rain forest. In youth especially it is very graceful, with thread-like branches hanging undivided for as much as 60cm/2ft, set with short needles. Later, as a mature tree, it forms a straight and slender, tapering stem with pendulous branches and tiny cypress-like foliage.

Like *Dacrydium*, *Phyllocladus* is in the family Podocarpaceae: but the two genera are very distinct in appearance, and indeed *Phyllocladus* is scarcely to be taken for a conifer at first sight. The whorled branches are set, not with needles or scale-like leaves, but with flattened, leaf-like structures known as cladodes, their shape suggested by the name 'celery topped pine' given to *P. asplenifolius*. In this tender species the cladodes are fan-shaped or rhombic, glaucous-green in colour. The alpine celery top, *P. alpinus*, is hardier, with greener, diamond-shaped cladodes; it makes a smaller tree, hardly more than a shrub but usually with a single main stem. The cultivar 'Silver Blades' is slower and smaller, with silvery-blue cladodes.

The largest cladodes in the genus are borne by the very tender *P. glaucus*; they are of two kinds, fan-shaped and toothed on the main stem, but on the branchlets arranged pinnate-fashion, each of the 'leaflets' – there are up to seventeen of them per axis – fan or diamond shaped. The specific epithet refers to the glaucous colouring of the undersides of the young cladodes. A similar arrangement of whorled branches and pinnate phylloclades is found in *P. trichomanoides*, the tallest species, in which, however, the cladodes are smaller; they are tawny-red on first emerging, later turning green. The male strobili in *Phyllocladus* species are catkin-like; carmine-red, they decorate the branch tips; the red fruits which follow the female strobili occur at the margins of the cladodes.

The genus *Podocarpus* is more widespread than *Dacrydium* or *Phyllocladus*, with species found not only in New Zealand and Australia, but also in Africa, South America, and in the northern hemisphere in China and Japan; other species too tender for our purposes occur in tropical areas. There are hardy, shrubby New Zealand species which need not concern us here, but also some very elegant trees. Least interesting are the often shrubby *P. totara* and closely allied *P. hallii*, with leathery, pointed leaves spiralling the stems; they are of a rather dirty yellowish or brownish green. The rare *P. spicatus* is more elegant, especially when young, for the branchlets are then slender and drooping; but the green or bronze-tinted needles are sparse and small. Also rare is *P. ferrugineus*, a graceful thing with yew-like foliage, though not of the intense black-green of *Taxus baccata*, borne on slender branchlets which droop at the tips. In a different class altogether is *P. dacrydioides*, a very tall tree in the wild but much smaller in captivity; the specific epithet suggests the slender, pendulous branchlets and small, narrow, rather bronzed leaves, arranged in two ranks on young trees, spirally on older specimens. It grows in swampy forest in New Zealand and clearly, in gardens, needs sheltered, moist woodland conditions to do well. *P. elatus*, an Australian species, is perhaps even more tender, a small and attractive tree with quite long, narrow, bright green leaves, longest of all (to 20cm/8in) on young, strongly growing plants. Species from the African continent that might be attempted with fair chance of success are *P. falcatus* from South Africa, which has leaves very variable in size and shape; and the elegant *P. gracilior*, from the mountains of Ethiopia, Uganda and Kenya, which has willow-like leaves. From Chile comes a hardier species, *P. salignus*, called the 'willow podocarp', on account, no doubt, of its attractive, abundant foliage of shining green. It is a very beautiful tree. *P. nubigenus*, with a wider range in South America, is hardier and more shrubby, with spirally-set, pointed leaves bright green above and glaucous beneath. Desirable though these are, however, it is before two of the Chinese and Japanese species that I find myself weak-kneed with admiration. One of them, *P. macrophyllus*, is actually among the hardiest in the genus; but with its glossy green, large and comparatively broad leaves, up to $20 \times 1 \cdot 2$cm/$8 \times \frac{1}{2}$in on vigorous plants, densely arranged in spirals along the stems, it has the look of something almost tropical. *P. nagi* is smaller in stature and in leaf, with leaves almost opposite, deep shining green above and paler, even whitish, beneath; it is a fine but none too hardy evergreen.

Rhododendrons

In writing about the trees which I have chosen to include in this chapter, I had to decide how far I would go in accepting those which, though needing a gentle climate, do not necessarily demand woodland conditions. Thus it is that a good many of them must be understood as helping to create such conditions rather than requiring them; light-loving trees such as the cherries will need siting at the margins of glades where the sun can reach them. By the time I came to consider shrubs, I could be more positively biased towards those needing, or at least preferring, woodland shelter, with dappled shade, and a deep, moist, humusy and most probably acid soil. This, of course, is especially true of the genus *Rhododendron*. By this stage of the chapter I am assuming that whatever you have selected from among the trees and shrubs have developed to the extent that you have areas beneath their branches where you will necessarily have to confine your choice to plants that enjoy warm shade, a more or less constantly humid atmosphere, and an organic soil enriched by years of leaf fall. If you cannot, or will not, grow rhododendrons, you can skip the next few pages to go straight to other woodland shrubs.

The genus *Rhododendron* has its heartland in the Sino-Himalayan regions, where for most of the year the atmosphere is misty, charged with moisture, if not actually precipitating it as rain or snow. It follows, therefore, that rhododendrons will scarcely thrive in areas of low rainfall where the air is dry; and if the soil is calcareous also, then you should forget them altogether. But in the mild south and west of Britain, on the Atlantic coasts of Ireland and France, and in other areas with similar soft, maritime or ever-humid climates, they will flourish wherever the soil is suitable. Though it is hard to pick out a manageable selection from so large, so varied, and in the main so addictive a genus, I must make the attempt. It may help to note which types of rhododendron I will not be considering: the hardy hybrids, without exception, valuable though they may be as shelter in the early years; the alpine types which in the wild grow at high altitudes or latitudes on more or less open slopes, snow-covered for many months in the year; and all the azaleas. Two groups, horticulturally speaking, stand out by contrast as ideally suited to the milder garden: the large-leaved species of subsections Falconera and Grandia, and the tenderish, often delectably fragrant species and hybrids of subsections Boothia and Edgeworthia. As well as these, I shall want to touch on a few species, other than the large-leaved, which are grown primarily for their foliage; some scarlet and blood-red species and their hybrid offspring; fewer yellow-flowered kinds; the exquisite *Lapageria*-flowered members of subsection Cinnabarina; the usually white or blush, often fragrant species in subsection Fortunea, together with some half-breed crosses; and a few oddments that I cannot reasonably coerce into any of these largely arbitrary and inconsistent categories.

Much though I love the fragrant Maddenia rhododendrons, I shall begin with the large-leaved kinds, to emphasize that rhododendrons can offer for our delectation several attributes other than flowers, once we move away from the laurel-leaved hardy hybrids. The rhododendrons of subsections Falconera and Grandia, to reach their most imposing dimensions in leaf, need shelter from wind, and a level of precipitation that is fairly constant, and fairly high, year round; conditions that combine to give a perpetually humid atmosphere. With this, they need acid, humusy soil, and a loose, leafy litter about their roots.

The most familiar of the large-leaved rhododendrons is *R. macabeanum*, in subsection Grandia. 'Macabe' forms a large, shrubby tree with leathery leaves as much as 30cm/12in long, dark lustrous green above and silvery-white beneath. The flowers are of the typical bulging bell shape of these, the most primitive species of rhododendron. In the best forms of *R. macabeanum* they are clear yellow with a red-purple basal blotch, but they may be a pale and wan primrose-cream; they are held in compact trusses of up to thirty blooms, set on a ruff of radiating leaves. The expanding growth buds in spring are striking also, the sealing-wax-red bud scales giving way to silvered young leaves. One of the characteristics of *R.*

macabeanum is that the best foliage is allied to the finest flowers, which may be helpful in deciding which seedlings to retain if you decide to acquire your plant in this way, rather than paying a big price for a known good form.

The leaves of *Rhododendron grande*, a tree to 9m/30ft, are even longer, up to 45cm/18in, though relatively narrower; they may be grey-white or fawn beneath, and are brightly silver-washed when young. The flowers, in similar hemispherical trusses, are always pale creamy-white with a purple basal blotch. *R. magnificum* is taller still, growing to 18m/60ft in the wild, the obovate leaves up to 35cm/14in long, dull green above and at first cobwebby with white hairs beneath. The flowers, more tubular in shape, vary in colour from pale to deep rosy-purple or even near-crimson, with purple blotches at the base. Of similar, though purer pink colouring, with carmine basal patches, are the stout bells of *R. montroseanum*, a shrubby tree of 5m/18ft with long, comparatively narrow leaves wrinkled above and shining silvery-white beneath. The long leaves of *R. protistum* var. *giganteum*, a tall tree, are densely brown-woolly beneath, the flowers deep carmine-pink. But it is *R. sinogrande*, the eastern counterpart of *R. grande*, that bears the noblest foliage, as much as 60cm/2ft long, emerging silvered, later dark, shining green above and grey on the undersides. Kingdon Ward wrote of it, in *Plant Hunting on the Edge of the World*, p. 277, 'its pale yellow globes were alight and shining brightly under the dark canopy of leaves ... The great spear-headed buds burst in July, and even in August one can pick out the trees a mile away by the plumes of silver foliage shooting up from ruby-red tubes'.

Many of the members of subsection Falconera have leaves that are felted beneath with a tan or fox-brown indumentum. Such is *Rhododendron falconeri* itself, with leaves up to 30cm/12in long. The cream or ivory to primrose, stout, asymmetrical bells last longer than those of any other rhododendron, up to a month. Its subspecies *eximium* differs in its flesh-pink or rosy bells, but also in the long-lasting cinnamon felt which coats both surfaces of the leaves for the whole of their first season. Both form trees to 12m/40ft. *R. basilicum* is often more shrubby, at 2·4m/8ft, but may develop into a 7m/22ft tree, with leaves tawny-felted beneath and close-packed trusses of up to twenty or more pale yellow bells flushed with pink and enhanced by crimson basal blotches. The flowers of *R. hodgsonii*, at their worse, can be a vile muddy mauve; at best, a clearer pink; they may also be fragrant. It will be some years before you discover which you have, if you acquire a seedling plant; meanwhile the handsome foliage is amply satisfying, up to 30cm/12in long, glossy metallic green above, and woolly brown-felted beneath. This species also has beautiful bark, peeling in sheets to reveal creamy-green, pink and crimson tones.

There remain, in this subsection Falconera, *Rhododendron rex* and its subspecies. *R. rex* itself has leaves up to 25cm/10in long, greyish or fawn beneath, and pink flowers, less striking than the deep rusty felt that backs the shining green leaves of ssp. *fictolacteum*, in which the flowers vary from white to blush to lilac and rose-pink, frilled at the edges. From drier areas than most large-leaved species, *R. rex*. ssp. *fictolacteum* should succeed better than most in conditions which are not ideal for these noble trees. *R. hodgsonii*, already mentioned, is another that is surprisingly easy-going, and to those we could add *R. rex* ssp. *arizelum*. Both Farrer and Kingdon Ward have written of this in the wild. Kingdon Ward, in *Plant Hunting on the Edge of the World*, p. 278, saw it in August when 'the young leaves project like silver spears powdered with bronze dust from amongst the tawny red and bottle green of the old leaves'. Farrer extolled the flowers: 'Typically, its blossoms [are] of a creamy white . . . But I have seen it vary to citron and once even to apricot-yellow, while there is no end to its developments into the loveliest rosy shades.' (*Gardener's Chronicle*, vol. 69 [1921] p. 274.)

The two subsections Falconera and Grandia are united in Fortune (*R. falconeri* ssp. *falconeri* × *R. sinogrande*), which has colossal, broad leaves, up to 45cm/18in long, pale tan beneath like those of *sinogrande* but more thickly felted, and large trusses of primrose-yellow flowers; the FCC form unites the foliage of *R. falconeri* with flower colour as good as a good *macabeanum*. It must be grafted, and is correspondingly scarce and expensive.

By contrast with the large-leaved rhododendrons, many of the lily-flowered, fragrant Maddenia species and hybrids are easy to raise from cuttings. Frost sensitivity aside, they are also much more adaptable, growing and flowering well even in containers, in a suitable compost. Nor are they all so tender as to need conservatory treatment in all but virtually frost-free gardens. Of the hardier species, *R. ciliatum*, for example, and some forms of *R. maddenii* spp. *crassum* (*R. crassum*) are rated H3–4 in the classification used by the Royal Horticultural Society's *Handbook of Rhododendrons*: H4 representing a rhododendron hardy anywhere in the British Isles, H3 one that is hardy in the south and west, along the seaboard and in sheltered gardens inland. The first is a low, dome-shaped shrub reaching 1–1·5m/3¼–5ft, with peeling bark, notably bristly leaves (whence its specific epithet), and wide open, nodding, fragrant bells, white to lilac-pink in colour, appearing in mid spring. *R. maddenii* ssp. *crassum* is a larger shrub, even a small tree to 6m/20ft in the wild, with thick, stiff, leathery leaves rather crowded at the shoot tips, and deliciously fragrant, funnel-shaped, white or pale pink flowers, sometimes flushed with yellow at the throat, appearing as late as midsummer and thereby escaping spring frosts. *R. maddenii* itself is even later to flower, from mid to late summer; the sweet-scented flowers are white, often flushed with pink outside, and stand wind remarkably well.

In the old classification of rhododendrons into series and subseries, *R. maddenii* and its subspecies *crassum*, alone of those I shall write of, were considered to form subseries Maddenii; the other species in the series (now subsection Maddenia) were formerly separated into subseries Ciliicalyx and subseries Megacalyx. Without making too much of relationships which are no longer stressed in the new classification (indeed, the revision has led to a reassessment of some species in the genus), I shall for all that allow myself to be guided by the old classification in describing these tender, fragrant species. Subseries Ciliicalyx, then, contained not only the hardy *R. ciliatum*, but also three species which depart from the traditional white to pink colouring. The purest yellow blooms belong to *R. valentinianum*, a shrub of $\frac{1}{2}$–1m/20in–$3\frac{1}{4}$ft, with small, bristly leaves clustered at the branch tips, and narrow canary-yellow bells at mid spring; it is about as hardy as *R. ciliatum*. Its near ally *R. fletcherianum* is hardier still; the flowers are paler and more widely flared, the leaves distinguished by scalloped margins, the habit more upright and less straggly than *R. valentinianum*. The form 'Yellow Bunting' gained an Award of Merit for its clear colouring. *R. valentinianum*, especially, needs full light – which does not mean full exposure – to remain compact. More tender than these is *R. burmanicum*, its fragrant, narrow bells pure yellow in the best forms, but varying to greenish-yellow or an appealing creamy-green.

R. ciliicalyx itself is taller, at 2·4m/8ft or so, than these, and bears large, wide-lobed flowers of pure white in spring; they are fragile, and easily spoiled by rough weather, while the shrub itself is much more tender than those so far described. Some species in subsection Maddenia are epiphytic in nature, such as *R. veitchianum*, which has white, frilly flowers tinged with green outside. It is now deemed to include the exquisite and tender *R. cubitii*, with white flowers, stained pink along the ribs, opening from tawny-pink buds. A good *cubitii*, as it might be the FCC clone 'Ashcombe', is one of the loveliest manifestations of these fragrant, lily-flowered rhododendrons. Easier, and hardier, is *R. johnstoneanum*, usually white with a warm pink flush along the ribs on the outside, or occasionally creamy-primrose; it is as fragrant as any. An aberrant fully double form 'Double Diamond', received an Award of Merit in 1956; but I cannot think this an improvement on the single, flared bells of the type. Eldorado, its hybrid with *R. valentinianum*, has acquired some of the yellow colouring of the smaller parent.

There remain a handful of lesser-known names belonging to white-flowered species: *R. lyi*, which is very like *R. johnstoneanum*; *R. pachypodum*, which is now considered to include *R. supranubium* and the good, tall, yellow-blotched *R. scottianum*; *R. parryae* which is even more boldly yolk-yellow stained; and *R. formosum*, among them. This last is not only a reliable scented white for mild gardens, but also a parent of several good hybrids: 'Sylvania', 'Sesterianum', huge-flowered 'Tyermannii', and the old, famous and still much valued 'Fragrantissimum', with pure white flowers and dark green, rugose leaves. 'Tyermannii' is *R. formosum* × *R. nuttallii*, which is a very tender, tall, sometimes epiphytic species in the old subseries Megacalyx. Listen to Arnold-Forster on *R. nuttallii*: 'half drooping, very fragrant waxen trumpets of great substance about 4 inches long, pale yellow ... splendidly modelled, with hollows near the base'. The white blooms of *R. megacalyx* itself are limp-textured and floppy; their fragrance suggested clove to Farrer, but to Kingdon Ward there was so strong an aroma of nutmeg about them that he nicknamed the species 'Nutmegacalyx'. With the exquisite *R. dalhousiae* we have another species with flowers as if 'moulded with wax, with hollows pressed by the moulder's thumbs; sulphur or sulphur-white, with green shading, it suggests the green light of the Himalayan jungle that it comes from' (Arnold-Forster). Epiphytic in the wild, it makes rather weak growth in captivity. *R. lindleyi*, with milk-white flowers as waxy as *dalhousiae*, has a fragrance of lemon and nutmeg; another epiphyte, it may grow to 3m/10ft. By contrast *R. taggianum* is quite small at 90–180cm/3–6ft, so that its marble-white, wide bells seem all the larger by contrast. And then there is the entirely lovely *R. dalhousiae rhabdotum*, its great lily-like trumpets cream-white with a crimson flush to the ribs; it is slow growing, tender and scarce. Hybrids in this group include Award of Merit cultivars such as 'Nutcracker' and 'Jane Hardy', both with *R. nuttallii* blood, and the famous 'Countess of Haddington', which is *R. ciliatum* × *R. dalhousiae* and has inherited some of the hardiness, and all of the good, rounded habit, of the former. The scented flowers, almost as large as those of *R. dalhousiae*, are pearly-white flushed with pink.

Subsection Maddenia, though it dominates, does not have a monopoly on tender, fragrant rhododendrons. *R. edgeworthii* has given its name to subsection Edgeworthia; it is a species varying in degree of hardiness, often epiphytic in the wild especially in damper climates, and includes the former *R. bullatum*. The names of some great plant collectors are attached to this species through their collectors' numbers, which can be a guide to hardiness: the most tender being Farrer 842 and Forrest 26618, both epiphytic. The former gained an Award of Merit in 1923, the latter a First Class Certificate in 1937, for their white, waxen, richly scented flowers. Kingdon Ward's pink form, also an AM plant, is hardier; the most frost resistant of them all is Joseph Rock's 59202. Both 'Lady Alice Fitzwilliam', an old FCC plant (the award granted in 1881) and the even older 'Princess Alice' (FCC 1862) are hybrids of *R. edgeworthii* with *R. ciliatum*, gaining thereby in hardiness. They are both of rather lanky habit, not too tall, with fine lily-like flowers, white stained with pink on the reverse of the ribs, opening from tinted buds; their rich far-carrying fragrance and ease of cultivation has ensured their survival and continuing popularity. 'Forsterianum' is R. *edgeworthii* × R. *veitchianum*, from which it has its large, frilled white flowers; the little-known 'Suave' is R. *edgeworthii* × R. *bullatum*, which is to say that two forms of the one species, as now recognized, have produced this compact, bushy, white-flowered clone.

The dwarf, very early flowering R. *leucaspis* is a hardy species in subsection Boothia; its milky-white, saucer-shaped flowers are enhanced by chocolate-brown anthers. Less frost-resistant, R. *boothii* is an uncommon species, small and rather lanky in habit, with wide, rich yellow bells in terminal clusters. The related R. *chrysodoron* is yellow also, as is R. *sulfureum* with saucer-shaped, bright yellow flowers faintly spotted inside, and smooth, tan-brown bark. Valaspis unites, as its name suggests, R. *leucaspis* and R. *valentinianum*; it has brown-felted stems and wide, canary-yellow bells. Though none can claim the voluptuous beauty of the lily-flowered species, these little rhododendrons are garden pets for anyone who, with little space to spare and suitable acid soil and shelter, wants a rhododendron that is devoid of either the heathy, open-air cast of the alpine species or the manicured smugness of R. *yakushimanum*.

With the rhododendrons of subsection Fortunea, we come to a group of tree-like species and hybrids, many with lily-like fragrant flowers: which is not to imply that they bear much resemblance to the Maddenia rhododendrons, with their swooning perfume from blooms as if moulded in wax or carved in marble. For a start, all the Fortunea group, except some forms of R. *griffithianum* and its offspring, are a good deal hardier, rating H3–4 on the RHS scale; they are bolder in leaf, though not to be compared with the members of subsections Grandia and Falconera; and several have beautiful bark, seen to advantage as they develop into trees with lovely strokeable limbs. Their relative hardiness notwithstanding, they all do best in sheltered, open woodland conditions. The central species, R. *fortunei*, was perhaps the first hardy Chinese rhododendron to be introduced to the west, so long ago as 1855, by Robert Fortune; it has thus been in cultivation long enough for more than one generation of its offspring to reach maturity, as we shall see. A sizeable shrub or small tree up to 5m/18ft tall, it has elliptic or oblong leaves, rounded at both ends, characterized by a red-purple petiole, and loose trusses of fragrant, bell-shaped flowers; lilac-pink in the type, they are blush fading to white in 'Mrs Charles Butler'. Its subspecies *discolor* (R. *discolor*) is taller and later, its very large trusses of fragrant, blush-white or pink funnel-shaped blooms opening after midsummer. At much the same season R. *diaprepes* comes into flower. From warmer, moister parts than many of the Fortunea group, it is at its best in a maritime climate, given suitable shelter. The large, fleshy white bells, faintly rose-tinted, are only slightly fragrant, but in other respects this is a very fine species. Its near ally *R. decorum* is variable in height, from 1·8m/6ft to 6m/20ft, and in the quality of its shell-pink or white, fragrant, funnel-shaped blooms, which open before midsummer in loose trusses.

The much earlier flowering *R. calophytum* and *R. sutchuenense*, though formerly in different subseries of the old classification as Series Fortunei, have to me a close family resemblance. Both are large, the first a tree to as much as 12m/40ft, their thick shoots capped with light green, narrow, radiating leaves that point downwards; at up to 30cm/12in long, they are scarcely shorter, though very much narrower, than those of some of the species always described as large-leaved. Upon these parasols of leaf sit large, lax trusses of white bells. Those of *R. sutchuenense* open first, in early spring, varying in colour from pale pink to a less pleasing rosy-mauve; purple freckled but unblotched in the type, they are chocolate-stained in var. *giraldii*, and blotched also in the closely allied, narrower-leaved *R. praevernum*. The flowers of *R. calophytum*, each held on a long, red stalk, are generally of a more appealing colour, ranging from white to blush with carmine-red basal blotch and a conspicuous, wide yellow stigma.

If a species is to be judged on its qualities as a parent, *R. griffithianum* would rank very highly; its blood is to be found even in many of the best hardy hybrids, even though it is itself by no means ironclad. But in its own right it is one of the most beautiful species that can be grown in mild, sheltered, woodland gardens. I recall a visit, on a day of drenching rain, to an old Irish garden, long neglected and only lately returning to caring hands, where the weather added to the lingering sense of desolation. A large *R. griffithianum*, probably at least as tall as the 6m/20ft it is said to attain in the wild, glowed in the downpour from across a stretch of black water: not its flowers, but the bark on its exposed trunk was the source of this rich streak of crimson. The flowers, indeed, were not yet ready to open on this spring day, which was as well, for their delicate white or faintest blush colouring would have been wrecked by the rain. Wide bells up to 15cm/6in across, they are sweetly, though not strongly scented.

The most famous of the *griffithianum* hybrids is the Loderi grex, of which *R. fortunei* is the other parent, as revealed in the purple petioles. Some say that the Loderi cultivars are at their most handsome as teenagers, when they form rounded, 2·4m/8–10ft bushes, their great fragrant trusses well displayed at eye and nose level. But as old, bare-limbed trees, though the flowers may be out of reach, all the Loderis are imposing, and reveal the peeling bark inherited from *R. griffithianum*. There are many cultivars: FCC winners are 'King George', opening blush to fade to pure white, and 'Pink Diamond', holding its colour well without fading; there is a 'White Diamond' too, also an FCC plant. 'Sir Joseph Hooker', though not granted this highest accolade, is as good as 'King George'; the blush, pink-veined flowers of 'Sir Edmund' are also very fine. The nearest to a yellow Loderi is 'Julie', in ivory-white suffused with creamy-sulphur; the deepest in colour, 'Venus', opens from deep pink buds to a paler, lilac-pink. Most of the Loderi cultivars have a faint green flash in the throat; in 'Patience', pink-budded opening to white, the green is enhanced with crimson.

Rhododendron griffithianum has united with *R. fortunei* ssp. *discolor* to produce the Angelo grex, with flowers like Loderi but later, and with more pronounced markings in the throat; there are several named clones, including the very fine 'Exbury Angelo', in white with green throat markings. A generation removed from *R. griffithianum*, the Albatross grex is *R. discolor* × Loderi; it has its large, richly fragrant flowers from the second parent, its height and late flowering from the first. Again, different clones, in blush or white, are to be had. Other fine hybrids of *R. griffithianum* are with species outside the subsection Fortunea. The old 'Beauty of Tremough' has as its other parent a blood-red form of *R. arboreum*, from which it has its early flowering, but the colour of its blooms, blush-pink with brighter margins, is essentially *griffithianum*. In Cornish Cross, it is *R. thomsonii* which has deepened to crimson-pink the shade of the narrow, waxy bells; a large, open shrub, it has attractive bark, as indeed it should with such parents. But perhaps the finest *R. griffithianum* hybrid – some say, the most beautiful rhododendron of any – is Penjerrick, which comes, without distinguishing clonal names, in creamy-primrose or pale pink. In either form the large bells are translucent; the yellow form is enhanced by coral buds and flower stalks, and crimson nectary spots at the base of the bell. The yellow colouring derives from *R. campylocarpum*, which we shall encounter later.

In Avalanche, Loderi has united with *R. calophytum* to produce a large, early flowering shrub with bold foliage and large trusses of large, fragrant, pure white flowers opening from blush-pink buds, contrasted with the red inner stain and conspicuous red stalks and bracts. 'Alpine Glow' differs in its delicate pink colouring. The last two hybrids with a Fortunea parent that I want to describe both have as the other parent *R. auriculatum*, a species in subsection Auriculata which has many of the garden qualities of the late-flowering Fortunea species. A tall shrub or even a tree to 4·5m/15ft, it derives its specific epithet from the characteristic auricles at the base of each long leaf. The fragrant white or blush flowers, in rounded trusses, open from tapering buds in high summer, and the new growths also are made so late that in cold areas they may fail to ripen. The lower part of the new shoot is clad with showy crimson scales. Crossed with *R. discolor*, this species has produced Argosy, a fine fragrant white, flowering a little ahead of Polar Bear, which is *R. auriculatum* × *R. diaprepes*, and the last of all to flower. A big shrub or even a tree, it does not flower when young, but once mature it should, in late summer, be well filled with very wide, lily-like trumpets of pure white, richly fragrant, and just speckled inside with green. It needs coolth, for the flowers brown quickly in hot weather.

The diversity of the genus *Rhododendron* is manifested in the contrast between the large, scented, white or blush flowers of subsection Fortunea and the lapageria-flowered species of subsection Cinnabarina. In the revision of the genus which resulted in the classification into sections and subsections in place of the old, familiar series and subseries, subsection Cinnabarina in particular has seen the loss of equally familiar specific names such as *concatenans*; almost everything in the subsection except *R. keysii* now seems to have been subsumed in *R. cinnabarinum* itself. The specific epithet well describes the colour of the waxy, tubular flowers, in their typical state a subtle, bloomy cinnabar-red, beautifully complemented by the blue-green, blunt-ended leaves. A variable species, especially since the recent revision, it includes the Blandfordiiflorum group with narrow bells red outside, yellow to citron within, in the manner of the liliaceous antipodean genus *Blandfordia*; and the Roylei group, with flowers of wine-crimson bloomed like a plum: the cultivar 'Vin Rosé' has flowers currant-red outside and blood-red within. Subspecies *xanthocodon* is deemed to include not only the warm yellow, glaucous-leaved former *R. xanthocodon* itself, but also varieties of *R. cinnabarinum* with colours ranging from pale to purplish tones, and the entirely lovely *R. concatenans*, which survives only as a group name, though clearly distinct in the mind and eye of growers. What used to be known as *R. concatenans* is a medium-sized shrub, smaller in stature than the often rather lanky *R. cinnabarinum*, with intensely blue-glaucous new growths and warm maize-yellow, waxy bells faintly shaded with purple on the outer surface. Kingdon Ward's introduction is described as having young leaves verdigris coloured; Collingwood Ingram's 'Copper' has flowers of Chinese coral suffused with red. As *R. concatenans* received a First Class Certificate from the RHS in 1935, it seems essential somehow to recognize it as a horticulturally distinct entity.

Of the near derivatives of *R. cinnabarinum*, the Lady Chamberlain grex is widely grown. Derived from a cross between *R. cinnabarinum roylei* and 'Royal Flush' orange form – itself *R. cinnabarinum* × *R. maddenii* – the Lady Chamberlain cultivars resemble a fine, large-flowered *R. cinnabarinum*. Different clones vary a little in colour from the typical mandarin-red to more orange tones, nearer to yellow in the red-tipped 'Gleam' and to pink in 'Chelsea'. The outstanding cultivar, if RHS awards are considered a reliable guide (remembering always that they are granted to material displayed on the show bench, not in the garden) is 'Exbury Lady Chamberlain', with warm yellow flowers overlaid salmon-rose. A different form of R. *cinnabarinum* crossed with 'Royal Flush' orange form produced 'Bodnant Yellow', which is nearer to buff-orange. Crossed with the pink form of 'Royal Flush', the result was the Lady Roseberry grex, differing in its soft to rich pink colouring. The now unrecognized R. *concatenans*, crossed with R. *cinnabarinum*, produced apricot 'Caerhays John' and rich ochre 'Caerhays Lawrence'; subspecies *blandfordiiflorum* was the *cinnabarinum* parent in 'Caerhays Philip', with more open bells. To Conroy, a grex name, R. *cinnabarinum roylei* and R. *concatenans* have bequeathed not only the first three letters of their names but also the very beautiful waxy, pale warm orange lapageria-like bells. 'Trewithen Orange' has the blood of R. *maddenii* also, for it is R. *concatenans* × Full House, which is R. *cinnabarinum blandfordiiflorum* × R. *maddenii*. The Trewithen hybrid, hardy as the Lady Chamberlain and Lady Roseberry grexes, has wider-flaring bells than those, of soft orange-brown suffused with rose-pink. But both Full House and the lovely 'Royal Flush' are more tender, especially in bud, needing the sheltered conditions which a mature garden in a mild area can offer.

I want to mention just two more rhododendrons in the subsection Cinnabarina or derivatives thereof. One is the hybrid 'Biskra', which is R. *cinnabarinum roylei* × R. *ambiguum*, making a large, slender and free-flowering shrub with narrow, soft vermilion trumpets recognizably of Cinnabarina design. The others is a species, which has curious flowers more reminiscent of *Fuchsia splendens* or of a correa than of a rhododendron, for they are narrow tubes of scarlet tipped with yellow and crimson. R. *keysii* makes a shrub of much smaller stature than R. *cinnabarinum*, seldom over 1·5m/5ft, though rarely it may reach twice that height. It is almost as unlike a rhododendron as R. *spinuliferum*, an upright shrub in subsection Scabrifolia with erect clusters of 2·5cm/1in, bright red tubular flowers, pinched in at the mouth through which the tuft of stamens protrudes. Crossed with R. *lutescens*, itself a slender shrub of great charm with narrow, pointed leaves often copper-tinted when young and flights of small primrose or lemon flowers in early spring, R. *spinuliferum* has given us 'Crossbill'. The flowers of this pretty hybrid are what you might expect from the cross, being narrowly tubular, of soft yellow stained apricot-red outside, with protruding stamens; they match precisely the apricot-flushed young growths of *Acer palmatum* 'Katsura'.

If I were to describe all the yellow flowered rhododendrons of more conventional form, the genus could entirely monopolize this chapter. Just a handful, then, will be allowed entry. One, already, has been mentioned: R. *campylocarpum*, a parent of Penjerrick. It forms a shrub of only 90–180cm/3–6ft, with leaves glossy deep green above and glaucous beneath, and clear yellow bells in spring. The form commonest in gardens in

Europe is taller, hence its horticultural epithet of *elatum*; the buds are scarlet-tinted, the corolla often blotched crimson at the base. Even brighter in bud is *R. caloxanthum*, a Farrer introduction now considered to be a subspecies of *R. campylocarpum*. From vermilion buds open sulphur flowers flushed with apricot and tipped with scarlet, fading to citron. In the same subsection Campylocarpa, *R. wardii* (*R. croceum*) has rounded leaves, glaucous beneath, and saucer-shaped flowers of clear yellow, sometimes decorated with a crimson basal stain. The species is now considered to include *R. litiense*, which has flowers more cupped in outline. Between them the various forms have received an array of awards and become parents of many fine hybrids. Crossed with Lady Bessborough (which is a very fine first cross, *R. campylocarpum* × *R. discolor*), it gave us Hawk, a beautiful shrub with large, primrose-yellow, funnel-shaped flowers, unblotched in 'Crest' and with a crimson flash in 'Jervis Bay', of which the *wardii* parent was Kingdon Ward's KW4170, nicknamed by him Lemon Bell. Smaller in stature is Damaris, a cross between *R. campylocarpum* and 'Dr Stocker', a *griffithianum* hybrid with ivory, maroon-stained flowers. The familiar clone of Damaris is 'Logan', a compact rounded shrub with bright glossy green foliage and wide bells, of a tint greener than primrose, opening in late spring. 'Dr Stocker' is a parent also of Mariloo, in which bold foliage is allied to large, slightly frilled lemon-yellow flowers tinged with green. The other parent is the beautiful but costive *R. lacteum*, a species with creamy-yellow flowers and leaves with a fawn, suede-textured undersurface.

If it is coloured indumentum you want, on a rhododendron smaller or less exigeant than the large-leaved kinds, there are others than the tricky *R. lacteum* to choose from. Some are perfectly hardy and do not, therefore, need the very mild conditions posited in this chapter; but they are too handsome to pass over entirely, and they thrive best in light shade with ample moisture, like most of the choicest rhododendrons. The slow-growing, compact *R. bureaui* (*R. bureavii*) is nothing in flower, and the tight trusses of less than pure pink are best viewed with a Nelson eye; but the dark green leaves, backed with bright rufous felt, more than compensate. *R. fulvum*, again, produces absurd little trusses of rose-pink bells that contrast rather disagreeably, in their short season, with the cinnamon indumentum of the very dark green leaves; a more gawky shrub, or even a small tree, it will when mature be tall enough for you to walk beneath its branches and look up at those vivid leaf backs. Some forms of the tree-like *R. arboreum* are also tawny-felted, others silvery beneath, varying also in flower from white through pink to deep blood-red, these last the most tender and the most desirable. The very handsome 'Sir Charles Lemon', usually attributed to *R. arboreum*, combines bright russet-backed leaves and dark maroon stems with fine white, dark-

anthered flowers on a large tree-like shrub. It is now suggested that it may
be a hybrid with *R. campanulatum*, a tall shrub which in its best forms has
glossy dark green foliage backed with tawny-red tomentum, and wide
bell-shaped flowers varying from white, through purple-pink to a good
lavender-blue, as in 'Knap Hill' and 'Graham Thomas'. Its subspecies
aeruginosum has flowers of less clear colouring, but is vividly striking in
spring when the foliage unfolds in verdigris and glaucous, metallic hues.

Even the bluest-flowered *R. campanulatum* cannot compare in colour
with the finest forms of *R. augustinii*. Here we have a tall, small-leaved
shrub of more open, airy nature than anything so far described, the flowers
like flights of lavender to violet-blue butterflies, sometimes splashed with
citron-green. It is a hardy species, though the deepest blue forms need
more shelter than the washed-out, pale lilac variants. 'Electra' is a fine
award-winning violet-blue cultivar with the sought-after acid-yellow
flare; it derives from a cross between the type and var. *chasmanthum* which
flowers two weeks later.

In allowing the blue-flowered *R. campanulatum* to lead me to *R. augustinii*, I have been sidetracked from my pursuit of rhododendrons with
tawny or fawn indumentum backing the leaves. Both *R. fulgens* and *R.
mallotum* combine foliage of this type with blood-red flowers, and must
lead me to a final group of species and hybrids, those with pure scarlet or
cardinal red flowers. In mild areas those that flower very early in spring
can be relied upon, whereas in colder climates the blooms are all too often
destroyed by frost. A fine tree of *R. barbatum*, with chocolate-crimson
bark peeling to a smooth, grey-blue lining, leaves deeply veined on the
upper surface, and dense rounded trusses of rich scarlet-crimson bells in
early spring, is every bit as good as the best blood-red *R. arboreum*. *R.
strigillosum* is related to *R. barbatum*, a large shrub with bright scarlet or
carmine flowers in early spring. Shilsonii is an old, blood red *barbatum*
hybrid, flowering a little later: due, no doubt, to the influence of the other
parent, *R. thomsonii*, from which the waxen texture of the flowers must
also have derived. Shilsonii itself, crossed with *R. arboreum* blood-red,
produced the magnificent, and very early flowering, Cornubia, which
thus unites the three great red-flowered Himalayan species; it has the neat,
rounded truss of *arboreum* but the individual corollas are larger. Another
fine early scarlet-crimson hybrid is Barclayi, its flowers shaped like those
of *R. thomsonii*, with a conspicuous, self-coloured calyx and black nectaries.
R. thomsonii itself flowers in late spring, when the waxy, blood-red or
wine-crimson bells are beautifully set off by the rounded, bright glaucous
leaves which mature to dark green above, blue-white beneath. Like *R.
barbatum*, the tree-like *R. thomsonii* also has strokeable bark, smooth and
flaking off in patches to make a pattern of plum and fawn and apricot,
grey and creamy-pink. Much less common than *R. thomsonii* is the related,

and more tender, R. *hookeri*, named for the great Sir Joseph Hooker and introduced as long ago as 1850. The flowers may be blood-red, or a less desirable pink.

Subsection Parishia includes some tender species which produce their glowing scarlet flowers late in the season, at or even after midsummer. R. *facetum* is now considered to include the former R. *eriogynum*, which from the gardener's point of view may be a shame, as the R. *facetum* introductions are rain forest natives and even more tender than the erstwhile R. *eriogynum*. The foliage is beautiful also, large, and bright silver-white when unfolding, shining out from the dark forest undergrowth. R. *elliottii* is similar, with glossy leaves, but flowers earlier, before midsummer; it starts very late into growth, and needs sheltered woodland conditions. Both these frost-sensitive species are the parents of many fine, and hardier, hybrids, such as 'Tally Ho' (R. *facetum* × R. *griersonianum*), 'Romany Chal' (R. *facetum* × 'Moser's Maroon') or 'Fusilier' (R. *elliottii* × R. *griersonianum*). But if I allow myself to expatiate on these also, we shall never be through with rhododendrons; and besides, fine though they are, I feel that one can easily overdose on scarlet rhododendrons. The mention of R. *griersonianum* does prompt me to commend this very lovely Chinese species, on account of its lanceolate, matt green leaves, buff felted beneath, its long tapering buds – a character shared only by R. *auriculatum* – and above all the quality of its clear, geranium-lake flowers. This is a soft scarlet quite unlike the colour of any other species, demanding dappled shade, so that shafts of sunlight can filter through to illumine the flowers.

An equally desirable species, which must bring me near to the end of the genus *Rhododendron*, is R. *neriiflorum*, more variable in colour from deep rose to scarlet, but always with its narrow leaves bright glaucous-white beneath. In the same subsection Neriiflora, R. *beanianum* also varies from the usual blood-red or scarlet to carmine or pink, its fleshy corollas marked with black nectaries, its glossy foliage thickly cinnamon-felted beneath. The bizarre little R. *dichroanthum* rates a mention chiefly for its colouring, varying from maize-orange, bronze and cinnabar to 'mar-malade or mustard-pickle' (Bean); you may or may not care for this, but it has the quality, as a parent, of dominating the blueing tendencies of so many red or pink rhododendrons to produce such delights as 'Nereid', a natural hybrid with R. *neriiflorum*, of compact growth with waxy, soft salmon-apricot bells. In colder gardens, and especially in public areas, we are unlikely to escape the blight of banks of hardy hybrids in puce and magenta and so-called scarlet, fading disgracefully towards purple; but for the gardener in favoured, milder areas, pure reds abound.

It is only right, before I leave the genus, to mention that lately there have been problems in many gardens with the fungal disease powdery mildew. At first thought to affect only susceptible species such as R.

cinnabarinum, it is now found to attack virtually any rhododendron; and it is worst in the very conditions that best suit the less hardy types, shade and a moist atmosphere, especially after a wet late summer and autumn. The disease attacks the young foliage, manifesting itself as brown patches on the underside of the leaf, with matching paler areas on the upper surface; there may also be greyish powdery marks. The leaves may turn yellow and fall prematurely; in extreme cases all the leaves fall, and the plant may even be killed. It spreads fast, and a regular programme of control, spraying alternately with two fungicides once a month from late spring to autumn, is essential to keep your rhododendrons in good health. If you have a serious attack, you may even have to get rid of your *R. cinnabarinum*. Avoid, if possible, planting rhododendrons under the drip of other trees, and keep them as much in the open as is consistent with the amount of shelter and shade they need to protect the growths and the flowers.

Camellias and other shrubs

Unless you are single-mindedly devoted to rhododendrons, you are likely to wish to grow them with other shrubs needing similar conditions of shade, shelter, humidity and acid soil. The genus *Camellia*, except that most species need more light, shares these requirements, and has the further similarity that (although it is a very much smaller genus) it ranges from wild, untamed species to an ever-increasing number of cultivars which themselves vary from informal shrubs to highly bred creations needing protection for their blooms of exquisite formality.

The species which is best known in cool temperate regions is *C. japonica*. It is as hardy as laurel, which is all I propose to say about it, except in passing. Almost as hardy is *C. saluenensis*, an evergreen, densely leafy shrub which may grow to 3m/10ft or more, the glossy leaves more pointed than those of *C. japonica*. The frail-seeming flowers are pale pink with deeper veining and appear in great masses in early spring. The flowers of *C. reticulata* are larger, and the leaves show the network of veins which gave the plant its specific name. The wild type, with large rose-pink flowers, at first trumpet shaped before expanding fully in their late winter and early spring season, is also virtually hardy, as is the semi-double form 'Captain Rawes' which, being the first to be introduced to the west (by Robert Fortune, in 1820), is regarded as the type of the species. Both make large shrubs; I have seen a 'Captain Rawes' two storeys high on a wall. And both are much tougher than the named cultivars, which have voluptuous flowers of great size, semi-double, double or paeony form, in shades of pink, crimson and wine-red. As my own taste runs more to wildlings than to flowers that look as if bred to make a corsage on an ample bosom, I will leave you to choose your own from the show bench, the catalogue, or the nursery rows.

The cross between *C. saluenensis* and *C. reticulata* known as 'Salutation' is a fine thing, making a medium-sized shrub with matt green leaves and soft pink semi-double flowers in late winter and early spring. The same parents gave rise to 'Inamorata', less hardy, looking like *C. reticulata* but with the flowers of *C. saluenensis.*

The winter-flowering, fragrant *C. sasanqua* is said to need sun to flower freely, although the wood, once mature, is fairly hardy. In the Devon garden I looked after there were two mature plants, one of a deep pink single-flowered cultivar growing in full sun on a wall, the other the lovely 'Narumi-gata' tucked away in a wooded clearing. It was, during winter and spring, always full of its large creamy-white flowers, just blushed with pink at the margins of the petals, while the pink *sasanqua* always looked scorched and unhappy, flowering sparsely from late autumn onwards. Granted that 'Narumi-gata' is known for its reliability, and that the pink-flowered cultivar I inherited might simply have been a poor variety, I would still be inclined to plant my sasanquas in a clearing unless I lived in the far north (or south, if in the southern hemisphere) where the light intensity is low.

'Narumi-gata' used to be known in commerce as *C. oleifera*, but the true *C. oleifera* is a distinct species, its name derived from the oil extracted from its fruits and used in toiletries. The leaves are stiff, with a lustreless finish; the small fragrant flowers are white and appear in spring. The cultivar 'Jaune', which has a large centre of yellow petaloides with a few, darker yellow stamens, is optimistically known as Fortune's Yellow Camellia. There is, as it happens, a species with truly yellow flowers, *C. chrysantha*, a native of southern China and Vietnam and hopelessly tender in the British climate; but in the warmer parts of California it has borne flowers.

Two species from Hong Kong are also distinctly tender. *C. granthamiana* is exceedingly rare in the wild, and is said to form a large shrub with leaves bronzed at first, later distinct in their deeply impressed veins; the solitary, 15cm/6in wide flowers are white with golden anthers and appear in autumn and early winter. *C. hongkongensis*, botanically close to *C. japonica*, is also handsome when the young growths display their metallic bronze and steely tones; the small cup-shaped flowers are deep red.

In mild maritime climates the tea plant, *C. sinensis*, should survive to make a small shrub with glossy leaves, and nodding white flowers on thick stalks. The related *C. taliensis* is larger, with bright green toothed leaves and creamy-white flowers opening from globular buds to reveal the yellow stamens. Of similar hardiness is *C. tsaii*, a large and graceful shrub with glossy dark green leaves, unfolding in shades of copper and bronze (paler than those of C. *cuspidata* which it resembles), and small white flowers borne in great abundance.

In the same family, Theaceae, as the camellias, are the tree-like stuartias. Most are hardy, and for reasons of space I must pass them by with no more than the observation that they are graceful trees for acid-soiled woodland, many with richly coloured leaves in the fall and marbled, flaking bark. Less than fully hardy is *Stuartia malacodendron*, its snow-white flowers, distinct in their purple filaments and blue anthers, appearing in high summer. More than most other stuartia species, it appreciates coolth at the root but its head in full light; the sunny edge of a clearing, with an underplanting of some of the low shrubs shortly to be described, should suit it well. The semi-evergreen *S. pteropetiolata* is less hardy still, needing warm, moist semi-shade; the white flowers are very like those of *Camellia sinensis* and are set off by dark glossy foliage.

Also potentially tree-like are the species of *Schima*, which bear white or cream flowers like small camellias. In the mild, woodland gardens of Cornwall, *Schima khasiana* forms a medium-sized tree, with bold toothed leaves up to 18cm/7in long, lucent dark green above, among which the small white, camellia-like flowers with yellow central tuft of stamens are borne in early autumn. *S. argentea* presumably has its specific epithet from the glaucous undersurface of the gleaming dark green leaves; often a wide-spreading shrub in cultivation, it may make a tree of 18m/60ft in the wild. The clustered, cupped, creamy flowers open in late summer. The more tender *S. wallichii*, with a range extending from Sikkim and Nepal to the East Indies, has glossy leaves which are reddish when unfolding, and fragrant white or red-flushed cream flowers opening from red buds in late summer. A tall tree in the wild, it is smaller in cultivation; the leaves are very large on strong young suckers, up to 25cm/10in long. *S. noronhae* is given by some authors as synonymous, by others as a distinct, and very tender, species from tropical Asia, with cream flowers and bloomy, pointed leaves.

Ternstroemia gymnanthera, though it may make a small tree in the wild, is usually seen as a medium-sized shrub in cultivation, with stout, red-brown branches and thick, obovate leaves clustered at the ends of the shoots. In the type they are dark, varnished green; 'Variegata' has leaves grey-marbled at the centre, with a broad cream margin stained with rose-pink in autumn. The very small, fragrant cream flowers are borne in summer. This is just one species in a large, mainly tropical genus, related to both *Eurya* and *Cleyera*, as the synonymy often reveals. The plant currently, I believe, known as *Cleyera japonica* has been known also as *C. ochnacea*, *Eurya ochnacea*, and *Ternstroemia japonica*. A slow-growing shrub to 3m/10ft or so, it has leathery, glossy deep green leaves which often turn red in winter, borne on rigid, spreading branches, and small white flowers aging to creamy-yellow, rather inconspicuous in their late spring season. In *C. fortunei* the foliage is variegated in much the same fashion as in *Ternstroemia gymnanthera* 'Variegata', marbled with grey at the centre and broadly edged with cream, flushed with deep rose. The green form is unknown; this is a garden form introduced from Japan in 1861.

Last of the genera in Theaceae that I want to include, *Gordonia* is an Asiatic and American genus needing lime-free soil and a sheltered position. The American species, *G. lasianthos* or loblolly bay, is – as the vernacular name implies – rather like a magnolia, tree-like to 15m/50ft or more, with polished deep green leaves and white flowers in high summer. The fragrant creamy flowers of *G. chrysandra* are smaller, and appear in late winter. The season of *G. axillaris* is long; from late autumn through to late spring the cream flowers are borne among dark green, varnished leaves. If cut by frost it has the ability to regenerate from the base.

This character it shares with *Clethra arborea*, a Madeiran species growing in mountain forests. In cultivation it forms a dense evergreen shrub or small tree with nodding sprays of fragrant white, lily-of-the-valley flowers in late summer. Given shade, shelter and an acid soil it is easy to grow, often sowing itself. Even wood that has apparently been killed by cold may shoot again, so despite its look of dereliction after an exceptionally cold winter it is worth leaving untouched all but the remotest tips of the branches. The Tasmanian and Australian *Atherosperma moschatum* is also a plant of temperate forests, not so tender as the clethra, but like it a handsome evergreen, with narrow, leathery dark green leaves that are whitish on the reverse, and creamy white flowers with apricot stamens, borne singly in the leaf axils in late winter. The whole plant is aromatic, yielding an essential oil.

The Mediterranean *Styrax officinalis* yields an aromatic resin, storax, used as incense, and formerly in perfumes. A shrub or small tree needing a warm, sheltered position in moist, lime-free soil, it bears clusters of white, nodding, fragrant bells, large for the genus (up to 3cm/1in +) at midsummer. Virtually all the other snowbells are hardy, so that although they are charming shrubs or small, spreading trees for woodland gardens, I cannot allow myself the indulgence of describing them all. One that is not fully hardy is the Chinese *S. dasyantha*, its white or creamy-yellow flowers with orange anthers hanging in slender racemes after those of *S. officinalis*.

Any plant belonging to the family Lauraceae is likely to be aromatic, and so it is with *Lindera megaphylla*, an evergreen shrub or tree with large, highly glossed, very dark green leaves as much as 20cm/8in long, with a rusty felting or glaucous bloom on the underside; the young shoots are bright red. It has been likened, by various authors, to *Daphniphyllum*,

Cinnamomum, or (Arnold-Forster) 'a large smooth-edged holly'; any of which comparisons give an idea of its quality. It needs a sheltered position in moist, acid, humusy soil. I have not seen the deciduous *L. rubronervia*; but it sounds good, with leaves polished above and glaucous beneath, turning orange and red in autumn. Nor have I seen anything but a tiny specimen of *Rhodoleia championii*, a relative of *Hamamelis* (though now, I believe, given its own family Rhodoleiaceae) suitable only for the mildest woodland garden. It will apparently, if suited, make a large shrub or even a small tree to 10m/33ft, with thick glossy leaves, glaucous on the undersides, crowding the shoot tips, and deep pink, black-anthered flowers emerging from silky, many-coloured bracts in late winter.

As with *Stuartia* and *Styrax*, so with *Enkianthus* the presence of a tender species in a genus that is mainly hardy gives me the excuse to bring to your attention that here is another group of shrubs of particular charm for acid-soiled woodland gardens, bringing grace and lightness among the heavier rhododendrons and camellias. *E. quinqueflorus* is semi-evergreen, a small shrub reaching perhaps 1.5m/5ft, with leaves emerging red before maturing to deep green. The hanging clusters of pink bells are held in the axils of large pink bracts in late spring.

There are, apparently, three species in the genus *Gevuina*, but I know only one, *G. avellana*, the Chilean hazel. It derives this name from the edible nuts that are borne in autumn; bright red at first and cherry-sized, they are covered with a thin layer of flesh which turns black when ripe, but it is the large nut within which you eat. Otherwise, the name is a misnomer; the plant is Chilean, admittedly, but it has nothing to do with hazels, being a member of the protea family. In gardens it is valued chiefly for its spectacular foliage; pinnate or bipinnate, it looks at first glance like some exceptionally fine mahonia, dark and glossy green and lacking only the sharp spines. The whole frond may be 45cm/18in or more long, the individual leaflets varying from 15cm/6in long to a bare 2½cm/1in; the rachis and petioles, and the young shoots, are brown-felted. The finest foliage belongs to plants that are not flowering, a condition you can induce in older specimens by cutting hard back from time to time, when the shrub will produce long, flexible stems (ideal for layering, though it grows easily from cuttings also). A flowering tree – mine was 12m/40ft or more tall, and solid enough to climb – bears abundant narrow racemes of many ivory-white flowers, the narrow petals recurved into an intricate, typically proteaceous structure, in late summer.

Another tree in the protea family that I know only as a young plant is *Knightia excelsa*, a native of New Zealand. Even when small, it is handsome, with stiff, narrow, toothed leaves. The brown-crimson flowers, with petals 'curled up like shavings, and white stamens' (Arnold-Forster) are borne in spikes up to 10cm/4in long. From New Zealand also comes *Pseudowintera colorata* (*Drimys colorata*), a dense evergreen shrub that, if you can give it a moist humus-rich soil and almost full light, at the edge of a woodland clearing perhaps, will develop extraordinary metallic tones to the leaves, of old-gold above and steely blue beneath, freckled with rose and margined with blackcurrant-purple.

The Chilean *Desfontainea spinosa* is fairly hardy – much more so, certainly, than *Gevuina avellana* – but grows very much better in mild, moist woodland areas than where the atmosphere is dry; for in the wild it grows in the shade of tall *Fitzroya patagonica* in the rain forest. Until it flowers, it is very like a holly, with dark, polished, spiny foliage, except that holly bears alternate leaves, while those of the desfontainea are opposite. The flowers are bright scarlet, narrow trumpets, with rounded yellow lobes, borne in late summer. The form 'Harold Comber', named for its collector, has richer red flowers.

Neither the pseudowintera nor the desfontainea is wholly calcifuge, though they do not do well in chalk soils and need ample humus. For those whose woodland garden is on a neutral or slightly limy soil, there are many good shrubs to compensate for the inability to grow rhododendrons and camellias. True, it is easier to find compensation in the matter of foliage than in flowers; but then foliage is with us for much longer than flowers, and even if your taste runs to the brightest variegations it is impossible with leaves to achieve the jarring clashes of colour that results from indiscriminate rhododendron planting.

With the discreet *Loropetalum chinense* you risk no clashes, for the late winter flowers of this smallish evergreen shrub are pale greenish cream, with petals like short thin ribbons in the manner of the Hamamelidaceae to which it belongs. Although they are too well-known to merit description here, it is worth mentioning that the species and cultivars of *Hamamelis* itself do well in clearings in sheltered woodland; where the atmosphere is clean and always humid, they acquire a coating of grey-green lichen which contrasts prettily with the yellow or orange-red flowers, especially if you contrive a backdrop of dark evergreen foliage.

In an earlier chapter I promised you one more *Osmanthus*, too tender to qualify for planting among shrubs in the open border except in the mildest areas. *O. fragrans* is well named, for its white flowers (or, in the cv. 'Aurantiacus', pale to rich orange) are intensely perfumed in their summer season: they are used by the Chinese to add fragrance to tea. The evergreen leaves are handsome in the manner of the genus, oblong-lanceolate and finely toothed, of leathery texture. *Persea borbonia*, in Lauraceae, is essentially a foliage plant, an evergreen tree reaching 10m/33ft, with lustrous dark green leaves, glaucous beneath. Although you could scarcely expect ripe fruits, you might hope for *P. americana* (*P. gratissima*), the avocado, to survive at least until an exceptional winter proved too much for it; one grew for several years in the Devon garden I cared for, though it was killed (in the great frosts of 1947) before I knew the garden, and the diary did not tell how tall it had become nor to what extent a normal winter damaged it. Anyone who has suspended a stone from the oily, delicious fruit over a jar of water, and watched the great seed produce a young avocado plant, will know that the leaves are very handsome, up to 20cm/8in long, polished dark green above and bluish beneath.

One of the prettiest evergreen shrubs for mild gardens is the Tasmanian *Anopterus glandulosus*, which is related to the escallonias of South America. The tough, glossy leaves, long and narrow and margined with large rounded teeth, are bunched at the end of the branches; the white or blush flowers are borne in long racemes in spring. In the same family, *Carpodetus serratus* forms a large shrub or small tree with rounded, 3cm/1in leaves on juvenile plants, which as so often in New Zealand natives have interlacing, zigzag branches; the leaves become longer and narrower on mature specimens, which have a graceful habit. The small white flowers are borne in sprays in summer.

Eugenia is a genus closely related to the myrtles, and like *Myrtus* (in the wider sense) it spans the continents; though as most species are found in the tropics, there are few that we can consider for our purposes. The Australian *E. smithii* has the charmingly dotty vernacular name of lilli pilly, which scarcely suggests, to me at least, the tall tree that it may become. The tapering evergreen leaves are myrtle-like, coppery when young, and the massed creamy, fluffy flowers are followed by berries ripening in winter from white to pale or deep violet. *E paniculata* (*E. myrtifolia*) varies from shrubby to tree-like in form, a handsome evergreen with lacquered, long-pointed green leaves and panicles of white flowers in spring with the bright mahogany-red young shoots. The flowers are followed by pinkish red fruits. The Brazilian *E. pungens* is so named on account of the sharp thorny tip to the light green, privet-like leaves. A medium-sized shrub with solitary white flowers and downy fruits, it has not the allure of its Australian cousins.

Blue fruits belong also to *Elaeocarpus cyaneus*, an Australian member of a largely tropical genus, forming a medium-sized shrub with sprays of creamy white flowers, fringed like those of a *Chionanthus*, in summer; they are pretty, but less showy than the bright turquoise-blue fruits. *E. dentatus*, from New Zealand, suffers in *Hilliers' Manual of Trees and Shrubs* from the damning phrase 'of botanical interest'; it is, however, a pleasant evergreen tree of as much as 12m/40ft, with tapering dark green leaves clustered at the branch tips, and white flowers borne in drooping racemes in winter. The fruits that follow are a subdued shade of slate blue. The related *Aristotelia serrata*, also from New Zealand, is a small deciduous tree of graceful habit, with long, heart-shaped, deeply toothed leaves. It is very pretty in flower, the little pink blossoms borne in short panicles; they are followed by dark red fruits.

Even in the moist shady glades of a woodland garden you may plant an *Olearia*, a genus chiefly associated with open, sunny plantings in windswept gardens. *O. argophylla* prefers cool, moist soils, lightly shaded, but is not very frost-resistant, so that the shelter of mature woodland suits it admirably. A tall evergreen shrub, it is very beautiful in leaf, the young shoots and unfolding leaves, held like candle flames, covered with a gleaming, silvery felt, which persists on the undersides of the musk-scented leaves. The creamy white flowerheads, grouped into wide hanging clusters at midsummer, are very freely borne. Another olearia that I prefer to grow in shelter, though it is remarkably wind hardy, is *O. paniculata*, so like a pittosporum in its fresh green, rather hard, wavy-edged leaves that almost everyone is fooled at first encounter. The insignificant little flowers that come in autumn are sweetly scented. Given shelter, *O. paniculata* will grow into a tree big enough to climb.

The familiar fuchsias that derive from South and Central American species are grown primarily for their flowers, but the New Zealand species have a different appeal. *Fuchsia excorticata* grows into a small tree, with peeling, papery bark; the undersides of the leaves are silvery glaucous with a faint purple flush. The flowers are short and stubby, with sombre or greenish-purple petals and bright blue pollen. *F. colensoi* has similar, though smaller, flowers, borne on a low rambling shrub.

Macropiper excelsum is an aromatic shrub in the pepper family which is abundant in the forests of New Zealand in gullies and on shaded rocky outcrops. The zigzag branches are swollen into knuckles at the nodes; the almost succulent, leathery leaves are heartshaped and pointed. In fruit it is handsome also, the close-packed erect spikes of flower turning to a solid column of orange-red berries.

Shrubs and plants of the understorey

Many of the shrubs and even trees that I have described in this chapter form part of the understorey in the rain forests of their native lands. At a lower level again come the plants of the forest floor, where there is light enough for lowly plants to grow. In our gardens there are likely to be plenty of places below trees and among shrub plantings for some of these little things. In acid-soiled woodland, gaultherias and vacciniums can join the rhododendrons and camellias. Both genera include some taller species, which I will consider first. *Vaccinium urceolatum* is a striking evergreen reaching 1·5m/5ft, with thick, leathery, pointed leaves, the dark green upper surface marked by deeply impressed veins. The pink flowers, of the usual urn shape, are borne at midsummer, and are followed by black fruits. The Madeiran species *V. padifolium* (*V. maderense*) is taller, up to 1·8m/6ft in cultivation and even forming a small tree in its native mountain habitat. The net-veined leaves are seldom shed before late winter; the little yellow-green bells faintly striped with red are borne in clusters at midsummer, and are followed by blue-black whortleberry fruits. Another species hardier than its origins suggest is *V. cylindraceum*, from the Azores, a large semi-evergreen shrub with narrowly cylindrical yellow-green flowers flushed with red, opening from red buds, hanging in bright clusters along the branches in late summer. The last flowers are still opening when the first of the oblong, bloomy black fruits are ripening. Still more surprising is that *V. floribundum* (*V. mortinia*) is hardy although it comes from Ecuador, which lies on the Equator. It is a pretty, spreading shrub growing to 1·2m/4ft, with fronds of small, crowded dark green leaves, mahogany-red when young, and dense clusters of tubular pink flowers on the undersides of the branches at midsummer, followed by plum-red bilberries. The Himalayan *V. glaucoalbum* is only hurt by frost in very cold areas, but is too appealing to omit, with its arching, suckering shoots reaching 1·2m/4ft, set with large, oval leaves that are grey-green above and bright blue-white beneath, setting off pale pink cylindrical flowers emerging from silvery-pink bracts in late spring. The black fruits are covered with a glaucous-white bloom and last well into winter. The more tender *V. gaultheriifolium* is more delicate in habit, with slender, pointed leaves glossy green above but no less glaucous beneath, and white flowers in late summer. Smallest of the species I want to include is *V. nummularia*, a wide-spreading shrublet no more than 30cm/12in tall, much-branched, with nodding branches set with small, rounded, bristly leaves neatly arranged in a double row; the young growths are bronzed. The little rosy-pink tubular flowers are held in clusters at the shoot tips in late spring; the rounded black fruits are edible.

The genus *Gaultheria* also offers a little creeping species suitable for a shady bank or mossy tree stump. *G. nummularioides* is of more modest size than the vaccinium, with very small bristly leaves set in two regular rows and diminishing in size towards the shoot tips. The flowers are quite hidden by these sprays of foliage, and the little fruits are blue-black. The genus runs rather, however, to blue or white fruits, formed by the calyx swelling into a fleshy 'berry' surrounding the true fruit. *G. tetramera*, for example, is a small spreading shrub of 45cm/18in or so, with quite large, bristly, leathery leaves, the expected small greenish-white urn-shaped flowers, and bright violet or china-blue fruits. *G. semi-infera* differs in being taller, with shiny foliage and indigo or violet-blue fruits. *G. codonantha* is an Assamese species introduced by Kingdon Ward, with gracefully arching branches and quite large toothed leaves arranged in two ranks to make a decorative pattern. The white cupped flowers are sometimes red-striped, and appear in late autumn. Taller still, sometimes even forming a small tree in its native Himalayan foothills and Burmese heights, is G. *fragrantissima*, named for the sweet perfume of its greenish-yellow, hanging bell-shaped flowers in spring. The tapering leaves are as much as 10cm/4in long, the fruits pale or bright blue. The field note for G. *wardii*, like G. *codonantha* also introduced by the eponymous Kingdon Ward, reads: 'flowers snow white, in masses. Berries blue with white bloom; undershrub growing on sunny boulders, in thickets'. It is a smallish shrub, up to 90cm/3ft or so, with bristly branches, the leaves bristly on both surfaces with the veins distinctly indented on the upper side. 'Sunny boulders' suggests that it would do better in an open clearing than under the skirts of taller shrubs, though gaultherias are usually quite happy in shade.

Another bristly-hairy species is *Gaultheria hispida*, usually growing to 1m/3¼ft though occasionally twice as tall. The finely-toothed leaves are quite large, and the short spikes of tubby white bells are followed by pure white, fleshy fruits. Unlike those already described, it is an antipodean species. So, self-evidently, is G. *antipoda*, a shrub often of erect habit though sometimes quite prostrate. The little white bells are followed by fleshy white or red fruits set among small, leathery, dark green leaves. G. *oppositifolia* is also variable in habit, usually with arching branches to 1m/3¼ft; the glossy, net-veined leaves are normally opposite, an unusual feature in a genus where alternate ranking is the rule. The white bell-shaped flowers are borne very freely in terminal panicles in late spring, and are followed by white fruits.

Much rarer in cultivation than these, the few *Agapetes* (*Pentapterygium*) taxa are seductive epiphytic shrubs from the eastern Himalaya and the Khasia mountains, needing sheltered shade and a lime-free, humus-rich soil. A. *serpens* is a shrub with a thickened rootstock and long, flexuous stems closely set with narrow leaves. The flowers, shaped like five-sided lanterns pinched in at the mouth, hang the length of the branches in winter and early spring; they are clear red with darker, angled pencillings. A. *incurvata* (A. *rugosa*) is a shorter, stiffer shrub with larger, broader, deep green leaves, reddish when first unfolding, and whitish lanterns shaded with red at the angles and marbled with red-purple. The hybrid between the two is the splendid 'Ludgvan Cross', intermediate in growth between the parents, with crimson-pink lanterns tipped with greenish-white and pencilled with deeper V marks, in crimson calyces. Lastly, A. *buxifolia* has glossy green, oblong leaves and bright red waxy tubular flowers in early spring.

Demonstrating once again how plants in Epacridaceae parallel, in the southern hemisphere, species in Ericaceae, the Tasmanian *Prionotes cer-*

inthoides is an epiphytic, sprawling or climbing evergreen shrub with thick, curved, dark green leaves, bluntly toothed, and tubular red 2·5cm/1in, narrow-mouthed bells hanging from the upper leaf axils. It is slow-growing, and needs shade, in a peaty or humus-rich, moist yet free-draining soil.

There are, of course, small, shade-loving shrubs other than in these calcifuge genera, needing the warm and sheltered conditions of a woodland garden. In the dense shady forests of its native India, Malaysia and Japan, *Chloranthus glaber* (*C. brachystachys*) forms a spreading shrub up to 90cm/3ft or so, with glossy green, oblong leaves and insignificant greenish flowers in short spikes; they are followed by bright orange fleshy berries. In both flower and fruit *Ardisia japonica* is attractive. A low shrub, probably no more than 45cm/18in tall, it has white or pale reddish, starry, fragrant flowers in short hanging racemes in late summer, and vivid red fruits.

The appeal of *Ruscus hypophyllum* and *R. hypoglossum* lies not in flower or even in fruit, but in the pattern formed by their broad, glossy cladodes, the structures that in Ruscaceae take the place of true leaves in more conventional plants. Like the hardier butcher's broom, *R. aculeatus*, they slowly form suckering patches of green stems, and if plants of both sexes are grown you may see bright red fruits on the females. The hybrid between the two, *R. × microglossus*, is elegant in its slender, pointed clad-odes, but is – so far as I know – always represented in cultivation by a male form. All will grow in the dry, rooty places that defeat most plants.

The related *Philesia magellanica*, formerly in Liliaceae and now in its own family Philesiaceae, is far from being so tolerant. It is quite hardy, but needs a moist, humusy soil in shade, with a constantly moist atmosphere; I have seen an established plant almost killed by a hot dry summer, even though its roots were shaded by a large boulder and the soil remained cool and moist. At the same time, if in too dense shade it will scarcely flower. It forms a suckering thicket, or will even climb mossy rocks or tree trunks. The wiry stems are set with narrow, stiff leaves, very dark green above and glaucous beneath; the flowers are nodding, tubular bells, waxy and fleshy like those of the related *Lapageria* but of a deeper, pinkish-crimson or occasionally paler pink. The hybrid between *Philesia* and *Lapageria*, × *Philageria veitchii*, is no less desirable, a scrambling shrub with narrow, leathery, three-veined leaves (those of *Philesia* are single-veined), with hanging waxy bright pink bells borne in late summer and autumn. Also from South America, *Luzuriaga radicans* is a more modest shrublet, with thin wiry shoots lying on the ground or climbing to 1m/3¼ft on a mossy rock or tree trunk. The narrow green leaves are two-ranked; the little starry flowers, borne only on climbing plants, have a prominent central cone of yellow stamens and are followed by pea-sized, bright orange or red fruits. *L. marginata* is similar, with purple fruits and fragrant flowers.

Not all the plants that will do well among shrubs and trees are shrubby themselves. Although they will grow in the open provided they are not baked dry, the astelias prefer a humusy soil, and at least dappled shade. Their colouring, of grey-green leaves markedly silvery-white beneath, is unusual among shade-loving plants, a contrast to the prevailing glossy greens. The arching sword-like leaves of *Astelia nervosa* var. *chathamica* are among the boldest in the genus; 'Silver Spear' is a fine named selection. *A. nervosa* itself is smaller, with rosettes of up to 60cm/2ft high and perhaps 90cm/3ft wide. *A. petriei* and *A. nivicola* are similar, with arching leaves green above and silvery or buff beneath. Do not expect anything exciting in the way of blooms; but orange fruits may follow the greenish or chestnut-brown flowers which are borne in upright panicles. Another species, *A. banksii*, is rather larger, and the fruits are purple-black. The same warm shade suits *Begonia evansiana* (*B. grandis*); here it can develop without sun or wind scorch the largest leaves, of the typical lopsided begonia shape, green with red veining, borne on succulent red stems. The flowers are magenta-pink, or white in 'Alba', where the pink pedicel and calyx delightfully set off the nodding crystalline bloom. Both can be increased quickly from the little bulbils which form in the axils of the leaves, especially if you collect them and grow them on in a pan of peaty compost until they have grown a little; at first the leaves are half the size of a little finger nail and very vulnerable to an over-enthusiastic weeder.

Unlikely though it may seem, *Senecio candicans* also needs moisture and at least half shade. It looks, with its broad silvery paddles, like something which should grow in full hot in the hottest, driest soil; but nothing will kill it more quickly. I lost my first plant in this way; the second went into humusy soil just above water level by a stream, and throve. At its feet I set *Parochetus communis*, which quickly spread a carpet of its clover-like leaves down to the water's edge and even in the shallows. The pea-shaped flowers are bright turquoise-blue. The late Percy Picton, who had worked for William Robinson in the garden at Gravetye, told me that the old man used to plant clumps of *Parochetus* at the waterside, in the hope that sooner or later it would spread and naturalize itself along the Medway.

Almost in the water, I planted drifts of *Schizostylis coccinea* in its various colour forms, already described in Chapter III. In the gritty but damp stream margins it increases very fast, and as it will also grow in drier soil the drifts can be extended up the bank to link the streamside with the woodland. Much the same is true of the white arum lily, *Zantedeschia aethiopica*. 'Crowborough' is a hardy form that is well known even in quite cold gardens, but in milder areas you can experiment with the half-

sized 'Little Gem' or the very fine 'White Sail', or add 'Green Goddess'
to the lush greenery of the streamside. Even more exciting than the white
arum lilies are the coloured species such as *Z. rehmannii*, with narrow
leaves and pink spathes reaching to 60cm/2ft, or *Z. elliottiana* which has
the typical dark green arrowhead leaves, freckled with white, to set off
bright canary-yellow spathes. Hybrids between these two, some with the
blood of *Z. angustiloba* (*Z. pentlandii*), from which they have their dark
purple throat, come in a wide colour range from the dusky pinks and
magnolia-purples of 'Majestic Red', 'Pacific Pink' and 'Dusky Pink' to
the rich yellow of 'Afterglow', in which the throat is apricot, orange
'Aztec Gold', yellow 'Golden Affair' or the wholly desirable 'Black
Magic', which is lemony-primrose with deepest maroon flush in the
throat. 'Regal Charm' is yellow flushed with red.

In a quiet pool, open to the sky, you could plant the fragrant, winter-
flowering *Aponogeton distachyos*, which has elegant foliage and edible white
flowers with black anthers, shaped rather like a pair of stubby spaghetti
tongs. A more insidious occupant of a pool is *Azolla caroliniana*, which
looks for all the world like a little floating fern, and often turns to rich
crimson; but it is exceptionally fast-growing, especially in warm water,
quickly making a dense blanket. Frost may knock it back, but you cannot
count on that in a mild garden.

Above water level, *Iris wattii* and *I. confusa* both quickly made fine
clumps of their fresh green leaf fans. Those of the larger, more tender *I.
wattii* are borne on bamboo-like stems. Their branching flower stems are
topped with frilled ice-white or palest lilac flowers, each marked with
deeper lilac or blue and decorated with the orange crest typical of the
Evansia irises. Even more successful were the species of *Dianella*, spreading
to form wide, weed-excluding sweeps of dark green blades above which,
in spring, the airy sprays of small, pale blue flowers lit by yellow stamens
promised plenty of berries in autumn. There is nothing else among non-
woody plants like these oblong, ultramarine or lapis lazuli, gleaming
fruits, which unless stripped by curious visitors last long on the stems.
There are several species, and I have never fully come to grips with the
differences between them, but I doubt if you would be disappointed with
any. The tall (1·2m/4ft) *D. tasmanica* is, I believe, more often seen than *D.
revoluta*, which is scarcely half its height; but perhaps the most widely
grown is *D. caerulea*, also growing to about 60cm/2ft. There is a pleasant
variegated form, with understated vertical cream striations, ascribed variously to this species or to *D. intermedia*.

If variegations in a woodland setting do not jar on your sensibilities,
then you may like to plant *Farfugium japonicum* (more descriptively known
as *Ligularia tussilaginea*) 'Argenteo-variegata', which has the broad, colts-
foot-shaped leaves implied by its former name, cleanly margined with

creamy white. 'Aureo-maculata' is a monstrous thing with spots of yellow on the leaves as though someone had been careless with weedkiller.

In complete contrast to these broad, bold leaves are the fronds of ferns, all of which do admirably in woodland settings. The tree ferns will be described in the next chapter, although they could just as well belong here. Of those that do not form a thick trunk, *Woodwardia radicans* is a graceful tall fern, with arching fronds as much as 1·8m/6ft long, mounding up to 90cm/3ft or more. The pinnae make a strong decorative pattern of fresh green; each frond bears a bud at its tip which if held down by a stone will root to make a new plant. The appeal of *Blechnum chilense* lies as much in its hard, sub-prickly texture as in its bold looks, the broad fronds set with wide pinnae, lightly bronzed when first unfurling. The fertile fronds bear recurved pinnae. There seems some confusion over the naming of this fern; we all used to call it *B. tabulare*, and it is still so called by many authors, but others suggest that *B. tabulare* of gardens is in fact *B. magellanicum*. There is a slighter version with narrower pinnae, said by some to be the true *B. tabulare*. The holly fern, *Cyrtomium falcatum*, is also hard-textured; it derives its vernacular name from the broad, deep green, glossy pinnae on fronds reaching 60cm/2ft; 'Rochfordianum' is especially luxuriant. *C. fortunei* has narrower pinnae.

At the edge of a clearing, the tall spires of *Nicotiana sylvestris* gleam in the half light, the long, drooping white trumpets powerfully fragrant at night. Growing more than head high in the woodsy soil that suits it, it forms a wide weed-excluding rosette of pale green, clammy leaves. The best plants are those that are sown in autumn and overwintered to flower the following summer and autumn. Fleeting shade and shelter also suit *Helleborus lividus*, similar to the more familiar *H. argutifolius* (*H. corsicus*), but that its leaves are subtly veined and marbled with grey and that the fragrant, bowl-shaped flowers range in colour from green-tinted pink to the pinkish-grey of a wood pigeon's feather. I once, accidentally but felicitously, planted it with *Athyrium niponicum* 'Metallicum' (*A. goeringianum* 'Pictum'), a hardy fern with pewter-grey fronds flushed with maroon. Another companion might be *Saxifraga cuscutiformis*, which spreads by throwing out thread-like runners bearing a baby plant at their tips, in the manner of a strawberry; the rounded, hairy leaves are dark marbled green, the starry flowers white. A brighter, more tender trailing plant, half woody, that might join this group is *Heterocentron elegans* (*Heeria elegans*), from the mountains of Mexico and Central America; the solitary, 2·5cm/1in four-petalled flowers are vivid magenta.

Sprawlers and climbers

The dividing line between sprawlers that will cover the ground like these and climbers that must run upwards is no clearer than that between trees and shrubs; plants grow as they will, not as we decree they must. Several plants that may decide to climb, if a congenial support presents itself, have already been mentioned. Thus with three woody, Chilean gesneriads. *Mitraria coccinea* will grow in the manner of ivy of northern woods, covering the ground or hoisting itself up through supporting neighbours; though it lacks the aerial roots of ivy. The neat, small leaves form a dark green setting for the vermilion-scarlet, bellied tubular flowers in summer and autumn. It is a good deal easier to grow than *Asteranthera ovata*, which does have rather feeble aerial roots to draw itself up to a height of 6m/20ft or so on living or fallen trees in its native temperate rain forest. The rounded, bristly leaves are thin-textured when the plant grows in deep shade, thicker when it is in the open; in the shrubby state each pair of leaves is set at right angles to the next, but when it begins to climb they flatten into one plane. The tubular, lipped flowers are rich raspberry-pink with deeper veinings and a white throat, and appear from midsummer onwards. In the wild it commonly forms thick carpets beneath *Desfontainea spinosa*. It needs a rich humusy soil and a constantly moist atmosphere. In the wild *Sarmienta repens* grows like *Mitraria*, preferring moist mossy rocks and tree trunks; but the almost circular leaves are semi-succulent, so that it can withstand a short period of dryness. Like *Asteranthera* it is stem rooting, and may even reach to the tops of tall forest trees. The bulging carmine tubular flowers open in summer.

Also Chilean, *Berberidopsis corallina* is easier to grow than these last, though it too needs a deep moist soil and at least half shade, with shelter from cold or drying winds. An evergreen, climbing shrub with holly-like leaves, though lacking the fierce spines, it bears hanging sprays of crimson flowers opening from round buds like blood-red beads on deep red stalks in summer and early autumn. Red and green is the colour-scheme of the Californian *Ribes viburnifolium*, an evergreen, thornless shrub quite unlike the usual flowering currant or gooseberry, with long, scandent, wine-red stems and leaves that smell of lemon verbena (or, some authors say, of turpentine, which just goes to show how subjective the sense of smell can be). The little dark terracotta, saucer-shaped flowers with five creamy anthers are borne in short upright racemes in spring, and are followed by red fruits.

The climbing hydrangea relatives *Decumaria sinensis*, which is evergreen, and deciduous *D. barbara*, both need moist humus-rich soil and some shelter, though they are quite frost-hardy. They climb by aerial roots, and have white flowers; those of *D. sinensis* open first, in late spring, and like the summer flowers of *D. barbara* are honey-scented. Both have pleasant glossy foliage, and could be encouraged to clothe a tree trunk rather as their hardier relative *Hydrangea petiolaris* will.

The queen of climbers for woodsy soil where the atmosphere is always humid is *Lapageria rosea*. A Chilean twining evergreen, it has thin, stiff shoots set with leathery, three or five-veined dark green leaves, and narrowly flared, high-shouldered bells of solid, waxy texture, carmine-pink in the type and white in the exquisite var. *albiflora*, hanging in ones and twos from the leaf axils. The only named cultivar that I knew until recently was 'Nash Court', which has large soft pink bells with deeper marbling; but as lapagerias can be raised from seed, nurserymen have selected other fine forms – 'White Cloud' (which seems to me an inappropriate name for a flower so firm in texture), 'Flesh Pink', 'Penheale'. Although the usual recipe for success is the humusy soil and moist atmosphere I too recommend, it is only fair to say that I know of at least one plant growing on an east wall facing the morning sun and, what is worse, fierce salt-laden and drying winds; yet it thrives, and flowers. Another is regularly baked in a glasshouse, where it is neglected for weeks on end by absentee owners; again, though some of the leaves are browned, it tolerates this maltreatment. It is worth carefully removing old, dead stems, to ensure that the young growths are uncluttered and flower freely.

Some species of *Metrosideros*, those that are tolerant of salt spray and wind, have already been described. But there are other species which grow, in their native New Zealand, in the forests, often forming self-clinging climbers reaching to the tops of tall trees. *M. robusta* might have been described in Chapter II with other wind-resistant species, for it is tolerant of sea winds in its mature state; yet its habit of growing as an epiphyte in the top of a tree, whence it sends down roots through the moss covering its host's bark, also fits it for this chapter. In youth it has thin-textured leaves on bright red stems, but in maturity they are thicker and tougher, and comparatively broader. The coppery-scarlet flowers are borne earlier in the life of the plant than those of *M. umbellata*, and are followed in high summer by the rich red young shoots. Arnold-Forster describes the 13·5m/45ft tree that grew at Ludgvan until the severe winter of 1938 in words that reveal his artist's eye: 'evening light was adding a fiery glow to the vermilion on the sunny side of the mass of flowers. Half way round towards the shadow, light caught the edges of the flower-heads; and further round still, the redness of the flowers and the green of the pines were muted by full shadow'.

New Zealand nurserymen have selected dwarf forms of *M. carminea*, typically a tall climbing evergreen with slender stems and bright carmine-red flowers among rounded leaves. Both 'Carousel' and 'Ferrous Wheel' are said to grow no taller than 1m/3¼ft, with the same deep carmine flowers in summer; 'Carousel' has glossy leaves margined with yellow, altogether too jazzy for a woodland setting. *M. parkinsonii* is more suitable, naturally forming a straggling, half-prostrate shrub in forest though it will make a slender tree in the open. The deep crimson flowers, composed of the usual bunch of showy stamens, are borne among thick, leathery leaves, which are sometimes flushed with red. As its name implies, *M. fulgens* also has red flowers. One of the best species for shaded gardens is *M. diffusa*, which will climb by aerial roots up a tree or dark rock face where the sun never strikes, or may be planted on a mossy tree to grow as an epiphyte. At the immature stage the leaves are thin-textured; Arnold-Forster recommends growing only a plant raised from cuttings of the mature form, perhaps because at this stage the thicker texture of the leaves makes it less vulnerable to frost damage. The flowers are carmine, the stamens tipped with yellow pollen. The genus also includes some species with pink or white flowers, such as *M. perforata*, which may be either pink or white, the rather ineffective *M. hypericifolia*, and *M. albiflora*, which has large heads of clear white flowers. In foliage too this is very distinct from any other species; the leaves are large, glossy, and pale green.

VIII

The Tropical Look

ALTHOUGH you can hardly grow many of the plants in the previous chapter without some 'woodland', even if it is only two or three trees and a belt of sheltering shrubs, you can create an exotic, subtropical if not truly tropical look in a very small space. All you need is an area of maximum shelter from wind, in the corner of two walls perhaps: I have seen some very tropical looking plantings even in London window boxes. Then there are plants which will take a little exposure, but which are so alien in appearance that they conjure up images of the jungle or of steamy tropical towns. And there are those, such as the tree ferns, which seem visually to belong here, although I should perhaps have included them with other woodland plants, for they definitely need overhead shelter from wind and sun, a humid atmosphere, and a climate in which frosts are only slight and infrequent.

Striving to achieve the tropical look in non-tropical climes implies adjustments of scale. Very large leaves, especially those of bold outline whether divided or entire, immediately give an alien, jungly feeling. Palm trees and cycads, bananas and tree ferns, and many species in Araliaceae, have this quality. It has much less to do with flowers, because if a flowering plant is so 'exotic', in the popular if not the pedantic sense of the word, as to conjure up steamy tropical countries, it will almost certainly be too tender to survive even a degree of frost.

Certain hardy plants can contribute to the tropical look, if their foliage or their deportment have the quality we seek. Thus, for example, *Ailanthus altissima*. The tree of heaven is perfectly hardy; yet, as you can see in many a corner of London, a young plant (frequently self-sown into a pavement crack) or one that is cut to the ground each year produces huge fronds that seem to have nothing to do with a northern city. *Paulownia tomentosa* is not often seen in London, but is sometimes grown in English gardens, where as a flowering tree it is not a great success, lacking the fierce summer ripening that encourages it to produce plenty of its violet-blue foxgloves. But stooled each year it will throw up stout shoots bearing enormous leaves as much as 60 cm/2 ft across. Even the thick furry shoots of *Hydrangea sargentiana*, if the plant is given the shade, shelter and moisture that it prefers, can develop dark velvety leaves nearly 30 cm/1 ft wide, over which the large pale purple flower heads with few whitish ray florets swim like little purple turtles in the submarine gloom.

Rather less hardy than these, *Melia azedarach* needs a sunny, sheltered corner. A deciduous tree or large shrub, it bears very large, bipinnate leaves as much as 75 cm/$2\frac{1}{2}$ ft long, the many small leaflets dark green above and paler beneath. The loose panicles of fragrant, lilac flowers are borne in late spring, followed in hot countries by clusters of yellow bead-like fruits which do not fall until well after the leaves.

Most members of Araliaceae seem to do well in shade, though many will tolerate sun and some are wind-resistant also. The hardy *Fatsia japonica*, which dominates many a small, shady courtyard in London, growing to 3 m/10 ft or more, bears large, dark green, glossy palmate leaves up to 30 cm/1 ft wide, with seven to nine narrow lobes. In autumn, handsome creamy white panicles of rounded flower clusters form at the shoot tips, bursting out of fat pale green buds. There is a fine variegated form in which the leaves are discreetly outlined with creamy white. *Tetrapanax papyrifer* is less hardy, and not so massive; it has thick stems bearing wide, deeply cut palmate leaves which are white or russet felted on the undersides, and should be treated with care to preserve this felty coating and the sharp, clean-cut integrity of their outline. The small white flowers are borne in large downy panicles in summer. Less hardy again, *Schefflera impressa*, like the tetrapanax, is an Asiatic species, a tree-like evergreen with seven-parted palmately lobed, leathery leaves on very long petioles, giving it the typical parasol appearance. The New Zealand *S. digitata* is a small, spreading evergreen tree with compound leaves of three to nine leaflets, thin and soft-textured, with sharply toothed margins. The drooping flower heads are greenish.

The most bizarre variations on the Araliaceae theme are found in the genus *Pseudopanax*. The Chinese *P. davidii* is still recognizably an araliad, especially in greenish-yellow flower and black fruit. It forms a slow-growing, ultimately large evergreen shrub with leathery, dark polished green leaves, varying in form from a simple lanceolate leaf with three longitudinal veins, to two leaflets, the larger with two veins and the smaller with only one, or three similarly sized leaflets each with a single vein. Both *P. arboreus* and the closely related *P. laetus* are from New Zealand. They quickly form large rounded shrubs or small trees, with glossy green, coarsely toothed leaflets borne in threes, fives or sevens at the end of the main stalk. The drooping leaflets of *P. laetus* are much larger and relatively broader, on red-purple petioles; yet despite these big leaves it is surprisingly wind-tolerant. For all that, the best specimen I ever saw was in dark, still woodland in an Irish garden, where it made a wide and tall mound of beautiful, jungly foliage. *P. arboreus* often starts life as an epiphyte on tree ferns, its roots ultimately reaching down to root in the soil. Its greenish flowers are followed by handsome black fruits.

We have already met *P. lessonii* on account of its variegated form 'Gold Splash' and hybrid 'Purpureum'. The type is a branching evergreen shrub growing to 3 m/10 ft or more, with the typical thick branches of the family, and three to five parted leaves clustered at the shoot tips; they are smooth shining green, distinctly veined on both surfaces. The related *P. discolor*, also from New Zealand, is more tender; the leathery leaves are bronzed or yellow-green. There are many hybrids or selections of, probably, *P. lessonii*, raised in New Zealand and recommended as architectural specimens for tubs and patios. 'Trident' has very bold, three-lobed leaves, glossy and leathery, of bronze to deep green, on upright rather narrow growth to 3 m/10 ft. It is slightly more tender than 'Sabre', which has long narrow juvenile foliage as much as 30 cm/12 in long, of glossy deep purplish-green with orange midribs. Despite its looks it is tolerant of both wind and drought, but needs shelter and is best in part shade. The smaller 'Linearifolius' tolerates deep shade; it has very elegant, long, narrow, five-parted juvenile leaves with toothed margins. In maturity the leaves are broader, but still show the highly polished sheen of the young foliage. 'Adiantifolius' implies to me something much more delicate than the broadly palmate, deep rich green, waxy-polished leaves of this rather tender cultivar. The stiffer 'Cyril Watson' is hardier, and has five-lobed, glossy, leathery leaves on a shrub of neat, multi-stemmed habit. Even as youngsters, which is how I know them, all these cultivars are striking foliage plants, needing the simplest of settings: a white wall, some paving or gravel, and a restrained accompaniment of plants.

I am inclined to leave until later the most bizarre manifestations of the genus *Pseudopanax*, in order to consider now some of the plants you might set with 'Trident' or 'Sabre' or 'Adiantifolius' if you are building up a small subtropical grouping by a patio, say, or in a sheltered border. The bulbous *Eucomis pallidiflora* is one of the most striking of the genus in leaf, the 15 cm/6 in wide blades rich shining green. Any of the cannas described in Chapter III, except perhaps the modest *Canna glauca*, could be used to add broad paddle-shaped leaves in green or purple; most striking of all is *C. musaefolia*, which bears foliage indeed very much like the immense blades of *Musa*, the banana; they are deep sea-green in colour, with reddish midribs and margins. I have not seen blooms on this canna, nor would I mind if it never flowered. The true bananas are even more substantial than this. The Japanese *Musa basjoo* grows to 4·5 m/15 ft, with leaves up to

3 m/10 ft long and 60 cm/2 ft wide, bright glossy green on both surfaces. They are borne on a tree-like stem which in fact is not at all woody, but is composed of the sheathing leaf bases; the leaves and flower stalks, in common with other species in the genus, spring from the rhizomatous roots. To preserve such huge leaves, wind-shelter is essential; they are easily frayed at the edges, or torn into wide strips. Even in comparatively cool gardens, as it might be in the south-west of England, it produces its dense hanging inflorescence and even bears triangular, 7·5 cm/3 in fruits. The Chinese *M. acuminata* is shorter in growth, with smaller leaves of bluish-green; the flower clusters are brightened by red, leathery bracts, and the yellow fruits, longer than those of *M. basjoo*, are sweet and edible. Despite its origins in Abyssinia, *Ensete ventricosum* (*Musa ensete*) is also surprisingly hardy, rated Z10, which implies a need for ample shelter but the ability to survive light frosts, which indeed it may experience from time to time in the open mountain forests of its native land. The bottle-shaped stem may grow as tall as 10 m/33 ft, but even plants of more modest size bear a handsome crown of enormous leaves, up to 6 m/20 ft long, bright green with a crimson midrib. You would need a very large patio to accommodate a mature specimen, but all the bananas grow fast and can be raised from seed when obtainable, or in the case of *Musa basjoo*, by detaching the suckers.

Other plants that are habitually raised from seed and can be discarded at season's end may add their quota of foliage. The familiar castor oil plant, if well grown (which is not invariably the case) is a bold and handsome foliage plant to contrast with bananas and cannas. *Ricinus communis* var. *gibsonii* is a the familiar form with metallic, red-purple foliage, and there are newer varieties also. 'Carmencita' has deep brown foliage and red flower buds, and 'Impala' leaves of maroon-carmine when young and sulphur-yellow flowers – not that the flowers are the reason for growing the castor oil plant, in this context at least. Young plants of *Eucalyptus globulus* (or stooled specimens of other species, such as *E. pulverulenta* or *E. perriniana*) add a note of bright glaucous foliage, and the Atlantic Island geraniums could be added for their wide mounds of finely cut, bright green foliage.

With all this bold foliage, the narrow sword leaves of phormiums and cordylines or the spiky rosettes of yuccas make a rather obvious contrast; but the obvious is not always to be scorned. Cordylines have a habit of developing into tall trees, in which state they are scarcely suitable for the corner of the average patio, but certainly bring an alien note to the rounded outlines of broadleaved trees or the needles and scales of conifers. I have described them, in an earlier chapter, as they are in youth, before they form a stem. In seaside resorts they are planted in full exposure to develop into trees but can look rather wind-battered. In open though more sheltered settings, you can admire a tall branching *Cordyline australis*, each stem bearing great tufts of rapier leaves, full of its wide branching panicles of fragrant creamy flowers in spring; the shorter, stumpier *C. banksii*, with very narrow leaves often red-veined, and larger, laxer sprays of highly perfumed creamy flowers; or the finest of them all, *C. indivisa*, grown past its stemless adolescence to form a branching tree with great rosettes of greyish blades.

These are often referred to as palms, though they are not members of Palmae but of (depending on your views) Liliaceae or Agavaceae, making them botanically not so far distant from phormiums (Agavaceae or, new-style, Phormiaceae) and yuccas (Agavaceae, or formerly Liliaceae). The true palms that can be grown out of doors in mild but not wholly frost-free gardens are comparatively few, but we need not limit ourselves to *Trachycarpus fortunei* from China and the European native palm, *Chamaerops humilis*. The first, which has also been known as *Chamaerops excelsa*, grows to anything from 4·5 to 12 m/15–40 ft, the upper portion of its cylindrical stem clothed in a thick matting of coarse fibres from the remains of the old leaf bases. The much divided leaves, forming large, nearly circular fans held on long stems clustered at the top of the stem, are tough and fibrous but can be badly frayed and broken by strong winds, so that the plant is best set in a sheltered position. It is surprisingly handsome in flower and even in fruit, the large curving panicles of many small yellow flowers in early summer followed by blue-black fruits. Although it comes from the mountain slopes above the coast in south-western Europe, *Chamaerops humilis* is less hardy than its Chinese cousin. It is much smaller, sometimes forming a short trunk or occasionally many-stemmed. The stiff fan-shaped leaves, cleft to the base into many segments, are bluish- or greyish-green and are held on long thorny stems; the yellow flowers are borne in stiff panicles. Plant it in the sun, in a loamy soil, with shelter from wind and cold.

In a garden in Torquay, on the south Devon coast of England, the Chilean *Jubaea chilensis* has formed a splendid tall tree. Three specimens were planted in about 1900; the tallest was measured at 23 ft (7 m) in 1972, and when I last saw them a few years ago one was undoubtedly taller than this. The thick, straight, smooth stem is topped by long, pinnate leaves, the stiff pinnae pointing in different directions. Apparently the fruit is a small coconut; but the tree is appreciated for another purpose in Chile, where it is cut down and the abundant sugary sap boiled down to make 'palm honey'. In a public park in Torquay grows a good specimen of *Phoenix canariensis*, a Canary Island species which also thrives in some Cornish gardens. A palm with a relatively thin, short stem, it is topped by a crown of narrow leaves with many slightly folded, deep green pinnae, giving it a more airy elegance than the *Jubaea*. Another species of *Phoenix* that is worth trying is the African *P. reclinata*, of which a specimen once grew to 9 m/30 ft at Penzance on the Atlantic tip of Cornwall. A thin-trunked, often multi-stemmed palm, it bears gracefully nodding fronds composed of two rows of narrow, stiff, sharp-tipped leaflets. Even the date palm, *P. dactylifera*, has been found growing on a rubbish tip in Cornwall, young plants presumably germinated from the discarded seeds of a box of imported dates.

I have not seen *Washingtonia filifera* growing out of doors in the British Isles, although its hardiness zone rating is 9 as against 10 for *Phoenix reclinata*. The washingtonia grows to 6 m/20 ft or more in mild climates, and is distinct in the crown of circular fans of deeply pleated leaves, the edges of the segments fringed with the filaments which gave it its specific epithet. The petiole is unkindly set with hooked marginal thorns.

Many cycads have somewhat the appearance of palms, though they are in their own family Cycadaceae, survivors of the vegetation of 100 million years ago or more; generally far too tender for gardens where even a degree or two of frost can be expected, the genus *Cycas* includes one species, *C. revoluta*, which is rated Z8. It surprises me that a sago palm (so called) should receive this rating, but it does suggest that it is worth trying out of doors in a sheltered position; certainly it is very handsome, the glossy deep green herringbone leaves up to 75 cm/$2\frac{1}{2}$ ft long each with up to one hundred leaflets.

Despite their hard, leathery texture, the cycads are also likened to tree ferns. The true tree ferns are of course in the same family as the holly fern, the maidenhair and the cosmopolitan bracken, but unlike these they form, in time, a 'trunk'. This is not a woody trunk in the manner of a conventional tree; indeed, if your tree fern has grown too tall for your taste, you can cut it down, and replant the top portion after reducing the stem to the length you want, for it is the root fibres which slowly build up into a trunk-like structure, and remain capable of functioning even if cut. *Dicksonia antarctica*, the hardiest of the tree ferns, is said to have been introduced to Britain at the time of the Great Exhibition of 1852, 'shipped as dry logs collected after bush fires from the hills of New South Wales' (Arnold-Forster). It can grow very tall, as much as 10 m/33 ft, with a dark brown 'trunk' topped by very large, tripinnate green fronds. The old fronds fall without breaking off, to shelter the trunk as the young croziers unfurl; especially where this fern may be growing at the limit of its climatic tolerance, it is wise to leave these old fronds or even to tie them to the trunk as added protection, rather than tidily stripping them off.

There are two other species of *Dicksonia* that you might try. *D. squarrosa* has a slender, almost black 'trunk', and large, finely cut, rather stiff fronds that are held almost horizontally outwards from the crown on dark red-purple stipes; it grows more quickly than other species, soon reaching

3 m/10 ft or more. The softer-textured D. *fibrosa* has a golden-brown trunk and a crown of arching light green fronds. Both are rated Z10 in the hardiness tables, as against Z8 for D. *antarctica*.

Surprisingly, *Cyathea dealbata* is also rated Z8. Known as the silver tree fern on account of the glaucous-white bloom on the underside of its great dark green fronds, it may grow a stem of as much as 12 m/40 ft in the wild. It is said to prefer a drier location than the dicksonias. The more tender C. *cooperi* and closely allied C. *australis* grow to only half the height of the silver tree fern, forming a straight stem topped by a spreading head of tripinnate leaves. The black tree fern, *Cyathea medullaris*, forms a crown of twenty to thirty curving fronds, each up to 2 m/6$\frac{1}{2}$ ft long, topping the stout trunk, which is covered in dense black fur extending up the rachis of the fronds, inviting you to stroke it.

At all stages the tree ferns are beautiful. When young they form wide stemless rosettes; later as the accumulation of root fibres develops into a trunk you find yourself first looking straight into the immense fronds, and in time standing beneath them. If they can be sited where dappled shade allows shafts of sunlight to reach them, yet where they have ample protection from wind and a humid atmosphere, then you will be able, as your tree ferns grow tall, to look up into the much-divided fronds, haloed by the light. The young croziers, unfurling, may be furred with golden or deepest umber hairs.

The size of mature tree-fern fronds makes it easy to imagine oneself in some prehistoric jungle. But when it comes to the stranger species of *Pseudopanax*, one expects to see a pterodactyl, or some other proto-bird long since extinct, perched in their branches. P. *crassifolius* and P. *ferox* are both New Zealand natives, and like so many plants from those islands their juvenile and mature forms differ. Not content with just two styles of growth and of leaf, they pass through four distinct stages during their life cycle. At the seedling stage, P. *crassifolius* has coarsely toothed, diamond-shaped leaves. For the next twenty years or so it forms a straight, unbranched main stem with very stiff and leathery, down-pointing, narrow leaves, shaped like toothed swords as much as 90 cm/3 ft long, dark green with a red midrib and maroon reverse. Once past its teens, the tree begins to branch, the leaves now erect or spreading, some of them divided into three or five leaflets, others similar to the jagged swords of the younger plant but only one third as long. It is at this stage that the inconspicuous flowers and black fruits are borne. Finally, at maturity, the leaves revert to a simple, linear outline, toothless or with a few teeth at the apex. The leaves of P. *ferox* at the second stage are bronzed, narrow 45 cm/18 in blades that might have been cut from thick, stiff leather, edged with knobbly hooked teeth. Like those of P. *crassifolius*, they are sharply angled downwards.

The Tasmanian species of *Richea* are almost as strange, for although they are in the family Epacridaceae they have parallel-veined leaves like a monocot. Indeed, the specific names may suggest their visual affinities: *R. dracophylla*, *R. pandanifolia*. The first is a large shrub from moist, low altitude mountain slopes, with long blade-like leaves clustered at the stem ends, *Cordyline*-fashion. The white flowers are borne in branching panicles, contrasting with the long, pointed brown bracts; while those of *R. pandanifolia* are red, the dense clusters hidden in the axils of the very hard, horny leaves. *R. milliganii* is a woodland plant with yellow-green flowers, less striking than the others. The other species I have grown, *R. scoparia*, is a small, spreading shrub which has been likened to a dwarf monkey puzzle or to a *Dracaena* species, the stems densely set with stiff, curved, sharp-pointed leaves. The flowers are clustered into spiky, erect racemes in spring; rather like the little bells of *Erica cinerea* in shape, they are usually white, but may be pink, crimson or orange; cultivated plants are less frequently white than coloured. *R. scoparia* needs a moist acid soil, and will grow in sun or shade; in the wild, in eucalypt forests, it becomes taller, up to 3 m/10 ft, and looks rather like a *Cunninghamia*, while in the open it forms a big untidy hummock.

In complete contrast are the big pale green leaves of *Firmiana simplex*, which was formerly, and more descriptively, known as *Sterculia platanifolia*. It is deciduous, like the African hemp, *Sparmannia africana*, which is better known for its tolerance of the maltreatment it receives in cafés than for its frost-hardiness. Where it is allowed to grow without the hazards of coffee grounds and cigarette stubs, in a very sheltered corner outside, it is a fine thing, making a thicket of stems with large, soft, lobed, pale green leaves and wide white flowers with yellow stamens, borne in showy clusters in spring. I have never seen the flowers of *Entelea arborescens*, said to be white with a central tuft of yellow stamens, and borne in loose heads in late spring. But as a foliage plant this large shrub is handsome, the broad heartshaped leaves, double-toothed at the margins, drawn out to a long point. The wood, we are told, is even lighter than cork. Related to *Sparmannia*, it finds its way into this chapter because of its need for shelter, both from frost and to protect the rather pale, fresh green leaves from damage. Despite their appearance this is an evergreen.

Perhaps it is stretching my very loose definition of 'tropical' a little far to include here a couple of not fully hardy bamboos, for these great woody grasses have become entirely familiar in many gardens of cool temperate regions, and indeed many species are extremely hardy, with zone ratings of 4 or 5. For all that, the two I want to mention seem to fit in this chapter better than elsewhere. *Arundinaria falconeri* is one of very few species still admitted in the genus since the latest revision; it has also been known as *Thamnocalamus falconeri*. Reaching 8 m/26½ ft, it has very slender, round canes, olive-green in shade and yellow in the sun, stained with brown-purple at the joints; they are clustered in dense crowded clumps, and do not spread by suckering in the manner of some bamboos. The foliage is bright fresh green with glaucous reverse, each blade long and narrow and of fragile texture; the effect is graceful and elegant. The leaves of *Chimonobambusa hookeriana* (*Arundinaria hookeriana*) are much larger, up to 30 cm/12 in long and 3·75 cm/1½ in wide, borne on canes up to 4·5 m/15 ft high, or even more in the wild, glaucous often striped with olive-green and pink when young and maturing to yellow.

APPENDIX 1
Some more plants for the milder garden

The Early Years (CHAPTER II)

Ceanothus griseus offers another selection, 'Louis Edmonds'; it sounds good, with prostrate main branches and erect side shoots making a shrub 1·8 m/6 ft high by up to 6 m/20 ft wide.

Garrya fremontii is an uncommon species similar to *G. elliptica*, less hardy, but equally wind-resistant; the leaves are generally obovate, and the shorter male catkins appear in late spring.

Olearia angustifolia is very like *O. chathamica*, but larger, with narrower leaves.

O. colensoi. I once indulged myself by collecting every *Olearia* species I could obtain. But one that I could admire only vicariously, through the words of Arnold-Forster, is this species. A shrub of up to 4·5 m/15 ft, it forms an important component of the vegetation near the sea in its native Stewart Island, so it should be resistant to salt winds; hardier forms might be introduced from higher altitudes. The leaves, it seems, are very large and leathery, 'of splendid design', looking like grey-green velvet when newly expanded at midsummer; earlier, the young shoots are intensely silvered. There is, though, a greener form; Arnold-Forster says, as though both were easy to obtain, 'choose the grey one', described as 'a plant for massing . . . amongst grey granite rocks'.

O. × *excorticata* is a hybrid of *O. arborescens*; the second parent is the recalcitrant *O. lacunosa*. The offspring is intermediate between the two, with dark green, gleaming leaves, virtually untoothed, but relatively shorter and broader than those of *O. lacunosa*.

O. lyallii, closely allied to *O. colensoi*, is taller and more tree-like still, with young shoots so white as to be very conspicuous against the dark grey-green leaves.

O. pachyphylla resembles a more robust, larger leaved form of *O. furfuracea*, the untoothed, leathery, apple-green leaves similarly wavy at the edges and silvered below.

Mixed Borders (CHAPTER III)
Alstroemeria chilensis is, of course, Chilean; but being promiscuous, it is seldom seen true to type in cultivation. It should have bright rose to creamy-white flowers on 75 cm/$2\frac{1}{2}$ ft stems in early summer.

A. pelegrina, from Peru, is shorter at 30 cm/12 in, with lilac pink, dark-freckled flowers. The lily of the Incas, its white form 'Alba', is exquisite, with the same dark markings.

A. violacea is a Chilean species with violet-mauve flowers in early summer on 45 cm/$1\frac{1}{2}$ ft stems.

Bomarea andimarcana is a non-twining species in a largely climbing genus closely related to the alstroemerias. It has flowers of typically tubular shape, with pale pink outer petals tipped with green, and brighter inner petals speckled with crimson.

Canna lutea has flowers as dainty as those of *C. glauca*, and of the same clear yellow, but the narrow leaf blades are green.

Crocosmia aurea is the tender species that has passed on to many of its offspring its wide, nodding flowers on 90 cm/3 ft stems and clear, warm yellow colouring.

Hedychium flavescens is pale yellow, and endowed with a perfume as rich and spicy as *H. gardnerianum*.

Homoglossum watsonianum is a South African cormous plant resembling a gladiolus, with hooded scarlet flowers, the upper segments paler, on 30 cm/12 in stems. Hybrids between *Homoglossum* and *Gladiolus* are known as Homoglads; one of the most famous is 'General Smuts', in vivid scarlet.

Kniphofia isoetifolia is an Abyssinian species, remarkably hardy but unsuited to cold gardens because of its late flowering season, the buds damaged by autumn frosts except where the growing season is long. The curving, orange-salmon florets are arranged in a dense mophead with the upper florets opening first.

K. 'Zululandii' is now uncommon, but valued in mild gardens for its very early season, from midwinter onwards, and its bright colouring of clear orange to coppery-scarlet.

Mimulus. The Californian monkey musks include a range of large-flowering, semi-shrubby hybrids in many colours, from cream and primrose to crushed strawberry and blackcurrant, tan, crimson, and the brilliant magenta of 'Verity Hybrid'.

Nemesia foetens is a semi-shrubby perennial from South Africa, with a long season of lilac-mauve flowers on 60 cm/2 ft stems.

Phormium 'Maori Maiden' has upright leaves, drooping at the tips, of rich rosy salmon-pink and coral; it reaches 90 cm/3 ft.

P. 'Maori Queen' is of similar stature, with rose red stripes on bronzed-green.

P. 'Maori Sunrise' has slender arching leaves of soft pinkish-red margined with bronze; 75 cm/2½ ft.

S. coccinea has slender spikes of pure scarlet flowers in purple calyces, borne over a long summer season on 60 cm/2 ft stems.

S. elegans (*S. rutilans*), the pineapple sage, is valued for the delicious fruity aroma of its soft, dark-veined leaves. The narrow flowers are rich red and appear from late winter on 60 cm/2 ft stems.

S. 'Indigo Spires' (*S. farinacea* × *S. longispicata*) has flower spikes as much as 75 cm/2½ ft long, of deeper blue than *S. farinacea*, to a height of 180 cm/6 ft overall.

Tropaeolum majus 'Hermione Grashof' is a double scarlet nasturtium, propagated by cuttings. Of trailing habit, it is suited to tubs or windowboxes as well as to the front of the border.

Tulbaghia violacea has a pale form, 'Pallida', which I would not waste garden space on, and an exquisite, and expensive, variegated form, for some reason known as 'Maritima'; the flowers are of the same gentle lavender-mauve as the type, and the narrow leaves are striped with cream so as to leave scarcely any of their original glaucous colouring.

Wachendorfia thyrsiflora is said to be available in a hardier form than the usual seed-raised plants; it has grown outside for many years in the Cornish garden of Trengwainton.

Shrubs (CHAPTER IV)
Cinnamomum glanduliferum has thicker and more leathery leaves than *C. camphora*, glossy green above and glaucous beneath; it is often used as a street tree in the eastern Black Sea region.

Peumus boldus is a small Chilean tree that likes full light and is unhappy where the soil is too moist. It appeals to the senses of both smell and taste, for the lustrous dark green leaves are agreeably aromatic when crushed, and the small fruits are said to be sweet to eat.

Xylosma japonicum is a shrub said by E. H. Wilson to be 'one of the finest evergreens of China', but by Krüssman to have no garden merit. This may be due to its being grown in a climate that is uncongenial to it, though as it is widespread in Japan, Formosa, China and the Ryukyu Islands, it should be adaptable enough. The creamy yellow flowers are inconspicuous but fragrant in their early autumn season.

Climbers and Wall Shrubs (CHAPTER V)

It may be that the global warming we are daily warned of could before long allow us to grow many plants previously too tender for our gardens. Many of the shrubs and climbers that follow are in this category.

Alstroemeria caryophyllea is a rare and tender Brazilian species. The large, fragrant flowers, scarlet-striped with white or all scarlet, are borne in spring on short stems.

Boronia pinnata has aromatic fern-like foliage and fragrant pink nodding flowers. You might also try lilac-pink *B. polygalifolia* and magenta-pink *B. elatior*. This last is one of several shrubs with heath-like foliage.

Burchellia bubalina, from South Africa, grows slowly to 1·5 m/5 ft, and bears coral-red, swollen tubular flowers in tight clusters in late spring, set off by dark green, glossy, wavy-edged leaves. Try it in the shelter of a wall, in full sun.

Calliandra tweedii is a Brazilian shrub of 1·8 m/6 ft with bipinnate leaves and furry, yellow-green flowers with red stamens. This bald description does not really do it justice; its generic name tells of its decorative value.

Calothamnus quadrifidus comes from western Australian regions and may grow to 2·4 m/8 ft; it needs full sun to flower freely, and is very pretty when the deep crimson stamens crowd the underside of the shoots in a one-sided spray. Even more attractive is *C. villosus*, which has greyish woolly needle leaves and deep red flowers.

Ceratopetalum gummiferum is a large evergreen shrub with small, lanceolate leaves and panicles of small white flowers; the bracts, at first creamy-white, mature through brick-red to crimson.

Chamaelaucium uncinatum, another member of the myrtle family from western Australia, is usually seen as a shrub of 1 m/3¼ ft or so, but may grow to a tree-like 6 m/20 ft; the needle leaves are curled into a hook at the tip. The clusters of white, pink or lilac flowers appear in spring, spaced along the branches.

Darwinia macrostegia (*Genetyllis tulipifera*) is a straggling shrub of 60–90 cm/2–3 ft, with small dark leaves, and nodding flowers in spring at each branch tip, the colourful bracts resembling a little creamy-yellow, red-streaked tulip.

Dryandra floribunda is an Australian member of the protea family, a rounded shrub with dark green, toothed, wedge-shaped leaves and primrose-white balls of flower in winter and spring. There is also the brighter, taller *D. formosa* with tangerine flower-heads.

Fortunella japonica (*Citrus japonica*) is the round kumquat, an evergreen shrub with white flowers, and fruits as round, and no larger than, yellow cherries; the branches are thorny.

Iochroma is a tender solanaceous genus, of which two species rated Z10 might just be worth a try: the scarlet *I. coccineum*, and deepest indigo-blue *I. cyaneum*. Both have long, tubular, nodding flowers in clusters in summer.

Justicia rizzinii (*Jacobinia pauciflora*, *Libonia floribunda*) is a subshrub of 60 cm/2 ft or so from Brazil with tubular flowers, scarlet-orange tipped with yellow, held horizontally on short axillary stems in autumn.

Lambertia formosa, of the protea family, has whorls of needle leaves and erect clusters of red flowers in red bracts during most of the year.

Marcetella moquiniana is a shrubby burnet with decorative pinnate foliage, composed of the same style of toothed leaflets as the hardy herbaceous burnets but, in this Canary Island species, pale glaucous blue in colour. The spikes of purplish flowers are a disappointment.

Ochna atropurpurea (*O. serrulata*), from South Africa, is grown as a conservatory shrub in cool climates; it may become tall but is usually seen as a low shrub with finely toothed leaves and yellow five-petalled flowers, followed by black pea-sized fruits hanging from bright crimson-red, waxy calyces.

Passiflora × *tresederi* 'Lilac Lady' (*P. caerulea* × *P.* × *caerulea-racemosa*) has large lilac-pink flowers in late summer and autumn, and bold, narrow-lobed leaves.

Pelargonium. These are always thought of in cool temperate gardens as tender; yet the ivy-leaved kinds will survive year after year on sunny walls in maritime Cornwall and Devon, pink 'Madame Crousse' and others making sheets of colour from ground to eaves.

Petraea volubilis is an evergreen twiner with long narrow trails of violet-blue or lilac flowers held in starry, paler calyces. It is rated Z10, and its range extends from the West Indies and Central America to Mexico; but many of us have succeeded with other Z10 plants and have found that they will cope with a degree or two of frost if well-sheltered and well-ripened.

Plumeria spp, the frangipanis, are also Z10 shrubs or small trees, shedding their leaves in winter, which might make them easier to tuck up in a cosy, frost-proofing blanket if you decide to give them a try. The waxy flowers of *Plumeria rubra* vary from crimson or pink to soft yellow or white; they are borne in summer, and are valued even more for their swooning fragrance than for their broad propellor-shaped petals opening from spiralled buds, typical of the periwinkle family to which they belong.

Stenocarpus sinuatus is the spectacular Queensland firewheel tree, which can grow to 30 m/100 ft, but will produce its umbels of vermilion flowers while still shrubby. The large leaves are often deeply pinnately lobed.

Tibouchina urvilleana (*T. semidecandra* of gardens) is generally seen in greenhouses in temperate areas, but is hardier than its glamorous appearance might suggest. The leaves are handsome even without the flowers, large, prominently veined and velvet-downy; but the flat royal-purple blooms themselves are magnificent, up to 7·5 cm/3 in wide in the type and twice as large in 'Grandiflora'. They come in succession over a long summer and autumn season, opening from red buds.

Tristania neriifolia is perhaps the most frost-resistant of a tender genus; it is a slender shrub with sprays of small yellow stars.

Hot and Dry (CHAPTER VI)

Acacia armata is another of the mimosas with needle-like leaves, and sharp needle-like spikes at each joint – as the specific name suggests. At around 3 m/10 ft, it is one of the smaller species. The rich yellow mimosa bobbles strung along the branches contrast in their spring season with the dark green foliage.

A. rhetinodes is a taller species, to 6 m/20 ft, with narrow linear phyllodes and pale yellow flowers in small round heads. In the Midi this is known as the 'Mimose de quatre saisons' on account of its almost uninterrupted flowering season. It is more lime tolerant than most acacias.

A. riceana (*Racosperma riceana*) is a tall and graceful mimosa growing to 10 m/33 ft, with slender pendulous shoots and spine-tippped needle-like phyllodes. The pale clear yellow flowers are borne in slim spikes, elegantly arched, in spring. Arnold-Forster suggests planting it on the top of a bank, with 'Erica mediterranea superba, or rosemary, or early blue ceanothus'; Ernest Lord finds that it prefers cooler, moister conditions than most others. Its seedling 'Exeter Hybrid', of which the pollen parent was *A. longifolia*, is also known as 'Veitchiana'. By whatever name you find it, it is an admirable mimosa, very free-flowering, with long, narrow, tapering leaves and abundant slender fluffy spikes of pale yellow.

Calodendron capense, the Cape chestnut, is probably too tender for even the mildest oceanic garden.

Hymenosporum flavum, from Australia, is related to *Pittosporum*; it forms an evergreen narrow-crowned tree with dark foliage and sprays of very fragrant flowers shaped like jasmine, opening pale creamy-white and aging to warm buff-yellow.

Jacaranda mimosaefolia is a tree with finely divided leaves and lavender-blue flowers with a curious zoo-like smell.

Leucadendron argenteum is a densely leafy, silver-plated proteaceous tree from South Africa which should be given the hottest, driest spot you can contrive.

Sophora secundiflora, from the states of Texas and New Mexico and from northern Mexico, is a beautiful evergreen tree up to 10 m/33 ft in height, with shining pinnate foliage and racemes of violet-blue pea-flowers, scented like sweet violets, in spring. As its origins suggest, it needs full sun and shelter; the Mediterranean climate suits it well.

Sterculia acerifolia (*Brachychiton acerifolium*), the flame tree, bears its vermilion-scarlet flowers on leafless branches.

Ursinia chrysanthemoides 'Geyeri' resents wet winters; where it can be grown in sharply-drained soil, it forms a clump of finely cut grey-green foliage contrasting with brilliant red daisies.

Westringia fruticosa is a shrub of eastern Australian coastal regions, found often on exposed cliffs; it is better, and more expressively, known as *W. rosmariniformis*. Growing to around 1·5 m/5 ft, it has narrow rosemary-like leaves white beneath, and white flowers faintly tinted with lilac and speckled with brown, very freely borne in late spring and summer. It needs maximum sun and free drainage. The plant known as *W. raleighii*, or those referred to as the Raleighii group, belong to *W. brevifolia*, in which the leaves are shiny above and silvery beneath, and the flowers white. Others that are offered are *W. rigida*, a small, stiff shrub with light green leaves and white to pale lavender flowers almost all year; and *W. angustifolia* which is a more straggling shrub with mauve to white flowers.

The Mature Milder Garden (CHAPTER VII)

Ixerba brexioides is endemic to New Zealand, growing in the forest interior where it forms a bushy tree with narrow, leathery leaves with toothed margins, highly glossed on the upper surface, and greenish-white flowers with five green stamens standing erect from the five petals.

Myosotideum hortensia (*M. nobile*) is the Chatham Island forgetmenot, with vivid blue flowers borne in wide dense heads over leaves as bold as a large leaved hosta, of rich, shining green, deeply ribbed. Although a plant of the seashore, which would suggest it should belong in Chapter II, it is not easy to please; abundant summer moisture, a diet of seaweed and even of rotting fish, and shelter, may (but are not guaranteed to) help it thrive. Its height varies from 45 cm/$1\frac{1}{2}$ ft to 90 cm/3 ft.

Podocarpus species from the African continent which might be attempted include *P. falcatus* from South African, which has leaves very variable in size and shape; and the elegant *P. gracilior*, from the mountains of Ethiopia, Uganda and Kenya, which has willow-like leaves.

APPENDIX 2
Note on plant availability

Few of the plants described in these pages are widely offered commercially in the United Kingdom. However, with patience almost all of them can be obtained sooner or later, either from small specialist nurseries who do not list in their catalogues the plants of which they have only a few available for sale, or from plant stalls in private gardens open only occasionally for charity. *The Plant Finder*, published annually by Headmain Ltd in association with the Hardy Plant Society, lists over 40,000 plants (some of them mentioned in this book) from over 300 nurseries in the UK; the special interests of the nurseries are mentioned, which may be a guide to the plants that they may have available but unlisted. Another source of unusual plants is provided by the catalogues of seedsmen such as Chiltern Seeds of Bortree Stile, Ulverston, Cumbria, who specialize in species from Australia and New Zealand, California and South Africa. The National Council for the Conservation of Plants and Gardens (NCCPG) arranges frequent plant sales at which many uncommon and interesting plants are to be found in small quantities; information on membership and forthcoming events from NCCPG, the Pines, c/o Wisley Garden, Working, Surrey GU23 6QB. The specialist societies such as the Hardy Plant Society (which despite its name does not confine itself to cold-hardy plants), the International Dendrology Society, and many others, also offer seeds and the opportunity to exchange plants. Exchange of plant material, indeed, is often the most rewarding way of obtaining new species or cultivars. No one, therefore, should be deterred if at first they cannot find a source of a particular plant. After all, the author of this book has, without any exceptional resources, obtained and grown most of the plants here described.

Bibliography

ALLAN, H. H. et al.: *Flora of New Zealand* Vol I. Wellington, New Zealand, 1961

ARNOLD-FORSTER, W.: *Shrubs for the Milder Counties* Country Life, 1948

BAILEY, L. H. & E. Z. & STAFF OF L. H. BAILEY HORTORIUM, CORNELL UNIVERSITY: *Hortus Third* Macmillan, 1976

BEAN, W. J.: *Trees & Shrubs Hardy in the British Isles* 4 vols, 8th (revised) ed. John Murray, 1976–80

BEAN, W. J.: Supplement to 8th ed. John Murray, 1988

BERGER, ALWIN: *Hortus Mortolensis* London, 1912

BOULLEMIER, L. B.: *Checklist of Species, Hybrids & Cultivars of the Genus Fuchsia* Blandford Press, 1985

CHALK, D.: *Hebes and Parahebes* Christopher Helm, 1988

CHATTO, BETH: *The Dry Garden* J. M. Dent, 1978

CHITTENDEN, F. J. (ed): *The Royal Horticultural Society Dictionary of Gardening* Oxford University Press, 1965

COX, P. A.: *The Larger Species of Rhododendron* Batsford, 1979

COX, P. A. & K. N. E.: *Encyclopedia of Rhododendron Hybrids* Batsford, 1988

CROWE, SYLVIA: *Garden Design* Thomas Gibson, 1981

CULLEN, J. & CHAMBERLAIN, C. F.: *Revision of Rhododendron. Notes from the Royal Botanic Garden Edinburgh* Vol. 39, 1 & 2 1980 and 1982

CURTIS's *Botanical Magazine* (now *The Kew Magazine*) 1787 et seq.

CURTIS, W. M.: *A Student's Flora of Tasmania* Government Printer, Hobart, 1956–67

EDLIN, HERBERT: *Atlas of Plant Life* Heinemann 1973

ELEY, CHARLES: *Twentieth Century Gardening* Country Life, 1939

EWART, R.: *Fuchsia Lexicon* Blandford Press, 1982

FISHER, M. E., SATCHELL, E. & WATKINS, J. M.: *Gardening with New Zealand Plants, Shrubs & Trees* Collins, 1970

GALBRAITH, J.: *Field Guide to the Wild Flowers of South-East Australia* Collins, 1977

Gardeners Chronicle

HARRISON, R.: *Handbook of Trees & Shrubs for the Southern Hemisphere* R. E. Harrison & Co, 1959

HAWORTH-BOOTH, M.: *Effective Flowering Shrubs* 2nd ed. Collins, 1970

HEALY, A. J. & EDGAR, E.: *Flora of New Zealand* Vol III. Wellington, New Zealand, 1980

Hillier's Manual of Trees & Shrubs David & Charles, 1977

241

INGRAM, COLLINGWOOD: *A Garden of Memories* Witherby, 1970

INNES, C.: *The World of Iridaceae* Hollygate International, 1985

KELWAY, CHRISTINE: *Gardening on Sand* Collingridge, 1965
  Gardening on the Coast David & Charles, 1970
  Seaside Gardening Collingridge, 1962

KRÜSSMANN, GERD: *Manual of Cultivated Broad-leaved Trees & Shrubs* 3 vols. Eng. ed. trs. Michael Epp, Batsford, 1984–6
  Manual of Cultivated Conifers Eng. ed. trs. Michael Epp, Batsford, 1985

LLOYD, C.: *Foliage Plants* Collins, 1972
  The Adventurous Gardener Allen Lane, 1983
  The Well Chosen Garden Elm Tree Books, 1984
  The Well Tempered Garden Collins, 1970

LORD, ERNEST E.: *Shrubs & Trees for Australian Gardens* Lothian Publishing, 1964

MACKENZIE, COMPTON: *My Life & Times Octave Four, 1907–1914* Chatto & Windus, 1965

MUNZ, P. A.: *A Californian Flora* University of California Press 1959

New Flora & Silva Dulau, London, 1929–40

DE NOAILLES & LANCASTER, R.: *Mediterranean Plants & Gardens* Floraprint, 1977

PAGE, R.: *The Education of a Gardener* Collins, 1962

PEREIRE, A. & VAN ZUYLEN, G.: *Private Gardens of France* Weidenfeld & Nicolson, 1983

PHILIP, C. & LORD, TONY: *The Plant Finder* Headman Ltd for The Hardy Plant Society, 1989

ROBINSON, W.: *The English Flower Garden* 8th ed. John Murray, 1900, and revised Amaryllis Press USA, 1984

ROWNTREE, L: *Flowering Shrubs of California* Stanford University Press, 1939
  Hardy Californians Macmillan, New York, 1936

SALLEY, H. E. & GREER, H. E.: *Rhododendron Hybrids: A Guide to Their Origins* Batsford, 1986

SALMON, J. T.: *New Zealand Flowers & Plants in Colour* Reed, 1963
  The Native Trees of New Zealand Reed, 1980

Plantsman RHS London

ROYAL HORTICULTURAL SOCIETY: *The Rhododendron Handbook – Rhododendron Species in Cultivation* RHS, 1980

ROYAL HORTICULTURAL SOCIETY's *Journal* (now *The Garden*)

TAYLOR, J.: *Collecting Garden Plants* Dent, 1988
  Kew Gardening Guides: *Climbing Plants* Collingridge, 1987
  Kew Gardening Guides: *Tender Perennials* Collingridge, 1990

THOMAS, G. S.: *The Art of Planting* Dent, 1984
  Perennial Garden Plants 2nd ed. Dent 1982
  Climbing Roses Old & New rev. ed. Dent, 1978
  Shrub Roses of Today Dent, 1962

THURSTON, E.: *Trees & Shrubs in Cornwall* Cambridge University Press, 1930

TREHANE, PIERS: *Index Hortensis* Vol I: Perennials. Quarterjack Publishing, 1989

TRESEDER, NEIL G.: *Magnolias* Faber & Faber, 1978

VAN RENSSELAER, M. & McMINN, PROF. H. E.: *Ceanothus* California, 1942

WALTERS, S. M. (ed) et al.: *The European Garden Flora* Vols I & II Cambridge University Press, 1984 & 1986

WARD, F. KINGDON: *Plant Hunter in Manipur* Jonathan Cape, 1952
  Plant Hunter's Paradise Jonathan Cape, 1937
  Plant Hunting on the Edge of the World Gollancz, 1930

WRIGLEY, J. W.: *Australian Native Plants* Collins 1979

General Index

Abbotsbury, 99
Aberconway, Lord, 186
Anderson, E. B., 172
Archeopterix, 66
Arnold-Forster, W., 1, 29, 34, 37, 96, 102, 117, 122, 126, 138, 139, 146, 147, 155, 197, 210, 221, 222, 228, 232

Bean, W. J., 1
Bodnant, 186
Boscawen, Canon, 19, 212
Bowles, E. A., 101, 158

Chaparral, 18, 120, 153, 160, 171–2, 176
Chatto, Beth, 138
Comber, Harold, 10, 121, 122
Crowe, Dame Sylvia, 35

Farrer, Reginald, 195, 197, 203
Forrest, George, 16, 182, 184, 185

Fortune, Robert, 198, 206

Garrigue, 15, 150, 160
Great Dixter, 74

Hadden, Norman, 80, 118, 134
Haworth-Booth, M., 17
Hidcote, 60
Highdown, 45
Hooker, Sir Joseph, 16, 205

Ingram, Capt. Collingwood, 164, 201

Jekyll, Miss G., 51, 61, 85

Lloyd, Christopher, 74
Lobb, William, 172
Ludgvan, 19, 121, 126, 221

Mackenzie, Compton, 61, 63
Maquis, 15, 103, 150, 160, 163, 168, 172, 185

Myddelton House, 158

Picton, Percy, 217
Priory, The, 85
Pterodactyl, 229

Robinson, William, 217
Rock, Joseph, 16

Slieve Donard, 78, 80
Stern, Sir Frederick, 45

Talbot de Malahide, Lord
Trengwainton, 94
Tresco Abbey, 18, 29, 111, 167, 235

Ward, F. Kingdon, 16, 102, 118, 119, 170, 179, 184, 185, 188, 194, 195, 197, 210, 203, 214, 215
Wilson, E. H., 16, 183, 236

Index of Plant Names

North American Zones are indicated in square brackets

ABELIA Caprifoliaceae
  floribunda Dcne [Z8], 18,
    137
  schumanni Rehd. [Z7], 105
ABIES Pinaceae, 189
  religiosa (HBK) Schlecht.
    [Z9], 18
ABUTILON Malvaceae
  'Margharita Manns' see *A.
    ochsenii*
  megapotamicum St. Hil. &
    Naud. [Z8], 141
  megapotamicum hybrids:
    'Cynthia Pike', 141
    'Kentish Belle', 141
    'Patrick Synge', 141
  × *milleri* hort. [Z8], 141
  ochsenii Phil.
    (*CORYNABUTILON*)
    [Z8], 108
  pictum Walp., 141
  × *suntense* Brickell
    (*CORYNABUTILON*)
    [Z8], 108
    'Jermyns', 108
    'Violetta', 108
    'White Charm', 108
  vitifolium Presl.
    (*CORYNABUTILON*)
    [Z8], 5, 10, 107–8
    'Veronica Tennant',
      107–8
    'Veronica Tennant
      White', 108
  hybrid cultivars:
    'Ashford Red', 141
    'Boule de Neige', 141
    'Canary Bird', 141
    'Cerise Queen', 141
    'Golden Fleece', 79, 141

'Louise Marignac', 141
'Nabob', 141
ACACIA Leguminosae, 13,
  20, 160, 163, 165
  armata R.Br. [Z8], 237
  baileyana F.v. Muell. [Z8],
    62, 161
  cultriformis G.Don [Z8], 162
  cyanophylla Lindl., 161
  dealbata Link [Z8], 161
  'Exeter Hybrid', 238
  × *hanburyana* hort., 162
  juniperina Willd., 162
  longifolia Willd. [Z8], 162
  melanoxylon R.Br. [Z8],
    161–2
  podalyriifolia G.Don. [Z8],
    62, 162
  pravissima F.v. Muell. [Z8],
    162
  pycnantha Benth. [Z8], 161
  rhetinodes Schlecht. [Z8],
    237
  riceana Henslow [Z8], 237–
    8
  verticillata Willd. [Z8], 162
Acanthus, 15
ACCA Myrtaceae
  sellowiana (Berg) Burret
    [Z8], 11, 109–10
ACER Aceraceae, 17, 184,
  187
  albopurpurascens Hayata
    [Z8], 185
  campbellii Hook.f. &
    Thoms. [Z7], 185
  cinnamomifolium Hayata
    [Z8], 185
  craibianum Delendick [Z8],
    185

flabellatum Rehd. [Z5], 185
  yunnanense Fang., 185
  hookeri Miq. [Z8], 185
  laevigatum Wall. [Z8], 185
  lanceolatum Molliard, 185
  oblongum DC [Z7], 185
  palmatum Thunb. [Z5]
    'Katsura', 202
  paxii Franch. [Z8], 185
  pentaphyllum Diels. [Z6],
    185
  sikkimense Miq. [Z7], 185
  wardii W.W.Sm. [Z5],
    185
ACIDANTHERA bicolor
  Hochst. see *Gladiolus
    callianthus*
  murielae Hoog see *Gladiolus
    callianthus*
ACRADENIA Rutaceae
  frankliniae Kipp. [Z8], 13,
    98
ADENANDRA Rutaceae
  fragrans Roem & Schult.
    [Z8], 124
  umbellata Willd. [Z8],
    124
  uniflora Willd. [Z8], 124
ADENOCARPUS
    Leguminosae
  anagyrifolius Coss &
    Balansa [Z8], 163
  decorticans Boiss. [Z8], 163
  foliolosus (Ait) DC [Z8],
    163
AEONIUM Crassulaceae, 15
  arboreum L., 160
    'Atropurpureum', 85,
      160
    'Schwartzkopf', 85

AGAPANTHUS Alliaceae, 14, 115, 131
africanus (L.)
  Hoffmannsegg, 64
  'Ardernei Hybrid', 64
campanulatus F.M.Leighton
  mooreanus hort., 64
  patens (F.M.Leighton)
    F.M.Leighton, 64
Headbourne Hybrids, 64
inapertus Beauv., 64
  pendulus (L.Bolus)
    F.M.Leighton, 64
  'Phantom', 64
praecox Willd., 64
  orientalis (F.M.Leighton)
    F.M.Leighton
    'Albatross', 64
umbellatus hort., 64
AGAPETES Ericaceae
buxifolia Nutt. [Z8], 215
incurvata (Griff.) Sleum.
  var. *incurvata* [Z8], 215
  'Ludgvan Cross' [Z8], 215
rugosa (Hook) Sleum [Z8], 215
serpens (Klotzch) Sleum.
  see *A. incurvata* var.
  incurvata
AGATHIS Araucariaceae, 189
australis (D.Don) Salisb.
  [Z9], 190
AGAVE Agavaceae, 18
americana L. [Z8], 157
  'Marginata', 157
  'Mediopicta', 157
parryi Englem. [Z8], 157
AGONIS Myrtaceae
flexuosa Lindl., 139
marginata Schau, 139
AILANTHUS
  Simaroubaceae
altissima Swingle [Z5], 223
ALBIZIA Leguminosae
lophantha (Willd.) Benth.
  [Z8], 162
Alder, 25
ALNUS Betulaceae
glutinosa Gaertn. [Z3], 25
ALOE Aloeaceae, 14
arborescens Mill. [Z9], 158
aristata Haworth [Z9], 158
vera L., 158

ALOYSIA Verbenaceae
triphylla (L'Herit.) Britt.
  [Z8], 11, 145
ALSTROEMERIA
  Alstroemeriaceae, 11
caryophyllea Jacq., 235
chilensis Cree, 233
pelegrina L., 138, 233
  'Alba', 138, 233
pulchella L.f., 59
violacea Philippi, 233
ALYOGYNE Malvaceae
huegelii (Endl.) Fryx
  'Santa Cruz', 73
× *AMARCRINUM*
  Amaryllidaceae
howardii Coutts, 76
memoria-corsii (Ragioneri)
  H.E.Moore, 76
× *AMARINE*
  Amaryllidaceae
tubergenii Sealy, 76
  'Zwanenburg', 76
× *AMARYGIA*
  Amaryllidaceae
parkeri (W.Watson)
  H.E.Moore, 76
  'Alba', 76
  'Tubergen's Var.', 76
AMARYLLIS
  Amaryllidaceae
belladonna L., 76, 166
  'Beacon', 76
  'Elata', 76
  'Hathor', 76
  'Rubra', 76
AMICIA Leguminosae
zygomeris DC [Z9], 84
AMOMYRTUS Myrtaceae
luma (Mol.) D.Legrand &
  Kausel [Z9], 97
ANAGYRIS Leguminosae
foetida L. [Z8], 163
ANEMONE Ranunculaceae
pavonina Lamarck, 15, 166
ANOPTERUS
  Escalloniaceae, 13
glandulosus Labill. [Z8], 212
ANTHYLLIS Leguminosae
Barba-jovis L. [Z8], 163
APONOGETON
  Aponogetonaceae
distachyos L., 218

ARAUCARIA
  Araucariaceae, 189
araucana K. Koch [Z8], 190
bidwillii Hook. [Z9], 190
cunninghamii D.Don. [Z9], 190
  'Glauca', 190
heterophylla (Salisb.) Franco
  [Z9], 190
ARAUJIA Asclepiadaceae
sericofera Brot. [Z9], 137
ARBUTUS Ericaceae, 160
andrachne L. [Z8], 18, 186
× *andrachnoides* Link [Z8], 186
arizonica (A.Gray) Sarg.
  [Z6], 187
menziesii Pursh. [Z8], 18, 186–7
texana Buckley, 187
unedo L. [Z8], 15, 33, 95, 186
  rubra, 95, 186
xalapensis HBK [Z8], 187
ARCTOSTAPHYLOS
  Ericaceae, 18, 172
andersonii A. Gray [Z8], 177
bicolor (Nutt.) A.Gray [Z7], 177
canescens Eastw. [Z7], 176
diversifolia see
  Comarostaphylis
  diversifolia
glauca Lindl. [Z8], 176
manzanita Parry see *A.*
  pungens ssp. *manzanita*
mariposa Dudley, 177
nevadensis A. Gray [Z6], 176
patula Greene [Z6], 177
pungens HBK [Z8]
  manzanita (Parry)
    J.B.Roof, 176
tomentosa (Pursh) Lindl.
  [Z8], 176
uva-ursi Spreng. [Z4], 176
viscida Parry [Z6], 177
ARCTOTIS Compositae, 14, 154
  'Apricot', 155
  'Flame', 155
  'Wine', 155

ARDISIA Myrsinaceae
  japonica BL [Z8], 215
ARGEMONE Papaveraceae,
  18
  grandiflora Sweet, 159
  mexicana L., 159
  platyceras Link & Otto,
    159
ARGYRANTHEMUM
  Compositae
  foeniculaceum (Willd.)
    Webb & Schultz-Bip,
    15, 71
  frutescens (L.) Schultz-Bip,
    15, 61
  maderense (D.Don) C.J.
    Humphries, 61
  hybrid cultivars:
    'Brontes', 61
    'Chelsea Girl', 71
    'Crimson Pompon', 70
    'Jamaica Primrose', 61
      dwarf form, 61
    'Levada Cream', 61
    'Mary Wootton', 69
    'Mrs Sanders', 71
    'Overbecks', 80
    'Pink Beauty', 70
    'Rollason's Red', 70
    'Royal Haze', 71
    'Snowflake', 71
    'Surprise', 70
    'Vancouver', 69
    'Wellwood Park', 69
ARISTEA Iridaceae, 14
  ecklonii Baker, 63
  major Andrews, 63
ARISTOTELIA
  Elaeocarpaceae, 109
  chilensis (Mol.) Stuntz [Z8],
    109
    'Variegata', 109
  macqui L'Her. see *A.
    chilensis*
  serrata W.R.Oliv. [Z8], 12,
    212–13
ARTEMISIA Compositae
  arborescens L. [Z8], 15, 81
    'Faith Raven', 81
    'Powis Castle', 81, 151
ARTHROPODIUM
  Anthericaceae
  cirrhatum R.Br., 12
Arum lily, 5, 14

ARUNDINARIA
  Gramineae
  falconeri (Munro) Duthie,
    230–1
  hookeriana Munro see
    *Chimonobambusa
    hookeriana*
  japonica Sieb. & Zucc. [Z7]
    (*Pseudosasa japonica*
    [Steudel] Makino), 34
  simonii A. & C. Riv. [Z7]
    (*Pleioblastus simonii*
    [Carr.] Nakai), 34
ASTELIA Asteliaceae
  banksii A.Cunn [Z8], 217
  chathamica (Skottsb.) L.B.
    Moore see *A. nervosa
    chathamica*
  nervosa Hook.f. [Z8], 217
    var. *chathamica* Skottsb.
    [Z8], 217
    'Silver Spear', 217
  nivicola Cockayne ex
    Cheesem., 217
  petriei Cockayne [Z8], 217
ASTER Compositae
  albescens (DC) Hand.-
    Mazz. [Z8], 70
ASTERANTHERA
  Gesneriaceae
  ovata (Cav.) Hanst. [Z8],
    10, 220
ASYSTASIA bella see
    Mackaya bella
ATHEROSPERMA
  Atherospermataceae
  moschatum Lab. [Z8], 93,
    209
ATHROTAXIS
  Taxodiaceae, 13, 189
  cupressoides, D.Don. [Z8–
    9], 190
  laxifolia Hook. [Z8–9], 190
  selaginoides D.Don [Z9],
    190
ATHYRIUM Woodsiaceae
  goeringianum hort. see *A.
    niponicum*
  niponicum (Mett.) Hance
    'Pictum', 219
ATRIPLEX Chenopodiaceae
  halimus L. [Z8], 26
AZARA Flacourtiaceae
  dentata Ruiz & Pav. [Z8], 96

integrifolia Ruiz & Pav.
    [Z8], 96
  lanceolata Hook.f. [Z8], 96
  microphylla Hook.f. [Z8],
    96
    'Variegata', 96
  petiolaris (D. Don)
    Johnston [Z8], 96
  serrata Ruiz & Pav. [Z8], 96
AZOLLA Azollaceae
  caroliniana Willd. see *A.
    filiculoides*
  filiculoides Lam., 218

BACCHARIS Compositae
  halimifolia L. [Z5], 34
  patagonica Hook. & Arn.
    [Z8], 11, 26, 34
Bamboo, 230
Banana, 223, 225, 226
BANKSIA Proteaceae, 13
  canei J.H.Willis, 147–8
  coccinea R.Br. [Z8], 147
  grandis Willd., 147
  integrifolia L.f. [Z8], 147
  marginata Cav. [Z8], 147
  serrata L.f. [Z8], 147
  verticillata R.Br., 147
BAROSMA Rutaceae
  pulchella Bartl. & Wendl.
    [Z10], 124
BAUERA Baueraceae
  rubioides Andr. [Z9], 146
BAUHINIA Leguminosae
  densiflora Franch. [Z9], 143
  yunnanensis Franch. [Z8],
    143
BEAUFORTIA Myrtaceae
  decussata Ait., 141
  sparsa R.Br., 141
Beech, southern, 183
BEGONIA Begoniaceae
  evansiana Andr. see *B.
    grandis*
  grandis Dryand., 217
    'Alba', 217
Belladonna lily, 4
BERBERIDOPSIS
  Flacourtiaceae
  corallina Hook.f. [Z8], 10,
    220
BERBERIS Berberidaceae
  hypokerina Airy-Shaw
    [Z8], 102

ilicifolia Forst. [Z8]
insignis Hook.f. & Thoms.
　[Z8], 102
× *ottawensis* Schneid.
　'Superba' [Z4], 86
valdiviana Phil. [Z8], 102
BERGENIA Saxifragaceae
ciliata (Haw.) Sternb., 51
BESCHORNERIA
　Agavaceae
yuccoides K.Koch. [Z8], 18,
　50, 51, 58, 59, 61, 78,
　156, 157
BIDENS Compositae
ferulaefolia (Jacq.) DC, 79
BIGNONIA Bignoniaceae
capreolata L. [Z8], 135
BILLARDIERA
　Pittosporaceae, 13
longiflora Labill. [Z8], 140
scandens Sm. [Z8], 140
BILLBERGIA Bromeliaceae
nutans Wendl., 158
Bird of Paradise, 11, 141
BLANDFORDIA Liliaceae,
　13, 201
grandiflora R.Br., 142
nobilis Sm., 142
punicea (Labill.) Sweet, 142
BLECHNUM Blechnaceae
chilense (Kaulf.) Mett., 219
magellanicum (Desv.) Mett.,
　219
tabulare hort. see *B.*
　magellanicum
Bluebell creeper, 140
BOMAREA
　Alstroemeriaceae, 11
andimarcana Bak., 233
caldasii (HBK) Asch. &
　Graebn., 140
× *cantabrigiensis* Lynch, 140
kalbreyeri Bak., 140
BORONIA Rutaceae
elatior Barth., 235
　'Heaven Scent', 138
heterophylla F.v.Muell., 138
megastigma Nees, 138
　'Lutea', 138
pinnata Sm., 235
polygalifolia Sm., 235
Bottlebrush, 13, 109, 139
BOUGAINVILLEA
　Nyctaginaceae, 160, 170

BOUVARDIA Rubiaceae
ternifolia (Cav.) Schlect.
　[Z9], 142
triphylla Salisb. see *ternifolia*
BOWKERIA
　Scrophulariaceae
gerardiana Harv. [Z9], 138
BRACHYCHITON
　Sterculiaceae
acerifolium F.v. Muell., 238
BRACHYGLOTTIS
　Compositae, 12, 36, 48
　'Alfred Atkinson', 100
bidwillii (Hook.f.) B. Nord
　[Z9], 36
buchananii (Armstr.) B.
　Nord., 36
compacta (Kirk) B. Nord
　[Z9], 35
　Dunedin Hybrids [Z8–9],
　36
　'Sunshine', 36, 154
elaeagnifolia (Hook.f.) B.
　Nord. [Z9], 27
greyi (Hook.f.) B. Nord.
　[Z9], 100
hectoris (Buchan) B. Nord.
　[Z9], 100
huntii (F.v. Muell.) B.
　Nord., 101
　'Joseph Andrews', 36
laxifolia (Buchan.) B.
　Nord. [Z9], 36
　'Leonard Cockayne', 100
monroi (Hook.f.) B. Nord.
　[Z9], 36, 154
perdicioides (Hook.f.) B.
　Nord., 100
repanda J. R. & G. Forst.
　[Z8], 33
rotundifolia J. R. & G. Forst.
　[Z9], 27, 36, 43, 53, 100
Bramble ornamental, 16
BRIDGESIA spicata Hook. &
　Arn. see *Ercilla volubilis*
BRODIAEA Alliaceae, 141
Broom, 15, 22, 169
　Tenerife, 163
BRUNSVIGIA
　Amaryllidaceae
josephinae (Redouté) Ker-
　Gawl., 76
BUDDLEJA Loganiaceae,
　107, 131

asiatica Lour. [Z8], 17, 116,
　143
auriculata Benth. [Z8], 14,
　61
candida Dunn. [Z8], 106
caryopteridifolia W.W.Sm.
　[Z8], 106
colvilei Hook.f. & Thoms.
　[Z8], 17
　'Kewensis', 58, 78
crispa Benth. [Z8], 70, 106
davidii Franch. [Z6], 17,
　106
fallowiana Balf. f. &
　W.W. Sm. [Z8],16,106
　'Alba', 106
　'Lochinch' [Z7–8], 106
farreri Balf. f. & W.W.Sm.
　[Z7], 106
forrestii Diels. [Z7], 106
globosa Hope [Z8], 26,
　106
× *lewisiana* Everett [Z8]
　'Margaret Pike', 143
lindleyana Fort. [Z8], 106
madagascariensis Lam. [Z9],
　143
　'Nicodemus' see
　B. × *lewisiana*
officinalis Maxim. [Z8], 116
pterocaulis A.B.Jacks. [Z7],
　106
salviifolia (L.) Lam. [Z8],
　106
× *weyeriana* Weyer, 106
　'Elstead Hybrid', 106
　'Moonlight', 106
　'Sungold', 106
Bull bay, 179
BUPLEURUM Umbelliferae
fruticosum L. [Z8], 26
BURCHELLIA Rubiaceae
bubalina Sims, 235

CAESALPINIA
　Leguminosae
gilliesii (Hook.) Benth.
　[Z8], 11, 141
japonica Sieb. & Zucc. [Z8],
　141
CALANDRINIA
　Portulaceae
umbellata Hook. & Arn.,
　159–60

CALCEOLARIA
Scrophulariaceae
arachnoidea Graham, 74
integrifolia Murr. [Z8], 11,
78
'Camden Hero', 83
'Kentish Hero', 83
mexicana Benth., 79
Californian lilac, 120
CALLIANDRA
Leguminosae
tweedii Benth. [Z8], 235
CALLICARPA
Verbenaceae, 75
CALLISTEMON
Myrtaceae, 13, 109, 110
citrinus Skeels [Z9], 110, 111
'Splendens', 110
linearis (Sm.) DC [Z9],
110
pallidus (Bonpl.) DC, 110
phoeniceus Lindl., 110
rigidus R.Br. [Z9], 110
salignus (Sm.) DC [Z9], 110
viridiflora F.v.Muell.
[Z9], 110
sieberi DC [Z9], 110
speciosus (Simms) DC [Z9],
110
subulatus Cheel, 110
viminalis Cheel [Z9], 110
hybrid cultivars:
'Burning Bush', 111
'Captain Cook', 111
'Hannah Ray', 111
'Mauve Mist', 111
'Perth Pink', 111
'Reeve's Pink', 111
CALLITRIS Cupressaceae,
189
oblonga Rich. [Z9], 190
rhomboidea R.Br. ex
L.C. Rich [Z9], 190
CALOCEPHALUS brownii
(Cass.) F.v.Muell. see
Leucophyta brownii
CALODENDRON
Rutaceae
capense (L.f.) Thunb. [Z9–
10], 238
CALOTHAMNUS
Myrtaceae
quadrifidus Ait. [Z9], 235
villosus Ait., 235

CALYSTEGIA
Convolvulaceae
pubescens Lindl., 138
CALYTRIX Myrtaceae
alpestris see *Lhotskya
alpestris*
sullivanii F.v.Muell., 139
tetragona Labill., 139
CAMELLIA Theaceae, 16, 17
chrysantha (Hu) Tuyama,
207
cuspidata Veitch, 208
Fortune's Yellow see *C.
oleifera* 'Jaune'
granthamiana Sealy, 207
hongkongensis Seem. [Z8],
207
'Inamorata', 207
japonica L., 186, 206, 207
oleifera Abel [Z8], 207
'Jaune', 207
reticulata Lindl. [Z8], 206,
207
'Captain Rawes', 206
saluenensis Stapf. [Z7], 206,
207
'Salutation', 207
sasanqua Thunb. [Z8], 16,
207
'Narumi-gata', 207
sinensis (L.) Ktze [Z8], 207,
208
taliensis (W.W.Sm.)
Melchior, 207
tsaii Hu [Z8], 207–8
CAMPHOROSMA
Chenopodiaceae
monspeliaca L. [Z8], 154
CAMPSIS Bignoniaceae, 137
grandiflora (Thunb.) K.
Schum. [Z7], 17, 135
radicans (L.) Seem. [Z5],
135
flava (Bosse) Rehd., 135
× *tagliabuana* Rehd. [Z5]
'Madame Galen', 135
CANDOLLEA cuneiformis
Labill. see *Hibbertia
cuneiformis*
CANNA Cannaceae, 78, 226
× *generalis* L.H.Bailey
'Le Roi Humbert', 85
'The President', 85
'Wyoming', 85

glauca L., 59, 61, 225, 235
indica L.
'Purpurea', 85
iridiflora Ruiz & Pav., 11,
66
lutea Mill., 235
musaefolia, 225
CANTUA Polemoniaceae
buxifolia Juss. [Z9], 137
Cape
heath, 14, 138–9
hyacinth, 79
CARMICHAELIA
Leguminosae, 12, 125
australis R.Br. [Z8], 126
flagelliformis Colenso [Z8],
126
glabrata Simpson, 126
grandiflora (Benth.) Hook.f.
[Z7–8], 126
odorata Colenso, 126
williamsii T. Kirk. [Z8], 126
Carob, 165
CARPENTERIA
Philadelphaceae
californica Torr. [Z8], 175
'Ladham's Var.', 175
CARPOBROTUS
Aizoaceae, 14
acinaciformis (L.) L.Bolus,
42, 154
edulis (L.) L.Bolus, 42, 154
CARPODETUS
Escalloniaceae
serratus Forst., 12, 212
CARYOPTERIS
Verbenaceae
× *clandonensis* Simmonds
[Z8], 65, 74
'Arthur Simmonds', 65
'Ferndown', 65
'Heavenly Blue', 65
'Kew Blue', 65
CASSIA Leguminosae
candolleana Vogel, 109
corymbosa Lam. [Z8], 108–9
CASSINIA Compositae, 12
fulvida Hook.f. see *C.
leptophylla*
leptophylla R.Br. [Z8], 122
fulvida Hook.f. [Z7], 28,
122
vauvilliersii Hook.f. [Z8]
albida Kirk, 122

retorta Cunn. ex DC [Z8], 122
CEANOTHUS
Rhamnaceae, 18, 20, 160, 172
arboreus Greene [Z8], 174
'Ray Hartman', 174
'Treasure Island', 174
'Trewithen Blue', 174
'Winter Cloud', 174
cyaneus Eastw. [Z8], 174
dentatus Torr. & Gr. [Z8], 172
floribundus (Hook.) Trel., 172
lobbianus see
C. × *lobbianus*
divergens Parry [Z8], 172
foliosus Parry [Z8], 172
austromontanus Abrams., 172
gloriosus J.T.Howell [Z8], 153
griseus (Trel.) McMinn [Z8], 40
horizontalis = 'Yankee Point', 40, 153
'Louis Edmonds', 232
impressus Trel. [Z7], 172, 173, 174
'Puget Blue', 173
incanus Torr. & Gr. [Z8], 120
integerrimus Hook. & Arn. [Z8], 120
jepsonii Greene [Z8], 173
× *lobbianus* Hook. [Z8], 172
megacarpus Nutt. [Z7], 120
papillosus Torr. & Gr. [Z8], 173
'Concha', 173
roweanus McMinn, 173
prostratus Benth. [Z7], 172
purpureus Jepson [Z8], 173
ramulosus (Greene) McMinn, 173
fascicularis McMinn, 173
rigidus Nutt. [Z8], 40, 173
'Snowball', 173
sorediatus Hook. & Arn. [Z8], 174
spinosus Nutt.

'Theodore Payne', 174
thyrsiflorus Eschsch. [Z8], 174
repens McMinn, 40, 153, 172
× *veitchianus* Hook. [Z8], 172
velutinus Hook. [Z8], 120
hybrid cultivars:
'A.T.Johnson' [Z8], 174
'Autumnal Blue' [Z6–7], 174
'Burkwoodii' [Z8], 174
'Burtonensis' [Z8], 174
'Cascade' [Z8], 174
'Cynthia Postan', 173–4
'Delight' [Z8], 73
'Dignity', 173
'Italian Skies' [Z8], 172–3
'La Purissima' [Z8], 173
'Yankee Point' see C. *griseus* var. *horizontalis*
CENTAUREA Compositae, 15, 83
candidissima Lam. see C. *rutifolia*
cineraria L., 81
'Colchester White', 81
gymnocarpa Moris & de Notaris see C. *cineraria*
rutifolia Sm., 81
CERATONIA Leguminosae
siliqua L. [Z8], 165
CERATOPETALUM
Cunoniaceae
gummiferum Sm., 235
CERATOSTIGMA
Plumbaginaceae
abyssinicum Aschers., 73
griffithii C.B.Clarke [Z9], 17, 109
willmottianum Stapf. [Z7], 73, 109
CERCIS Leguminosae
siliquastrum L. [Z6], 15, 166
CERCOCARPUS Rosaceae, 172
CESTRUM Solanaceae, 18, 116, 144
aurantiacum Lindl. [Z8], 59, 146

elegans (Brongn.) Schlecht. [Z8], 72, 73, 146
smithii (hort.) Bailey, 72
fasciculatum (Schlecht.) Miers [Z8], 146
'Newellii' [Z8], 146
nocturnum L., 146
parqui L'Herit. [Z8], 108
roseum HBK, 72
'Ilnacullen', 72
CHAMAECYPARIS
Cupressaceae
lawsoniana Parl. [Z6], 32
CHAMAELAUCIUM
Myrtaceae
uncinatum Schau.[Z9],235–6
CHAMAEROPS Palmae
excelsa Thunb. see
Trachycarpus fortunei
humilis L. [Z8], 227
CHASMANTHE Iridaceae
aethiopica (L.) N.E.Br., 83
floribunda (Salisb.) N.E.Br., 83
duckitii Lewis, 83
Chatham Island forgetmenot, 239
Chilean hazel, 210
CHILIOTRICHUM
Compositae
amelloides DC see C. *diffusum*
diffusum (Forst.) Kuntze [Z8], 63
rosmarinifolium Lessing see C. *diffusum*
CHIMONOBAMBUSA
Gramineae
hookeriana (Munro) Nakai, 231
CHIONANTHUS Oleaceae, 212
CHLORANTHUS
Chloranthaceae
brachystachus Blume see C. *glaber*
glaber Makino [Z9], 216
CHOISYA Rutaceae
ternata HBK [Z8], 18, 55, 99
'Sundance', 50, 55
CHORDOSPARTIUM
Leguminosae, 12
stevensonii Cheesem. [Z8],125

CHORIZEMA Leguminosae
  cordatum Lindl. [Z10], 141
  ilicifolium Labill. see *C.
    cordatum*
Christmas bells, 13, 142
CHRYSANTHEMUM
  foeniculaceum (Willd.)
    Desf. see *Argyranthemum
    foeniculaceum*
  frutescens L. see
    Argyranthemum frutescens
CINNAMOMUM
  Lauraceae, 210
  camphora (L.) Nees [Z9], 17,
    91, 185, 234
  glanduliferum (Wendl.)
    Meissm. [Z9], 234
CISSUS Vitaceae
  striata Ruiz & Pav. [Z8],
    131
CISTUS Cistaceae, 15, 20,
    22, 25, 40, 47, 48, 150,
    160, 165
  × *aguilari* Pau [Z8], 164
    'Maculatus', 164
  albidus L. [Z8], 151
    'Anne Palmer', 151
    'Blanche', 164
  × *corbariensis* Pourr. [Z8],
    152
  creticus L. [Z8], 151
  crispus L. [Z8], 35, 151
    'Sunset', 151
  × *cyprius* Lam. [Z8], 164
    'Elma', 164
  × *florentinus* Lam. [Z8],
    152
  hirsutus Lam. [Z8], 152
  incanus L. see *C. creticus*
  ladanifer L. [Z8], 164
  laurifolius L. [Z8], 164
  × *lusitanicus* Maund. [Z8]
    'Decumbens', 152
    'Paladin', 164
  palhinhae Ingram [Z7], 164
  parviflorus Lam. [Z8], 35,
    151
    'Pat', 164
    'Peggy Sammons', 151
  × *purpureus* Lam. [Z8], 151
    'Betty Taudevin', 152
  salvifolius L. [Z8], 35, 151,
    152
    'Prostratus', 150–1

'Silver Pink', 151
  × *skanbergii* Lojac. [Z8],
    35, 151
  villosus L. see *C. creticus*
CITRONELLA Icacinaceae
  mucronata (Ruiz & Pav.) D.
    Don [Z9], 90
CITRUS Rutaceae, 171
  japonica Thunb. see
    Fortunella japonica
  'Meyer's Lemon', 171
CLEMATIS Ranunculaceae
  armandii Franch. [Z8], 132
    'Apple Blossom', 132
    'Snowdrift', 132
  australis T. Kirk., 133
  brachiata Thunb., 133
  cirrhosa L. [Z8], 133
  florida Thunb.
    'Sieboldii', 138
  fosteri J.F.Gmel, 133
  indivisa Willd. see *C.
    paniculata*
  montana DC [Z5–6], 133
  napaulensis DC [Z8], 133
  paniculata Gmel. [Z8], 133
  phlebantha L.H.L.Williams,
    17, 133
  uncinata Benth. [Z6], 17
CLETHRA Clethraceae
  arborea Ait. [Z8], 15, 209
  delavayi Franch. [Z7–8], 17,
    119
CLEYERA Theaceae, 17
  fortunei Hook. f. [Z8], 209
  japonica Thunb. [Z8], 17,
    208–9
  ochnacea DC see *C. japonica*
CLIANTHUS Leguminosae
  puniceus Banks & Soland.
    [Z8], 12
COLEONEMA Rutaceae
  album (Thunb.) Barth &
    Wendle. [Z9], 138
  pulchrum Hook. [Z9], 138
COLLETIA Rhamnaceae
  armata Miers [Z8], 118
    'Rosea', 118
  cruciata Gil. & Hook. see *C.
    paradoxa*
  infausta N.E.Br. [Z8], 118
  paradoxa (Spreng.)
    Escalente [Z8], 118
  spinosa Lam., 118

COLQUHOUNIA Labiatae
  coccinea Wall. [Z8], 17, 108
    mollis Prain see *C. c.
      vestita*
    vestita (Wall.) Prain, 108
COMAROSTAPHYLIS
  Ericaceae
  diversifolia (Parry) Greene
    [Z7], 177
CONVOLVULUS
  Convolvulaceae
  althaeoides L., 70, 138
  cneorum L. [Z8], 73, 151
  elegantissimus Miller, 70, 73,
    138
  mauritanicus Boiss. see *C.
    sabatius*
  sabatius Viviani, 70, 73, 151
  tenuissimus Sm. see *C.
    elegantissimus*
COPROSMA Rubiaceae
  acerosa A. Cunn. [Z8], 123
  baueri Endl., 34
    'Beatson's Gold' [Z8–9], 55
  brunnea (Kirk.) Cheesem.
    [Z8], 123
  × *cunninghamii* Hook.f.
    [Z8], 124
  kirkii Cheesem., 123
    'Variegata', 123
  lucida J.R.&G.Forst. [Z8],
    34
  petriei Cheesem. [Z7], 123
  propinqua A. Cunn. [Z8],
    124
  repens A.Rich, 34, 87, 123
    'Coppershine', 87
    'Picturata', 57
    'Pink Splendour', 57
    'Silver Queen', 57
    'Variegata', 57
  rhamnoides A. Cunn., 123–4
  robusta Raoul, 124
    'Williamsii Variegata',
      57
  rotundifolia A. Cunn., 123
  rugosa Cheesem., 123
CORDYLINE Agavaceae,
    226, 230
  australis Hook.f. [Z8], 33,
    227
    'Atropurpurea', 87
    'Purpurea', 87
    'Torbay Red', 87

banksii Hook.f. [Z9], 227
indivisa (Forst.f.) Steud. [Z9], 227
CORNUS Cornaceae
capitata Wall. [Z8], 16, 178
chinensis Wanger [Z8–9], 16, 179
mas L. [Z5], 179
COROKIA Cornaceae, 29
buddleioides A. Cunn. [Z8], 29
cotoneaster Raoul [Z8], 124
macrocarpa T. Kirk. [Z8], 29
× *virgata* Turnill [Z8], 29
'Bronze King', 29, 87
'Bronze Knight', 87
'Bronze Lady', 87
'Red Wonder', 29
'Yellow Wonder', 29
CORONILLA Leguminosae
glauca L. [Z9], 62, 163
'Citrina', 62
'Variegata', 62
valentina L. [Z9], 163
CORREA Rutaceae, 202
alba Andrews [Z8], 145
backhousiana Hook. [Z8], 146
calycina, 146
decumbens F.v.Muell. [Z8], 146
'Dusky Bells', 146
'Harrisii' [Z8], 146
lawrenciana Hook. [Z8], 146
magnifica hort., 146
'Mannii', 146
pulchella Sweet see *C. reflexa*
reflexa (Labill.) Venten [Z8], 146
virens Hook., 146
schlechtendalii Behr., 146
speciosa J.Don. ex Andr. see *C. reflexa*
ventricosa Nichols, 146
Corsican pine, 32
CORYNOCARPUS Corynocarpaceae
laevigatum J.R.&G.Forst. [Z10], 186
COSMOS Compositae
atrosanguineus (Hook.) Stapf., 69

COTINUS Anacardiaceae
coggygria Scop. 'Royal Purple' [Z5], 86
COTONEASTER Rosaceae
glaucophyllus Franch. [Z6–7], 31
lacteus W.W.Sm. [Z7], 31
pannosus Franch. [Z6], 31
Crape myrtle, 170
CRINODENDRON Elaeocarpaceae, 10, 119
hookerianum Gay [Z8], 33, 94
patagua Mol. [Z7], 94
CRINUM Amaryllidaceae
bulbispermum (Burman f.) Milne-Redhead & Schweickerdt, 77
capense Herb. see *C. bulbispermum*
longifolium Thunb. see *C. bulbispermum*
moorei Hook.f., 76, 77
× *powellii* Baker, 76, 77
'Album', 77
'Ellen Bosanquet', 77
'Haarlemense', 77
'Krelagei', 77
CROCOSMIA Iridaceae, 14, 84
aurea (Pappe ex Hook.) Planch., 83, 233
hybrid cultivars:
'Canary Bird', 59
'Carmin Brillant', 83
'Citronella', 59, 84
'Emily Mckenzie', 83
'His Majesty', 83
'Jackanapes', 83
'James Coey', 83
'Lady Hamilton', 59
'Queen of Spain', 83
'Solfatare', 59
'Star of the East', 83
CROWEA Rutaceae
exalata F.v.Muell., 124–5
CUNNINGHAMIA Taxodiaceae, 230
CUPRESSUS Cupressaceae
cashmeriana Royle ex Carr. [Z9], 17, 189
duclouxiana Hickel. [Z8–9], 189

guadalupensis S. Wats [Z9], 189
lusitanica Mill. [Z9], 18, 189
'Glauca', 189
'Glauca Pendula', 189
macrocarpa Hartweg [Z8–9], 18, 32
'Donard Gold', 32
'Goldcrest', 32
'Lutea', 32
sempervirens L. [Z8]
'Stricta', 161
CURTONUS Iridaceae, 83
CYATHEA Cyatheaceae
australis (R.Br.) Domin. [Z8], 229
cooperi (F.J.Muell) Domin. [Z10], 229
dealbata (G.Forst.) Swartz [Z8], 229
medullaris G.Forst. [Z10], 229
CYATHODES Epacridaceae
colensoi Hook.f. [Z8], 125
juniperina (J.R.&G.Forst.) Dunce [Z8], 125
robusta Hook.f. [Z8], 125
Cycads, 223, 228
CYCAS Cycadaceae
revoluta Thunb. [Z8], 228
Cypress, 160
Leyland, 32
Kashmir, 189
Monterey, 18
Tecate, 189
CYRTANTHUS Amaryllidaceae
purpureus (Ait.) Herb. ex Traub, 142
CYRTOMIUM Dryopteridaceae
falcatum (L.f.) C.Presl., 18, 219
'Rochfordianum', 219
fortunei J.Smith, 219
CYTISUS Leguminosae, 15, 125
battandieri Maire [Z7–8], 15, 108
canariensis (L.) O. Kuntze, 162
× *kewensis* Bean, 153
maderensis Masf. var.

CYTISUS Leguminosae –
    cont
  magnifoliosus Briq. [Z9],
    162
  'Porlock', 163
  × *praecox* Wheeler [Z7],
    40, 153
  'Allgold', 40
  proliferus L.f. [Z9], 163
  racemosus Nichols, 162
  × *spachianus* Webb [Z9],
    162
  stenopetalus (Webb.)
    Christ. [Z9], 162

DACRYDIUM
  Podocarpaceae, 12, 190,
    191
  biforme (Hook.) Pilger
    [Z9], 190
  colensoi Hook. [Z9], 190
  cupressinum Sol. ex Lamb.
    [Z9], 190–1
  franklinii Hook.f. [Z9], 190
  intermedium Kirk. [Z9], 190
DAHLIA Compositae, 18
  coccinea Cav.
    'Bishop of Llandaff', 85
  merckii Lehm., 71
DAPHNE Thymelaeaceae,
  125
  bholua Buch-Ham [Z8],
    116
  odora Thunb. [Z8], 116
DAPHNIPHYLLUM
  Daphniphyllaceae, 209
  macropodum Miq. [Z7],
    90
DARWINIA Myrtaceae
  macrostegia Benth., 236
DATURA Solanaceae
  arborea L. [Z9], 142
  chlorantha Hook., 142
  cornigera Hook. [Z9], 142
    'Knightii', 142–3
  inioxia Mill., 142
  meteloides (DC) Dunal see
    D. inioxia
  sanguinea Ruiz & Pav. [Z9],
    142
  stramonium L., 143
  suaveolens Humb. & Bonpl.
    ex Willd. [Z9], 142
  'Flore Pleno', 142

versicolor Lagerh. [Z10], 142
  'Grand Marnier', 142
DECUMARIA
  Hydrangeaceae
  barbara L. [Z7], 220–1
  sinensis Oliv. [Z8], 220–1
DENDROMECON
  Papaveraceae, 18
  harfordii Kell. [Z9], 175
  rigida Benth. [Z8], 175
DESFONTAINEA
  Loganiaceae
  spinosa Ruiz & Pav. [Z8],
    10, 184, 211, 220
  'Harold Comber', 211
DESMODIUM
  Leguminosae
  praestans Forr. [Z9], 136
DIANELLA Phormiaceae, 13
  caerulea Sims, 218
  intermedia Endl., 218
    'Variegata', 218
  revoluta R.Br., 218
  tasmanica Hook.f., 218
DIASCIA Scrophulariaceae,
  14, 75
  barberae Hook. f., 67
  elegans see *D. vigilis*
  felthamii see *D. fetcaniensis*
  fetcaniensis Hilliard & Burtt,
    67
  flanaganii Hiern see *D.
    stachyoides*
  rigescens E. Meyer ex
    Benth., 67
  stachyoides Schleicht. ex
    Hiern, 67
  vigilis Hilliard & Burtt, 67,
    69
DICENTRA Fumariaceae
  chrysantha (Hook. & Arn.)
    Walp., 140
DICHELOSTEMMA
  Alliaceae
  volubile (Kellogg) A.
    Heller, 140–1
DICHROA Hydrangeaceae
  febrifuga Lour., 119
DICKSONIA Cyatheaceae
  antarctica Labill. [Z8], 184,
    228, 229
  fibrosa Colenso [Z10], 229
  squarrosa (G.Forst.) Swartz
    [Z10], 228

DIERAMA Iridaceae
  pendulum (L.f.) Baker
    pumilum, Baker, 72
  pulcherrimum (Hook.f.)
    Baker, 72
  'Blackbird', 72
  'Plover', 72
  'Windhover', 72
DIETES Iridaceae
  iridioides (L.) Sweet, 63
  robinsoniana (F.v.Muell.)
    Klatt., 63
DIGITALIS
  Scrophulariaceae
  obscura L., 59
DIOSMA pulchella hort. see
  Barosma pulchella
  uniflora L. see *Adenandra
    uniflora*
DIOSTEA Verbenaceae
  juncea (Gillies & Hook.)
    Miers, 11
DIPLADENIA splendens
  (Hook.f.) A.DC see
  Mandevilla splendens
DISELMA Cupressaceae,
  13
DODONAEA Sapindaceae
  viscosa (L.) Jacq. [Z9]
  purpurea, 86
Dogwood, 16
DORYCNIUM
  Leguminosae
  hirsutum Ser. [Z8], 70, 106,
    151
Douglas fir, 33
DOXANTHA Bignoniaceae
  capreolata Miers, 135
DRACAENA Agavaceae,
  230
DRIMYS Winteraceae, 11
  lanceolata (Poir.) Baill. [Z8],
    93
  winteri J.R.&G.Forst.
    [Z8], 92–3, 94, 184
  andina Reiche, 92
  latifolia Miers, 92
DRYANDRA Proteaceae
  floribunda R.Br. [Z9],
    236
  formosa R.Br. [Z9], 236
DUDLEYA Crassulaceae
  farinosa (Lindl.) Britt. &
    Rose [Z10], 155

ECCREMOCARPUS
Bignoniaceae
scaber Ruiz & Pav. [Z8], 11,
135–6
aureus, 136
carmineus, 136
ECHEVERIA Crassulaceae,
18
secunda W.B.Booth var.
glauca (Bak.) Otto
[Z10], 155
ECHIUM Boraginaceae, 15
candicans L.f., 169
fastuosum Jacq., 169
nervosum Ait., 169
pininiana Webb & Berth.,
169
× *scilloniensis*, 169
'Tresco Blue', 169
wildpretii H.H.W.Pearson
ex Hook.f., 169
EDGEWORTHIA
Thymelaeaceae
chrysantha Lindl. [Z8], 116
rubra, 116
ELAEAGNUS Elaeagnaceae
angustifolia Kuntze [Z2–3],
30
× *ebbingei* Boom. [Z6],
30
glabra Thunb. [Z8], 30
macrophylla Thunb. [Z8],
. 30
pungens Thunb. [Z7], 30
'Maculata', 30
× *reflexa* Morr. & Dcne
[Z7], 30
umbellata Thunb. [Z3], 30
ELAEOCARPUS
Elaeocarpaceae
cyaneus Sims [Z9], 212
dentatus (J.R.&G.Forst.)
Vahl. [Z9], 212
ELYTROPUS Apocynaceae
chilensis Muell. [Z9], 131
EMBOTHRIUM
Proteaceae, 10, 112
coccineum Forst. [Z8], 96
'Eliot Hodgkin', 96
lanceolatum O. Kuntze
[Z8], 96–7
'Norquinco Valley',
96
Longifolium Group, 96

EMMENOPTERYS
Rubiaceae
henryi Oliv. [Z8], 183
ENKIANTHUS Ericaceae
quinqueflorus Lour. [Z8],
210
ENSETE Musaceae
ventricosum (Welv.)
Cheesem. [Z10], 226
ENTELEA Tiliaceae
arborescens R.Br. [Z9–10],
230
EPACRIS Epacridaceae, 125
'Diadem', 139
longiflora Cav. [Z9–10], 139
impressa Labill. [Z9], 139
'Mont Blanc', 139
purpurascens R.Br. [Z9–
10], 139
EPILOBIUM Onagraceae
canum (Greene) P.H.Raven
[Z8], 18, 78
'Dublin', 78, 79
'Solidarity Pink', 66
ERCILLA Phytolaccaceae
volubilis A. Juss. [Z9], 131
EREMURUS
Asphodelaceae, 61, 63
ERICA Ericaceae
arborea L. [Z9], 166
australis L. [Z9], 166
'Mr Robert', 166
canaliculata Andr. [Z10],
14, 139, 166
cinerea L. [Z6], 230
erigena R.Ross [Z9], 166
lusitanica Rudolf [Z9], 166
mediterranea hort. see *E.
erigena*
pageana Bolus [Z10], 14,
139
scoparia L. [Z9], 166
umbellata L. [Z9], 166
× *veitchii* Bean [Z9]
'Exeter', 166
ERIGERON Compositae
glaucus Ker-Gawl., 42
ERIOBOTRYA Rosaceae
japonica Lindl. [Z9], 6, 89
ERIOSTEMON Rutaceae
buxifolius Sm., 124
crowei F.v.Muell. see
Crowea exalata
lanceolatus Gaertn., 124

neriifolius Sieb., 124
ERYSIMUM Cruciferae
'Bowles' Mauve', 70, 156
capitatum (Douglas)
Greene, 156
linifolium (Pers.) Gay, 156
'Variegatum', 68
ERYTHRINA Leguminosae
crista-galli L. [Z9], 84
ESCALLONIA
Escalloniaceae, 43, 47,
212
bifida Link & Otto [Z9],
117
'C. F. Ball', 26
× *exoniensis* Veitch, 26
'Ingramii', 26
montevidensis DC see *E.
bifida*
'Newryensis', 26
punctata DC see *E. rubra*
revoluta Pers. [Z9], 26
rubra (Ruiz & Pav.) Pers.
[Z9], 26
macrantha (Hook. &
Arn.) Reiche [Z9], 11,
25, 26, 34
'Crimson Spire', 26
'Red Hedger', 26
EUCALYPTUS Myrtaceae,
13, 20, 48, 93
calophylla R.Br. ex Lindl.
'Rosea', 167
citriodora Hook. [Z9], 168
coccifera Hook.f. [Z9], 48,
167
cordata Labill., 168
dalrympleana Maiden, 167
ficifolia F.v.Muell. [Z9], 167
glaucescens, 167
globulus Labill. [Z9], 168,
226
gunnii Hook.f. [Z9], 167
leucoxylon F.v.Muell.,
'Rosea', 167
nichollii Maiden & Blakely
[Z8], 168
niphophila Maiden &
Blakely [Z7], 167
perriniana Rodway, 167,
226
pulverulenta Sims, 167, 226
urnigera Hook.f. [Z9], 167
viminalis Labill. [Z8], 167

EUCOMIS Hyacinthaceae
  comosa (Houttuyn) hort. ex
    Wehrhahn, 68
  pallidiflora Baker, 225
  punctata L'Hérit. see *E.
    comosa*
EUCRYPHIA
  Eucryphiaceae, 11
  cordifolia Cav. [Z9], 93, 94,
    184
  cordifolia × lucida [Z9], 94
  glutinosa Baill. [Z9], 93
  × *hillieri* Ivens [Z9], 93–4
    'Penwith', 94
    'Winton', 94
  × *intermedia* Bausch. [Z9]
    'Rostrevor', 94
  lucida (Labill.) Baill. [Z9],
    93, 94
    'Pink Cloud', 93
  milliganii Hook.f. [Z9], 93
  moorei F. v. Muell. [Z9],
    93, 94
  × *nymansensis* Bausch.
    [Z9], 93
    'Mount Usher', 93
    'Nymansay', 93
EUGENIA Myrtaceae
  myrtifolia Sims see *E.
    paniculata*
  paniculata Banks ex Gaertn.
    [Z10], 212
  pungens Berg. [Z10], 212
  smithii Poir. [Z10], 212
EUONYMUS Celastraceae,
    91
  frigidus Wall. [Z9], 91
  japonicus Thunb. [Z8], 25,
    26, 34, 54
    'Aureopictus' see
      'Aureus'
    'Aureovariegatus' see
      'Ovatus Aureus'
    'Aureus', 55
    'Duc d'Anjou', 55
    'Latifolius
      Albomarginatus',
      55
    'Macrophyllus Albus'
      see Latifolius
      Albomarginatus'
    'Ovatus Aureus', 55
  lucidus D.Don. [Z9], 17, 91
  wilsonii Sprague [Z9], 91

EUPATORIUM
  Compositae
  ligustrinum DC [Z10], 18,
    107
  micranthum Lessing see *E.
    ligustrinum*
  weinmannianum Regel &
    Koern see *E. ligustrinum*
EUPHORBIA
  Euphorbiaceae
  characias L. [Z10], 101
    wulfenii (Hoope ex
      Koch) A Radcliffe
      Smith [Z9], 101
    sibthorpii, 101
    'Lambrook Gold', 101
  dendroides L. [Z10], 156
  mellifera Ait. [Z10], 101
  rigida Bieb., 155
EURYA Theaceae, 17, 208
  ochnacea (DC) Szysz. see
    Cleyera japonica
EURYOPS Compositae
  abrotanifolius (L.) DC, 171
  chrysanthemoides, 171
  pectinatus (L.) Cass., 171

FABIANA Solanaceae
  imbricata Ruiz & Pav. [Z9],
    11
FARFUGIUM Compositae
  japonicum Kitamura, 17
    'Argentea', 218–19
    'Aureo Maculata', 219
FASCICULARIA
  Bromeliaceae, 11
  bicolor (Ruiz & Pav.) Mez,
    158
  pitcairniifolia (Verlot) Mez,
    158
FATSIA Araliaceae
  japonica Dcne & Planch.
    [Z7], 224
    'Variegata', 224
FEIJOA see *ACCA*
FELICIA Compositae, 14, 83
  amelloides (L.) Voss, 63, 115
    'Santa Anita', 63
    'Variegata', 63
  amoena (Schulz-Bip)
    Levyns, 63, 82
  pappei (Harv.) Hutch. see
    F. amoena
FENDLERA Philadelphaceae

  rupicola Gray var. *wrightii*
    Gray [Z7], 175
Fern, holly, 219
  tree, 12
FERRARIA Iridaceae, 14
FICUS Moraceae
  pumila L. [Z9], 131
    'Minima', 131
FIRMIANA Sterculiaceae
  platanifolia (L.f.) Schott &
    Endl. [Z9], 230
  simplex (L.) Wright see *F.
    platanifolia*
FITZROYA Cupressaceae
  cupressoides Johnston [Z8–
    9], 211
  patagonica Hook.f. see *F.
    cupressoides*
FORTUNELLA Rutaceae
  japonica Swingle [Z10], 236
Foxglove, 15
Frangipani, 237
FREESIA Iridaceae, 14
  alba (G.L.Meyer)
    Gumbleton, 166
  lactea Klatt., 166
  refracta (Jacq.) Ecklon ex
    Klatt see *F. alba*
FREMONTODENDRON
  Sterculiaceae
  californicum (Torr.) Kov.
    [Z9], 174–5
    'California Glory' [Z9],
    175
  mexicanum Davidson [Z10],
    174–5
FREYLINIA
  Scrophulariaceae
  cestroides Colla see *F.
    lanceolata*
  lanceolata G.Don, 14, 116
FUCHSIA Onagraceae, 11,
    77, 78
  arborescens Sims, 143
  boliviana Carr, 142
  cordifolia Benth. see *F.
    splendens* 'Karl Hartweg'
  colensoi Hook., 213
  excorticata L.f. [Z9], 12, 213
  fulgens Moç & Sesse ex DC,
    82
    'Genii', 84
  magellanica Lam., 11, 30
    gracilis Bailey, 31

paniculata Lindl., 143
'Riccartonii', 31
splendens Zucc., 82, 202
'Karl Hartweg', 82
triphylla L., 18, 82, 137
Triphylla hybrids:
'Billy Green', 82
'Fanfare', 82
'Gartenmeister
Bonstedt', 86
'Koralle', 82
'Mary', 86
'Thalia', 86
FURCRAEA Agavaceae, 157
bedinghausii C.Koch, 156
longaeva Karw. & Zucc.,
156

GALTONIA Liliaceae
candicans Decne, 79
viridiflora, 79
GARRYA Garryaceae
elliptica Lindl. [Z9], 33,
232
fremontii Torr. [Z9], 232
× *thuretii* Carr. [Z9], 33
GAULTHERIA Ericaceae,
213
antipoda Forst. f. [Z9], 215
codonantha Airy Shaw [Z9],
214–15
fragrantissima Wall. [Z9],
215
hispida R.Br. [Z9], 215
nummularioides D.Don.
[Z9], 214
oppositifolia Hook.f. [Z9],
215
semi-infera Airy-Shaw, 214
tetramera W.W.Sm. [Z9],
214
wardii Marquand & Shaw
[Z8], 215
GAZANIA Compositae, 14,
83, 171
× *hybrida* hort.
'Cream Beauty', 60
'Silver Beauty', 83
GELSEMIUM Loganiaceae
sempervirens Ait.f. [Z7–9],
131
GENETILIS tulipifera Schau
ex Hook. see *Darwinia
macrostegia*

GENISTA Leguminosae, 15,
125
aetnensis DC [Z9], 163
cinerea DC [Z9], 163
ephedroides DC [Z9], 163
falcata Brot. [Z9], 163
fragrans hort., 162
monosperma (L.) Lam. [Z9],
163
tenera O. Kuntze [Z9], 163
virgata Link see *G. tenera*
GERANIUM Geraniaceae,
226
anemonifolium L'Herit. see
G. palmatum
canariense Reuter, 67
maderense Yeo, 67
palmatum Cav., 15, 67
traversii Hook.f.
elegans Cockayne, 70
GERBERA Compositae, 14
jamesonii Hook., 171
GEVUINA Proteaceae, 10
avellana Mol. [Z9], 10, 210,
211
GLADIOLUS Iridaceae, 14,
233
callianthus Marais, 69
cardinalis Curt., 68
carinatus Ait., 138
carmineus C.H.Wright, 68
'Christabel', 140
citrinus Klatt, 140
× *colvillei* Sweet, 68
'Nanus' hybrids, 68, 140
'Blushing Bride', 68
'Nymph', 68
'The Bride', 68
natalensis (Ecklon)
Reinwardt ex Hook., 65
primulinus Bak. see *G.
natalensis*
tristis L., 68, 140
concolor (Salisb.) Baker, 140
undulatus L., 138
GLAUCIUM Papaveraceae
flavum Crantz, 159
grandiflorum Boiss. & Huet,
159
phoenicium Crantz, 159
Gloriosa lily, 140
GORDONIA Theaceae
axillaris (Roxb.) D.Dietr.
[Z9], 209

chrysandra Cowan [Z9], 209
lasianthos Ellis [Z9], 209
GREVILLEA Proteaceae, 13,
112
alpina Lindl. [Z9], 112
asplenifolia Knight &
Salisb., 112
'Robin Hood', 112
juniperina R.Br. [Z9]
sulphurea (A.Cunn.)
Benth. [Z9], 112
lanigera A.Cunn., 112
robusta A. Cunn. ex R.Br.
[Z9], 19, 112
'Robyn Gordon', 112
rosmarinifolia A. Cunn.
[Z9], 112
'Canberra Gem', 112
'Jenkinsii', 112
× *semperflorens* F.E.Briggs
ex Mulligan [Z9], 60,
112
thelemanniana Huegel
[Z10], 112
GRINDELIA Compositae
chiloensis (Cornelisson)
Cabrera [Z9], 11, 84
GRISELINIA Cornaceae
littoralis Raoul [Z9], 24, 26,
32, 34, 44, 89
'Bantry Bay', 54
'Brodick', 54
'Dixon's Cream', 54
'Variegata', 54
lucida Forst.f. [Z7], 89

HAKEA Proteaceae
epiglottis Labill., 168
gibbosa Cav., 168
laurina R.Br. [Z10], 168
lissosperma R.Br. [Z10],
168
microcarpa R.Br. [Z9], 168
saligna Knight, 168
sericea Schrad. & J.Wendl.
[Z10], 168
suaveolens R.Br. [Z10], 169
× *HALIMIOCISTUS*
Cistaceae
'Ingwersenii' [Z9], 153
revolii (Coste & Soulié)
Dansereau [Z9], 153
sahucii Janchen [Z9], 153

× *HALIMIOCISTUS*
 Cistaceae – *cont*
 wintonensis O. & E. F.
  Warb., 145
  'Merrist Wood Cream',
  145
HALIMIUM Cistaceae
 atriplicifolium Spach [Z9],
  164
 halimifolium (L.) Willk. &
  Lange [Z9], 153
 lasianthum Spach [Z9], 153
  formosum Willk., 153
  concolor, 153
 libanotis Willk. & Lange,
  153
 ocymoides (Lam.) Willk. &
  Lange [Z9], 153
 umbellatum (L.) Spach [Z9]
HAMAMELIS
 Hamamelidaceae, 211
HAMILTONIA pilosa
 Roxb. see *Leptodermis*
 pilosa
HARDENBERGIA
 Leguminosae
 comptoniana Benth. [Z10],
  144
  'Rosea', 144
 violacea (Scheev.)
  F.C.Stern [Z10], 144
 Hawthorn, 18
HEBE Scrophulariaceae, 13,
  24, 33, 47
 albicans Ckn [Z8], 38
 × *andersonii* Ckn [Z10]
  'Variegata', 39
  'Ann Pimm' [Z10], 39
 armstrongii Ckn. & Allen
  [Z7], 38
 brachysiphon Summerhayes
  [Z7]
  'White Gem', 38
  'Carnosula' [Z7], 38
  'Clarkii' [Z7], 38
 colensoi (Hook.f.) Wall.
  'Glauca' [Z7], 38
 cupressoides Ckn. & Allen
  [Z7], 38
 dieffenbachii Ckn. & Allen
  [Z9], 27
 × *franciscana* Souster [Z9–
  10]
  'Blue Gem', 27, 34

 'Variegata', 39
 hulkeana (F.v.Muell.) Ckn
  & Allen [Z9], 107, 155
  'Fairfieldii', 107
  'Hagley Park', 107
 lavaudiana Ckn & Allen
  [Z10], 107
 ochracea M B Ashwin [Z7],
  38
  'James Stirling', 38
 'Pagei' [Z7], 38
 'Pewter Dome' [Z7], 38
 rakaiensis Ckn. [Z7], 38,
  152
 raoulii Ckn. & Allen, 107
 recurva Simp. & Thom.
  [Z8], 38
 salicifolia Pennell [Z7], 27,
  39
 speciosa R.Cunn. [Z10], 39,
  77, 107
 'Tricolor' see 'Purple
  Tips'
 'Speciosa Hybrids' (all
  [Z10]), 13, 38, 40
  'Alicia Amherst', 39
  'Gauntlettii', 39
  'Gloriosa', 39
  'La Séduisante', 39
  'Pink Pearl' see
   'Gloriosa'
  'Purple Queen', 39
  'Purple Tips', 39
  'Royal Purple' see
   'Alicia Amherst'
  'Simon Delaux', 39
  'Veitchii' see 'Alicia
   Amherst'
 subalpina (Ckn.) Ckn. &
  Allen see *H. rakaiensis*
 topiaria L.B.Moore [Z8], 38
 whipcord, 38
 hybrid cultivars:
  'Amy' [Z10], 39
  'Autumn Glory' [Z9], 39
  'Blush Wand' [Z9–10],
   39
  'Carnea' [Z9–10], 39
  'Carnea Variegata'
   [Z10], 39
  'Great Orme' [Z9], 39
  'Midsummer Beauty'
   [Z8–9], 39, 40
  'Mrs Winder' [Z9], 38, 87

  'Pink Wand' [Z9–10], 39
  'Violet Wand' [Z9–10],
   39
  'Waikiki' [Z9], 38, 87
  'White Wand' [Z9–10],
   39
HÉDYCHIUM
 Zingiberaceae, 16, 78
 coccineum Buch.-Ham.
  'Tara', 79
 densiflorum Wall.
  'Assam Orange', 79
  L S & H 17393, 79
  'Stephen', 79
 flavescens W.Carey, 233
 flaviflorum see *H. flavescens*
 gardnerianum Sheppard ex
  Ker-Gawl., 61, 233
  pallidum (Regel) Baker,
  61
 greenei W.W.Sm., 59, 79,
  85
 spicatum Smith ex Buch.-
  Ham., 61
HEERIA elegans Schlecht. see
 Heterocentron elegans
HELICHRYSUM
 Compositae
 antennaria (DC) F.v.Muell.
  ex Benth. [Z9], 122
 ericeteum W.M.Curtis see
  H. ledifolium ssp.
  ericeteum
 ledifolium (DC) Benth.
  [Z9], 122–3
  ericeteum W.M.Curtis,
  123
 microphyllum Cambess. see
  Plecostachys serpyllifolia
 petiolare Hilliard & Burtt,
  14, 21, 51, 59, 66, 74,
  81, 122
  'Limelight', 52, 79, 84
 populifolium DC, 66
 purpurascens (DC)
  W.M.Curtis [Z9],
  123
 rosmarinifolium (Labill.)
  Steud. ex Benth. [Z9],
  123
  'Silver Jubilee', 123
  'Sussex Silver', 123
 thyrsoideum (DC) Willis &
  Morris [Z9], 123

HELIOTROPIUM
Boraginaceae
arborescens L.
'Chatsworth', 74
'Lord Roberts', 74
'Princess Marina', 74
HELLEBORUS
Ranunculaceae
argutifolius Viviani, 219
lividus Ait., 219
HESPERALOE Agavaceae
parviflora (Torr.) J. Coult.,
158
HETEROCENTRON
Melastomataceae
elegans (Schlecht.) O.
Kuntze [Z10], 126, 219
HIBBERTIA Dilleniaceae
cuneiformis (Labill.) Sm.,
145
dentata R.Br. [Z9], 145
scandens (Willd.) Dryand.
ex Hoogl. [Z9], 145
volubilis Andr. see *H.*
scandens
HIBISCUS Malvaceae
hamabo Sieb. & Zucc.
[Z10], 141
syriacus L., 141
trionum L., 80
HIPPEASTRUM
Amaryllidaceae, 84
aulicum (Ker-Gawl.) Herb,
84
'Acramanii', 84
HIPPOPHAE Elaeagnaceae
rhamnoides L. [Z3], 25
HOHERIA Malvaceae, 12
angustifolia Raoul [Z9], 117
glabrata Sprague &
Summerh. [Z9], 116–17
'Glory of Amlwch', 117
lyallii Hook.f. [Z9], 117
populnea A. Cunn. [Z9],
117
'Albovariegata', 117
'Foliis Purpureis', 117
'Osbornei', 117
'Variegata', 117
sexstylosa Col. [Z9], 117
HOLBOELLIA
Lardizabalaceae
coriacea Diels. [Z9], 131
latifolia Wall. [Z9], 131

Holly, 17, 33, 210, 211
New Zealand, 27
Holly fern, 18, 228
Holm oak, 33, 185
HOMERIA Iridaceae, 14
breyniana (L.) G. Lewis see
H. collina
collina (Thunb.) Venten., 61
aurantiaca (Zuccagni) G.
Lewis, 61
ochroleuca (Salisb.) G.
Lewis, 61
Homoglads, 233
'General Smuts', 233
HOMOGLOSSUM
Iridaceae
watsonianum (Thunb.)
N.E.Br., 233
Honeysuckle, 132
Horned poppy, 159
Hottentot fig, 5, 42
HUNNEMANNIA
Papaveraceae
fumariifolia Sweet, 159
Hyacinth, Roman, 166
HYDRANGEA
Hydrangeaceae, 38, 48,
119
aspera D. Don [Z7], 95
macrophylla (Thunb.) Ser.
[Z8], 31
'Joseph Banks', 41
Hortensias
('Mopheads'), 113–14
'Ami Pasquier', 114
'Ayesha', 114
'Générale Vicomtesse
de Vibraye', 114
'Goliath', 114
'Hamburg', 114
'Heinrich Seidel', 114
'La Marne', 114
'Mme Mouillère', 114
'Maréchal Foch', 114
'Mousseline', 114
'Oriental', 114
'Preziosa', 114
'Westfalen', 114
petiolaris Sieb. & Zucc.
[Z5], 221
sargentiana Rehd. [Z7], 95,
224
seemanii Riley, 132
villosa Rehd. see *H. aspera*

HYMENANTHERA
Violaceae
angustifolia R.Br. [Z7], 126
crassifolia Hook.f. [Z7], 126
obovata T. Kirk [Z7], 126
HYMENOSPORUM
Pittosporaceae
flavum F.v.Muell. [Z9], 238
HYPERICUM Guttiferae,
114
calycinum L. [Z5–6], 109
chinense L. see *H.*
monogynum
grandiflorum Choisy [Z10],
109
hookerianum Wight & Arn.
[Z7–8], 109
'Rogersii', 109
leschenaultii Choisy [Z10],
109
monogynum L. [Z10], 109
'Rowallane' [Z9], 109

ILEX Aquifoliaceae
× *altaclarensis* Dallim. [Z8],
34
aquifolium L. [Z7], 34, 37
kingiana Cockerell [Z9], 90
latifolia Thunb. [Z7], 90
perado Ait. [Z9], 15
ILLICIUM Illiciaceae
anisatum L. [Z7–8], 91
floridanum Ellis [Z7–8], 91
henryi Diels. [Z8], 91
verum Hook.f., 91
IMPATIENS Balsaminaceae
tinctoria A. Rich, 68
INDIGOFERA
Leguminosae
pulchella Roxb., 106
IOCHROMA Solanaceae
coccineum Scheidw. [Z10],
236
cyaneum (Lindl.)
M.L.Green [Z10], 236
IPOMOEA Convolvulaceae
acuminata Roem. & Schult.,
171
learii Paxt. see *I. acuminata*
IRESINE Amaranthaceae
herbstii Hook., 85
IRIS Iridaceae
confusa Sealy, 218
Evansia, 16

IRIS Iridaceae – *cont*
Oncocyclus, 63
Regelia, 63
unguicularis Poiret, 166
wattii Baker, 218
ISOPLEXIS
Scrophulariaceae, 147
canariensis (L.) Lindl. ex
G.Don [Z10], 146
sceptrum Steud., 146
ITEA Iteaceae
ilicifolia Oliv. [Z9], 102–3
yunnanensis Franch. [Z9],
103
IXERBA Escalloniaceae
brexioides A. Cunn. [Z10],
239
IXIA Iridaceae, 14
viridiflora Lam., 166

JACARANDA Bignoniaceae
mimosaefolia D.Don, 238
JACOBINIA pauciflora
Benth. & Hook. see
Justicia rizzinii
JASMINUM Oleaceae, 132
angulare Vahl [Z9], 133
azoricum L. [Z9], 133
dispermum Wall. [Z8], 133
floridum Bge [Z9], 134
lineatum, see *J.*
simplicifolium ssp.
suavissimum
mesnyi Hance [Z8–9], 16,
134
nudiflorum Lindl., [Z6], 96,
134
polyanthum Franch. [Z9],
16, 133
primulinum Hemsl. see *J.*
mesnyi
sambac (L.) Ait. [Z10], 133
'Grand Duke', 133
simplicifolium G. Forst. ssp.
suavissimum (Lindl.)
P.S.Green, 133
suavissimum Lindl. see *J.*
simplicifolium ssp.
suavissimum
Jerusalem sage, 14, 152, 160
Jimson weed, 143
JOVELLANA
Scrophulariaceae

violacea (Cav.) G.Don [Z9],
11, 105
JUBAEA Palmeae
chilensis (Mol.) Baill. [Z8],
227
Judas tree, 15, 166
JUNIPERUS Cupressaceae
conferta Parl [Z6], 35, 36
horizontalis Moench [Z3–
9], 35
JUSTICIA Acanthaceae
rizzinii Wassh., 236

KADSURA Schisandraceae
japonica Dun. [Z9], 131
Kaffir lily, 77
KENNEDIA Leguminosae
coccinea Venten., 144
eximia Lindl., 144
macrophylla Meissn., 144
prostrata R.Br. ex Ait.f.
[Z10], 144
rubicunda (Scheev.) Venten.
[Z10], 144
nigricans Lindl. [Z10], 144
KNIGHTIA Proteaceae
excelsa R.Br., 210
KNIPHOFIA
Asphodelaceae, 14, 21,
78, 106, 131
caulescens Baker, 42
citrina Baker, 78
comosa Hochst., 63
galpinii hort. see *K.*
triangularis
ichopensis Bak. ex Schinz,
79
isoetifolia A. Rich, 233
leichtlinii Bak., 63
multiflora J.M.Wood &
Evans, 61, 63
rooperi (Moore) Lem., 84
rufa Baker, 81
thomsonii Baker
snowdenii (C.H.Wright)
Marais, 81
triangularis Kunth, 81
uvaria (L.) Hook., 42
hybrid cultivars:
'Ada', 80
'Atlanta', 42
'Apricot', 61, 80
'Bees' Lemon', 79
'Bees' Sunset', 80

'Bressingham Comet',
81
'Bressingham Flame', 81
'Bressingham Gleam', 81
'Bressingham Glow', 81
'Bressingham Torch', 81
'Brimstone', 79
Buckshaw Hybrids, 80
'Canary Bird', 78
'Chartreuse', 79
'Chrysantha', 78
'Comet,' 80
'Corallina', 86
'Dawn Sunkiss', 65
'Enchantress', 65
'Erecta', 86
'Gold Else', 78
'Goldfinch', 80
'Green Jade', 79
'Green Lemon', 78
'Green Magic', 66, 79
'Jenny Bloom,' 65
'John Benary', 86
'July Glow', 80
'Limelight', 79
'Little Elf', 81
'Little Maid', 60, 61
'Lord Roberts', 86
'Maid of Orléans', 60,
61, 79
'Mermaiden', 60, 79
'Modesta', 65
'Painted Lady', 80
'Pfitzeri', 86
'Primrose Beauty', 80
'Prince Igor', 79, 86
'Red Admiral', 84
'Redstart', 80
'Royal Standard', 83,
158
'Samuel's Sensation', 84
'Strawberries & Cream',
65
'Sunningdale Yellow',
78
'Timothy', 65
'Toffee Nosed', 61, 80
'Torchbearer', 61, 79
'Tubergeniana', 80
'Underway', 61, 80
'Vanilla', 80
'White Fairy', 61
'Wrexham Buttercup',
78

'Yellow Hammer', 78
'Zeal Primrose', 80
'Zululandii', 233–4

LAGERSTROEMIA
Lythraceae
indica L. [Z10], 170
LAMBERTIA Proteaceae
formosa Sm., 236
LAMPRANTHUS
Aizoaceae, 14
aurantiacus (DC)
Schwantes, 154
aureus (L.) N.E.Br., 154
blandus (Haw.) Schwantes,
154
coccineus (Haw.) N.E.Br.,
154
glaucus (L.) N.E.Br., 154
multiradiatus (Jacq.)
N.E.Br., 154
roseus (Willd.) Schwantes
see *L. multiradiatus*
spectabilis (Haw.) N.E.Br.,
154
'Tresco Apricot', 154
'Tresco Brilliant', 154
'Tresco Red', 154
zeyheri (Salm-Dyck)
N.E.Br., 154
LAPAGERIA Philesiaceae,
131, 216
rosea Ruiz & Pav. [Z9], 10,
221
albiflora, 221
'Flesh Pink', 221
'Nash Court', 221
'Penheale', 221
'White Cloud', 221
LARDIZABALA
Lardizabalaceae
biternata Ruiz & Pav. [Z9],
131
LATHYRUS Leguminosae
pubescens Nutt. ex Torr. &
Gray, 138
Laurel
bay, 186, 187
cherry, 33
Chilean, 186
Portugal, 33
LAURELIA
Atherospermataceae
serrata Bertero [Z9], 10, 186

LAURUS Lauraceae
azorica (Seub.) Franco
[Z10], 33, 186
nobilis L. [Z9], 33, 186
angustifolia (Nees)
Markgraf, 165
'Aurea', 165
Laurustinus, 15, 56, 95
LAVANDULA Labiatae,
150, 151, 160, 165
dentata L. [Z10], 165
lanata Boiss. [Z9], 165
stoechas L., 165
LAVATERA Malvaceae
arborea L. [Z9], 34
assurgentifolia Kell, 34
bicolor Rouy see *L. maritima*
maritima Gouan [Z9], 72,
73, 106
olbia hort. see *L. thuringiaca*
thuringiaca L., 40
'Barnsley', 40
'Bressingham Pink', 40
'Kew Rose', 40
'Peppermint', 40
'Rosea', 40
'Shorty', 40
Lemon verbena, 11, 145
Lentisk, 160, 168
LEONOTIS Labiatae
leonurus R.Br. [Z10], 82
'Harrismith White', 60,
82
LEPTODERMIS Rubiaceae
kumaonensis Parker [Z9],
119
oblonga Bunge, 120
pilosa Diels. [Z9], 119
purdomii Hutchins., 120
LEPTOSPERMUM
Myrtaceae, 9, 13
cunninghamii Schau. [Z9]
see *L. lanigerum*
ericoides A.Rich, 121
flavescens Sm., 121
obovatum Sweet, 121
grandiflorum Lodd. see *L.
rodwayanum*
laevigatum F.v.Muell., 121–
2
lanigerum (Ait.) Sm. [Z9],
121
'Cunninghamii', 121
'Silver Sheen', 121

liversidgei R.T.Baker &
H.G.Sm., 121
nitidum Hook.f., 121
'Macrocarpum', 121
rodwayanum Summerh. &
Comber., 121
scoparium J.R. & G.Forst.
[Z9], 46, 113, 120
'Blossom', 113
'Boscawenii', 121
'Burgundy Queen', 113
'Chapmanii', 113
'Cherry Brandy', 113
'Fascination', 113
'Gaiety Girl', 113
'Keatleyi', 121
incanum Ckn, 120
'Leonard Wilson', 113
'Martinii', 121
'Nanum', 113
'Nanum Huia', 113
'Nanum Kiwi', 113
'Nicholsii', 113
'Nicholsii
Grandiflorum', 113
'Pink Cascade', 121
'Pink Champagne', 113
'Red Damask', 113
'Ruby Glow', 113
'Snow Flurry', 113
'Winter Cheer', 113
sericeum Labill., 121
stellatum Cav. [Z9], 121
LEUCADENDRON
Proteaceae
argenteum R.Br. [Z10], 238
LEUCOPHYTA
Compositae
brownii Cass., 82, 160
LEYCESTERIA
Caprifoliaceae
crocothyrsos Airy-Shaw
[Z9], 16, 118
Leyland cypress, 32, 34
LHOTSKYA Myrtaceae
alpestris (Lindl.) Druce, 139
LIBERTIA Iridaceae
formosa R.Graham, 43
grandiflora (R.Br.) Sweet,
43
ixioides (Forst.f.) Spreng.,
43
peregrinans Ckn & Allen, 43
'Gold Leaf', 43

LIBONIA floribunda K.Koch
    see *Justicia rizzinii*
LIGULARIA tussilaginea
    (Burm.f.)
    Mak. see *Farfugium
    japonicum*
LIGUSTRUM Oleaceae
    confusum Dcne [Z9], 90
    lucidum Ait.f. [Z8–9], 186
    ovalifolium Hassk. [Z6], 34
        'Argenteum', 34
        'Aureum', 34
Lillipilly, 212
LINDERA Lauraceae
    megaphylla Hemsl. [Z9], 209
    rubronervia Gamble, 210
LINUM Linaceae
    arboreum L. [Z10], 164
LIPPIA citriodora HBK see
    Aloysia triphylla
LITHOCARPUS Fagaceae
    pachyphyllus (Kurz) Rehd.
    [Z10], 186
LITHODORA Boraginaceae
    rosmarinifolia (Ten.) Johnst.
    [Z9], 165
LITHOSPERMUM see
    LITHODORA
LOBELIA Campanulaceae, 18
    laxiflora HBK, 78, 84
    × *speciosa* Sweet
        'Bees' Flame', 85
        'Brightness', 85
        'Cherry Ripe', 85
        'Dark Crusader', 69, 85
        'Mrs Humbert', 75
        'Queen Victoria', 69, 74,
        85
        'Russian Princess', 75
        'Will Scarlet', 85
    tupa L., 60
Loblolly bay, 209
Lobster claw, 12
LOMATIA Proteaceae, 11,
    112
    dentata R.Br. [Z9], 99
    ferruginea (Cav.) R.Br.
    [Z9], 10, 99
    fraxinifolia F.v.Muell., 99
    hirsuta (Lam.) Diels. [Z9],
    99
    ilicifolia R.Br., 99
    myricoides (Gaertn.)
        Dorrien [Z9], 99

    silaefolia (Sm.) R.Br., 99
    tinctoria (Labill.) R.Br.
    [Z9], 99
LONICERA Caprifoliaceae
    giraldii Rehd., 133
    hildebrandiana Coll. &
    Hemsl. [Z9], 17, 133
    splendida Boiss. [Z9],
    133
LOPHOMYRTUS
    Myrtaceae
    bullata (Soland. ex
    A.Cunn.) Burret [Z9],
    12, 98
        'Gloriosa', 98
    obcordata (Raoul) Burret,
    98
        'Pinkalina', 98
    × *ralphii* (Hook.f.) Burret,
    98
        'Kathryn', 98
        'Lilliput', 98
        'Pixie', 98
        'Sundae', 98
        'Variegata', 98
        'Versicolor', 98
LOPHOSPERMUM
    Scrophulariaceae
    erubescens D. Don, 78
Loquat, 5, 89
LOROPETALUM
    Hamamelidaceae
    chinense (R.Br.) Oliv. [Z9],
    17, 211
LOTUS Leguminosae
    berthelotii Masf., 80
    maculatus Breitfeld, 81
LUCULIA Rubiaceae
    grandifolia Chose [Z9], 143
    gratissima Sweet [Z10], 143
    pinceana Hook. [Z9], 143
LUMA Myrtaceae
    apiculata (DC) Burret [Z9],
    5, 11, 33, 97, 187
        'Glanleam Gold', 55
        'Penwith', 55
    chequen (Mol.) A.Gray
    [Z9], 97
LUPINUS Leguminosae
    arboreus Sims. [Z8], 40
    albifrons Benth. [Z9], 176
    chamissonis Escs. [Z9], 176
LUZURIAGA Philesiaceae,
    10

    marginata Benth. & Hook.,
    217
    radicans Ruiz & Pav. [Z10],
    216–17
LYCIUM Solanaceae
    chinense Mill. [Z6], 25
LYONOTHAMNUS
    Rosaceae
    floribundus A. Gray
    asplenifolius (Greene)
        Brandegee [Z9], 100

MACHILUS ichangensis
    Rehd. & Wils. see *Persea
    ichangensis*
MACKAYA Acanthaceae
    bella Harv., 137
MACROPIPER Piperaceae
    excelsum (G.Forst.) Miq.,
    213
Madrona, 18, 187
MAGNOLIA Magnoliaceae,
    187
    ashei Weatherby [Z7], 180
        'Caerhays Belle', 183
    campbellii Hook.f. &
        Thoms. [Z9], 181, 182
        alba hort. [Z9], 182
        'Betty Jessel', 182
        'Charles Raffill', 182
        'Darjeeling', 182
        'Kew's Surprise', 182
        'Lanarth', 182
        mollicomata F.K.Ward
        [Z9], 181
        'Charles Coates', 181
    coco (Lour.) DC [Z9], 183
    dawsoniana Rehd. & Wils.
    [Z9], 182
        'Chyverton', 182
    delavayi Franch. [Z9], 16,
    179
    denudata Desrouss. [Z6], 17,
    182, 183
    globosa Hook.f. & Thoms.
    [Z9], 180–1
    grandiflora L. [Z6–7], 179
        'Exmouth', 179
        'Ferruginea', 179
        'Goliath', 179
    grandiflora × *virginiana*
        'Maryland', 180
    hypoleuca Sieb. & Zucc.
    [Z6], 180, 181

MAGNOLIA
    Magnoliaceae – *cont*
    macrophylla Michx. [Z6],
        180
        ashei Weatherby see *M.*
            ashei
    nitida W.W.Sm. [Z9], 180,
        183
    obovata Thunb. see *M.*
        hypoleuca
    officinalis Rehd. & Wils.
        [Z8], 180
    rostrata W.W.Sm. [Z9],
        180
    sargentiana Rehd. & Wils.
        [Z9], 182
        robusta Rehd. & Wils.
            [Z9], 182, 183
    sieboldii K. Koch [Z7–8],
        180, 181
    sinensis Stapf. [Z8–9], 180
    × *soulangiana* Soulange-
        Bodin [Z5], 179
    sprengeri Pampan [Z9], 182
        diva Stapf., 183
            'Burncoose', 183
            'Claret Cup', 183
            'Copeland Court',
                183
        elongata Stapf., 182–3
    × *thompsoniana* C de Vos,
        180
    tripetala L. [Z5], 180, 181
    × *veitchii* Bean [Z7], 182
        'Isca', 182
        'Peter Veitch', 182
        'Veitchii Rubra', 182
    virginiana L. [Z5], 180
    × *watsonii* Hook.f. see
        M. × *wiesneri*
    × *wiesneri* Carr. [Z6], 181
MAHONIA Berberidaceae,
    17, 18
    acanthifolia G.Don. [Z9], 94
    fremontii (Torr.) Fedde
        [Z9], 175–6
    haematocarpa (Woot.)
        Fedde [Z9], 175
    japonica DC [Z7], 17
    lomariifolia Takeda [Z9], 94
    napaulensis DC [Z9], 94
        'Maharajah', 94
    nevinii Fedde [Z9], 175
    siamensis Takeda [Z10], 95

swaseyi (Buchl.) Fedde
    [Z9], 175
trifoliata (Moric.) Fedde
    [Z9]
    glauca I.M.Johnston, 175
MALLOTUS Euphorbiaceae
    japonicus (Thunb.) Muell.-
        Arg. [Z9], 127
MALVASTRUM Malvaceae
    lateritium Nichols., 66, 80
Mandevilla Apocynaceae
    × *amabilis* 'Alice du Pont'
        [Z10], 144
    splendens (Hook.f.)
        Woodson, 144
    suaveolens Lindl. [Z9], 144
MANGLIETIA
    Magnoliaceae
    hookeri Cubitt & W.W.Sm.
        [Z9], 183
    insignis (Wall.) Bl. [Z9], 183
Manzanita, 160
Maple, 17
MARCETELLA Rosaceae
    moquiniana (Webb &
        Berth.) Svent., 236
MAURANDYA
    Scrophulariaceae
    barclaiana Lindl., 78
    erubescens (D.Don) A.Gray
        see *Lophospermum*
        erubescens
    scandens (D.Don) A.Gray
        see *Lophospermum*
        scandens
MAYTENUS Celastraceae
    boaria Mol. [Z8–9], 186
    magellanica (Lam.) Hook.f.
        [Z9], 186
MELALEUCA Myrtaceae,
    13, 109
    armillaris (Soland, ex
        Gaertn.) Sm., 111
    decussata R.BR. [Z9], 111
    elliptica Labill., 111
    ericifolia Sm. [Z9], 111
    gibbosa Labill., 111
    hypericifolia (Salisb.) Sm.
        [Z9], 112
    lateritea Otto & Diels., 111–
        12
    leucadendron L. [Z9], 111
    squamea Labill., 111
    squarrosa Sm., 111

stypheloides Sm. [Z9], 111
wilsonii F.v. Muell. [Z9],
    111
MELIA Meliaceae
    azedarach L. [Z9], 224
MELIANTHUS
    Melianthaceae
    major L. [Z10], 14, 66
MELICOPE Rutaceae
    ternata J.R.&G. Forst., 127
MELICYTUS Violaceae
    ramiflorus J.R.&G.Forst
        [Z9], 126
MELIOSMA Sabiaceae
    myriantha Sieb. & Zucc.
        [Z9], 127
    veitchiorum Hemsl., 127
METROSIDEROS
    Myrtaceae, 29, 139
    albiflora Sol., 222
    carminea W. Oliver [Z10],
        221
    'Carousel', 221–2
    'Ferrous Wheel', 221
    diffusa (Forst.f.) Sm. [Z9],
        222
    excelsa Sol. ex Gaertn., 29,
        30
    florida Sm. [Z9], 222
    fulgens Sol. ex Gaertn. see
        M. florida
    hypericifolia Cunn., 222
    kermadecensis
        W.R.B.Oliver, 30
        'Radiant', 30
        'Variegata', 30
        'Minstrel', 30
    lucida A. Rich. see *M.*
        umbellata
    parkinsonii Buch., 222
    perforata (J.R. & G.Forst)
        A.Rich., 222
    robusta A. Cunn. [Z9], 221
    scandens Sol. ex Gaertn. see
        M. perfoliata
    tomentosa A. Rich. see *M.*
        excelsa
    umbellata Cav. [Z9], 12, 29,
        221
    villosa Kierk see *M.*
        kermadecensis
Mexican orange blossom, 55
MICHELIA Magnoliaceae
    compressa Sarg. [Z9], 104

MICHELIA Magnoliaceae –
    cont
doltsopa Buch-Ham.
    [Z9], 103
    'Silver Cloud', 104
figo (Lour.) Spreng. [Z9],
    104
fuscata Bl. see *M. figo*
MICROGLOSSA albescens
    B.Clarke see *Aster
    albescens*
Mimosa, 169, 171
MIMULUS
    Scrophulariaceae
aurantiacus Curtis [Z9], 59
glutinosus J.C.Wendl. see
    M. aurantiacus
longiflorus (Nutt.)
    A.L.Grant [Z9], 59
puniceus (Nutt.) Steud.
    [Z9], 59
    'Verity Hybrid', 234
MITRARIA Gesneriaceae
coccinea Cav. [Z7], 10, 220
MODIOLASTRUM
lateritium see *Malvastrum
    lateritium*
Monterey
    cypress, 18
    pine, 7, 18, 32
MORAEA Iridaceae, 14
Muehlenbeckia Polygonaceae
complexa Meissen. [Z9], 12,
    26
    trilobata Cheesem. [Z9],
        26
MUSA Musaceae, 225
acuminata Colla [Z10], 226
basjoo Sieb. & Zucc. [Z10],
    6, 17, 225–6
cavendishii Lamb. & Paxt.
    see *M. acuminata*
ensete Gmel. see *Ensete
    ventricosum*
Musk, 18
MUTISIA Compositae
clematis L. [Z9], 147
decurrens Cav. [Z9], 147
ilicifolia Cav. [Z9], 147
oligodon Poepp. & Endl.
    [Z9], 147
MYOPORUM Myoporaceae
laetum Forst.f. [Z10], 19,
    30

MYSOTIDEUM
    Boraginaceae
hortensia Baill., 239
nobile Hook. see *M.
    hortensia*
MYRICA Myricaceae
cerifera L., 127
MYRSINE Myrsinaceae
africana L. [Z9], 103
australis Allan, 104
chathamica F.v.Muell. [Z9],
    103
Myrtle, 15, 160, 165, 212
MYRTUS Myrtaceae, 11,
    212
apiculata Niedenz. see *Luma
    apiculata*
bullata Soland. ex A. Cunn.
    see *Lophomyrtus bullata*
chequen Spreng. see *Luma
    chequen*
communis L. [Z8], 97, 165
    'Flore Pleno', 165
tarentina L., 165
    'Variegata', 165
lechleriana (Miq.) Sealy see
    Amomyrtus luma
luma Mol. see *Luma
    apiculata*
obcordata (Raoul) Hook.f.
    see *Lophomyrtus obcordata*
× *ralphii* (Raoul) Hook.f.
    see *Lophomyrtus × ralphii*
ugni Mol. see *Ugni molinae*

NARCISSUS
    Amaryllidaceae
tazetta L., 166
    'Avalanche', 166
    'Grand Monarque', 166
    'Grand Primo', 166
    'Grand Soleil d'Or', 166
    'Paper White', 166
    'Scilly White', 166
NEMESIA Scrophulariaceae
foetens Vent., 234
NEOLITSEA Lauraceae
glauca (Sieb.) Koidz. see *N.
    sericea*
sericea Koidz. [Z9], 17, 104
NERINE Amaryllidaceae, 14,
    20, 76
    'Aurora', 75
bowdenii W.Wat., 75, 76

'Alba', 75
'Blush Beauty', 75
'Fenwick's Variety', 75
'Manina', 75
'Pink Triumph'
'Quinton Wells', 75
'Hera', 75
'Paula Knight', 75
'Rushmere Star', 75
NERIUM Apocynaceae
oleander L. [Z9], 164
New Zealand holly, 27
NICODEMIA
madagascariensis (Lam).
    R N Packer see *Buddleia
    madagascariensis*
NICOTIANA Solanaceae, 85
glauca Graham [Z10], 19,
    171
langsdorfii Weinm., 79, 84
sylvestris Speg. & Comes,
    219
NIEREMBERGIA
    Solanaceae
frutescens Durieu [Z9], 73
NOTELAEA excelsa Webb.
    & Bert. see *Picconia
    excelsa*
NOTHOFAGUS Fagaceae,
    11
betuloides (Mirbel) Bl. [Z9],
    183
dombeyi (Mirbel) Bl. [Z9],
    184
cliffortioides (Hook f.)
    Oerst. [Z9], 184
cunninghamii Oerst. [Z9],
    93, 184, 190
fusca (Hook. f.) Oerst. [Z9],
    184
menziesii (Hook. f.) Oerst.
    [Z9], 184
solanderi Oerst. [Z9], 184
NOTOSPARTIUM
    Leguminosae, 12
carmichaeliae Hook.f. [Z9],
    125–6
glabrescens Petrie [Z9], 126
    'Woodside', 125

Oak, Kermes, 103, 165
OCHAGAVIA
    Bromeliaceae
lindleyana (Lem.) Mez, 159

OCHNA Ochnaceae
  atropurpurea DC [Z10],
    236
  serrulata Walp. see *O.*
    atropurpurea
OLEA Oleaceae
  europaea L. [Z9], 171
Oleander, 164
OLEARIA Compositae, 12,
    13, 100
  albida Hook.f. [Z9], 28
  albida hort. see *O.*
    avicennifolia 'Talbot de
    Malahide'
  algida N.A.Wakefield, 122
  angustifolia Hook.f. [Z9],
    232
  arborescens Ckn. & Laing
    [Z9], 28, 232
  angustifolia Cheesem. see
    O. cheesemannii
  argophylla (Labill.) Bent.,
    213
  avicenniaefolia Hook.f.
    [Z9], 27, 32, 36
    'Talbot de Malahide',
      27
    'White Confusion', 27,
      36
  capillaris Buchan., 28
  chathamica Kirk [Z9], 38,
    232
  cheesemannii Ckn. & Allen,
    36
  colensoi Hook.f., 232
  cunninghamii hort. see *O.*
    rani
  erubescens Dipp. [Z9], 103
  ilicifolia (DC) Bean [Z9],
    103
    × *excorticata* Buchan., 232
  floribunda Benth., 122
  frostii (F.v.Muell.)
    J.H.Willis, 73
  furfuracea Hook.f., 28, 233
  gunniana (DC) Hook.f. see
    O. phlogopappa
    × *haastii* Hook.f. [Z9], 27
    'Henry Travers' [Z9], 37,
      103
  ilicifolia Hook.f., 36, 37
  insignis Hook.f. [Z9], 10,
    107, 155
    minor Cheesem., 155

  lacunosa Hook. f. [Z9],
    37, 232
  ledifolia (DC) Benth., 122
  lyallii Hook.f., 232–3
  macrodonta Baker [Z9], 27,
    28, 37, 53
    'Major', 28
    'Minor', 37
  mollis hort., 36
  moschata Hook.f. [Z9], 36
  myrsinoides (Labill.) Benth.,
    103
  nummulariifolia (Hook.f.)
    Hook.f. [Z9], 37
  odorata Petrie [Z9], 28
    × *oleifolia* Kirk. see *O.*
    'Waikariensis'
  pachyphylla Cheesem., 233
  paniculata Druce [Z9], 29,
    213
  phlogopappa DC [Z9], 69
    'Comber's Blue', 69
    'Comber's Pink', 69
    'Master Michael', 69
  pinifolia (Hook.f.) Benth.
    [Z9], 122
  ramulosa Benth. [Z10], 122
  rani (A.Cunn.) Druce, 36
  rotundifolia (Lessing) DC,
    102
    'Rowallane Hybrid', 28
    × *scilloniensis* Dorrien Smith
    [Z9], 37, 50, 62
  semidentata Decne see *O.*
    'Henry Travers'
  solanderi Hook.f. [Z9], 28,
    37, 122
  speciosa Hutch., 101
  stellulata DC [Z9], 13
  tomentosa DC, 102
  traversii Hook.f. [Z9], 28,
    34, 43, 44, 48
  virgata Hook.f. [Z7]
    lineata Kirk [Z7], 28
    'Waikariensis', 36
    'Zennorensis' [Z9], 37
Olive, 6, 160, 165, 166, 171
OMPHALODES
  Boraginaceae
  linifolia (L.) Moench, 160
ORTHROSANTHUS
  Iridaceae
  chimboracensis (HBK)
    Baker, 63

  multiflorus Sweet, 63
OSMANTHUS Oleaceae
  aquifolium Sieb. & Zucc. see
    O. heterophyllus
  armatus Diels [Z9], 89
  delavayi Franch. [Z8–9], 89
    × *fortunei* Carr [Z8–9], 89
  fragrans Lour. [Z9], 89, 211
    'Aurantiacus', 211
  heterophyllus P.S.Green
    [Z7], 89
  ilicifolius (Hook.f.) Mouille
    f. see *O. heterophyllus*
  serrulatus Rehd. [Z9], 89
  yunnanensis (Franch.)
    P.S.Green, 89
OSTEOMELES Rosaceae
  schweriniae Schneid. [Z9],
    120
  subrotunda K. Koch [Z9], 120
OSTEOSPERMUM
    Compositae, 9, 14, 83,
    171
  barberae hort. see *O.*
    jucundum
  ecklonis (DC) Norl. [Z9]
    'Prostratum', 63, 72
    'Weetwood', 64
  jucundum (E.Phillips) Norl.,
    42, 43, 67, 72
  hybrid cultivars:
    'Bloemhof Belle', 68, 72
    'Blue Streak', 64
    'Brickell's Hybrid', 72
    'Buttermilk', 59, 80
    'Cannington Roy', 72
    'Hopley', 43, 67, 72
    'Lady Leitrim', 43, 72
    'La Mortola', 72
    'Langtrees', 43, 67, 72
    'Nairobi Purple' see
      'Tresco Purple'
    'Pale Face' see 'Lady
      Leitrim'
    'Peggii' see 'Tresco
      Purple'
    'Pink Whirls', 72
    'Silver Sparkler', 63, 73
    'Whirligig', 64, 72
    'Tresco Purple', 67
OTHONNOPSIS
    Compositae
  cheirifolia (L.) Benth. &
    Hook. [Z10], 155

OXYPETALUM
  Asclepiadaceae
  caeruleum Dcne [Z10], 73,
    137
OZOTHAMNUS antennaria
  Hook.f. see Helichrysum
    antennaria ericifolius
  Hook.f. see Helichrysum
    led. folium ssp. ericeteum
  ledifolius Hook.f. see
    Helichrysum ledifolium
  purpurascens DC
    see Helichrysum
    purpurascens (DC)
    W.M.Curtis
  rosmarinifolius DC see
    Helichrysum
    rosmarinifolium
  thyrsoideus DC see
    Helichrysum thyrsoideum

PACHYSTEGIA insignis
  (Hook.f.) Cheesem.
  see Olearia insignis
PAEONIA Ranunculaceae
  officinalis L., 15
Palm, 223, 227, 228·
  sago, 228
PANDOREA Bignoniaceae
  jasminoides (Lindl.)
    K.Schum. [Z10], 135
PARAHEBE
  Scrophulariaceae
  perfoliata R.Br. [Z9], 70
PAROCHETUS
  Leguminosae
  communis Buch.-Ham. ex
    D.Don, 217
Parrot's bill, 12
PARSONSIA Apocynaceae
  heterophylla A.Cunn.,144–5
PASSIFLORA
  Passifloraceae, 144
  'Allardii' [Z9], 134
  antioquiensis Karst. [Z9],
    135
  caerulea L. [Z7], 134, 236
    'Constance Elliott', 134
    × caerulea-racemosa Sabine
      [Z9], 134, 236
    × caponii 'John Innes', 134
  edulis Sims [Z9], 134
    × exoniensis L.H.Bailey
      [Z10], 134, 135

mollissima (HBK)
  L.H.Bailey [Z10], 134,
    135
quadrangularis L., 134
racemosa Brot. [Z10], 134
  × tresederi 'Lilac Lady', 236
umbilicata Hams., 134
Passion flower, 132, 138
PAULOWNIA
  Scrophulariaceae
  tomentosa (Thunb.) Steud.
    [Z6], 223–4
PELARGONIUM
  Geraniaceae, 5, 236
  'Madame Crousse', 236
PENSTEMON
  Scrophulariaceae, 18
  cordifolius Benth., 82
  heterophyllus Lindl., 64
    'Blue Gem', 64
    'Blue Springs', 64
    'True Blue', 64
  isophyllus Robs., 82
  hybrid cultivars:
    'Andeken an Friedrich
      Hahn', 74, 86
    'Apple Blossom', 75
    'Burgundy', 75
    'Castle Forbes', 86
    'Chester Scarlet', 86
    'Evelyn', 74
    'Firebird' see
      'Schönholzeri'
    'Garnet' see 'Andeken an
      Friedrich Hahn'
    'George Home', 86
    'King George', 86
    'Hidcote Pink', 75
    'Newbury Gem', 86
      'Pennington Gem'. 75
    'Phyllis' see 'Evelyn'
    'Port Wine', 75
    'Purple Bedder', 75
    'Rich Ruby', 74, 86
    'Rubicunda', 75, 86
    'Schönholzeri', 86
    'Sour Grapes', 75
    'Southgate Gem', 86
    'Stapleford Gem', 75
    'Taosensis', 82
Pepper tree, 11, 168
PERICALLIS Compositae
  aurita (L'Hérit.) B. Nord.,
    73

lanata Webb & Berth., 73,
  74
PERILLA Labiatae
  'Nankinensis', 85
PERSEA Lauraceae
  americana Mill. [Z10], 211–
    12
  borbonia Spreng. [Z9], 211
  gratissima Gaertn. see P.
    americana
  ichangensis (Rehd. & Wils.)
    Kostermans [Z9], 104,
    187
PERSOONIA Proteaceae,
  112
  toru A.Cunn, 99
PETREA Verbenaceae
  volubilis L. [Z10], 237
PEUMUS Monimiaceae
  boldus Molina [Z10], 235
PHARBITIS learii Lindl. see
  Ipomoea acuminata
PHILADELPHUS
  Philadelphaceae, 175
  coronarius L. [Z5]
    'Aureus', 84
  coulteri hort. see P.
    mexicanus
  mexicanus Schlecht. [Z9]
    'Rose Syringa', 108
× PHILAGERIA
  Philesiaceae
  veitchii Mast. [Z9], 216
PHILESIA Philesiaceae
  magellanica Gmel. [Z9], 10,
    216
    'Rosea', 216
PHILLYREA Oleaceae
  latifolia L. [Z9], 33, 185
PHLOMIS Labiatae, 14, 60,
  150, 153
  cashmeriana Royle ex
    Benth., 106, 152
  chrysophylla Boiss. [Z9],
    152
  fruticosa L. [Z8–9], 152
    'Edward Bowles', 152
  italica L. [Z9], 70, 152
  purpurea L. [Z10], 152
PHOENIX Palmae
  canariensis Chabaud [Z9],
    227
  dactylifera L. [Z10], 228
  reclinata Jacq. [Z10], 228

PHORMIUM Phormiaceae,
9, 12, 43, 51, 226, 227
colensoi Hook.f. see *P.*
cookianum
cookianum Le Jolis [Z9], 41,
42, 52
'Cream Delight', 52
'Tricolor', 42, 52
'Variegatum', 52
tenax J.R. & G. Forst. [Z9],
41, 42, 52
'Atropurpureum', 41
'Burgundy', 52
'Dark Delight', 52
'Guardsman', 53
'Jack Spratt', 52
'Maori Chief', 53
'Purple Giant', 41, 52
'Purpureum', 41
'Radiance', 52
'Sundowner', 53
'Surfer', 52
'Tom Thumb', 52
'Tricolor', 42, 52
'Variegatum', 42, 52
'Veitchii', 52
'Williamsii', 52
'Yellow Queen', 52
hybrid cultivars:
'Apricot Queen', 53
'Aurora', 53
'Bronze Baby', 52
'Dazzler', 52
'Maori Maiden', 234
'Maori Queen', 234
'Maori Sunrise', 234
'Pink Panther', 52
'Smiling Morn', 53
'Sunset', 53
'Thumbelina', 52
'Yellow Wave', 52
PHOTINIA Rosaceae
arbutifolia Lindl. [Z9],
172
davidiana (Dcne) Cardot
[Z7], 34
davidsoniae Rehd. & Wils.
[Z9], 91
× *fraseri* Dress. [Z9], 104
'Red Robin', 91
'Robusta', 91
glabra (Thunb.) Maxim.
[Z9], 91
'Rubens', 91

nussia (D.Don) Kalkman
[Z9], 17, 91
serratifolia (Desf.) Kalkman
[Z9], 91
serrulata Lindl. see *P.*
serratifolia
PHYGELIUS
Scrophulariaceae, 14
aequalis Hiern., 14, 60, 79
'Yellow Trumpet', 14,
79, 80
capensis Benth. [Z9], 14, 60,
79
× *rectus* Coombes
'African Queen', 82
'Devil's Tears', 82
'Moonraker', 80
'Pink Elf', 65
'Salmon Leap', 60
'Winchester Fanfare', 60
PHYLLOCLADUS
Podocarpaceae, 189, 191
alpinus Hook.f. [Z9], 191
'Silver Blades', 191
aspleniifolius (Labill.)
Hook.f. [Z9], 191
glaucus Carr. [Z9], 191
trichomanoides D. Don [Z9],
191
PICCONIA Oleaceae
excelsa DC [Z9], 185
PICEA Pinaceae
abies Karst [Z5], 33
PIERIS Ericaceae, 91
PIMELEA Thymelaeaceae
drupacea Labill., 125
ferruginea Labill., 125
Pine
Aleppo, 161
bishop, 32
chilghoza, 189
Corsican, 32
kauri, 190
Monterey, 32, 189
Norfolk Island, 190
Scots, 32
umbrella, 160, 161
PINUS Pinaceae, 47
ayacahuite Ehren. [Z7], 18,
189
canariensis C.Smith [Z9],
15, 189
gerardiana Wall. [Z8–9],
189

halepensis Mill. [Z8–9], 161
insignis Dougl. ex Loud. see
P. radiata
maritima Poir. see *P. pinaster*
montezumae Lambert [Z9],
18, 188
hartwegii (Lindl.) Engel.
[Z9], 188
lindleyi Loud. [Z9], 188
rudis (Engl.) Shaw [Z9],
188
muricata D.Don [Z8], 32,
188
nigra Arnold
maritima Melv. [Z4], 32
patula Schl. & Cham. [Z9],
18, 188
pinaster Ait. [Z8], 32, 161
pinea L. [Z8–9], 161
radiata D.Don [Z8–9], 18,
32, 43, 156, 176, 188
roxburghii Sarg. [Z9], 189
sylvestris L. [Z2], 32
wallichiana A B Jacks [Z7],
189
PISTACIA Anacardiaceae
lentiscus L. [Z9], 15, 168
terebinthus L. [Z9], 168
PITTOSPORUM
Pittosporaceae, 213, 238
adaphniphylloides Hu &
Wang [Z9], 92
anomalum Laing & Gourlay
[Z9], 124
colensoi Hook.f. [Z9], 33
cornifolium A. Cunn., 102
crassifolium Banks &
Soland. ex A. Cunn.
[Z9], 26, 43, 102
'Variegatum', 56
dalli, Cheesem. [Z9], 92
divaricatum Ckn. [Z9], 124
eugenoides A. Cunn., 56, 92
'Platinum', 56
'Variegatum', 56
'Garnettii', 57
heterophyllum Franch. [Z9],
102
patulum Hook.f. [Z9], 124
phillyreoides DC [Z9], 92
ralphii T. Kirk. [Z9], 26, 33,
43
'Variegatum', 56
revolutum Ait. [Z9], 92

PITTOSPORUM
  Pittosoraceae – cont
  rigidum Hook.f., 124
  tenuifolium Gaertn. [Z9],
    26, 33, 54, 56, 92
    'Abbotsbury Gold', 54
    'Deborah', 53, 57
    'Eila Keightley', 54
    'Golden King', 54
    'Irene Patterson', 57
    'James Stirling', 56
    'Katty', 56
    'Limelight', 54
    'Margaret Turnbull', 54
    'Purpureum', 54, 86
    'Saundersii', 57
    'Silver Magic', 57
    'Silver Queen', 56
    'Silver Sheen', 56
    'Snow' see 'Irene
      Patterson'
    'Sterling Gold', 54
    'Tom Thumb', 52, 54,
      86
    'Variegatum', 56
    'Warnham Gold', 52, 54
    'Wendle Channon', 54
    'Winter Sunshine', 54
  tobira Ait. [Z9], 56, 92
    'Variegatum', 56
  undulatum Vent. [Z9], 92
  viridiflorum Sims [Z9], 102
PLAGIANTHUS Malvaceae
  betulinus A. Cunn. [Z9], 117
  divaricatus J.R. & G.Forst.
    [Z9], 124
PLECOSTACHYS
  Compositae
  serpyllifolia (Berg.)
    O.M.Hilliard &
    B.L.Burtt, 66
PLUMERIA Apocynaceae,
  238
  rubra L. [Z10], 236
PLUMBAGO
  Plumbaginaceae
  auriculata Lam. [Z10], 73,
    137
  capensis Thunb. see *P.*
    auriculata
PODALYRIA Leguminosae
  calyptrata Willd. [Z10],
    143
  sericea R.Br., 143

PODOCARPUS
  Podocarpaceae, 12, 189
  dacrydioides A. Rich. [Z9],
    191
  elatus R.Br. ex Mirb. [Z9],
    192
  falcatus R. Br. ex Mirb.
    [Z9], 192
  ferrugineus G. Benn ex
    D.Don [Z9], 191
  gracilior Pilger [Z9], 192
  hallii Kirk. [Z9], 191
  macrophyllus (Thunb.)
    D.Don [Z9], 192
  nagi (Thunb.) Zoll &
    Moritzi ex Makino [Z9],
    192
  nubigenus Lindl. [Z9], 192
  salignus D.Don [Z9], 192
  spicatus R.Br. ex Mirb.
    [Z9], 191
  totara G. Benn ex D. Don
    [Z9], 191
POINCIANA gilliesii Hook.
  see *Caesalpinia gilliesii*
POLYGALA Polygalaceae
  'Dalmaisiana' [Z9], 170–1
  myrtifolia hort.
    'Grandiflora' see *P.*
    'Dalmaisiana'
  virgata Thunb. [Z10], 171
POLYGONUM
  Polygonaceae
  capitatum Buch.-Ham. &
    D.Don, 73
POMADERRIS
  Rhamnaceae
  apetala Labill. [Z10], 140
  elliptica Labill. [Z10],
    140
  kumeraho A.Cunn., 139
  phylicifolia Lodd. [Z10],
    139
Pomegranate, 8, 16, 170
Poplar, 25
Poppy
  horned, 159
  prickly, 18, 159
  tree, 18
  tulip, 159
POPULUS Salicaceae
  alba L. [Z3], 25
  trichocarpa Hook. [Z5], 25
Portugal laurel, 33

PRIONOTES Epacridaceae
  cerinthoides R.Br., 215–16
PROSTANTHERA
  Labiatae, 107
  'Chelsea Pink', 69
  cuneata Benth., 105
  lasianthos Labill. [Z9], 105
  melissifolia R.Br. [Z9]
    parvifolia Sealy, 69, 105
  nivea A. Cunn., 105
  rotundifolia R.Br. [Z9], 69,
    105
    'Rosea', 69
  sieberi hort. see *P.*
    melissifolia parvifolia
  walteri F.v.Muell., 105–6
PRUNUS Rosaceae
  campanulata Maxim [Z8],
    17, 188
  cerasoides D.Don [Z9]
    rubea Ingram, 16, 188
  ilicifolia Walp. [Z9], 103
  laurocerasus L. [Z7], 33
  lusitanica L. [Z7], 33
  lyonii (Eastw.) Sarg. [Z8],
    103
PSEUDOPANAX
  Araliaceae, 12, 225
  arboreus W.R.Philipson,
    224, 225
  crassifolius (A.Cunn.)
    C.Koch [Z9], 229
  davidii (Franch.)
    W.R.Philipson, 224
  discolor (Kirk) Harms [Z9],
    225
  ferox T.Kirk [Z9], 229
  laetus (T.Kirk)
    W.R.Philipson [Z9],
    224–5
  lessonii (DC) C.Koch [Z9],
    225
    'Gold Splash', 55, 225
    'Purpureum', 52, 55, 225
  hybrid cultivars:
    'Adiantifolius', 225
    'Cyril Watson', 225
    'Linearifolius', 225
    'Sabre', 225
    'Trident', 225
PSEUDOTSUGA Pinaceae
  menziesii Franco, 33
PSEUDOWINTERA
  Winteraceae

colorata Dandy [Z9], 12, 210–11
PSORALEA Leguminosae
  glandulosa L., 145
  pinnata L. [Z10], 145
PUNICA Punicaceae
  granatum L. [Z9], 8, 170
    'Albo Plena', 170
    'Flore Pleno', 170
PUYA Bromeliaceae
  alpestris (Poepp. & Endl.) Gay [Z8], 159
  berteroniana Mez, 159
  chilensis Molina [Z9], 159
  coerulea Lindl., 159
  mirabilis (Mez) L.B.Smith, 159
  raimondii Harms., 159
PYROSTEGIA
  Bignoniaceae
  venusta Miers, 135

QUERCUS Fagaceae
  alnifolia Poech [Z8], 103
  coccifera L. [Z9], 103, 165
  ilex L. [Z8], 14, 31, 33, 43, 47
  incana Roxb. [Z8], 103
  phillyraeoides Gray [Z6], 33
QUILLAIA Rosaceae
  saponaria Molina [Z8], 94

Red hot poker, 42
REEVESIA Sterculiaceae
  pubescens Mast. [Z9], 187
  thyrsoidea Lindl. [Z9], 187
REHMANNIA
  Scrophulariaceae, 16
RHAMNUS Rhamnaceae
  alaternus L. [Z7], 165
    angustifolia (Mill.) Ait. [Z8], 165
RHAPHIOLEPSIS
  Rosaceae
  × *delacourii* Andre [Z9], 105
    'Coates Crimson', 105
    'Enchantress' [Z8], 105
  indica (L.) Lindl. [Z9], 104
    'Springtime', 104–5
  umbellata (Thunb.) Mak. [Z9], 105
RHAPHITHAMNUS
  Verbenaceae

cyanocarpus Miek. see *R. spinosus*
spinosus (Juss.) Moldenke [Z9], 11, 103
RHODOCHITON
  Scrophulariaceae
  atrosanguineum Rothm., 18, 137
  volubile Zucc. see *R. atrosanguineum*
RHODODENDRON
  Ericaceae, 16, 48, 192
  ambiguum Hemsl., 202
  arboreum W.W.Sm. [Z9], 103, 185, 203
    'Album', 203
    'Blood Red', 16, 200, 203, 205
  augustinii Hemsl. [Z6], 204
    chasmanthum (Diels) Cullen [Z7], 204
    'Electra', 204
  Auriculata subsection, 200
  auriculatum Hemsl. [Z6], 200, 205
  barbatum Wall. [Z8], 204
  basilicum Balf. f. & W.W.Sm. [Z8], 194
  beanianum Conway [Z8], 205
  Boothia subsection, 193, 198
  boothii Nutt. [Z9], 198
  bullatum Franch. see *R. edgeworthii*
  bureaui Franch. [Z6], 203
  burmanicum Hutchins [Z9], 196
  calophytum Franch. [Z6], 199, 200
  caloxanthum Balf. f. & Farrer see *R. campylocarpum* ssp. *caloxanthum*
  campanulatum D.Don [Z6], 204, 204
    aeruginosum (Hook.f.) Chamberlain [Z6], 204
    'Album', 204
    'Graham Thomas', 204
    'Knap Hill', 204
  Campylocarpa subsection, 203

campylocarpum Hook.f. [Z7], 200, 202–3
  caloxanthum (Balf.f. & Farrer) Chamberlain [Z7], 203
  elatum hort., 203
chrysodoron Hutch., 198
ciliatum Hook.f. [Z8], 195, 196, 197
ciliicalyx Franch. [Z9], 196
Cinnabarina subsection, 193, 201, 202
cinnabarinum Hook.f. [Z8], 201, 202, 206
  Blandfordiiflorum group, 201, 202
  Roylei group, 201, 202
    'Vin Rosé', 201
  xanthocodon (Hutch.) Cullen, 201
  Concatenans group, 201, 202
    'Copper', 201
crassum Hook.f. see *R. maddenii* ssp. *crassum*
croceum Balf.f. & W.W.Sm. see *R. wardii*
cubittii Hutch. see *R. veitchianum*
dalhousiae Hook.f. [Z9], 197
  rhabdotum (Balf.f. & Cooper) Cullen [Z9], 197
decorum Franch. [Z7], 199
delavayi Franch. see *R. arboreum* ssp. *delavayi*
diaprepes Balf.f. & W.W.Sm. [Z8], 198–9, 200
dichroanthum Diels. [Z8], 205
discolor Franch. see *R. fortunei* ssp. *discolor*
Edgeworthia subsection, 193, 197
edgeworthii Hook.f. [Z10], 197, 198
  Farrer 842, 197
  Forrest 26618, 197
  Kingdon Ward's pink form, 197
  Rock 59202, 197
elliotii Wat. & W.W.Sm. [Z9], 205

RHODODENDRON
Ericaceae – cont
eriogynum Balf. f. &
W.W.Sm. see R. facetum
eximium Nutt. see R.
falconeri ssp. eximium
facetum Balf. f. & Ward
[Z9], 205
Falconera subsection, 193,
194, 195, 198
falconeri Hook.f. [Z9], 194
eximium (Nutt.)
Chamberlain [Z9], 194
fletcherianum Davidian, 196
'Yellow Bunting', 196
formosum Wall., 197
inaequale C.B.Cl.
Fortunea subsection, 193,
198, 200, 201
fortunei Lindl. [Z7], 90, 198,
199
discolor (Franch.)
Chamberlain [Z7],
198, 200, 203
'Mrs Charles Butler', 198
fulgens Hook.f. [Z7], 204
fulvum Balf.f. & W.W.Sm.
[Z7], 203
grande Wight [Z9], 194
Grandia subsection, 193,
195, 198
griersonianum Balf.f. & Farr.
[Z8], 205
griffithianum Wight [Z9–
10], 198, 199, 200, 203
hodgsonii Hook.f. [Z9], 194,
195
hookeri Nutt. [Z8–9], 205
johnstoneanum Watt ex
Hutch. [Z7–8], 196
'Double Diamond', 196
keysii Nutt. [Z7], 201, 202
lacteum Franch. [Z7], 203
leucaspis Tagg. [Z8], 198
lindleyi T. Moore [Z9–10],
197
lutescens Franch. [Z7], 202
lyi Lévl., 196
macabeanum Balf.f. [Z8],
193–4, 195
Maddenia subsection, 193,
195, 196, 197, 198
maddenii Hook.f. [Z9–10],
195–6, 201, 202

crassum (Franch.) Cullen
[Z9], 195, 196
magnificum Ward. [Z9], 194
mallotum Balf.f. & Ward
[Z7], 204
megacalyx Balf.f. & Ward
[Z9], 197
mollyanum Cowan &
Davidian see R.
montroseanum
montroseanum Davidian
[Z7], 194
Neriiflora subsection, 205
neriiflorum Franch. [Z7],
205
nuttallii Booth [Z10], 197
pachypodum Balf.f. &
W.W.Sm., 196
Parishia subsection, 205
parryae Hutch. [Z10], 196
ponticum L. [Z6], 24, 31, 44,
189
praevernum Hutch. [Z6],
199
protistum Balf.f. & Forr.
[Z9–10]
giganteum (Tagg)
Chamberlain, 194
rex Lévl. [Z7], 194, 195
arizelum (Balf.f. & Forr.)
Chamberlain [Z8],
195
fictolaceum (Balf.f.)
Chamberlain [Z8],
195
rhabdotum Balf. f. & Cooper
see R. dalhousiae ssp.
rhabdotum
Scabrifolia subsection, 202
scottianum Hutch. see R.
pachypodum
simsii Planch., 17
sinogrande Balf.f. &
W.W.Sm. [Z8], 194,
195
spinuliferum Franch. [Z8],
202
strigillosum Franch. [Z8],
204
sulfureum Franch., 198
supranubium Hutch. see R.
pachypodum
sutchuenense Franch. [Z6],
199

giraldii Hutch., 199
taggianum Hutch. [Z10],
197
thomsonii Hook.f. [Z8],
200, 205
valentinianum Forr. [Z9],
196, 198
veitchianum Hook.f. [Z9],
196, 198
'Ashcombe', 196
wardii W.W.Sm. [Z7], 203
KW4170, 203
yakushimanum Nakai, 198
hybrid cultivars:
Albatross, 200
Angelo, 200
'Exbury Angelo', 200
Argosy, 200
Avalanche, 200
'Alpine Glow', 200
Barclayi, 204
Beauty of Tremough,
200
'Biskra', 202
'Bodnant Yellow', 202
'Caerhays John', 202
'Caerhays Lawrence',
202
'Caerhays Philip', 202
Conroy, 202
Cornish Cross, 200
Cornubia, 204
'Countess of
Haddington', 197
Crossbill, 202
Damaris, 203
'Logan', 203
'Dr Stocker', 203
Eldorado, 196
'Forsterianum', 198
Fortune, 195
FCC form, 195
'Fragrantissimum', 76,
197
Full House, 202
'Fusilier', 205
Hawk, 203
'Crest', 203
'Jervis Bay', 203
'Jane Hardy', 197
'Lady Alice Fitzwilliam',
197–8
Lady Bessborough,
203

Lady Chamberlain, 201, 202
  'Chelsea', 201
  'Exbury', 201–2
  'Gleam', 201
Lady Roseberry, 202
Loderi, 199, 200
  'Julie', 200
  'King George', 199
  'Patience', 200
  'Pink Diamond', 199
  'Sir Edmund', 200
  'Sir Joseph Hooker', 199–200
  'Venus', 200
  'White Diamond', 199
Mariloo, 203
'Moser's Maroon', 205
'Nereid', 205
'Nutcracker', 197
Penjerrick, 200, 202
  Cream Form, 200
  Pink Form, 200
Polar Bear, 200–1
'Princess Alice', 197–8
'Romany Chal', 205
'Royal Flush', 201, 202
Sesterianum, 197
Shilsonii, 204
'Sir Charles Lemon', 203–4
'Suave', 198
'Sylvania', 197
'Tally Ho', 205
'Trewithen Orange', 202
'Tyermannii', 197
Valaspis, 198
RHODOLEIA
Hamamelidaceae/Rhodoleiaceae
  championii Hook. [Z9], 210
RHUS Anacardiaceae, 160, 172
  succedanea L. [Z5], 127
RIBES Grossulariaceae
  viburnifolium Gray [Z9], 220
RICHEA Epacridaceae, 13
  dracophylla R.Br., 230
  milliganii F.v.Muell., 230
  pandanifolia Hook.f., 230
  scoparia Hook.f. [Z9], 230
RICINUS Euphorbiaceae
  communis L.

'Carmencita', 226
'Gibsonii', 85, 226
'Impala', 226
Roman hyacinth, 166
ROMNEYA Papaveraceae, 18, 159
  coulteri Harv., 175
  trichocalyx (Eastw.)
    Jepson, 175
  trichocalyx Eastw. see *R. coulteri* var. *trichocalyx*
ROSA Rosaceae
  'Anemone', 132–3
  banksiae Ait. [Z8], 169
    'Lutea' [Z9], 108, 169
    lutescens Voss [Z9], 169
    normalis Regel [Z9], 169
  'Belle Portugaise', 169, 170
  bracteata Wendl. [Z7], 17, 132
  cabbage, 116
  'Climbing Devoniensis', 169, 170
  'Cooper's Burmese' see *R. laevigata* 'Cooperi'
  damask, 116
  'Fortune's Double Yellow', 169
  × *fortuniana* Lindl. [Z9], 169
  gallica L., 116
  gigantea Collet ex Crép. [Z9], 115, 132, 170
  hemisphaerica Herrm. [Z6], 170
  laevigata Michx. [Z7], 132
    'Cooperi', 132
  'La Follette', 169
  'Maréchal Niel', 170
  'Ramona', 133
  rugosa Thunb. [Z2], 34
  'Super Star', 115
  Tea, 106, 113, 114–15, 160, 169
    'Anna Olivier', 115
    'Archiduc Joseph', 115
    'Baronne Henriette de Snoy', 115
    'Catherine Mermet', 115
    'Dr Grill', 115
    'Duchesse de Brabant', 115
    'Freiherr von Marschall', 115

'Général Schablikine', 115
    'Lady Hillingdon', 115
    'Mme Berkeley', 115
    'Mme Bravy', 115
    'Maman Cochet', 115
    'Marie van Houtte', 115
    'Monsieur Tillier', 115
    'Niphetos', 170
    'Papa Gontier', 115
    'Perle des Jardins', 115
    'Safrano', 115
    'Souvenir d'Elise Vardon', 115
    'Triomphe du Luxembourg', 115
    'William R Smith', 115
Rose
  Cherokee, 132
  Macartney, 17, 132
Rosemary, 15, 150, 151, 160, 165
ROSMARINUS Labiatae
  lavandulaceus Turrill [Z9], 165
  officinalis L. [Z7–8], 165
    'Benenden Blue', 165
    'McConnell's Blue', 165
    'Prostratus', 165
    'Severn Sea', 165
    'Tuscan Blue', 165
Rowan, 184, 187
RUBUS Rosaceae
  australis Forst. [Z9], 127
  × *barkeri* Cock., 128
  cissoides A. Cunn. [Z9], 127
    pauperatus Kirk. see *R. squarrosus*
  lineatus Reinw. [Z9], 16, 128
  parvus Buch. [Z9], 128
  schmidelioides A. Cunn., 127
  squarrosus Flitsch. [Z9], 127
Ruby chard, 85
Rue, 150
RUSCUS Ruscaceae, 131
  aculeatus L. [Z6], 216
  hypoglossum L. [Z8], 216
  hypophyllum L. [Z9], 216
  × *microglossus* Bertoloni [Z9], 216

Sacred fir, 18
Sage, 15, 150

Salix Salicaceae
  acutifolia Willd. [Z4], 25
  caprea L. [Z5], 25
  daphnoides Wimm. [Z5],
    25
SALVIA Labiatae, 18, 78, 172
  africana-lutea L., 59
  ambigens hort. see *S.*
    guaranitica 'Blue
    Enigma'
  argentea L., 51, 74
  aurea L. see *S. africana-lutea*
  azurea Michx. ex Lam., 62
  blepharophylla Brand. ex
    Epling, 79
  buchananii Hedge, 72
  cacaliifolia Benth., 62
  coccinea Juss. ex Murr., 234
  coerulea Benth. see *S.*
    guaranitica 'Black and
    Blue'
  concolor Lam. ex Benth.,
    62
  confertiflora Pohl, 59
  discolor HBK, 73
  dorisiana Standl., 71
  elegans Vahl, 234
  farinacea Benth., 234
    'Victoria', 74
  fulgens Cav., 79
  gesneriiflora Lindl. & Paxt.,
    79
  grahamii Benth. see *S.*
    microphylla var. *neurepia*
  greggii A.Gray, 71
    'Peach', 71
  guaranitica A.St.Hil. ex
    Benth., 62
    'Black and Blue', 62
    'Blue Enigma', 62
  'Indigo Spires', 234
  involucrata Cav., 71, 75
    'Bethellii', 71
    'Boutin', 71
    'Hadspen', 71
    'Mrs Pope', 71
  leucantha Cav., 71
  longispicata Mart. & Gall.,
    234
  microphylla HBK, 71
    neurepia (Fern.) Epling,
    71
    'Oxford Variety', 71
    wislizenii A.Gray, 71

  neurepia Fern. see *S.*
    microphylla var. *neurepia*
  officinalis L.
    'Icterina', 153
    'Purpurascens', 151
  patens Cav., 62
    'Cambridge Blue', 62, 73
  rutilans Carr see *S. elegans*
  uliginosa Benth., 84
SANDERSONIA
  Colchicaceae
  aurantiaca Hook., 140
SANTOLINA Compositae,
  151
SAPIUM Euphorbiaceae
  sebiferum Roxb. [Z9], 187
SARCOCOCCA Buxaceae
  saligna (D.Don) Muell.-
    Arg. [Z9], 116
SARMIENTA Gesneriaceae,
  10
  repens Ruiz & Pav. [Z9],
    220
SASSAFRAS Lauraceae
  albidum Nees [Z5], 187–8
  tzumu (Hemsl.) Hemsl.
    [Z9], 188
SAXIFRAGA Saxifragaceae
  cuscutiformis Lodd., 219
SCHEFFLERA Araliaceae
  digitata J.R. & G. Forst
    [Z10], 224
  impressa (C.B.Clarke)
    Harms. [Z9], 224
SCHIMA Theaceae
  argentea Pritz. [Z9], 208
  khasiana Dyer [Z9], 208
  noronhae Reinw. ex Blume
    [Z9], 208
  wallichii (DC) Korth. [Z9],
    208
SCHINUS Anacardiaceae
  dependens Ort. see *S.*
    polygamus
  molle L. [Z9], 11, 168
  polygamus (Cav.) Cabrera
    [Z9], 168
Schizostylis Iridaceae
  coccinea Backh. & Harv.,
    77, 87, 217
    'Alba', 77
    'Cardinal', 87
    'Jennifer', 77
    'Major', 87

    'Mrs Hegarty', 77
    'November Cheer', 77
    'Pallida', 77
    'Professor Barnard', 77
    'Sunrise', 77
    'Tambara', 77
    'Viscountess Byng', 77
    'Zeal Salmon', 77
SCILLA Hyacinthaceae
  peruviana L., 15
Sea buckthorn, 25
SEDUM Crassulaceae
  dendroideum Moç & Sessé ex
    DC, 160
  maximum (L.) Suter see *S.*
    telephium ssp. *maximum*
  telephium L.
    maximum (L.) Korck.
      'Atropurpureum', 85
      'Munstead Red', 85
SEMELE Ruscaceae
  androgyna (L.) Kunth.,
    131
SENECIO Compositae
  'Alfred Atkinson' see
    Brachyglottis 'Alfred
    Atkinson'
  bicolor Willd.
    cinerarea DC, 81
      'Cirrus', 81
      'White Diamond', 81
  bidwillii Hook.f. see
    Brachyglottis bidwillii
  buchananii Armstr. see
    Brachyglottis
    buchananii
  candicans DC, 10, 217
  compactus Kirk see
    Brachyglottis compacta
  Dunedin Hybrids see
    Brachyglottis Dunedin
    Hybrids
  elaeagnifolius Hook.f. see
    Brachyglottis
    elaeagnifolia
  glastifolius L.f., 137
  greyi Hook.f. see
    Brachyglottis greyi
  hectoris Buchan. see
    Brachyglottis hectoris
  heritieri DC see *Pericallis*
    lanata
  huntii F.v.Muell. see
    Brachyglottis huntii

'*Joseph Andrews*' see
  Brachyglottis 'Joseph
  Andrews'
kirkii Hook.f., 100
laxifolius Buchan. see
  Brachyglottis laxifolius
'Leonard Cockayne' see
  Brachyglottis 'Leonard
  Cockayne'
leucostachys Baker see *S.
  vira-vira*
maderensis DC see *Pericallis
  aurita*
monroi Hook.f. see
  Brachyglottis monroi
perdicioides Hook.f. see
  Brachyglottis
  · *perdicioides*
pulcher Hook. & Arn., 75
reinoldii Endl. see
  *Brachyglottis
  rotundifolia*
rotundifolius (J.R. &
  G.Forst.) Hook.f. see
  Brachyglottis rotundifolia
vira-vira Hieron., 11, 60,
  74, 81
SETCREASEA purpurea
  Boom. see *Tradescantia
  pallida* 'Purpurea'
Seville orange, 171
SMILAX Smilacaceae
  aspera L. [Z9], 132
  excelsa L, 132
SOLANUM Solanaceae
  aviculare Forst.f. [Z9], 136
  crispum Ruiz. & Pav. [Z9],
    107, 108
  'Glasnevin', 107
  jasminoides Paxt. [Z9], 136
    'Album', 136
  laciniatum Ait. [Z9], 73, 136
  rantonettii Carr [Z10], 136
  valdiviense Dunal [Z9],
    136
  wendlandii Hook.f. [Z10],
    137
SOLLYA Pittosporaceae
  drummondii Morr. see *S.
  parviflora*
  fusiformis Payer see *S.
  heterophylla*
  heterophylla Lindl. [Z9],
    140

parviflora Turcz [Z9], 140
SOPHORA Leguminosae,
  11, 12, 118–19
  macrocarpa Sm. [Z9], 119
  microphylla Ait. [Z9], 119
  prostrata Buch. [Z8], 119
  secundiflora (Ort.) Lag. ex
    DC, 238
  tetraptera J.Mill [Z9], 119
    'Gnome', 119
SORBUS Rosaceae, 184
  harrowiana (Balf.f. &
    W.W.Sm.) Rehd. [Z9],
    16, 184
  insignis (Hook.f.) Hedl.
    [Z9], 16, 184
    KW7746, 184
Southern beech, 11, 183
Southern rata, 29
SPARAXIS Iridaceae, 14,
  166
SPARMANNIA Tiliaceae
  africana L. [Z10], 230
SPARTIUM Leguminosae
  junceum L. [Z8–9], 25, 150
SPARTOCYTISUS
  Leguminosae
  nubigenus Webb & Barth.,
    163
SPHACELE Labiatae
  chamaedryoides Briquet
    [Z9], 105
SPHAERALCEA Malvaceae
  fendleri A.Gray [Z9], 59
  munroana Spach, 65, 66
SPREKELIA Amaryllidaceae
  formosissima (L.) Herb., 142
STACHYURUS
  Stachyuraceae
  himalaicus Hook.f. &
    Thoms. ex Benth. [Z8],
    17, 119
  lancifolius Koidz. see *S.
    praecox* var. *matzusakii*
  praecox Sieb & Zucc. [Z7]
    matzusakii (Nakai)
      Makino [Z9], 17, 119
STAUNTONIA
  Lardizabalaceae
  hexaphylla Dcne., 130, 131
STENOCARPUS
  Proteaceae
  sinuatus (A.Cunn.) Endl.
    [Z10], 237

STERCULIA Sterculiaceae
  acerifolia A. Cunn., 238
  platanifolia L.f. see *Firmiana
    platanifolia*
Strawberry tree, 15, 33
STREPTOSOLEN
  Solanaceae
  jamesonii (Benth.) Miers
    [Z10], 147
STRANVAESIA davidiana
  Dcne. see *Photinia
    davidiana*
  nussia Dcne. see *Photinia
    nussia*
STUARTIA Theaceae, 210
  malacodendron L. [Z9], 208
  pteropetiolata Cheng, 208
STYRAX Styracaceae, 210
  dasyantha Perkins [Z9],
    209
  officinalis L. [Z9], 209
SUTERA Scrophulariaceae
  grandiflora (Galpin) Hiern,
    138
SUTHERLANDIA
  Leguminosae
  frutescens (L.) R.Br. [Z10],
    142
Sweet bay, 180
Sycamore, 18

TACSONIA Passifloraceae,
  134, 135
  vanvolxemii Lem. see
    Passiflora antioquiensis
TAMARIX Tamaricaceae
  gallica L. [Z7], 31
  hispida Willd. [Z8], 107
  juniperina Bunge [Z6], 31
  parviflora DC [Z5], 31
  pentandra Pall. [Z5], 31, 107
    'Pink Cascade', 107
    'Rubra', 31, 107
  ramosissima Ledeb. [Z2], 31,
    107
  tetrandra Pall. [Z6], 31
TAXUS Taxaceae
  baccata L. [Z6], 191
Tea rose, 106, 113, 114
TECOMANTHE
  Bignoniaceae
  speciosa W.R.B.Oliver
    [Z9], 135

TECOMARIA Bignoniaceae
capensis (Thunb.) Spach.
[Z9], 135
'Apricot', 135
'Coccinea', 135
'Lutea', 135
'Salmonea', 135
TELOPEA Proteaceae, 13,
112
mongaensis Cheel, 97
oreades F.v.Muell., 97
speciosissima (Sm.) R.Br.
[Z9], 97
truncata R.Br. [Z9], 97
TERNSTROEMIA
Theaceae, 17
gymnanthera (Wight &
Arn.)Sprague[Z10],
208
'Variegata', 208, 209
japonica Thunb. see *Cleyera
japonica*
TETRAPANAX
Araliaceae
papyrifer (Hook.) K.Koch
[Z8], 224
TEUCRIUM Labiatae
fruticans L., 152
'Azureum', 152
THAMNOCALAMUS
falconeri Munro see
Arundinaria falconeri
Thorn apple, 143
Thuya, 32
TIBOUCHINA
Melastomataceae
semidecandra hort. see *T.
urvilleana*
urvilleana (DC) Cogniaux
[Z10], 238
'Grandiflora', 237
Tobacco plant, 5, 11
TRACHELOSPERMUM
Apocynaceae
asiaticum (Sieb & Zucc.)
Nakai [Z9], 130
crocostemon Kanitz, see *T.
asiaticum*
divaricatum Stapf., see *T.
asiaticum*
jasminoides (Lindl.) Lem.
[Z9], 17, 130
'Variegatum', 130
majus Stapf., 130

TRACHYCARPUS Palmae
fortunei (Hook.) Wendl.
[Z9], 227
TRADESCANTIA
Commelinaceae
pallida (Rose) Hunt
'Purpurea', 18, 85, 160
Tree fern, 184, 219, 223, 225,
228, 229
Tree heath, 150, 166
Tree lupin, 22, 40, 47, 176
Tree poppy, 18, 175
TRISTANIA Myrtaceae
neriifolia R.Br., 237
TROCHODENDRON
Trochodendraceae
aralioides Sieb. & Zucc.
[Z8], 90
TROPAEOLUM
Tropaeolaceae
majus L.
'Hermione Grashof', 81,
234
tricolor Sweet, 140
tuberosum Ruiz & Pav., 11,
80
'Ken Aslet', 80
TULBAGHIA Alliaceae
capensis L., 61
violacea Harv., 71, 73
'Maritima', 234
'Pallida', 234
'Variegata' see *T.
violacea* 'Maritima'
TULIPA Liliaceae
saxatilis Sieb. ex Spreng.,
166
TWEEDIA caerulea D. Don
ex Sweet see *Oxypetalum
caeruleum*

UGNI Myrtaceae
molinae Turcz. [Z9], 97
UMBELLULARIA
Lauraceae
californica (Hook. & Arn.)
Nutt. [Z9], 91
URSINIA Compositae, 155
chrysanthemoides (Less.)
Harv.
'Geyeri', 238

VACCINIUM Ericaceae
cyclindraceum Sm. [Z10],
15, 214

floribundum HBK [Z9], 214
gaultherifolium Hook.f.
[Z10], 214
glaucoalbum Hook.f. [Z9],
214
maderense Link. see *V.
padifolium*
mortinia Benth. see *V.
floribundum*
nummularia Hook. &
Thoms. [Z7], 214
padifolium Sm. [Z9], 15, 214
urceolatum Hemsl. [Z9],
213–14
VALLEA Elaeocarpaceae
stipularis L., 119
VALLOTA speciosa (L.f.)
Dur. & Schinz see
Cyrtanthus purpureus
VELLA Cruciferae
pseudocytisus L. [Z9], 163–4
Venidio-arctotis hybrids, 155
VENIDIUM Compositae,
14, 154
VERBENA Verbenaceae
× *hybrida* hort. ex Vilm.
'Huntsman', 86
'Lawrence Johnston', 68,
86
'Loveliness', 68
'Pink Bouquet', 68
'Silver Ann', 52, 68, 69
'Sissinghurst', 68
peruviana (L.) Druce, 86
'Alba', 68
tridens Lag. [Z9], 11
VERONICA perfoliata R.Br.
see *Parahebe perfoliata*
VESTIA Solanaceae
foetida Hoffmann [Z9], 118
lycioides Willd. see *V.
foetida*
VIBURNUM Caprifoliaceae,
17
cinnamomifolium Rehd.
[Z7], 89
cylindricum D.Don [Z6], 95
davidii Franch. [Z6], 89
erubescens Wall. [Z6], 118
gracilipes Rehd. [Z6], 118
japonicum Spreng. [Z7], 17,
89, 90
odoratissimum Ker-GawL.
[Z8], 17, 90

rigidum Vent. [Z9], 95
suspensum Lindl. [Z8], 95
tinus L. [Z7], 55, 95
  hirtum Ait., 95
  lucidum Ait., 95
  'Variegatum', 56
VILLARESIA mucronata
  Ruiz & Pav. see
  Citronella mucronata
VIOLA Violaceae, 126
VITEX Verbenaceae
  negundo L. [Z6], 117–18
    heterophylla (Franch.)
    Rehd., 118

WACHENDORFIA
  Haemodoraceae
  paniculata L., 147
  thyrsiflora L., 147, 234
WASHINGTONIA Palmae
  filifera (Linden) Wendl.
    [Z9], 228
WATSONIA Iridaceae, 14,
  78
  angusta Ker-Gawl. see *W.
    fulgens*
  ardernei Sander see *W.
    meriana*
  beatricis Math. & Bolus, 83
  bulbillifera Math. & Bolus,
    59
  fulgens (Andr.) Pers., 83
  knuysnana L.Bol., 68
  marginata (Eckl.) Ker-
    Gawl., 68
  meriana (L.) Mill., 68
    'Ardernei', 68

pillansii, 59
pyramidata (Andr.) Stapf.,
  68
'Stanfords', 83
stenosiphon L.Bol., 59
wilmaniae Math. & Bolus,
  68
WATTAKAKA
  Asclepiadaceae,
  sinensis Stapf., 17, 138
WEINMANNIA
  Cunoniaceae, 11
  racemosa L.f. [Z9], 98
  sylvicola Soland. ex
    A.Cunn. [Z9], 98
  trichosperma Cav. [Z9], 98
WESTRINGIA Labiatae
  angustifolia R.Br. 238
  brevifolia Benth. 238
    Raleighii group 238
  fruticosa (Willd.) Druce
    [Z9], 238
  rigida R.Br., 238
  rosmariniformis Sm. see *W.
    fruticosa*
Willow, 25
  goat, 25
WOODWARDIA
  Blechnaceae
  radicans Sm., 219

XYLOSMA Flacourtiaceae
  japonicum (Walp.) A.Gray
    [Z7], 235

YUCCA Agavaceae, 18, 226,
  227

baccata Torr. [Z6], 158
filamentosa L. [Z5], 51
flaccida Haw. [Z5], 50, 51
glauca Nutt. [Z5], 157
gloriosa L. [Z7], 50, 51
recurvifolia Salisb. [Z6], 51
whipplei Torr. [Z10], 18,
  157–8

ZANTEDESCHIA Araceae
  aethiopica (L.) Spreng., 217
    'Crowborough', 217
    'Green Goddess', 217
    'Little Gem', 217
    'White Sail', 217
  angustiloba Engl., 218
  elliottiana (W.Wats.) Engl.,
    218
  pentlandii (R.Whyte ex
    W.Wats.) Witt. see *Z.
    angustiloba*
  rehmannii Engl., 218
  hybrid cultivars:
    'Afterglow', 218
    'Aztec Gold', 218
    'Black Magic', 218
    'Dusky Pink', 218
    'Golden Affair', 218
    'Majestic Red', 218
    'Pacific Pink', 218
    'Regal Charm', 218
ZAUSCHNERIA
  Onagraceae
  californica Presl. see
    Epilobium canum
  cana Greene see *Epilobium
    canum*